NETWORKED MULTIMEDIA SYSTEMS
Concepts, Architecture & Design

S. V. Raghavan

Department of Computer Science and Engineering
Indian Institute of Technology Madras
Chennai, India

and

Satish K. Tripathi

University of Maryland, College Park
and
University of California, Riverside

PRENTICE HALL,
Upper Saddle River, New Jersey 07458

Library of Congress Cataloging-in-Publication Data

Raghavan, S. V.
    Networked multimedia systems: concepts, architecture, and
    design / S. V. Raghavan and Satish K. Tripathi. —
        p. cm.
    Includes index.
    ISBN: 0-13-210642-6
    1. Multimedia systems. 2. Computer networks. I. Tripathi, S. K.
    (Satish K.), 1951-   . II. Title.
    QA76.575.R34   1998
    006.7--dc21   97-27377
                                      CIP

Publisher: Alan Apt
Development Editor: Sondra Chavez
Editorial/Production Supervision: Barbara Kraemer
Managing Editor: Bayani Mendoza DeLeon
Editor-in-Chief: Marcia Horton
Assistant Vice President of Production and Manufacturing: David W. Riccardi
Art Director: Amy Rosen
Cover Designer: Heather Scott
Manufacturing Manager: Trudy Pisciotti
Manufacturing Buyer: Donna Sullivan
Editorial Assistant: Toni Holm

©1998 by Prentice-Hall, Inc.
Simon & Schuster / A Viacom Company
Upper Saddle River, New Jersey 07458

The author and publisher of this book have used their best efforts in preparing this book. These efforts include the development, research, and testing of the theories and programs to determine their effectiveness. The author and publisher make no warranty of any kind, expressed or implied, with regard to these programs or the documentation contained in this book. The author and publisher shall not be liable in any event for incidental or consequential damages in connection with, or arising out of, the furnishing, performance, or use of these programs.

Printed in the United States of America

10 9 8 7 6 5 4 3 2 1

ISBN 0-13-210642-6

Prentice-Hall International (UK) Limited, London
Prentice-Hall of Australia Pty. Limited, Sydney
Prentice-Hall Canada Inc., Toronto
Prentice-Hall Hispanoamericana, S.A., Mexico
Prentice-Hall of India Private Limited, New Delhi
Prentice-Hall of Japan, Inc., Tokyo
Simon & Schuster Asia Pte. Ltd., Singapore
Editora Prentice-Hall do Brasil, Ltda., Rio de Janeiro

We dedicate this book
To

The Lotus feet of Sri Sathya Sai Baba

- Raghavan

My Mother Gaura Devi Tripathi

- Satish K. Tripathi

Preface

The advent of processor technology, high speed networking, and special purpose high performance VLSI technology have opened new frontiers for computing applications. The user of a computer system is no longer limited to textual information. Audio, video, and graphics information can all be simultaneously accessed and displayed. The most exciting aspect of these systems is that they operate in both centralized and distributed environments.

Multimedia systems consist of information from multiple sources and representations. Designing a multimedia system involves understanding various technologies and making design decisions on issues that are still topics of research. There are many multimedia projects addressing various issues including creation, maintenance, and retrieval of different types of data.

Research and implementation in the field of multimedia are progressing simultaneously. Design of a multimedia system involves interfacing with many areas of computer and communication sciences. In this book, our goal is to systematize the multimedia design process, introduce the various subfields that are essential to understanding the problems, and give detailed state-of-the-art treatment to each of these topics.

The book is written with dual purpose in mind. The primary purpose is to develop a text book for senior undergraduate and graduate students who are interested in pursuing research or development careers in the general area of multimedia. In addition, we expect that this book will serve as a reference book for a large and growing population of professionals who design and use these systems. We assume that the reader is familiar with the basic concepts of computer systems and networking.

Chapter 1 introduces Multimedia systems from rudimentary notions of computing. The emphasis is on conveying the fact that multimedia systems have a different set of requirements as compared to computer systems. After introducing the two fundamental characteristics of multimedia, viz., high volume data and time synchrony, this chapter discusses the impact of these on system design.

Chapter 2 highlights the requirements of a multimedia system more quantitatively for the benefit of the reader. Each medium is considered separately and its impact on volume of data to be handled by the machine and its time characteristics are discussed. The discussions consider one medium at a time and then a set of media. This chapter also underlines why it is necessary to develop techniques to keep the volume of data as low as possible.

Chapter 3 addresses the issue of compact representation of multimedia information for the purposes of storage, transmission, and processing. As the most demanding media is video, the chapter discusses more on how to handle images and video. The coding and compression techniques required for doing so are explained with reference to the popular coding and compression standards: JPEG and MPEG.

Chapter 4 focuses on how I/O can be handled in multimedia systems. After a conceptual overview of what needs to be done to handle high volume and time-constrained data, storage architectures such as RAID and specific storage devices such as CD-ROMs, are discussed.

Chapter 5 explains the key technology behind the modern computing environment, viz., networking. After a brief presentation of history, motivation and standards, the chapter explains Ethernet, Fast Ethernet, FDDI, ISDN, Frame Relay, and ATM.

In the first five chapters, the reader will learn about the requirements and the availability of technology to meet these requirements. In chapter 6, the architecture and issues related to multimedia systems are presented. A taxonomy, which the multimedia systems can be represented with for better understanding, is also presented. The chapter concludes by highlighting all the areas to be addressed in designing a modern multimedia system. Issues such as traffic prediction, buffer design, traffic shaping, scheduling, and congestion control are introduced briefly in this chapter as a precursor to the set of chapters that follow, addressing each one of these issues at length. Chapters 7, 8, 9,10, and 11 concentrate on different aspects of multimedia system design. These five chapters will help the reader understand the interplay of various parameters in a modern high speed network.

Chapter 12 surveys the trends in system software design and enumerates a few design principles that may be important in the design of operating systems in future.

Appendix presents a short tutorial on Standards and standard bodies.

Many people have contributed during the writing of this book and without their help our task would have been very difficult. In particular, we want to thank Debanjan Saha, Marwan Krunz, Mahabala, Frank Miller, Suman Banerjee, Pravin Bhagwat, Radha, Selvakumar, Vishnu Priya, Swaminathan, Shankar, Williams, Ganesh, Krishna Prakash, and Ashok Agrawala for their suggestions and editorial help. Reviewers have been very helpful with their constructive comments. Alan Apt, Scott Barr, Barbara Kraemer, and Sondra Chavez of Prentice Hall deserve a lot of credit to get this project completed. Finally, Raghavan would like to thank Meena, Sriram, and Sairam, and Tripathi would like to thank Kamlesh, Manish, and Aashish for their understanding during the entire time of this endeavor.

Contents

Chapter 1

Multimedia Systems Primer

1.1 What is Multimedia?

Computers, as we understand them today, came into existence about three decades ago. Originally, the computers supported only the computations related to research. As time progressed and with the technological advances, the computers became powerful contrivances and today they are an integral part of our day-to-day life. Perception, memory, thought, and reason, which are considered the basic traits of human beings, are being mimicked today by special systems that are built using powerful computers. These systems are able to 'talk', 'see', 'understand', 'listen', 'think', and 'communicate' although to a much lesser degree of perfection when compared to human beings. Specialized systems are built to perform dedicated tasks such as a class teacher, a librarian, an aircraft pilot, a mining engineer, and numerous other specialized tasks.

All these developments have one thing in common. That is, to automate the following functions: perception, retention, reasoning, and presentation. All four functions directly relate to the sensory, memory, and reactionary modes of behavior of human beings. There are basically two types of systems that are attempted; those which act as replacement for human beings and those which act as facilitating contrivances for human beings. A flexible manufacturing system is an example of the former category. Cooperative computing and teleconferencing systems are examples of the latter category. In both types of systems, all four functions, i.e., perception, retention, reasoning, and presentation are performed but with a difference. In the case of a flexible manufacturing system all four functions are performed by computers, while in the case of teleconferencing systems the four functions are performed by computers and human beings simultaneously in a coordinated way. For example, in a teleconferencing application, perception, retention, and presentation are handled by the computers, and the reasoning is done by the participants. In both types of systems, if the participating agents are geographically distributed, a function called *transmission* comes in automatically. Therefore, in the case of distributed flexible manufacturing systems the functions to be performed by the systems become perception, retention, reasoning, transmission, and presentation and in the case of distributed teleconferencing systems, the functions become perception, retention, transmission, and presentation. The challenge to the computer technology, science, and engineering is in handling these functions efficiently; and the key to doing so is in understanding the nature of the information that is being perceived, stored, processed, and presented.

Information in the external world can be perceived in five different ways: sound, touch (or feel), scene (or visual), taste, and smell. Of these, only sound and scene are tangible information, and hence can be handled by systems. By 'tangible' we mean that the technology is available to capture the information in electronic (more specifically in digital) form. All other forms of information from the external world are presented to the system as enumerated data. Therefore, what is perceived using a system is either in visual, audio, or data form. When we refer to a visual or audio form, we mean that the corresponding digital information is recorded as a series of bits[1]. Depending on what was spoken or which picture was digitized, the series of bits will have different meanings. In fact, this is exactly what a computer scientist has been referring to as *video, audio,* and *data* related information or *multimedia* information. The multimedia systems that are built today handle essentially these three forms of information. The only variation, however, is in the design goals for these systems, which in turn depends on the ultimate use to which the systems are fielded. But all multimedia systems have to deal with issues related to representation or coding, storage or databases, resource allocation or scheduling, flow of information in different media form through the network, time synchronization across flows, and ultimately the performance of the entire system.

Today, it is more appropriate to refer to a computing environment instead of a computer system since the technology is moving rapidly towards total seamless integration of computing facilities all over the world. Internet is an ideal example of what confronts a computer user today. The user of the computing environment has the choice to store the information in digital form. If the user comes across a speech or a symphony, which the user

---

[1]Bit is a binary digit, the smallest unit that can be stored in a computer system.

would like to store and reproduce at a later point in time, the user can simply choose to store it as audio information. The same holds for a video picture; be it a single frame or a series of frames forming a movie. Moreover, the user is also provided with the flexibility (by the computing environment) to mix and match different types of information. It may be noted by the reader that we use the term *information* to refer to any digital data. Specifically, *information* could refer to a data file (the usual connotation in computer literature), digitized voice, or digitized video. Each type of information is referred to as a medium; a means to transport information; a particular way to render. From a computing perspective, media are means of communication between humans and computers and between humans using computers as communication tools. As there are several interpretations to the term 'multimedia', we would like to emphasize the meaning associated with the term 'multimedia' in this book. *A medium, as used here, refers to any one of data such as text, digitized voice, digitized video, still digitized images, and graphics.* Multimedia, as used here, refers to the combination of two or more of these media, of which at least one is a discrete medium (such as text, image) and one is a continuous medium (e.g., video, audio). Literally, multimedia means many media or multiple media.

The user of the computing environment today gets input in the form of data, voice, video, image, graphics, or a combination of these. Similarly, the user generates information in one or more of these media. We can visualize the user as the focal point in the computing environment, who constantly accepts input from the external world in multimedia form and interacts with the external world with multimedia information. Pictorially, a modern user deals with a computing environment shown in Fig. 1.1.

Currently, multimedia systems related research and development is being pursued by many research groups, often with different perspectives. There is a wide spectrum of work spanning creation, maintenance and retrieval of multimedia databases, synchronization and presentation of multimedia information, conferencing systems using multimedia, protocols for multimedia applications, networks for multimedia applications, performance of multimedia systems, and quality of service relating to multimedia systems. In all these studies, researchers and developers have considered two types of applications: those that deal with multimedia information that is *stored* on a disk and those that deal with multimedia information that is generated *live* such as a conversation shot through video cameras and speech captured using a microphone during a video conferencing session. The information that is retrieved from storage is also referred to as *persistent* information.

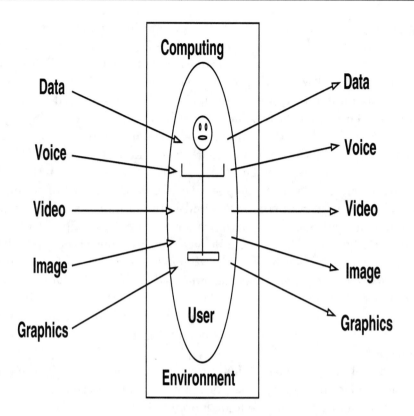

Fig. 1.1. User in a Modern Computing Environment

The term persistent refers to the information that is always available and not transient. The information that is generated *live* from devices such as video cameras or microphones are referred to as *non-persistent* information. The term *non-persistent* is used to refer to the information that is transient; there is no way to repeat if lost or corrupted.

1.2 Why Multimedia?

Human beings have the natural ability to *understand* the information presented in the form of speech, photographs, or video sequences. For example, we cannot only hear the conversation on a telephone, but also *identify* as to who is talking. A mother can recognize her baby in a crowded railway station platform, simply by the baby's voice or cry. Given a photograph of a baseball team, a baseball fan can recognize each player. If we see a video sequence of a place that we have visited several years ago, we start explaining many things related to the place, by a virtual walk through the memory lane. All these simply underline the fact that there are enough *cognitive reasons* as to why multimedia is being used increasingly in systems today.

Multimedia is the form in which the information is handled by the computing environment of today. Multimedia is much richer than the informative bits with which it is represented. For example, when we look at an organization's employee database, it is now possible to store the photograph of each employee, details such as age, salary, expertise, etc., and a short presentation by the employee himself. The database of today is very different compared to conventional databases. Also, for a user of this database, it is possible to flip through the photographs of the employees and pick up the details about an individual as opposed to a key-word search. In fact, the user of the multimedia database need not remember any specific detail regarding the employee other than a recollection of the face.

Another use of an employee database in multimedia form can be illustrated using the following scenario: If the presentations recorded by the employees contain the projects or assignments handled by the employee, then the employer can pick a team for a new project by searching through the voice presentation for relevant experience. The process of picking up a team for the new project is equivalent to having a meeting of all employees in which each employee makes a technical presentation highlighting his skills. This is made possible because when we store the information, different media retain their original form. While in the normal form of storage in a database, every piece of information is encoded as a bit or a byte or a group of bytes, with a preassigned relationship, thereby losing the original character of the information.

Let us consider yet another example that uses the current information-generation technology. Until now, conferencing using computers only meant that the screen was subdivided into as many units as there were participants in a conversation, each one typing in what they had to express as opinion on the subject matter under discussion. The same conferencing will dramatically change once the input changes from simple keyboard interaction to display of slides, transparencies, computer-generated graphics (possibly with animation), annotation with the voice of the participant or from an expert as an extract from a database, and so on. In fact, the possibilities are limited only by the imagination of the user of this new environment supporting multimedia conferencing.

1.3   What is a Multimedia System?

A multimedia system is characterized by processing, storage, generation, manipulation, and rendition of multimedia information. The information to be handled may involve time-dependent/continuous (e.g., audio and video) and time-independent/discrete (e.g., text and still images) media. Modern multimedia applications are geographically spread out, and therefore the *generation* and *replay* of the multimedia information are often at different physical locations. In such cases, a computer network is used to interconnect sources to destinations. Supporting multimedia applications over a computer network renders the application *distributed*. Distributed multimedia applications raise several requirements in communication support and operating system support. Besides, the user interactions may modify the communication requirements of applications.

It may be a good idea to recall the definition of a computer system at this point. A computer system is a machine that can accept data in digital form, process it as per the algorithmic procedure programmed, and give out results in digital form. For the sake of easy interaction, the input and output are mapped onto characters in the form of alphabets, numerals, and special symbols such as +, -, /, *, and so on. Now, let us try to define a multimedia system by comparison! A multimedia system is a computer that can accept information from the external world as data, voice, video, image, or graphics. Of these, only data are mapped to the character set as described earlier. The rest of the information are in their natural form (but recorded digitally) and hence mapping is not required. Also, the devices that are employed for input and output for each media are special and are designed specifically to be able to handle the respective media.

Why is this so? It is because there is an interesting feature of the multimedia information that makes it different from normal data. That is the *temporal relationship* which is peculiar to multimedia information. There are two temporal relationships - one is the right sequence within a medium and the other is across media, called *synchronization*. The idea of temporal relationship is best understood by means of a simple example. Let us assume that we have recorded a classroom lecture on "Introduction to Multimedia Systems" on a disk. Such a recording will have the image of the blackboard used by the instructor, the transparencies or the slides projected in the classroom, the picture of the classroom including the teacher as you would see in a movie, and the sound associated with the actual lecture. It is common knowledge that the teacher will speak about the transparency that is being projected. Also, if you observe the teacher and the lip movement closely, they should be in synchronism with what is being said. If not, on playback, there will be no match between what is being played out as lecture in voice form and what you actually see on the screen. This is what is meant by *temporal relationship!* It will be like seeing a Russian movie with voice coming in English translation. While such a mismatch is alright for a "dubbed" film, it will be very odd in a classroom lecture.

The key issues that are raised by these discussions are the following:

- How are the temporal relationships stored in the system?

- How will the multimedia information be played back so that the temporal relationships are strictly maintained?

- What is involved in doing so?

Handling of the multimedia information keeping this temporal relationship intact makes the multimedia systems different from ordinary computer systems. It is therefore essential for us to understand the nature of multimedia information.

1.3.1 Nature of Multimedia Information

The basic elements that compose multimedia information are data, audio, video, image, and graphics. They have their own 'physical' forms. Data has a physical form of a file. Audio has a physical form of speech that we can hear. Video has a physical form of a movie that we can see. Image has the physical form of a photograph. Graphics has the physical form of the output as displayed on a monitor. While their external manifestations are different, all of them look alike when they are stored in a computer system as a disk file. Suppose we want to store the word HELLO in each one of the media. If it is stored as data in a file, then it will be just five ASCII characters or 40 bits. If it is stored as audio as spoken by a person, it will still look like a series of 1's and 0's but will be a long sequence of bits. If it is stored as video (along with its audio) showing the picture of a person saying hello, it will be a longer sequence of bits. If it is stored as an image, then again it will be a sequence of bits with a length shorter than that of the video representation. If it is stored as graphics, it will be a short sequence of bits with which the word 'HELLO' can be drawn. All five representations are shown in Fig. 1.2. While all the representations in a computer system disk look like a series of bits, the *meaning* associated with the bit sequence in each file is different.

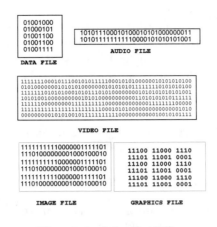

Fig. 1.2. Media Files

For example, data such as computer file have the inherent property that they consist of characters from the standard ASCII character set. In fact, such files are called ASCII files. There are classes of files that are called binary files. The executable images of programs belong to this category. When represented inside the storage of the computer system in digital form, the contents of ASCII files do not change (except for the control characters to indicate beginning, end, etc.) and the binary files are simply recorded as per the eight-bit counterpart in the ASCII character set.

The rest of the media such as audio, video, image and graphics are different. For example, human voice is sampled at the rate of 8000 samples per second and the value of each sample is represented using 8 bits, thereby giving rise to 64 kilobits per second. If we are storing a speech that lasts 5 minutes, then 300 such 64 bits of digital data (approximately 19.2 million bits) will have to be stored.

Video information is even more interesting. Let us assume that we are capturing the five minutes of speech referred to earlier as a part of the video coverage of the speaker. Motion picture or video operates on the principle that a fixed number of frames (equivalent to still pictures) is displayed every second. The number of frames is 30 per second for the United States of America and 25 per second in Europe and India. Each frame corresponds to what is displayed on the screen. This corresponds to a data rate of about 226.5 [2] megabits per second, and if we use efficient compression techniques, then the corresponding compressed data rate can be 0.5 million bits per

---

[2] 300 seconds * 30 frames per second * 1024 * 1024 pixels per frame * 24 bits color.

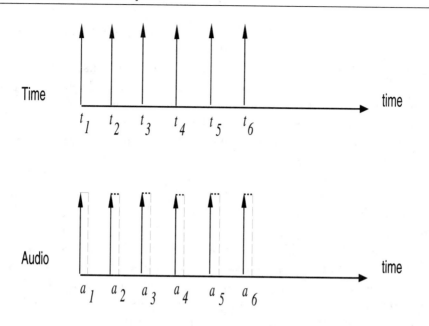

Fig. 1.3. Audio and Time

second for real-time full motion video. That means a total of 150 million bits are to be stored, for our example. How exactly such dramatic savings are brought about by compression is the subject matter for Chapter 3.

So far, we have only looked at the volume of information. In addition to this, there are two other attributes. One relating to the time constraints of the media itself and the other related to *inter-media synchronization*. The time dependency of the audio stream and the video stream are shown in Figs 1.3 and 1.4, respectively. There are two sets of arrows in each diagram. The top portion in each diagram is the time axis that is used for reference. In the time axis (the x-axis as shown), time increases as we move from left to right in the figure. Each arrow represents a time instant, when the sampling is done for either audio or video. The markings at the bottom of the axis t_i are to show the time instants. In Fig. 1.3, the second set of arrows corresponds to the audio. As is the case of the reference axis, here also time increases as we move from left to right. Each arrow corresponds to one *voice sample*. The annotations a_i denote the sample numbers. In the figure, they correspond one-to-one with the time instants that are marked. The dotted box adjoining the arrow represents the amount of information present in each sample, which in our case is 8 bits. We can also use such a diagrammatic representation to refer to different time intervals and the corresponding sizes. It can also be used to show higher-level information units which are aggregation of samples. For example, if we consider the arrows in the time axis to be spaced 1 second apart, then each audio information will represent 64 kilobits of audio information. On the other hand, if we consider the arrows in the time axis to be spaced 1/64 seconds apart, then each audio information will correspond to 1 kilobit of audio information. In Fig. 1.4, the second set of arrows represents video information corresponding to the time instants marked. Each unit of video information sample is a video frame. The video frames are 1/30th of a second apart. In the normal case, the amount of information carried as bits will be the same across all video frames. One size corresponding to a frame can be calculated as a product of the number of pixels along the x axis, the number of pixels along the y axis, the color of each pixel, and the grey level of each pixel. Basically, each frame is viewed as a grid of slots with different colors and intensities. As there is redundancy in the successive video frames, they are normally coded and thereby reduced in size. In Fig. 1.4, the third set of arrows represents such coded frames corresponding to a motion video sequence. The I, P, and B refer to different frame types that are produced when video is coded. The

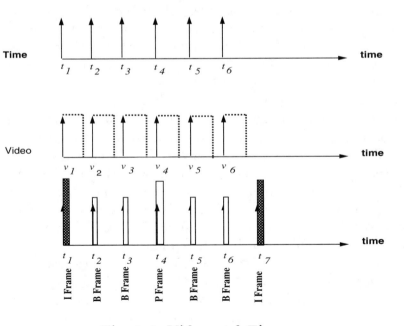

Fig. 1.4. Video and Time

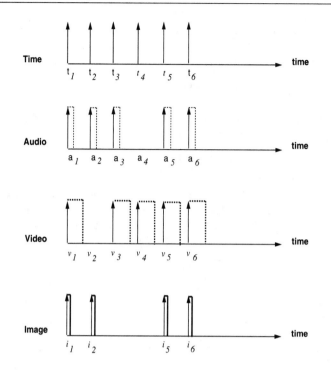

Fig. 1.5. Synchronization of Audio, Video, and Image

different frames are explained in Chapter 3, section 3.4. The difference in the heights of I,P, and B is indicative of the difference in the sizes of frames.

1.3.2 Synchronization of Multimedia Information

Multimedia information has inter-media synchronization as an inherent property. Let us look at the 5-minute-speech example once again. Assume that the speaker uses transparencies to illustrate a point, and that the transparencies are shown in a separate window in the display of the workstation of the viewer, for reasons of clarity. There will be at least two windows, one showing the video of the lecture hall and the other the image of the transparencies. We now have three different media, viz., *video* of the lecture hall, *image* of the transparencies, and *audio* of the lecture itself. As mentioned earlier, lip synchronization demands that the samples a_i and v_i be synchronized periodically. Also, as the transparencies are going to relate to the subject matter being discussed, the *image* should be synchronized with *audio* and *video*. Such an integrated picture will be as shown in Fig. 1.5.

Fig. 1.5 is a *snapshot* of a classroom lecture application that we have been citing as an example. The horizontal line in the figure represents time and it increases as we move from left to right. Vertically, there are four sets of arrows showing the audio, video, and image (top to bottom) at various time instants. There is a different meaning attached to the arrows in Fig. 1.5 as compared to Figs. 1.3 or 1.4. The arrows and the dotted box represent the change in content; for instance at a_1, a_2, and a_3 changes take place in audio stream corresponding to time instances t_1, t_2 and t_3; at a_4 there is no change. The series of information units/samples for each media is called a *stream*. The arrows for each one of the media, audio, video, and image represent *a change in that stream*. If we are listening to a lecture, then the *change* refers to the 'switching over' of the context of discussion from one idea to another. For example, in the audio stream there is a change at every time instant, excepting t_4. The reader should note that we are not dealing with individual samples in Fig. 1.5, but with changes of flow in each media stream. Between changes (or should we say between arrows), there may be a number of samples occurring. They could be fixed or variable in a particular stream as well as across streams. They are not shown in Fig. 1.5. Though the figure looks similar to the earlier Fig. 1.3 and 1.4, it should be noted that Fig. 1.5 deals with an aggregate of samples in each media stream.

Let us now consider the *audio stream*. At time instants t_1, t_2, t_3, t_5, t_6 the *audio* changes. That means the speaker is talking about a connected idea between t_1 and t_2, and then at t_2 changes to a different idea and stays on until t_3, and so on. At the same time, if we look at the *video stream*, there is no change at t_2. That means, the scene associated with the speaker does not change until t_3. Further on, there is a change at t_4, when the related speech still continues. Same is the case with the *image stream*. In this example, *inter-media synchronization* is required between audio and video at t_3, t_5, and t_6, between audio and image at t_2, t_5, and t_6, between image and video at t_5 and t_6, and between all three at t_5 and t_6. Of course, at the start (i.e., at t_1) all of the media are synchronized.

We should note that what we discussed so far is only a snapshot. If we consider a multimedia application, there will be several such snapshots appearing in a sequence during the lifetime of the application. There will also be several time instants when synchronization will be required between some or all streams of information.

1.3.3 Notion of Multimedia Formation

Due to the inherent nature of multimedia information and the synchronization requirements, a multimedia application can be essentially viewed as consisting of different media streams. The number of these streams, the amount of information in each stream, and the time instants of synchronization across the media streams may vary during the lifetime of an application. But if we divide the application lifetime into observation intervals, we will see snapshots similar to Fig. 1.5 successively. We refer to each one of them as a *multimedia formation*. Therefore, every multimedia application is going to consist of several such formations. Such a view, based on the streams, is shown schematically in Fig. 1.6. Though the multimedia formations are shown as being distinct objects in the schematic, in reality, they are indistinguishable, except for marking the observation intervals. These formations are retrieved from disks as stored data and are integrated from the output coming out of input devices such as video cameras, microphones, and so on. The individual streams in the formation may go through the same path through a communication network or may take entirely different paths. Depending on their path, the individual streams (and each sample or aggregate sample) may arrive at the receiving end at different times. This is likely to disturb the formation. Before replaying, the multimedia formation should be formed again at the receiver buffer and then displayed on the screen and/or output on the speaker. All of these issues naturally raise the question as to what are the desirable features of a multimedia system.

1.3.4 Desirable Features of a Multimedia System

The features that are expected of a computer system to support the demands of multimedia applications are essentially a phenomenal increase in the conventional capabilities and an additional ability to deal with time-related input and output. Some of the features are highlighted in the sequel.

Very high processing power: In the conventional computing scenario, the processing requirement was essentially derived from scientific computing, which emphasized better instruction execution capability and better number crunching capability. In contrast, in the modern multimedia context, we emphasize movement and processing of large amounts of data in *real-time*. It is presently a common design practice to include support hardware such as graphics and video adapters, digital signal processors, and special-purpose processors that carry out various compression techniques in microcode. CPU

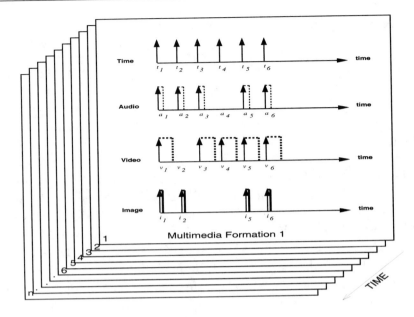

Fig. 1.6. Multimedia Formation

operates at speeds upwards of 150 MHz, when we consider machines of Pentium or higher order.

A file system capable of handling multimedia information: The speciality of multimedia information such as video is that it is a continuous[3] data as opposed to data files or program files. Conventional file systems tend to locate pieces of a file through successive pointer lookup, which means too many accesses to the storage device and therefore increased I/O time. This tends to defeat the goal of real-time processing of audio or video. Therefore, file systems should have the capability to deal with streams of data.

File formats that exploit the inherent properties of the multimedia information: This is closely related to the requirement we stated as desirable on the part of the file system. The file formats, on one hand, should be easy to handle from the file system point of view and on the other hand should naturally represent the isochronous nature of the media information to be handled. Streams and their variations are natural choices.

Efficient and high I/O rate: The input and output subsystem should be able to handle large storage, and the controller hardware should be able to

---

[3]They are sampled digital data, with a start time and an end time.

provide recording and reading of data from these storages in a manner that appears contiguous from the application viewpoint. For example, if there are four disks that are in an array, simultaneous reading and writing on all four should be possible. This will help in handling audio and video data which are inherently continuous and best handled as streams. Also, the capture and recording devices should incorporate the standard compression and coding techniques in the hardware for efficient handling.

Multimedia operating system: An efficient file system (to handle placement of continuous data) and efficient data structures are required to provide support for direct transfers from disk to NIU, real-time scheduling of tasks, fast interrupt processing, and streams. To support direct transfers from disk to network interface unit, real-time scheduling of tasks, fast interrupt processing, and support for streaming I/Os, an efficient file system to handle placement of continuous data and data structures to support them is needed.

Storage and memory: The storage (secondary) requirement in the multimedia context is of the order of 50-100 Gigabytes and correspondingly, the memory (primary) requirements are in the range of 50-100 Megabytes. Caches have to be larger and may have to be in a 2 or 3 level hierarchy for efficient management. Hardware that maps the working set of a program onto these hierarchical structures should be supported by the controller hardware.

Network support: It is common to apply the client-server paradigm [4] in building multimedia applications. The consequence is that we need high-speed support from the network subsystem, including the interface unit. It should be able to stream the data out of the disk directly. This is essential, as we try to minimize delay and jitter by improving the efficiency of subsystems that contribute to the delay, wherever possible.

Software tools: Need to be user friendly as they have to handle a variety of media at the same time. Also, to make things easier for the developer, tools should support object-oriented software design and development methodologies.

1.3.5 Operational View of a Multimedia System

Multimedia applications present the multimedia information as a series of multimedia formations to the computer system. The multimedia informa-

---

[4]Server: a program which offers a service that can be reacted over a network.
Client: a program which sends a request to a server and waits for response.

tion may be generated live or retrieved from storage. The system, while
processing the information, should preserve the time constraints *within* the
media as well as *across* the media. From the information viewpoint, the
different media are generated at constant rate and constant size, and should
be presented to the display device at constant rate and constant size. This
is true for each medium. For example, audio is at 8000 samples per second
and video is at 30 frames per second (each frame has a fixed number of
samples), which implies constant rate. Each audio sample is 8 bits in size
and each video frame is 620x560x24 bits. As the amount of information is
too large to store or retrieve or process or transmit, and because media such
as video have inherent redundancy, the multimedia information is encoded,
thereby changing its original formation. Compression reduces the size of
the formation. Moreover, if the source and destination are separated by a
communication network, then due to sharing of the communication bandwidth with other applications or users, *asynchrony* sets into the multimedia
formation. The asynchrony may affect different media streams in the multimedia formation differently, thereby disturbing the synchronization that
was present across the media streams at the source end. In addition to this
asynchrony there could be possible losses in transit. Both effects render the
problem of reconstructing the multimedia formation at the receiving end
more difficult. After reconstructing, the formation has to be decoded to obtain the original constant rate and constant size for display. An operational
view of the multimedia system may help the reader better appreciate the
problem.

1.4   Components of a Multimedia System

Multimedia systems have several components such as input (capture) devices, storage, communication network, computer systems, and composition
(display) devices. Table 1.1 presents examples of these components. In any
given multimedia system, the components used depend on the location of
multimedia information (source) and the location to which it is to be transported to for use (destination). For instance, if the source is in a device
such as CD-ROM and the destination is the display device on the same
workstation, then only the playback speed needs to be maintained to ensure
multimedia synchronization. In such cases, there is no need for any special
synchronization technique.

Devices	Examples
Capture devices	Video camera, video cassette recorder Audio microphone, keyboard, mouse, scabber etc.
Storage devices	CD-ROMs, disks
Communication network	Ethernet(10 to 100 Mbps), Token Ring (100 Mbps) FDDI (100 Mbps), ATM (up to 1 Gbps)
Computer systems	Pentium PCs, workstations, MPEG, DSP hardware
Display devices	CD-quality speaker(audio), HDTV, SVGA, HiRes monitors

Table 1.1. Examples of Multimedia Components

1.5 Types of Multimedia Systems

Multimedia systems that are available today appear to be of different types. But a careful analysis of the systems will show that a typical multimedia system can be thought of as consisting of a multimedia information storage subsystem, multimedia information processing subsystem such as MPEG hardware, and multimedia information display subsystem. These subsystems could appear as an integral part of a single system or can be spread over a network (LAN[5] or WAN[6]) with dedicated communication channels between the three subsystems or can be spread over a wide area network with high-speed switched access. The three representative scenarios are illustrated in Fig. 1.7.

The first part of Fig. 1.7 represents standalone multimedia systems that have the capability to handle voice and video. Such systems consist of components such as PCs with CD-ROMs, sound blaster card, and video blaster card. These are used commonly in authoring systems and multimedia **presentation** systems. The second part of the figure represents **peer-to-peer**

---

[5]Local Area Network.
[6]Wide Area Network.

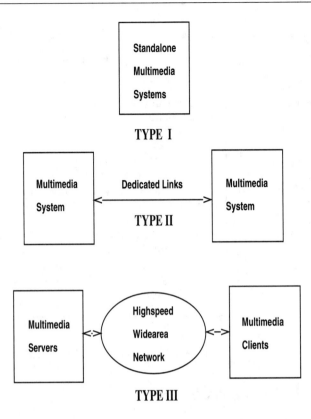

Fig. 1.7. Multimedia Systems - Different Possibilities

communication over a network using a virtual channel setup between the peers. Typical examples are multimedia workstations based conferencing systems that use local or wide area networks. The third part of the figure represents the situation as it exists in a large interconnected network. Internet and corporate networks are examples of this type of system. The servers generally have extraordinarily large storage capabilities, and the clients have the input and output capabilities for handling multimedia.

In our further discussions in this book, we will refer to standalone systems as Type I systems, systems using dedicated links as Type II systems, and systems using high-speed wide area networks as Type III systems. Workstation-based examples of multimedia systems of Types I, II, and III are shown pictorially in Figs. 1.8, 1.9, and 1.10 respectively. The computer system part contains a Central Processing Unit, Memory, Input/Output for disk, Network Interface Unit (NIU), and MPEG hardware. When the system is

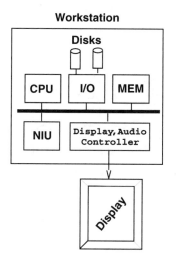

Fig. 1.8. Standalone Multimedia Systems

used as a standalone system, the entire flow of the multimedia information is within the system. When the system is configured with two workstations interconnected using a dedicated communication link, the NIUs play a role in transporting the multimedia information in either direction as is requested by the application. A dedicated link between the workstations implies that adequate bandwidth is assured. The most complex part is when the system is configured as a server and a client interconnected using a high-speed network, which is also likely to be serving other such pairs of servers and clients. In such a case, to guarantee all the transmission requirements of the application is a non-trivial design task, which is the main emphasis of this book.

1.6   Where are Multimedia Systems used?

Multimedia systems are used in a variety of situations. By and large they can be classified as *multimedia database systems, multimedia presentation systems, and multimedia conferencing systems.* These are the generic examples of multimedia systems which can be configured as customized systems tailored to specific applications.

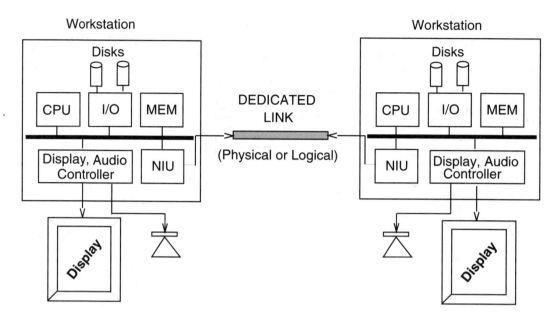

Fig. 1.9. Workstation Peers

1.6.1   Multimedia Database System

Multimedia database systems deal with creation, maintenance, manipulation, and retrieval of multimedia information. In general, the databases can be at several sites (normally referred to as *servers*) and will be connected to a number of workstations through a communication network. Multiple servers such as video servers, voice servers, and data servers can be realized in a single physical machine as well. The query generated by any of the clients will be internally translated into one or more queries to the different servers. The responses that are received from the individual servers are pieced together into one composite response by the workstation. Such a multimedia database system is shown in Fig. 1.11, where there are three servers, for video, voice, and data, connected to several clients through a communication subnetwork. The database may store information as video, voice, data, image, graphics, or a combination of these. Designing a multimedia database system poses a number of challenges. The sheer volume of data to be handled, structuring the data from different sources such as video and audio appropriately, and maintaining the synchronization information are all vital tasks. Once these problems are solved and the database is created, providing a proper query language that can be context sensitive,

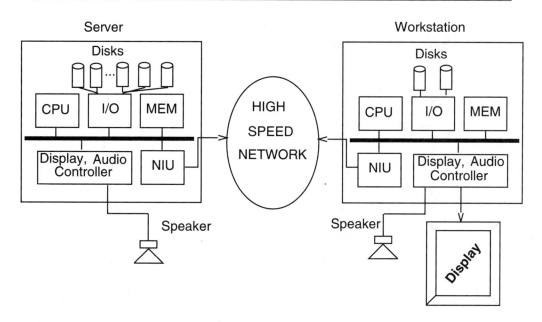

Fig. 1.10. Server-Client Configuration

media sensitive, and at the same time lead naturally to efficient searching will be necessary.

Example: Let us consider a simple application scenario in which a multimedia workstation accesses a multimedia database server. By nature, the database applications are half-duplex - that means the user station (called *Source*) sends a query first and then waits; the server station (called *Destination*) picks up the query, interprets it, collects and collates the information required to form a response, and finally sends it to the user station. If we follow the transaction from the very beginning, the query is sent by the *Source* to the *Destination* and the response is sent by the *Destination* back to the *Source*. At any point in time, it is either *Source* → *Destination* flow of multimedia information or *Destination* → *Source* and never both simultaneously.

Let us specify some more details about the workstation at the source. There are two windows in the query physically exhibiting an image and text.

The image (photograph) of a scientist delivering a talk shows the person and a snapshot of a video. The text provides supplementary information. The intention of the query is to identify when and where the scientist gave that talk, pick up the video clip, and play it for the benefit of the user.

When the reply is received, it will consist of the video clip, charts used in the talk in the form of images, the audio and the text to support the talk. Depending on the nature of the user's requirement, the database query can be interactive. For example, the user may choose to skip through the video clip quickly to locate a particular part of the lecture in fast forward mode and play from there onwards in the normal play mode. The user may also repeat a chosen (identified) sequence repeatedly for a specific end use.

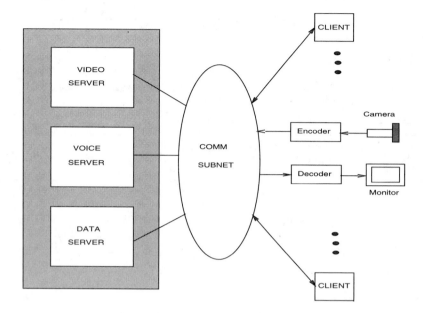

Fig. 1.11. Multimedia Database System

Another important point to be noted in this context is that the multimedia information is *non-persistent* when created and *persistent* when retrieved from the database for rendition. These two factors influence the design choice one makes to meet the challenges described earlier. The multimedia digital library system is a good example of a multimedia database system.

On-demand multimedia server, as an application, belongs to the generic class of multimedia database systems [1, 2]. A HDTV [7]-on-demand server provides services similar to those of a videotape rental store [3]. The server digitally stores video such as entertainment movies, educational documentaries, etc., on a large array of high-capacity storage devices (e.g., optical disks). Users can access the server by searching on the video's subject title, and can play the movie by retrieving the stored video from the server. Such a system lends itself naturally to two modes of operation; viz., *broadcast* and *on-demand*. In the broadcast mode, the server plays the role of a sender and many clients play the role of receivers simultaneously, receiving the same information. In the on-demand mode, the server plays the role of multiple senders simultaneously and each client communicates with one instantiation of the server. An example of an on-demand server is a multimedia database

---

[7]High Definition Television.

server with travel information about a country. In such cases, the information in the form of audio, video, text, and image, representing the scenic beauty of the country, are stored in databases. Such systems will have special functions for the users to access and search through the databases, playing the role of a 'virtual' tourist.

1.6.2 Multimedia Presentation System

A multimedia presentation system deals primarily with the problem of retrieving the multimedia information from a database for presentation on a user workstation with the user participation. The database of presentation material is created separately and stored as in the case of multimedia database systems. But the retrieval is under user control. This can also be seen as a special case of a multimedia database system, where the structure of the database and the query are fixed. Because of user participation, the information accessed may vary dynamically within a subset of the database. In addition to the challenges to be faced in the case of multimedia database systems design, handling the user interactions to control the sequence of presentations will be an additional problem to be tackled at design time. The interactions effectively amount to a VCR[7]-like function on several media simultaneously.

1.6.3 Multimedia Conferencing System

A multimedia conferencing system is an on-line real-time system where the multimedia information is generated, transmitted, and presented in real-time. Optionally, such systems may have a storage facility for later playback. As the number of participants and locations of the conference increase, the resource demands will also increase. Such a system primarily deals with creating digitized video, digitized voice, data, images, and graphics and transmitting such information across a communication network so that it reaches the destination(s) in real-time. The important point to be noted in this context is that the system deals primarily with *non-persistent* multimedia information. Besides, the design challenges identified earlier, namely, dealing with large quantities of non-persistent information in real-time (using appropriate buffering techniques) is an additional challenge.

---

[7]Functions such as Play, Reverse, Fast Forward, Skip, Pause, etc.

1.6.4   Classification of Multimedia Applications

Multimedia applications may also be classified as *orchestrated* and *live* based on the mode of generation of information. The classification stems from the fact that the multimedia information has a lifetime in the system depending on the way it is generated. For example, for a given application and a system, the multimedia information can be generated either by using multimedia devices such as video cameras and microphones(live) or by accessing stored information in databases (orchestrated or archived). In the live case, the multimedia information is transient (i.e., non-persistent) and in the archived case, it is permanent (i.e., persistent). A multimedia application is referred to as orchestrated if the information handled by that application is persistent. On-demand HDTV server and multimedia database applications fall under the orchestrated category and typically access stored information in large optical disks. On the contrary, a multimedia application is referred to as live if it processes information generated from devices such as a video camera, microphone, or keyboard. Multimedia teleconferencing applications fall under the live category.

1.6.5   Classification of Multimedia Information

Multimedia information can be classified as *discrete* and *continuous* based on the relationship of the information with respect to time. Media such as text, graphics, and image have a discrete relation to time with the exception of graphics with animation. On the contrary, media such as audio and video have a continuous relation to time. Multimedia applications, whether orchestrated or live, may deal with both discrete and continuous media.

It should be noted that the terms *continuous* and *discrete* do not refer to the internal data representation, but to the users' view of the data. Continuous media data (e.g., video) often consists of a sequence of discrete values which replace each other as time progresses. For example, in a video clip the persistence of vision, which is part of human vision, lets us see any image sequence with more than 16 images per second as continuous movement. When such time sequencing is added to discrete media such as graphics, *animation* will result.

1.7   Current Trends in Internet

The ubiquitous Internet has two interesting applications that are truly global with a harmonizing touch on the world-wide human population. They are

World Wide Web (WWW) and MBone - Multicast Backbone. The WWW technology enables integration of information sources around the world and MBone technology provides the equivalent of conventional radio and television on the Internet. WWW typically uses images along with text. MBone uses images, voice, video, and text. These two applications together signify a sea-change in the way applications are going to be, in the Internet. Currently, they are the most popular multimedia applications on the Internet. We discuss both WWW and MBone in this section.

1.7.1 WWW

World Wide Web (popularly known as WWW) is a cooperative project initiated in 1989 at CERN[8], Geneva, Switzerland, to design and develop a system for the integration of various types of information sources using *hypermedia* concepts. The motivation was to support collaborative research among physicists, who produce and exchange large volumes of information and are spread out geographically. Therefore, scalability and simplicity turned out to be the hallmark of the technology produced through this effort.

World Wide Web consists of the following:

- Technology to establish a WWW server. This includes the protocols to contact other servers and clients.

- Technology to establish clients to be parented to any server either statically or dynamically. A user-friendly GUI (Graphical User Interface) to enable interaction with the WWW.

- A protocol called http (hyper-text transfer protocol) as a part of the client as well as the server.

- A language called html (hyper-text markup language) to enable users to organize the information in the servers.

The interesting aspect of the WWW technology is the transparent access to any web site for information, thereby giving the user the impression of seamless inter-connectivity of information sources (known popularly as web servers) across LANs, WANs, Internet, or a combination of these. Though the technology appears to be uncontrolled and unregulated, there seems to be a voluntary adoption of discipline among the users. The information

---

[8]CERN is the European Laboratory for Particle Physics.

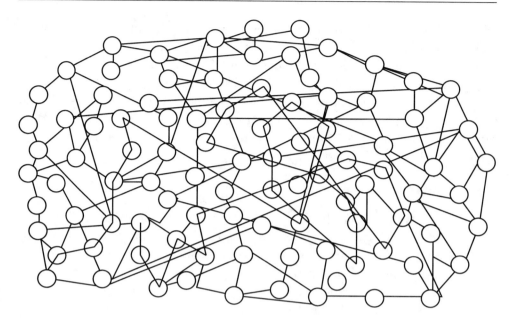

Fig. 1.12. An Attempt at Drawing the Linkages across all Web Sites

sources (often referred to as hyperspace, cyberspace, and so on) are linked among themselves, which when drawn on a sheet of paper looks like the web of a spider. For identification purposes, each unit of information that is linked into the cyberspace has an ID called Universal Resource Locator or URL. This idea has enabled a liberalized approach to information sharing - anybody can author a document and at the same time optionally refer to anybody else's document - leading to contribution of research results to the cyberspace. If we attempt drawing the graph interconnecting all the information sources in the WWW today, the picture may appear to be similar to what is shown in Fig. 1.12.

Let us look at the following scenario. A user working on System A runs browser software (browser is the client portion of WWW with GUI). During the web search on the 'local server', one of the pages has pointers to two different documents: one on the 'local server' and the other on the 'remote server', as depicted in Fig. 1.13. The 'local server' (also referred to as System A) has a local pointer corresponding to the first reference and a remote pointer to a document in 'remote server' (also referred to as System B). The user can 'click' his/her way through these documents, oblivious of the

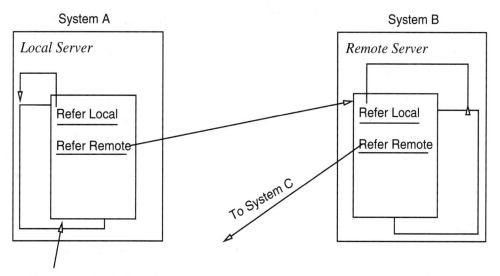

Fig. 1.13. Document Linkages on the Web

physical location of the documents. On reaching System B from System A through the use of hyperlinks, yet another link may take the user away to another System C (not shown in the figure) in a transparent fashion. What is more - these systems can be anywhere in the global Internet! In addition to providing electronic annihilation of distance, WWW technology also interfaces with the traditional databases with ease. For example, if a query needs to be answered after searching a database, then it is transparently done. You may want to look for screens where you accessed the same information (for example, the weather conditions in Alaska) more than once, but the answer you receive is different every time.

Let us take a few moments to understand the components of WWW.

Uniform Resource Locator: URLs specify how and where to get a document. The host where the document resides is identified by its name and not IP[9] address.

Hyper-Text Markup Language (HTML):   HTML provides a format for specifying simple logical structures and hyper-text links. Usual characteristics

---

[9]IP address is a globally unique address administered by the Internet Network Information Center. More information about IP appears in Chapter 5.

of documents, viz., headers, paragraphs, character highlighting, bullets, figures, photographs, graphics, special markers called anchor tags, and so on
are all possible. HTML also defines how URLs can be inserted. Recent
versions of HTML support form filling by users, tables, and mathematical
equations.

Hyper-Text Transfer Protocol (HTTP): HTTP is the protocol that supports the transfer of documents attached to WWW hyperlinks. HTTP normally operates on a *downloading* mode, but it can also operate in *real-time*
transmission mode when large continuous media documents are to be displayed.

1.7.2   MBone

MBone means **M**ulticast **Backbone**. Multicast is the process of sending
packets to a group of destinations as opposed to a single destination, in the
normal case. In several situations, this approach of selective communication
to a group is quite useful. Let us consider a simple example. A conference
on Multimedia Systems Design is taking place in California. There are a
couple of hundred researchers physically present at the conference location.
But there are at least another 100,000 researchers located in different countries who would like to listen to the talks and discussions that are going
on at the conference. How do we support it? This is where an ingenuous
solution based on the Internet comes into the picture. The IP substrate of
the Internet provides the necessary universal view and global reach. Moreover, the 100,000 researchers can be viewed as concentrated in a few groups;
some groups may be over 1,000 and some may be just 10. If we can elect
a representative for each one of these groups, and send all that is going on
at the conference to these representatives, then the problem is somewhat
simpler. It is assumed that it is the responsibility of these chosen representatives to transmit all the information to all the members of the respective
groups individually.

MBone protocol supports such a group communication over the Internet.
MBone is comprised of two things: a physical network, made of IP multicast
nodes spread over the globe and running over the standard Internet, and a set
of tools to announce audio and video programs broadcast over the networks
and to assist users in automatically joining such groups and automatically
launching necessary applications on their systems. The scenario that we
described earlier and the solution leading to MBone technology are shown
pictorially in Fig. 1.14. The examples that follow are brief descriptions of the

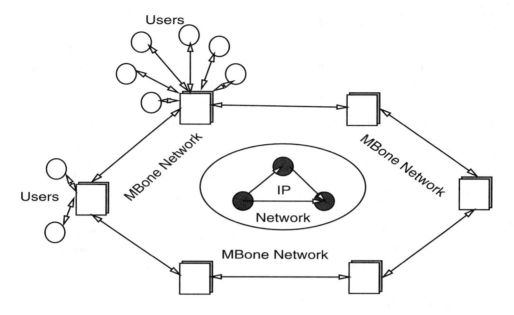

Fig. 1.14. MBone Example

software that use MBone to provide user-level applications on the Internet.

Example - sd (Session Directory): The session directory is an interface to the MBone. When sd is invoked, it displays the available conferences on the mbone that a user can join.

Example - vat (Visual Audio Tool): The visual audio tool allows users to send and receive sound across the mbone. Only a microphone and a speaker or headphones are needed. Since vat defaults the microphone to mute, a user must click the right mouse button anywhere in the vat's window or click on the mute button above the microphone to talk.

Example - wb (White Board): The white board allows users to send and receive imported post script, imported text, or various graphics and text images created on the white board across the mbone. When wb is started, two windows appear. The first one shows activity, participants, participants information, and network information, while the second window is the white board.

Example - nv (Network Video): nv allows users to send and receive video. In order to send video, a video camera and a video card are required. The software needed to receive video is an X-windows session on the workstation.

1.8 Enabling Technologies

Electronics and computer related technologies have been growing at a rapid rate. The increase in the capacity of computer and related equipment have encouraged users to think in terms of new applications. Multimedia is one such application. It demands more in terms of processing, storage, and communications from the computer system. In addition to these, there has been a tremendous growth in coding technologies, technologies for application support, and system integration technologies. We briefly discuss here some of these technologies as well as their impact on the evolution. Many of these technologies are discussed in detail later in the book.

- *Carrier Technology:* e.g., fiber, high capacity, high-speeds, high reliability. These technologies relate to the mechanism of transporting bits across a wide area network at high-speeds (typically multi megabits or gigabits per second). Mainly, optical fiber based technology is very reliable with a low bit error rate of the order of 10^{-10} to 10^{-12}.

- *Switching Technology:* These technologies relate to high-speed switching of basic units of information called cells or frames. The switches use the carrier technologies as input and output, and therefore operate at speeds of the order of gigabits per second or 2 million cells or frames per second. Some examples are the ATM, DQDB, FDDI, SMDS, frame relays, etc. (equivalent to network layer and below). These are further discussed in Chapter 5.

- *Protocol Technology:* e.g., new protocol suites, especially at the application level, to support multimedia applications. These technologies relate to providing generic services to the applications such as address location, address resolution, connection setup, multicasting, end-to-end control, quality of service, and so on. High-speed networks demand innovative lookahead schemes from protocol technology.

- *Application Technology:* e.g., new multimedia applications, user-friendly interface equipment, etc. Some examples are Head Trackball, Joystick, Movieworks, etc. These technologies act as the interface between the protocol technology and the applications themselves. Often these technologies are specific to a class of applications and require to be developed as communication subsystem independent and protocol independent technologies, for deployment in a wide variety of systems.

- *Sensor, Coding and Compression Technology:* e.g., digital video cameras, digital microphones, digital scanners, video codec, voice code, digital compression techniques for data, voice and video, etc. These technologies help in interfacing the input equipment for video, voice, and image. To conserve bandwidth and to eliminate redundancies, the input devices have the coding mechanisms built in as part of the device itself. The emphasis in designing equipment has been to suit high-fidelity reproduction of the original information.

- *Database Technology;* e.g., large databases, integrated databases, federated databases, active and proactive databases, etc. These technologies address the issue of storing multimedia information of the order of several gigabytes and retrieving them with multimedia keys. For example, from an employee database, one would like to pull out the record of an individual by presenting the photograph of the person as a search criterion. Moreover, when multimedia information is stored as an integral part of each record, the synchronization information should also be stored so that the original nature of the multimedia information is retained on retrieval.

- *Software Technology:* e.g., environments for distributed programming, parallel programming, etc. These technologies become vital in the modern computing environment as the development of multimedia applications require an appropriate development environment. One such environment is the object-oriented software development environment which is becoming popular today. Such an environment includes programming support, runtime library support for multimedia operations, a facility to integrate with protocol stacks [10], debugging with real-time event monitoring, and so on.

- *Computation Technology:* e.g., high-performance processors, distributed environments, server-client computing, etc. These technologies are fundamental to multimedia support. In fact, in sophisticated multimedia systems, there can be many processors dedicated to a specific task. The coordination between the processors to conform to the real-time constraints in processing is an interesting area of research in architecture.

---

[10] A set of protocols that are hierarchically arranged(as layers one above the other), such that a complex service is accomplished by segmenting it into a number of simpler services, is called a protocol stack.

- *System Integration Technology:* e.g., seamless integration of the technologies mentioned above for domain-specific application development. This is by far the most important requirement in the context of multimedia. Integration involves hardware, software, communication, sensor, coding, and compression technologies to coexist in the modern multimedia system and the whole system should have a simple and easy-to-use user interface.

The relationship between these technologies is shown in Fig. 1.15. This figure shows the carrier technology as the basis for the whole development. In fact, from the days of telephony several improvements have come about in this technology and today it is all set to integrate computer communication, television broadcasting, and telephony in digital. To provide seamless integration of these three technologies at the fundamental level requires redesign of the carrier technology itself. Of the several options tried out by various manufacturers, providers, and users, the option of transferring information asynchronously in small quantities called cells, but at high-speeds to simulate real-time, is gaining ground. Such a fundamental change will require redesign/rethinking at all other levels. Switching technology is closely coupled with carrier technology and should reflect how the new approach at carrier level is going to be used for setting up arbitrary paths between two parties or users. The ubiquitous telephone system provides interconnection between any two telephones, across the entire globe. Using the digital technology, as we go from continuous analog signal representation of voice in existing telephony to discrete digital representation, the problem of setting up paths, providing good quality speech, and carrying them within tolerable limits of human perception have been achieved.

Protocols were originally designed to ensure that the conversation between two computers is error free even in the presence of errors in the channels. These were refined to such an extent that logical operations such as bank transactions can be performed reliably over unreliable interconnections. As the variability in the systems became large, the specification, verification, development, and testing required special technologies for faster and reliable prototyping. Also, efficient implementation[11] of protocols is important at high-speeds, especially in multimedia networks. The protocol technology provides means of finding state-of-the-art solutions to modern switching en-

---

[11]Limiting or reducing the time to ensure reliable transfer (which is what a protocol does) enables one to deal with time constraints better while designing high-speed networks with multimedia support.

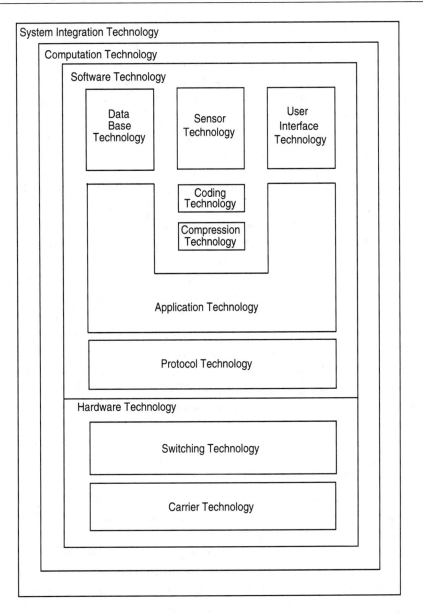

Fig. 1.15. Technology Relationships

vironment. At the same time, a protocol provides 'appropriate' services to
the applications.

Multimedia applications span a large spectrum. At one end of the spectrum we have a simple presentation tool and at the other end we have a doctor performing brain microsurgery with the help of a consultant doctor located at the other side of the globe, both of them sharing a common database in another geographical location - all in real-time. Such diversity demands two classes of support services from the protocols and protocol technology: one set of services common to all multimedia applications and another set particularly tailored to a specific class. The applications themselves are to be developed using a sophisticated environment, which makes available the features of a high-speed network, as a simple set of procedure calls.

But the application technology has to support applications and at the same time interface with the runtime environment consisting of network protocol call libraries, database interfaces, user interfaces (including the features of input and display devices), and the sensors (such as video camera and a microphone) with the attendant coding and compression technologies. All these interactions take place at the system level and require appropriate 'views' of data and operations. This implies that we have an environment in which such integration can be done in software, as a human being would deal with objects in the physical world around him.

The software technology, the required computational power, and the ultimate system integration permeate through all levels of a multimedia system. In fact, in Fig. 1.15 these three technologies encircle the entire system in all three dimensions.

1.9   The Magic Word - QoS

As we discussed earlier in this chapter, there are several aspects to a multimedia system. If we consider the three types of systems that we explained, the third system is by far the most complex and also most demanding. When we say 'complex' and 'most demanding', we simply refer to the basic requirement in the multimedia systems, which is maintenance of time synchronization across media. When the multimedia information goes through a communication network, the asynchrony introduced by the network disturbs the synchronization which is essential to multimedia information. Some part of synchrony is handled by additional information(such as markers) which is needed in transfer-store-play. But there is additional need when the store is eliminated, which is necessary for real-time.

To ensure strict adherence to synchronization, we need to ensure that sufficient guaranteed bandwidth is always available from the source to the destination. This is a simple and good strategy as long as the flow of information is uniform. As the flow of information itself is 'bursty' in nature, dedicating a large (peak) bandwidth for every flow will most often result in a significant(and avoidable) waste of resources. Therefore, network designers would like to operate with average values thereby maximizing the utilization of the network. Also, the end systems may be able to buffer the flow of information to a large extent, thereby ensuring the synchronization at the receiving end, even if it is disturbed during transmission over a communication network. But the extent to which such disturbances to synchronization can be tolerated is ultimately limited by human tolerance.

Based on the stream model of multimedia information explained earlier in Section 1.3.1, a disturbance in synchronization is simply a delay suffered by one (or more) of the streams during transmission. By buffering, one can compensate for the delay and reconstruct the multimedia formation as it was originally at the source end. But one more problem will come up! Because of the highly dynamic nature of the communication network (and the traffic handled by it), the *delay* may not be a constant delay for a given stream across the multimedia formation. That means, the receiver will experience not only a delay but also a *jitter* in the delay. In a multimedia system, the jitter should also be kept within limits. Delay and jitter together affect synchronization requirements. Besides, the system should ensure that *loss of packets* are minimized, if not completely eliminated. Requirements such as delay, jitter, percentage loss of packets, etc. are together referred to as the Quality of Service (QoS) expected of a communication network by a multimedia application.

In practice, QoS is not one fixed value but varies from application to application. It depends on the composition of the multimedia formation corresponding to the application. Each application will have a range of QoS bounded by preferred QoS and acceptable QoS. The preferred QoS corresponds to the ideal conditions under which the application would like to run. The acceptable QoS corresponds to the minimum acceptable situation, below which it does not make sense to run that application. These two extremes together define what is called a QoS spectrum, which is shown schematically in Fig. 1.16. Normally, a negotiation takes place between the application and the network service provider to decide the point of operation within this QoS spectrum. The operating point is referred to as guaranteed QoS.

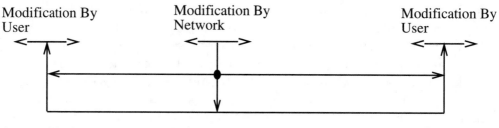

Fig. 1.16. QoS Spectrum

QoS Requirements: The QoS offered by the network to a multimedia application can be characterized by the values of the following performance parameters [4, 5, 6].

1. *Traffic throughput:* This QoS parameter is related to the amount of data that will be sent through the network per unit time, specifying the traffic communication needs in terms of the bandwidth required.

2. *Transmission delay:* This parameter specifies the delay that a transmitted data unit can suffer through the network. This parameter may be expressed either in terms of an absolute or a probabilistic bound.

3. *Delay jitter:* In addition to delay, a bound on the delay variation called the *delay jitter* can also be specified.

4. *Transmission reliability:* This parameter is primarily related to the buffering mechanisms involved in data transmission along the network. Because of the limited size of these buffers, some packets might be lost due to traffic congestion. A probabilistic bound on such losses influence the amount of resources required for the establishment of a connection.

5. *Synchronization:* Another consideration for multimedia applications is that a number of network channels are simultaneously required for transferring different media objects. In some cases, inter-channel synchronization has to be provided when separate channels are used for transferring media like audio and video. A channel group is described by a set of member channels along with the relationship that relates them. A channel is defined as a simplex end-to-end connection with traffic characterization and performance guarantees. Relationship

among the channels can be specified in terms of inter-channel bounds on QoS parameters (bounds on delay jitter, in the case of audio and video channels) or multicast relationship.

In the discussions we had so far, the fact that multimedia applications have a different set of requirements from the systems point of view and their impact on different aspects has been repeatedly underlined. We have also emphasized that these requirements are inherent to the multiple media information that is being handled by these systems. Now, let us elaborate on these requirements and their impact on different subsystems.

1.10 Impact on System Design

Multimedia systems have several unique requirements that should be met in any system design. Even though these systems are nothing more than so-phisticated computer systems, the fact that these systems are dealing with multimedia information make them more demanding. We can analyze the requirements from different points of view, viz., processing, storage, commu-nication, and input and output.

In terms of processing, multimedia information presents two types of challenges: one related to volume and the other related to time constraints. One example is the processing related to video information that is to be reconstructed from a coded representation. In such a case, the amount of data to be handled will be of the order of tens of megabytes.

In terms of storage, video information poses the maximum possible chal-lenges. Also, when we deal with more than one medium, the inter-media synchronization information should also be taken into account. Storing the multimedia information while keeping their inter-media relationships intact is a serious concern in design.

Why is this so? Let us consider an example of an application that com-prises video, voice, image, and graphics relating to a lecture on 'Molecular Modeling'. The four media may have different points at which to synchro-nize. Supporting the sequencing in the application requires that the an-imated molecular model of a certain protein be displayed along with the explanations of the properties of the molecule by a scientist. During this se-quence, the three media graphics, video, and audio will have to be synchro-nized in such a way that the animation is in synchrony with the explanation being given. When we capture the lecture by the scientist using a digital video camera with MPEG [12] output, video and audio will be recorded with synchronization information automatically. But we need an external marking or structuring technique to preserve the synchronization by the MPEG output with the animated graphics.

Earlier on we introduced the idea of three different types of multimedia systems: standalone, peer-to-peer with dedicated link, and client-server with high-speed wide area interconnection. In Type I system, one may not come across serious challenges in design arising out of the communication subsystem. But in Type II and Type III systems, the communication subsystem itself becomes a shared resource across many multimedia applications. Each multimedia application has a delivery requirement (expressed as a function of time) pertaining to *that* application. When many such requests are presented to the communication subsystem simultaneously, different levels of decisions have to be taken by the communication subsystem. For example, one such decision could be whether to allow a new multimedia application to start or not because the available resources might have been fully committed earlier or it may turn out that the new application requires a time-critical delivery guarantee that cannot be sustained by the communication subsystem at that point, given the commitments made earlier on. Also, the decision to allow an application is based on the Quality of Service demanded by the application at start. If an application exceeds the initial estimate during its lifetime, it could lead to problems inside the communication subsystem and may ultimately affect all the other applications that are currently sharing the communication subsystem. These and more such related issues are to be considered in designing a multimedia system.

From a systems viewpoint, we can consider the Type II and Type III systems as distributed systems and therefore the operating system environment should be sensitive to issues relating to resource sharing between processes in different physical systems. Fig. 1.17 pictorially shows the different parts of hardware and software of a multimedia system. For the system to be usable, the hardware must be supported by an operating system, a file system with utilities, device driver for all devices, and a set of run-time system routines which can be used to develop other software such as network and application support. When a multimedia system consists of more than one system, the networking part assumes more importance both in hardware and software. The network-related hardware should be able to interface to a high-speed

---

[12]MPEG: Moving Picture Experts Group standard for recording audio and video along with their(frame-wise) synchronization information.

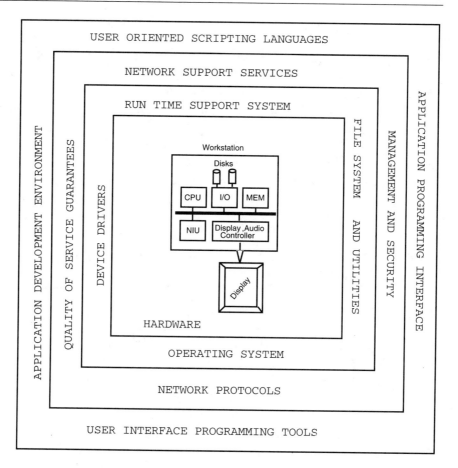

Fig. 1.17. Hardware and Software Organization

network and the network-related software should be able to coordinate all
the actions with the software executing in other remote systems. Such coordination is especially tricky when we have to negotiate for a quality of
service and maintain it during the lifetime of the applications. Let us therefore understand the role of each one of these subsystems that are realized
either in hardware or in software as a part of a multimedia system. We will
divide the system into *System Hardware*, *System Software*, and *Communication Support*. For each subsystem we will discuss the role to be performed
and the issues to be considered while designing these subsystems.

1.10.1   System Hardware

The system hardware is the core of a multimedia workstation. It consists of a central processing unit, memory, input/output system for disks, network interface unit, display controller, and audio controller. In addition, the system hardware contains a few disk drives, displays, microphones, and a speaker. All these hardware should have the capability to handle information of the size generated by multimedia applications and at the rate at which they are generated. Essentially, the central processing unit should have very high processing capability and the memory should be sufficiently large to hold several buffers of large volume information. As the size of the information handled by these systems is very high, the memory should have sufficient speed so that the transfers in and out of physical memory can take place at the desired rate. As and when the information is brought into the central processing unit, the CPU should be capable of processing it. That means the raw capacity of the CPU should be several million instructions per second. As the information has to be brought from the external storage medium such as disk, the input/output controllers should be capable of transfers at high-speeds with the capacity to buffer information of the order of a few million bytes during the transfer.

The display controller plays a crucial role of storing and displaying the information as and when it is delivered. In the same way the audio devices should be able to handle the information as it is delivered to them, the network interface hardware should be capable of directly interfacing with a high-speed network. Over and above these, there should be a high-speed network that is capable of interconnecting several such multimedia systems. Some of the multimedia systems which support desktop video and audio conferencing are given in Tables 1.2 through 1.4. These tables were obtained from the World Wide Web. This is a dynamic list changing frequently. A search through the World Wide Web can yield a more recent list. The software listed are available either on PCs, Mac, workstations such as SUN, or networks such as LAN or ISDN. The list was obtained from the Internet as a result of a search through Netscape. These are likely to change as time, technology, and access to technology, changes.

1.10.2   System Software

In general, system software encompasses the operating system, file system, compilers, and utilities. A typical multimedia application requires support in handling large files and the ability to interact with devices that handle

System	Applications
AT&T GIS Vistium 1300	Video / Audio/ Collaboration Tools
AT&T GIS Vistium 1200	Video / Audio/ Collaboration Tools
BeingThere	Video/Audio/Tools over LAN
BVCS (Bit-field Video Communication System)	Video/Audio over ISDN
C-Phone	Windows Desktop Video Conferencing System over LAN, ISDN, fractional T1, V.35, or Switched-56 digital lines.
Cameo Personal Video System	Video over Switched 56, ISDN, and Ethernet. Audio requires separate ISDN or Analog phone line.
Communicator-III	Video/Audio/Tools over Switched 56, ISDN, T1, Ethernet, or Token Ring.
Communique	Video/Audio/Tools over ISDN, Frame relay, FDDI, SMDS, Ethernet, ATM.
Connect 918	Video/Audio/Tools over Analog, Switched 56, ISDN, or Ethernet.
CU-SeeMe	Video/Audio over the Internet.
DECspin (DEC Sound Picture Information Network)	Video/Audio using standard network protocols.
Eris Personal Video Communications System	Video/Audio/Tools over ISDN or analog phone lines.
ES+F2F (Electronic Studio's Face 2 Face)	Video/Tools over ISDN, Analog, Ethernet. Audio requires ISDN or Analog phone line.
ICU Video Services	Audio/Video/Tools over LAN/WAN
InPerson	Video/Audio/Tools over ISDN, T1, Ethernet, FDDI
Interact	Windows Desktop Video Conferencing System over ISDN line or RS-449 interface.

Table 1.2. Desktop Video and Audio Conferencing Systems *Source: http://visviz.gmd.de/MultimediaInfo/*

video and audio. Besides, the operating system should employ techniques such as real-time scheduling in order to ensure that the relevant processes are executed in time.

While handling large files, the relationship between the 'logical unit' used by the application and the 'physical unit' used by the storage device such as disk assumes importance. Traditionally, the storage architectures

System	Applications
INTERVu	Video/Audio/Data over ISO-Ethernet (802.9), ISDN, Switched 56, or V.35/RS366.
InVision	Video/Audio/Tools over LAN/WAN (including Ethernet, Token Ring, FDDI, Frame Relay, ATM, ISDN, etc.) Also V.32 or faster modem.
IVS (INRIA Video-conferencing System)	Video/Audio over the Internet.
Mediafone/Fonewatch	Audio/Video/Tools over analog/digital phone lines and LAN/WANs.
Meet-Me	Video/Audio/Collaboration Tools over LAN (using ISO Ethernet) or ISDN.
MINX	Windows Desktop Video Conferencing System using Standard phone, ISDN, 56/64-T1/E1, or Switched-56 digital lines.
Ntv	Video/Audio/Tools over Ethernet and Token Ring.
nv (Network Video)	nv provides unicast and multicast video over the Internet.
Person To Person	Video/Tools over Analog, ISDN, Ethernet, or Token Ring. Audio requires separate ISDN or Analog phone line.
Personal Viewpoint	Video/Audio/Tools over Analog, Switched 56, ISDN, Ethernet, Token Ring.
PICFON	Video/Audio over Analog and ISDN phone lines.
PictureTel Live PCS 100	Video/Audio/Tools over Switched 56, ISDN
PictureTel Live PCS 50	Video/Audio/Tools over ISDN.
PictureTel LiveLAN	Video/Audio/Tools over Local Area Network

Table 1.3. Desktop Video and Audio Conferencing Systems (Contd.) *Source: http://visviz.gmd.de/MultimediaInfo/*

allow *unconstrained allocation* of 'physical units' called blocks on the disk. When large contiguous chunks are used to store video and audio information, guaranteeing bounds on access times and latency will become difficult. On the contrary, if *constrained block allocation* is used, factors such as *size of blocks (granularity)* and *separation between blocks (scattering parameter)* should be determined for ensuring bounds.

One of the problems faced in operating system design is the choice of a

System	Applications
Picture-Window	Video/Audio over the Internet.
Proshare Video System 150	Video/Audio/Tools over LAN
Proshare Video System 200	Video/Audio/Tools over LAN/WAN/ISDN.
PSVC (Paradise Software Video Conferencing)	Audio/Video/Tools over ISDN, Ethernet, ATM.
Share-Vision Mac 3000	Audio/Video/Tools over Analog phone line.
Share-Vision PC 3000	Audio/Video/Tools over Analog phone line.
ShowMe	Video/Audio/Tools over the Internet.
TelePro	Video/Audio/Tools over WAN (Analog phone lines and ISDN).
TeleView 1000C	Video over Analog phone lines.
VC8000	ISA PC multimedia communications card. Software applications packages from IBM, ICL or Olivetti provide the user interface. Allow Audio/Video/Tools over ISDN.
VicPhone	Video/Tools over Analog, ISDN phone lines, or Ethernet.
VidCall	Video/Tools over Analog, ISDN, Ethernet, Token Ring
VideoVu	Audio/Video/Tools over modem, LAN, or Internet
VISIT Video	Video/Tools over ISDN or Switched 56. Audio requires separate ISDN or Analog phone line.
Vivo320	Video/Audio/Tools over ISDN
VS1000	Video/Audio

Table 1.4. Desktop Video and Audio Conferencing Systems (Contd.) *Source: http://visviz.gmd.de/MultimediaInfo/*

scheduler. As the applications that handle multimedia information are extremely time-sensitive, they have to be scheduled at the right time. Scheduling essentially means that all the required resources for the execution of the process are made available. The uncertainties in the operating environment due to lack of *a priori* knowledge of the resource requirement of the processes and the external events called 'interrupt' make the decision on scheduling policy difficult. But the requirement is a guarantee that the multimedia application and the application-related tasks will be started 'on-time' and will be completed 'on-time'. When such features are built into the operating system, then they are called 'real-time' operating systems.

1.10.3 Communication Support

Supporting multimedia applications over a computer network raises a number of interesting issues. Communication requirements depend on the type of multimedia application and the multimedia formation for the application. Continuous media such as video demand high bandwidth, low end-to-end delays, bounded delay variations (jitter), and minimum packet loss for transferring the required information. Discrete media, such as images, do not have such stringent requirements. The digital video requires maximum bandwidth, especially in the uncompressed form. There are standard video coding and compression techniques available to reduce the bandwidth requirements [7,8]. Compression of video depends on the picture height, picture width, aspect ratio, frame rate, and inter-frame redundancy.

The services offered by the computer network should encompass establishment of communication between any pair of source and destination, conforming to a QoS. The present-day communication protocols have a layered architecture with facilities for supporting traditional applications like file transfer, electronic mail, and remote login. The low latency in the modern high-speed networks require protocols which are very different from the conventional layered ones.

The network technology today is matured to a level where it can support high bandwidth applications such as multimedia. Local area networks such as Ethernet and token ring support speeds of the order of 10 Mbps. When we move on to medium-speed networks such as FDDI [13], speeds of the order of 100 Mbps using a ring-type architecture is common. At the high end, ATM [14] networks scale up in speed and geographical coverage without sacrificing the Quality of Service.

1.11 Summary

In this chapter, we have introduced the concept of *multimedia* and explained the different components of a typical multimedia system. We also explained the two important features that distinguish the multimedia systems from conventional computer systems, viz., large volume of data and the time

---

[13] Fiber Distributed Data Interface.
[14] Asynchronous Transfer Mode.

synchronization between streams of data. We outlined the desirable features of a multimedia system, described the growth in technology and explained the hardware, software, and communication subsystems of a multimedia system. Further information about multimedia systems can be obtained from [9, 10, 11].

Over and above the features mentioned earlier, there are mechanisms to exploit the redundancy in the multimedia information by coding it, so that the resources required from the system become less. Obviously, coding at the source end has to have a counterpart called decoding at the receiving end and both have to be done on-the-fly to meet the stringent timing requirements of multimedia information. All these are essentially the subject matter of this book.

REFERENCES

1. T.D.C Little and A. Ghafoor. Synchronization and storage models for multimedia objects. IEEE Journal on Selected Areas in Communication, 8(3):413-427, April 1990.

2. P. Venkat Rangan, H.M. Vin and S. Ramanathan. Hierarchical conferencing architectures for intergroup multimedia collaboration. In Proceedings of the ACM Conference on Organizational Computing Systems (COCS'91), Atlanta, Georgia, November 1991.

3. H.M. Vin and P. Venkat Rangan. Designing a multi-user HDTV storage server. IEEE Journal on Selected Areas in Communication, Vol.11,N0.1, pp. 153-164, January 1993.

4. D. Ferrari and Dinesh Verma. A scheme for Real-Time Channel Establishment in WANs. IEEE Journal on Selected Areas in Communications, 8(3):368-379, April 1990.

5. D. Ferrari. Client requirements for real-time communication services. IEEE Communication Magazine, 31(1):15-19, January 1993.

6. D. Ferrari. Delay jitter control scheme for packet-switching internetworks. Computer Communications, 15(6):367-373, July/August 1992.

7. William B. Pennebaker and Joan L. Mitchell. JPEG: Still Image Data Compression Standard, Van Nostrand Reinhold, 1993.

8. Joan L. Mitchell, William B. Pennebaker, Chad E. Fogg and Didier J. Legall (Eds.). MPEG Video Compression Standard, Chapman & hall, 1997.

9. Ralf Steinmetz and Klara Nahrstedt. Multimedia: Computing, Communications and Applications, Prentice-Hall, Inc., 1995.

10. Francois Fluckiger. Understanding Networked Multimedia: Applications and Technology, Prentice-Hall, Inc., 1995.

11. A. Murat Tekalp. Digital Video Processing, Prentice-Hall, Inc., 1995.

Exercises

1. Compute the storage required for 5 minutes of speech that is sampled at 8 Kilo Hertz. Assume that one byte is required for every sample.

2. Calculate the time corresponding to the synchronization points between audio and video in a video clip of duration 10 minutes, if the audio changes at the following frames: 45, 80, 110, 190, 240, and 300.

3. Draw the timing diagram for the multimedia formation with three streams of audio, video and image given that audio information changes every 3 seconds, video information changes every 33.33 milliseconds, and image is stationary.

4. Imagine that you are making a multimedia version of the swearing-in ceremony of Bill Clinton as the President of the United States of America. You decide to show Capitol Hill in the backdrop, all the time. You are given the video clip of the entire ceremony. You also have access to the National Archives, from where you are free to include any episode as is appropriate. But the archived information is available only as newspaper clips. What are the media that you will use? Assume that there are three occasions that you show from the archives.

5. What is involved in making the Cartoon Channel as a multimedia channel? What are the media involved? Assume that the story given to you just consists of Tom chasing Jerry from the main door to his little house - just one scene! Draw the multimedia formation for the story. Mark the synchronization points, wherever appropriate.

6. Define Quality of Service parameters for a restaurant that delivers 'on order'. Some items on the menu they make and the rest they subcontract. The number of items listed on the menu is analogous to the number of media in multimedia.

7. Give examples for acceptable QoS, preferred QoS, and guaranteed QoS in the case of a hospital *when treating a patient for a minor bruises* and *when treating a patient for a heart attack.*

8. Try to locate Tables 1.2 through 1.4 on the Internet.

9. Identify synchronization and synchronization interval in the following cases:

   (a) In a restaurant, Pizza and Coke are served by different counters. You are in the Pizza queue and your friend is in the Coke queue.

   (b) You need to do a bus transfer to go from Place A to Place B at Place C. Buses R1 and R2 run from Place A to D and E to B through C, respectively. The schedule of R1 and R2 are such that they arrive at Place C every hour on-the-hour and every hour 10 minutes-past-the-hour, respectively.

10. You travel from New York to Seattle, changing flights at Chicago. At Chicago, the incoming flight and the outgoing flight are 30 minutes apart. Flight F1 is from London to Chicago through New York, and flight F2 is from Florida to Seattle through Chicago. During the winter, the flights normally land 10 minutes late, in the maximum. Draw the worst-case and best-case synchronization intervals for F1 and F2 at Chicago.

11. Look at the first screen after initiating Netscape. Identify all the media. In which order did they appear? Repeat it a second time. Is the number of media the same? Are the media the same as before? Was the sequence the same again?

Chapter 2

Multimedia Systems Requirements

2.1   What is Special about Multimedia?

Multimedia systems deal with generation, manipulation, storage, presentation, and communication of information in digital form corresponding to media such as data, audio, video, image, and graphics. Except for data, all the other media generate large quantities of digital information every second, with video generating the maximum amount of information for every second. In addition to large amounts of information, periodic synchronization of different media is essential as the media are integrated. In this chapter, we discuss how information is generated for each media and the impact of inter-media synchronization.

Multimedia information has intra-media and inter-media time constraints (also referred to as temporal relationships) as an integral property. The multimedia formation that we discussed in Chapter 1 reflects these temporal relationships. But, as the multimedia formation goes through the communication subsystem, it could undergo a *change* and as a result the temporal relationships could be disturbed. For display at the receiving end, the multimedia information has to be reconstructed in the same form as it was at the source end. Proper design of the receiving end of the multimedia systems can lead to a *tolerance of changes* to the multimedia formation, to a *certain extent*. Therefore, a discussion of multimedia system design focuses on the following questions:

- Given the characteristics of the source and the destination, how should the network be designed?

- Given the network, how should the destination be configured?

- Given a certain combination of source, destination, and network, what are the applications that can be supported?

To find answers to these questions, one needs to understand the requirements of the multimedia information in more depth.

The changes that the multimedia information go through in a communication subsystem are shown schematically in Fig. 2.1. The figure has three parts: a snapshot of the representation of the multimedia formations at input, the high-speed communication network, and a snapshot of the representation of the multimedia formations at the output. The streams that enter the communication network may take different paths, such as 1-2-3-7, 1-5-7, 1-4-6-7, through the communication network. Since the number of hops are different or due to the 'other' traffic handled by switches 1 through 7, the streams may arrive at output out-of-synchronization, as illustrated. This is what we have been referring to all along as the *asynchrony* that is likely to be introduced by the communication network.

One interesting point to note here is that the special media such as voice and video are ultimately for human consumption. Human-Computer-Interaction studies have shown that human beings do exhibit a 'limited tolerance' to delays and loss in the presentation of voice and video - they need not be delivered instantaneously. The implication of such tolerance on system design is that the individual streams can be delivered within certain

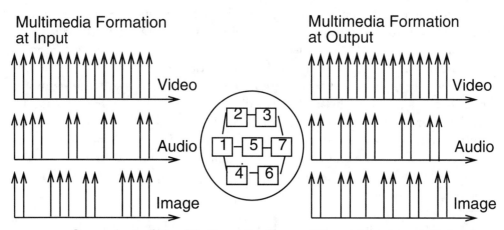

Snapshot of the Multimedia Formation at Input and Output

Fig. 2.1. Operational View of a Multimedia System

time delays. So, even though the network introduces asynchrony, it can still be admissible in a multimedia system, subject to the human tolerance. In this chapter, we discuss the digital form of each media and also the human tolerance times to these media, from rudimentary concepts. We organize the discussion on media in two parts, viz., discrete media and continuous media. We classify media such as data (text), image, and graphics under discrete media. We consider audio and video under continuous media.

2.2 Discrete Media

Discrete media are composed of time-independent information units. That is, there is no temporal relationship between successive units of information from the same media. From the application viewpoint, a discrete media such as a text file may be displayed according to a certain timing or sequence for being sensible to the application. But the point to be noted is that *time* by itself is not part of the *semantics* of discrete media.

2.3 Discrete Medium: Data or Text

The sources of this medium are the keyboard, floppies, disks, and tapes. In the case of keyboard, information flows in units called characters[1]. From other devices, which are basically for storage, information flows in different units such as characters, blocks, or files. Blocks have a fixed number of characters and files have a fixed number of blocks. To give an example, blocks are usually specified as consisting of 128 bytes, 512 bytes, or even 1024 bytes. Though files have a fixed number of blocks, the actual number of blocks will depend on the information stored in the file by the user or the application. In fact, it is more appropriate to say that a file consists of an integral number of blocks as opposed to a fixed number of blocks. To refer to the total quantity of information in a file, we will refer to the total number of bytes in a file. For example, when we refer to the size of a program file, we will say 500,000 bytes.

Interestingly, the information inside a file does not have any time constraints but they have an implied sequence; for example, the contents of a C program file or its executable image has no inherent time relationship within the data in the file but the sequence in which the statements appear in the program is extremely important. Therefore, when we transfer a data file from one place to another over a communication network, the delay that

---

[1] Each character occupies one byte (8 bits) of memory.

the data file suffers, if any, has no impact on its utility at the receiving end. While the data file can sustain arbitrary delay, it is highly sensitive to losses! For instance, even if one character is lost, the syntax may be completely affected and/or the semantics may completely change, depending on where the loss is inside the program.

If we consider a computer screen (i.e., a terminal), we have 24 lines and 80 characters per line. Let us assume that an electronic mail message fills the screen. That is $24 \times 80 = 1920$ bytes per screen of data. If some attributes are associated with each character, and if we assume that an additional byte per character will be required, then the total storage required for a screen will be $1920 \times 2 = 3840$ bytes.

The program files, electronic mail message files, and data files are referred to as ASCII files, implying that the ASCII representation of each character is stored in the file. The general format of ASCII files in a system is one of variable-length records separated by either LF (Line Feed) characters or CR-LF (Carriage Return - Line Feed pair).

2.4 Discrete Medium: Image

Image is a still picture represented as a bitmap[2] on a computer screen. As discussed earlier, a typical screen will consist of 640 x 480 pixels in the x and y axes. For a display, each pixel in the bitmap can be represented by a 256 level of gray (see also Section 2.10). That is, 1 byte is needed per pixel. Therefore, the total storage required per image will be $640 \times 480 \times 1 = 307200$ bytes. As in the case of data, there is no time constraint in this medium.

The scanning process for producing the image of an A4 page produces the same number of bits, irrespective of the contents of the page. Let us assume that we use only one bit to represent each pixel; that is, 0 means the pixel is *black* and 1 means that the pixel is *white*. Then for a 640 x 480 resolution, we will need just 307200 bits or 38400 bytes of storage, after scanning. Let us look at the case of scanning a page which has nothing in it - it is pure *white*. Then, after scanning, we will represent the page by 307200 bits which are all 1s. or 38400 bytes, which are all 255. What we have in the scanned image file is lot of redundant information, which is called spatial redundancy. By smart representation (coding), we can effect dramatic savings in storage. Let us say that we refer to the presence of 1s by 255 (a byte with all bits on). We

---

[2]Bitmap is a series of bits (pixels) in the x and y axes that form a grid.

succeed this byte by a count of 1s. In our example, we need 3 bytes (24 bits) to represent 38400; i.e., 00000101001000000000000. We just need a total of 4 bytes as opposed to 38400 bytes! In order to save disk space, such coding schemes are used in conjunction with the scanning process. The reader may also note that the coding we practiced led to a compression of 9600:1; this was primarily due to the contents of the page - a contradiction compared to the first sentence in this paragraph! In fact, both are true!! What it means is that *scanning* is *independent* of the contents and *compression* (consequence of coding) is *dependent* upon the contents and the coding method employed.

Supposing we want to see the contents of an A4 page on a VGA monitor whose resolution is 640 x 480, then the scanning may have to be done with the same resolution. Similarly, there are SVGA (800 x 600), XGA (1024 x 768), and large size image (1280 x 1024). If the monitors are color, then we need 3 bytes (or 24 bits) to represent 256 grey levels of each one of the colors R, G, and B.

2.5   Discrete Medium: Graphics

Graphics are constructed by the composition of primitive objects such as lines, circles, polygons, curves, and splines. Graphics can be generated manually with a graphics editor or automatically by a program. The storage form is in terms of objects. A graphics document can be viewed as an *editable* document as their format retains the structural information as objects and timing relationships. For moving graphics or animation, each view is computed at display time. Moreover, at the time of display, all objects are transferred to display memory.

The graphics display is constructed by treating the screen as a collection of dots (each dot corresponds to a pixel) and selectively lighting the dots corresponding to the bitmap maintained in the display memory. The pixels or dots on the screen are scanned progressively at a rate of 72 frames per second. Special graphics adapters accelerate this process. The graphics processor has to repeat the display of the picture at a certain rate, so that for the human eye it appears as if the picture screen is around permanently. In the case of a motion to be captured (called *animation* in graphics), the coded information available as bitmap is to be displayed on the screen and has to be changed in between the repetition (repeated scanning) of the display.

PHIGS[8] and GKS[9] are examples of graphics standards.

2.6   Continuous Media

Continuous media, such as audio and video, require continuous playout as time passes. In other words, time dependency between information units is part of the information itself. If the timing is changed or the sequence of the information units is changed, the meaning is altered. That means *time* is part of the *semantics* of continuous media. They are also referred to as time-dependent media. Before we actually start our discussions on audio and video, we will discuss the concepts related to analog signals, digital signals, and the process of converting an analog signal to the corresponding digital equivalent, as these ideas are employed in handling continuous media in computers or networks.

2.7   Analog and Digital Signals

2.7.1   What is an Analog Signal?

From the physical world, *sensors* transform the time-dependent or space-dependent physical variables into electrical signals. For example, a thermocouple will sense the temperature and transform it to a corresponding electrical signal. As the temperature varies, the transformed signal will continue to track the variation faithfully. In other words, the transformed electrical signal produced by the sensor is analogous to the original physical variable. That is why we say that the signal produced by a sensor is an *analog signal*. By nature, it is a continuous signal. Fig. 2.2 shows a vessel with a liquid which is being heated by a burner. The sensor is immersed in the liquid inside the vessel and two leads are shown to indicate that electrical signal (voltage for example) is produced corresponding to the temperature variation (rising as we are heating). If we connect a voltmeter, then the needle indicating the voltage will move to the right (We are assuming 0 volt mark on the left and 12 volt mark on the right. We are further assuming that the maximum range of voltage produced for the maximum range of temperature variation is 0-12 volts). If we plot the values on a graph sheet, we will get the plot shown in Graph A in Fig. 2.2. In fact, instead of a voltmeter, one could connect a plotter directly, so that the plotter pen will draw the curve shown in Fig. 2.2.

    If we extend our example for a cooling cycle, we can see some more interesting features exhibited by the *analog signals*. Let us assume that the

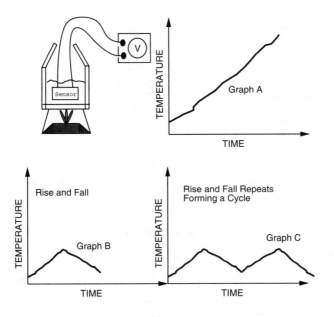

Fig. 2.2. Continuous Analog Signal from the Physical World

liquid we are using in our example cools at approximately the same rate[3] as it heated up. If the liquid is allowed to cool and the temperature is recorded as in the earlier case, we will see the curve as a *rise and fall* as shown in Fig. 2.2 (Graph B). Further, if we repeat this exercise once more, the curve will show a cycle as can be seen from Fig. 2.2 (Graph C). All these simply indicate that the variables in the physical world are continuously varying and that the changes in a physical variable can be recorded electronically. At the end of this exercise, what we have is an analog signal. However, the computers and modern electronics gadgets, which are all digital, do not understand this signal. What does one do under such circumstances?

2.7.2 Converting an Analog Signal to a Digital Signal

Unlike the physical world where everything is *continuous*, the digital world is *discrete* by definition. For example, the digital world has to represent anything and everything only with the help of *two values a bit can take*; viz., 0 and 1. There is nothing in between. Any higher order number is built up based on these two values by adding more bits, but the discontinuity continues. When we relate this to our 'temperature example', it is our ability

---

[3]We will conjure a property - we do not know if such a liquid exists! Perhaps it does.

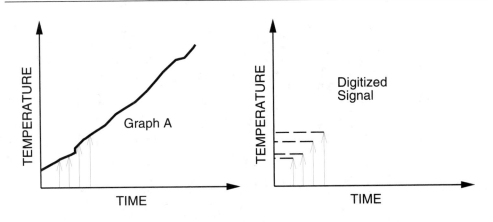

Fig. 2.3. Analog to Digital Conversion

to observe the temperature at specific instances of time such as 10:00:00, 10:00:05, 10:00:10, and so on; that is, at discrete time intervals and not continuously. If the value of the temperature at those instances were 35, 37, and 40, we really do not know how 37 was reached after 35 and how 40 was reached after 37. But what is under our control is the granularity with which we monitor. For instance, in our temperature example, we have indicated a granularity of 5 seconds. This could be reduced if we feel that there is too much variability in 5 seconds, or it could be increased if we find that the variability is *not too much*. By *variability* we mean all the changes that could occur to the value of the physical variable. A series of values such as 35, 35.2, 36.4, 36.4, 36.8, and 37 could be one such example for the temperature, if measured every second. Once we measure the values of the physical variables, we are dealing with the problem of representation of a number in the digital world. In our example, it is a question of representing 35, 37, or 40. The range of values that the physical variable can take may indicate the number of bits that one may require. When we look at Fig. 2.2, the three graphs (A, B, and C) have the same range but a different number of measurements.

2.7.3 Sampling and Sampling Interval

Whenever we discuss analog and digital signals, we also come across the terms *sampling* and *sampling interval*. Sampling refers to the process of digitizing. For instance, in the temperature example, the sampling was done at four points. The sampling interval was 5 seconds. The process of sampling and the samples are shown pictorially in Fig. 2.3. Each one of the values in the temperature example, viz., 35, 37, and 40, are called samples; the time instants 10:00:00, 10:00:05, and 10:00:10 are called sampling instants; and of course the interval between the time instants is called the sampling interval, which is 5 seconds in our example. There is *space discretization* as well as *time discretization*. After sampling, we say that we have a *digital* equivalent of the *analog* signal.

A curious question follows this: 'How do I know how often to sample?'. This is related to the behavior of the signal. When you sample, you get the value of the physical variable at that instant. If the sampling is done *as often as* the changes that are occurring in the physical world, *information will not be lost*. But, are there guidelines to identify the rate? How does it relate to the rate of change in the sampled signal? In other words, how do we sample without a loss of information? H. Nyquist showed, as early as 1924, that sampling a signal faster than twice the rate of change in the original signal is meaningless [1]. Claude Shannon [2] extended the work of Nyquist to the case of a communication channel subject to a random noise. Further details about the work of Nyquist and Shannon can found in [1, 2, 3, 4].

2.7.4   Quantization and Quantization Error

We have discussed the nature of a physical variable, the process of generating the analog signal, and the process of sampling to get the samples which can form the digital counterpart of the analog signal. We observed that the value we get at every sample will be represented in digital form. Thereby, a series of samples of an analog signal will represent the digital signal corresponding to the analog signal that was sampled. But in the digital domain, we need to represent these values, samples, or digits. To represent we have a *fixed* number of bits. Since the sample has been obtained from a domain which is continuous, while mapping to a corresponding value in the *discrete domain*, we may run into difficulty. As the name implies, in the discrete domain *not all the values you get in the continuous domain* can be found. This is because, by definition, discrete domain had discontinuities. In such cases, the value of the sample has to be mapped to the *nearest available representation* in the digital domain. For example, if we have 8 bits to represent temperature in the digital domain, then we can represent all values from -255 to +255, assuming that we use one bit to indicate the sign. If we get a value such as 36.4 or 120.7, there is no corresponding representation and we have to find the nearest possible representation, viz., 36 or 121. Obviously, we are introducing an *error* during the process. This is called *quantization error* and can be minimized by increasing the number of bits used for the representation and by allowing for enough bits to represent decimal values as well.

Example: For a picture or motion video to be processed by a computer, it needs to be converted to digital from analog representation. Stated simply, digitalization means sampling the grey level (or color) in the picture (or a frame of motion video) as M x N points. When we sample, the gray levels themselves may take any value in a continuous range, hence we need to quantize them. This essentially means that we have taken a continuous variable and replaced it by a K-interval counterpart, restricting the values that the sampled variable can take. For example, if the interval was from 1 to 10 and due to quantization, we say that only integers are allowed; thus we are essentially restricting the possible values to one of the ten (1, 2, 3, 4, 5, 6, 7, 8, 9, 10). So a value such as 4.4 has to be truncated to 4. This will introduce errors. Therefore, for the reconstructed picture to have good quality, the quantization level must be high. In the same example, if the interval was from 1 to 100 (1, 2, 3, 4, ... 99, 100), a value such as 4.4 will naturally fit into 44 without any loss of information.

2.7.5 Code-Word Generation

Another way of representing the sampled values in the digital domain is by using code-words. In this process, a code-word (in the form of binary digits) is assigned to every quantized value. For example, the sample at 10:00:00, which was 35, can be coded as 00010011. Note that this is also the binary representation of integer 35. *Code* basically uses a position-based numerical scheme. That is, the value of the coded variable may be retrieved by summing terms formed by the product of the *value* of the digit and a factor depending on the *position* of the digit. In our temperature example, the sampled value (35) is retrieved from the code-word using the following sum:

$$(0x2^7) + (0x2^6) + (1x2^5) + (0x2^4) + (0x2^3) + (0x2^2) + (1x2^1) + (1x2^0)$$

Strictly speaking, the whole process of sampling, quantization, and coding is called *digitization*. It may be noted that forms of coding such as octal, hexadecimal, excees-3, etc. may also be employed. Depending on the code, the bit pattern will also change.

2.8 Digitizing Audio and Video

What we discussed in this section is applicable to all continuous signals. If we have a speech of President Eisenhower recorded in the archives, we can now convert them into digital form. The famous Fifth Symphony of Beethoven can now be converted to digital form, recorded on digital storage devices such as CD-ROMs, and distributed. These are different forms of *audio* signals. The granularity of digital observation will relate the signal to its original continuous signal more closely and hence will lend itself to HiFi reproduction. What was presented in Section 2.3 refers to this process of analog to digital conversion. It is important to understand that the sound waves are actually converted to electrical form and the electrical signal is digitized.

How do we see a photograph, a movie, or an object? We see the *light incident on the object!*[4] The light rays get reflected from the object and reach our retina, which passes it on to a neural network in our brain that triggers an object recognition process. The signal received from the physical world is in the form of light energy. In the human body it goes in as an internal signal to the brain. To a photographic film, it goes as chemical transformations on a photographic paper. In a video camera, it gets converted to an electrical signal.

For both audio and video, since the signals have to be exchanged (either in the native form or in any transformed form), standard ways of digitizing, recording, and processing become necessary for reasons of compatibility. Some of these were discussed in this chapter, and a few other issues are discussed in Chapter 3.

2.9 Continuous Medium: Audio

Audio signals are continuous analog signals in their electronic form. To represent them in the equivalent digital form, the audio signal is sampled at 8 Kilo Hertz. Each sample is quantized with 8 bits, thereby leading to a digital audio stream of 64 Kilobits per second. In terms of storage requirement, this will translate into 8 Kilobytes per second. The samples are generated every 125 microseconds, as shown schematically in Fig. 2.4. The series of arrows on the time axis illustrate the samples obtained. In terms of quality of audio, an audio stream at 64 Kbps[5] is also referred to as near CD-quality audio. For full CD-quality audio, one requires sampling at 44.1 KHz[6] with 16-bit samples. This will amount to a total of 44100 $\times$ 16/8 = 176400 Kbps. Table. 2.1 gives some standards, their corresponding

---

[4]Obviously we do not see anything in the dark.

[5]kilobits per second.

[6]Kilo Hertz.

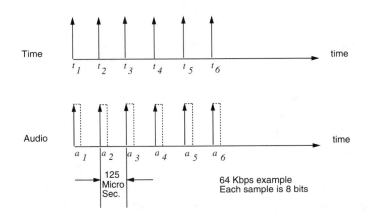

Fig. 2.4. Audio Samples

Coding	Sampling Rate	Data Rate
L16	48 KHz	768 Kbps
	44.1 KHz	705.6 Kbps
	22.05 KHz	352.8 Kbps
	11.025 KHz	176.4 Kbps

Table 2.1. Audio Encodings

sampling frequencies, and data rates.

L16 denotes uncompressed audio data, using 16-bit signed representation with 65535 equally divided steps between minimum and maximum signal levels ranging from -32768 to +32767. The value is represented in two's complement notation. L16 coding with a sampling rate of 44.1 KHz means that the spacing between samples is 22.7 microseconds, as illustrated in Fig. 2.5.

It should be noted that audio information takes the form of a continuous stream with equal spacing. It is also referred to as isochronous medium. In Figs. 2.4 and 2.5, we have represented each sample by an arrow and marked the samples as a_1, a_2, ..., a_n. The order of the samples has to be maintained

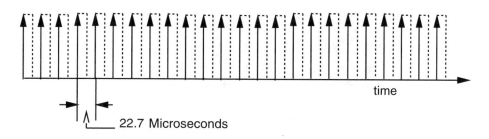

Fig. 2.5. Audio Samples at 44.1 KHz

while replaying. Once sample a_i is played at the receiving end, sample a_{i+1} must be played at a fixed interval (125 or 22.7 microseconds) later.

2.10 Seeing is a Process

2.10.1 How do we See an Object?

We 'sense' the light incident on an object. We need to understand this process with all its subtleties because the process of seeing is emulated in a camera (either photographic or video). In fact, a video camera acts as the sensor and produces electrical signals that can be sampled and digitized.

To explain 'seeing', we use the terms *light* and *object*. Light is a form of electro-magnetic radiation that can stimulate a human visual response. Light has a wavelength of 250-780 nanometers - this is also in the visible range. The human visual response system cannot see beyond this range. Different wavelengths produce different color impressions or sensations. A *light source* which is composed of a single wavelength is called a *monochromatic* source. Every monochromatic source has its own wavelength and *intensity*. *Intensity* is the energy a light source has. Other sources (non-monochromatic) are composed of a range of wavelengths, each having its own intensity.

The sensitivity of the human eye varies from color to color (or wavelength to wavelength) and also from person to person, for the same color. The same person may perceive two colors (or wavelengths) with the same intensity differently. Also, two different persons may perceive the same color (or wavelength) with the same intensity differently. Moreover, the human eye is more sensitive to yellow or yellow-green than to red or violet. They are in the middle of the famous rainbow colors VIB GY OR. The traffic signals, interestingly, adopt these colors as well.

Let us get back to our discussion on light and object. When light energy

Fig. 2.6. Gray Scale - Black to White

is incident on the object, the object reflects or transmits the incident light. When an object reflects less than 30% of the incident light, it is perceived as *black* by the human eye. When an object reflects more than 80% of the incident light, it is perceived as *white* by the human eye. For achromatic[7] objects, the human eye has a graded sensation between black and white called grey-scale. The gray scales are pictorially shown in Fig. 2.6.

We can define the process of seeing as the perceptual response of the human eye. *Luminance* is a measure of the overall response of the eyes to all the wavelengths contained in a source, in a given object, or in a scene mixing several illuminated objects and sources. *Brightness* is an attribute of the visual sensation indicating that an area emits more or less light, and it depends on the surroundings. *Lightness* is the level of grey. *Colors* are sensations, and a number of different spectral distributions may produce the same color. Any color may be obtained, theoretically, by mixing an appropriate amount of any three different colors. The human eye is less sensitive to colors than to lightness and brightness.

2.10.2   Role of RGB?

If any color can be produced by mixing any three different colors, what are the primary colors? Why are Red, Green, and Blue (RGB) important? While theoretically any three colors can be used as primaries, in practice certain colors in nature cannot be reproduced by mixing three primaries. Notwithstanding this limitation, various standards have been defined with RGB as primaries. The respective wavelengths are Red = 700 nanometers, Green = 546 nanometers, and Blue = 436 nanometers. An analog video camera produces three distinct continuous signals, one for each color component Red, Green, and Blue as shown pictorially in Fig. 2.7. Standardization by the Commission International de l'Eclairage is the reason for the RGB be-

---

[7]Objects with no color.

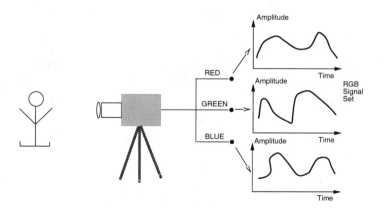

Fig. 2.7. RGB Output from Video Camera

ing quoted as primary colors. Video cameras and displays use the RGB for representing any color.

2.10.3 What are YUV?

Television transmission (for reasons of easy transmission) transforms the RGB signal set to three other signals, which together carry the *luminance* and *chrominance* [8] information. Luminance carries information on lightness and brightness as a single signal, and chrominance carries the color information as a set of two signals derived from the RGB set as a weighted difference. As the human visual system is less sensitive to color than to luminance, the color signal may be represented or transmitted with less accuracy. From the analog television broadcasting point of view, the two color signals can be transported using *lesser bandwidth* and with lower accuracy than the luminance signal. In TV, luminance signal is denoted by Y. The chrominance signals are denoted by U and V. While transmitting the two color difference signals, U and V are combined together to form the chrominance signal or chroma signal C. While actually broadcasting, only Y and C are transmitted. Obviously, the reverse process has to take place at the receiving end; that is, in the TV set at homes. The TV sets receive the Y and C signals and convert them back to Y, U, and V. In fact, in the case of color TV, Y and C are converted to Y, U, and V and in the case of black and white TV, Y and C are converted to Y only as shown in Fig. 2.8.

---

[8] Color related.

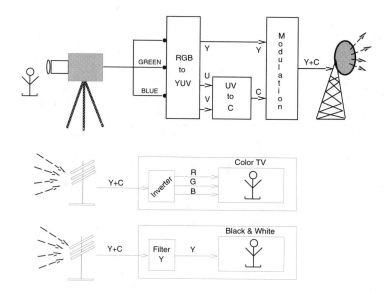

Fig. 2.8. TV Broadcast and Role of Y, U, and V

2.10.4   Analog Video Signal

The term "analog video signal" refers to a one-dimensional analog signal of time, where the spatio-temporal information is ordered as a function of time according to a *predefined scanning convention*. The signal captures the time-varying image intensity only along the scanned lines. The analog video signal also contains the timing information and the blanking signals needed to align the pictures correctly. The most commonly used scanning methods are *progressive scanning* and *interlaced scanning*. A progressive scan traces the complete picture called a *frame* every 1/72 seconds. This is illustrated in Fig. 2.9. This is used in computer monitors.

On the other hand, the TV industry uses 2:1 interlace where the odd numbered lines (shown as dotted lines in Fig. 2.9) and even numbered lines (shown as continuous lines in Fig. 2.9) are scanned separately. Each is called a *field*. The scanning raster for the field with odd-numbered lines, even-numbered lines, and the complete screen are shown in Fig. 2.9. The odd field is the scan from A to B and the even field is the scan from C to D. The scanning is done by a spot beam of electron and it flies back from P to Q in the horizontal direction and from B to C or D to A in the vertical direction.

The video signal for a frame looks as shown in Fig. 2.10. From the figure one can see a cycle consisting of a time-varying analog signal interspersed with pulses that essentially trigger horizontal retrace. The reader may want to spend some time and see the correlation between the signal in Fig. 2.10 and the process of reading the page you are holding right now. Let us say that your child is watching you and draws on a sheet of paper randomly with a Crayon pencil. The way the child draws is that the child makes a random up-and-down movement from left-to-right, as you read a line from left to right. As your head turns left[9], the child draws a sharp line upwards and back. Let the child repeat it a hundred times. If you now look at the paper, it will look similar to Fig. 2.10. Now let us let the child play and proceed with our discussion. It is important to note that the frame time includes the horizontal retrace time. Therefore, when we look at analog video signal as in Fig. 2.10, the actual signal occupies *less time* than the frame time as can be from the frame rate of either 25 or 30. When we sample this signal, only samples in this part will carry useful information. If we have a certain sampling rate (such as 13.5 MHz), which gives the equivalent number of samples as 858 per line (of scan in a frame), what is useful will only be a part of it. Of course, it is a very significant part; e.g., 720 samples as defined by the ITU-R 601 standard.

---

[9]When you are experienced, it is only the eye movement and not head movement - this is an example, so exaggeration is permitted to a limited extent!

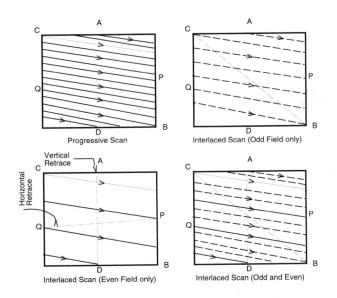

Fig. 2.9. Progressive and Interlaced Scanning

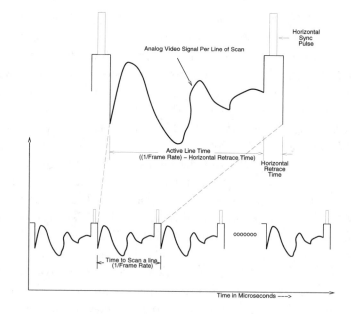

Fig. 2.10. Analog Video Signal

NTSC, PAL, and SECAM are the standards that define analog TV systems. ITU-R 601 and ITU-TS H.261 define the digital TV standard for studio quality and videoconferencing quality.

2.10.5   NTSC

NTSC (National Television Systems Committee) is a standard that defines the signal composition from RGB. The NTSC standard is in use in the American TV broadcasting system, Canada, Japan, and Latin America. The NTSC standard refers to luminance as the **Y** component and the two chrominance signals as **I** and **Q** components. They are calculated as follows:

Y = 0.30R + 0.59G + 0.14B

I = 0.74(R-Y) - 0.27(B-Y) = 0.60R + 0.28G + 0.32B

Q = 0.48(R-Y) + 0.41(B-Y) = 0.21R + 0.52G + 0.31B

NTSC uses 2:1 interlaced scanning and has an aspect ratio of 4:3 for horizontal to vertical. The scanning is 525 lines per frame at a rate of 29.97 frames per second. This is equivalent to 262.5 lines at the rate of 59.94 fields per second. NTSC analog transmission requires a 6 MHz analog channel for transmission, and in the U.S. 68 channels are assigned.

2.10.6 PAL

PAL (Phase Alteration Line) is another standard that defines the signal composition from RGB. PAL standard is in use in Europe and Australia. The PAL standard refers to luminance as the **Y** component and the two chrominance signals as **U** and **V** components. They are calculated as follows:

Y = 0.30R + 0.59G + 0.11B

U = 0.493(B-Y) = - 0.15R - 0.29G + 0.44B

V = 0.877(R-Y) = 0.62R + 0.52G + 0.10B

PAL uses 2:1 interlaced scanning and has an aspect ratio of 4:3 for horizontal to vertical. The scanning is 625 lines per frame at a rate of 25 frames per second. This is equivalent to 362.5 lines at the rate of 50 fields per second. PAL analog transmission requires a 8 MHz analog channel for transmission.

2.10.7 SECAM

SECAM (Systeme Electronique Color Avec Memoire) is yet another standard for color broadcast, used in France, Russia, and Eastern Europe. SECAM uses 2:1 interlaced scanning and has an aspect ratio of 4:3 for horizontal to vertical. The scanning is 625 lines per frame at a rate of 25 frames per second. This is equivalent to 362.5 lines at the rate of 50 fields per second. SECAM analog transmission requires a 8 MHz analog channel for transmission.

2.11 Continuous Medium: Video

Historical Background: We must remember that what we are trying to understand is a compressed version of TV technology development over several decades, impacted by fairly heavy investments in several TV technologies by different countries, and influenced significantly by global standardization processes. These processes are essential to interchange information between countries across the globe for the purpose of promoting international trade and commerce, which in turn is regarded as the backbone for overall development of nations. TV production, broadcasting, and reception (in individual homes) require that the equipment used by the three parties be compatible. That means, the output of one should act as input to the next level. We start from a natural scene, *production* process converts it to electronic form, *broadcasting* distributes it to homes, *TV receiver* at home displays it on a screen, and finally the user "sees" the natural scene. The chain of actions we described just now are illustrated in Fig. 2.8. Standards are required to take care of all these interfaces.

Another interesting aspect is the chronological order of availability of technologies and growth of these technologies. NTSC standards came into vogue in 1941 for black and white and in 1954 for color. PAL and SECAM standards were accepted in 1967. These three standards were not inter-operating in a significant manner until digital signal processing became fea-sible on a large scale in the 1980's. Around the same time, digital display technologies and networking technologies became popular. For example, it was possible to transmit across the Unites States at 1.544 Mbps speed as early as 1970. But it could be effectively utilized only when bitmap display technology started becoming available in the later part of the 1980's. Europe already had the ISDN capability as a regular commercial service, which trig-gered the interest in digital videoconferencing, adding a new dimension to the applications. At the dawn of the 1990's, the digital technology has vir-tually rendered all old standards in the analog TV world meaningless. But the fact is that the investment and reach is very heavy to change everything overnight. While today's technology makes it possible to *think digital* end-to-end, use of standards for reasons of *backward* compatibility will remain valid at least until the turn of this century.

Basics: Let us first understand what is meant by representing video on a computer. Basically, whatever we want to represent in the digital computer has to be converted to digital form; therefore the screenful of picture we see should have an equivalent representation inside the computer, called *bitmap*. A full screen image is viewed as a matrix of pixels in the X and Y directions. A digital image is represented by a matrix I_{video} of numeric values, each representing a *quantized* intensity value. The rows and columns of the matrix I_{video} represent the intensity of the corresponding *pixel* [10] on the screen.

Video, in its native analog form, is a sequence of frames where each frame has a corresponding analog signal. The video sequence is a series of such analog signals (Fig. 2.10), separated by pulses required for the scanning beam to fly back from right to left after scanning every line. Each retrace pulse also piggy-backs another pulse for horizontal synchronization at the receiving end. Similarly, between frames, there is a vertical retrace pulse with piggy-back pulse for vertical synchronization.

Handling video on computers involved sampling the analog video signal

---

[10] Pixel means a Picture Element.

at a certain sampling rate and representing each sample by a number, which typically is the value or amplitude corresponding to the sample.

Analog TV: The tri-stimulus theory of color states that almost any color can be reproduced by an appropriate mixing of three additive primaries: Red (R), Green (G), and Blue (B). Since display devices can only generate nonnegative primaries, and an adequate amount of luminance is required, there is in practice a constraint on the gamut of colors that can be reproduced. As human perception is more sensitive to brightness than any chrominance information, each frame is encoded as luminance (brightness) or Y and chrominance (color differences) or R-Y (U) and B-Y (V). Y is defined as (0.30R+0.59G+0.11B). The basic video bandwidth required to transmit luminance and chrominance signals as a single composite signal over a TV channel is 6 MHz for the NTSC standard.

Digital TV: Digital TV is a combination of analog TV technology, signal handling technology, and computer display technology, Analog TV technology presents the natural scene as a continuous analog signal that can be electronically recorded. This is described in Section 2.10. The signal handling technology enables one to convert an analog signal to digital signal through the processes of sampling, quantization, and coding. This is explained in Section 2.7. The computer display technology actually displays the digital information corresponding to the natural scene on a computer monitor or a digital TV monitor. The principle of operation of digital displays is presented at the beginning of this section. To produce a digital TV system, one has to integrate all these technologies.

Concept of Subsampling: The technique of transforming RGB into luminance and chrominance (color difference) signals applies to digital TV as well. As in the case of analog TV, the bandwidth and storage will be less if we reduce the bit-rate. The bit-rate can be reduced by controlling the sampling rate. Reducing sampling rate will imply loss of information. In line with analog TV principles, digital TV retains the sampling of luminance at the required rate and reduces that of chrominance signals to half the value. Let us denote the luminance signal by Y and chrominance by C_1 and C_2. In one standard, referred to as studio quality digital TV standard, the sampling rate of Y, C_1, and C_2 is in the ratio 4:2:2. Depending on the ratio, the bit-rate will also change. This technique is called *subsampling*, and basically reduces the bit-rate required for chrominance signals by 50% for each color difference signal. Since the luminance is unchanged, this amounts to an overall reduction of 33%. This bit-rate reduction is achieved without any noticeable degradation in the quality of the image.

Studio-Quality TV: ITU-R 601 standard specifies the resolution and frame rates in such a way that they are backward compatible with the existing analog TV standards. The sampling rates for Y, C_1, and C_2 are 13.5 MHz, 6.75 MHz, and 6.75 MHz, respectively. For the NTSC standard and for the luminance signal, for example, this is equivalent to 13,500,000 samples per second, 21600 samples per frame, or 864 samples per scanned line. Of the 864 samples, only those from the *active video signal part* represent the natural scene being captured and that is defined to be 720 samples per scanned line. The number of active lines per frame is 486 for NTSC.

Example: Let us consider the European NTSC standard, where video is defined by 525 lines and 30 frames per second. According to the ITU-R 601 definition (CCIR 601)[11], a studio standard for digital video, the sampling rate is 13.5 MHz for luminance Y and 6.75 MHz each for chrominance R-Y and B-Y. If the result is a uniform 8-bit coding of each sample, then the total data rate of (13.5+6.75+6.75) x 8 = **216 Mbps**. This is the rate of the multiplexed digital data stream.

Example: For NTSC, the samples per active line are 720 and the number of active lines per frame is 486. This amounts to 720 x 486 = 349920 samples per frame. These are samples which are representing the natural scene. These are obtained after accounting for the retrace (horizontal and vertical) pulse periods in every frame. If we use 8 bits to code each sample, then the bits per frame will be 2,799,360 bits. Since NTSC has 30 frames every second, this is equivalent to a bit-rate of 83,980,800 bits per second or approximately 84 Mbps. This is only for the luminance part. The color difference signals contribute as follows: 360 x 486 x 2 x 8 x 30 = 83,980,800 or approximately 84 Mbps. So, the total bit-rate required for studio-quality TV with a subsampling ratio of 4:2:2 is **168 Mbps**. This is shown pictorially in Fig. 2.11.

Example: Let us consider the European PAL standard, where video is defined by 625 lines and 25 frames per second. According to the ITU-R 601 definition (CCIR 601), a studio standard for digital video, the sampling rate is 13.5 MHz for luminance Y and 6.75 MHz each for chrominance R-Y and B-Y. If the result is a uniform 8-bit coding of each sample, then the total data rate of (13.5+6.75+6.75) x 8 = **216 Mbps**. This is the rate of the multiplexed digital data stream.

Example: For PAL, the samples per active line are 720 and the number of active lines per frame is 576. This amounts to 720 x 576 = 414720 samples per frame. These are samples which are representing the natural scene. These are obtained after accounting for the retrace (horizontal and vertical) pulse periods in every frame. If we use 8 bits to code each sample, then the bits per frame will be 3,317,760 bits. Since PAL has 25 frames every second, this is equivalent to a bit-rate of 82,944,000 bits per second or approximately 83 Mbps. This is only for the luminance part. The color difference signals contribute as follows: 360 x 576 x 2 x 8 x 25 = 82,944,000 or approximately 83 Mbps. So, the total

---

[11]Consultative Committee for International Radio.

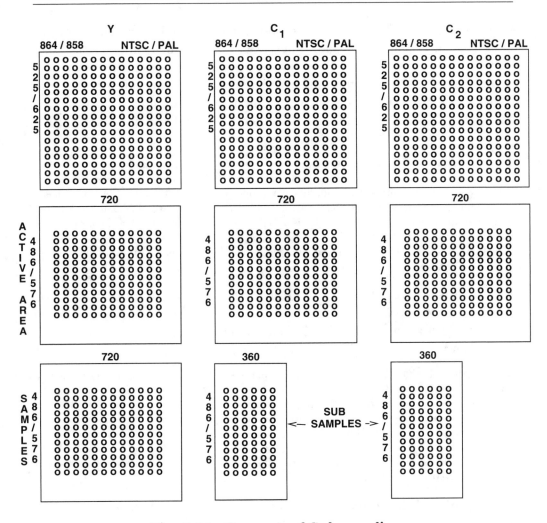

Fig. 2.11. Concept of Subsampling

bit-rate required for studio-quality TV with a subsampling ratio of 4:2:2 is **166 Mbps**. This is shown pictorially in Fig. 2.11.

Example: For US HDTV, if we assume 720,000 total pixels per frame, 24 bits per pixel, and a frame rate of 60 frames per second, the bit-rate will be **1.0368** gigabits per second. For European HDTV the same figure will be 870,000 pixels per frame and at 24 bits per pixel and a frame rate of 50 frames per second, the bit-rate will be **1.044** gigabits per second.

videoconferencing Quality - CIF: ITU-TS H.261 recommendation defines a format called *Common Interchange Format (CIF)*, with a frame size of 352 samples per line and 288 lines per frame, for luminance. Based on the subsampling principle, the color difference signals are defined as 176 samples per frame. Unlike the ITU-R 601 standard, the number of lines per frame is also halved to 144 for chrominance signals. As a result, subsampling provides a 50% reduction in the bit-rate. The CIF subsampling is also referred to as 4:1:1, meaning that each color difference signal has one-fourth of the spatial resolution of the luminance component.

Example: For CIF format, the samples per active line are 352 and number of active lines per frame is 288. This amounts to 352 x 288 = 101376 samples per frame. If we use 8 bits to code each sample, then the bits per frame will be 811,008 bits. Since CIF has a maximum of 30 frames every second, this is equivalent to a bit-rate of 24,330,240 bits per second or approximately 24 Mbps. This is only for the luminance part. The color difference signals contribute as follows: 176 x 144 x 2 x 8 x 30 = 12,165,120 or approximately 12 Mbps. So, the total bit-rate required for studio-quality TV with a subsampling ratio of 4:1:1 is **36 Mbps**.

videoconferencing Quality - QCIF: ITU-TS H.261 recommendation defines a *lower quality* format called *Quarter-Common Interchange Format (QCIF)*, with a frame size of 176 samples per line and 144 lines per frame, for luminance and the color difference signals.

Example: For QCIF format, the samples per active line are 176 and number of active lines per frame is 144. This amounts to 176 x 144 = 25344 samples per frame. If we use 8 bits to code each sample, then the bits per frame will be 202,752 bits. Since QCIF has a maximum of 30 frames every second, this is equivalent to a bit-rate of 6,082,560 bits per second or approximately 6 Mbps. This is only for the luminance part. The color difference signals contribute as follows: 176 x 144 x 2 x 8 x 30 = 12,165,120 or approximately 12 Mbps. So, the total bit-rate required for studio-quality TV with a subsampling ratio of 4:1:1 is **18 Mbps**.

videoconferencing Quality - Super-CIF: ITU-TS H.261 recommendation defines a *near studio quality* format called *Super-Common Interchange Format (Super-CIF)*, with a frame size of 704 samples per line and 576 lines per frame, for luminance and a subsampling ratio of 4:1:1 for the color difference signals.

VCR Quality - SIF: MPEG-1 motion video compression standard defines a *VCR quality* format called *Standard Interchange Format (SIF)*, with a frame size of 352 samples per line and either 240 (for NTSC) or 288 (for PAL/SECAM) lines per frame, for luminance. The color difference signals are sampled at half the frequency of the luminance - 176 samples per line and either 120 or 144 lines per frame. Thus, the MPEG-1 subsampling ratio is 4:1:1.

Media	Storage Required in KB
Data (typical)	50 - 500
Audio (1 second)	64 - 768
Video (1 second)	27648
Image or Graphics	307.2

Table 2.2. Storage Required for Each Media

2.12 Multimedia: Data, Audio, Video, Image, and Graphics

So far we have looked at the nature of each medium, one at a time, to understand the implications in terms of space and time. The reason is that the design of a multimedia system is going to deal with space and time. Therefore, it is important for us to know these and the tolerance limits for each medium. Table 2.2 summarizes the storage requirements across media. The audio rate is based on L16 coding and 48 KHz sampling rate, the video rate is based on 640 x 480, 24 bits per pixel, 60 frames, and the image (and graphics) is based on the size of a 640 x 480 pixel image. It is obvious that video requires a tremendous amount of storage and hence has to be dealt with as a special case. One interesting feature about these media is that there is a lot of redundancy in the information and it is possible to reduce the storage requirements by exploiting the redundancy. In fact, that is why the literature talks about coding and compression whenever media such as video is referred to. While dealing with system design for multimedia, reducing the storage requirements for video (compression) is the goal and coding is used as a means to achieve this goal. We will discuss more about coding and compression in Chapter 3.

2.13 Timing Analysis

When we consider the timing relationship across media and coding together, we need to ensure that the inter-stream synchronization is also coded. This makes the coding process go beyond compression and encompasses synchronization as well. In general, when the multimedia information goes through different subsystems, the timing relationships may be affected. For example, there could be a small variation δ between the time instants t_{i+1} and t_i when samples a_{i+1} and a_i are played. In the general case, the generated and replayed audio stream will be as shown in Fig. 2.12. The following conditions should be satisfied for faithful reproduction of generated audio at playing time:

$$t_{i+1} - t_i = \Delta$$
$$t'_{i+1} - t'_i = \Delta \pm \delta$$
$$t_i < t'_i < t'_{i+1}$$
$$\delta \ll \Delta$$

where,

t_i, t_{i+1} refer to time instants at the generating end,
t'_i, t'_{i+1} refer to time instants at the replaying end,
Δ is the inter-sample spacing at the generating end,
δ is the variation that can be tolerated at the replaying end.

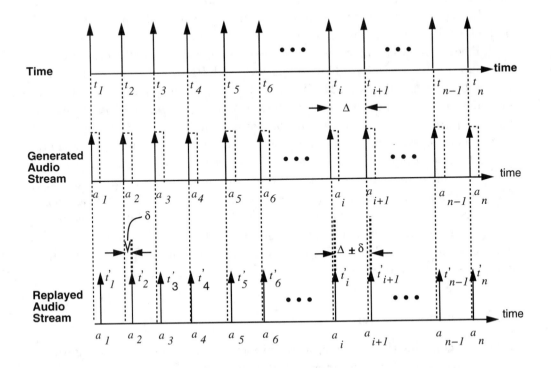

Fig. 2.12. Generated and Replayed Audio Streams

The physical significance of these conditions is that the condition $t_{i+1} - t_i = \Delta$ states that the generated stream has *constant rate* samples with rate $1/\Delta$. The condition $t'_{i+1} - t'_i = \Delta \pm \delta$ states that on the replaying side, there could be a variation in the rate (due to several system-related factors that we will discuss later), but should be limited to $\pm\delta$. $t_i < t'_i$ states that a sample cannot be replayed before it is generated. $t'_i < t'_{i+1}$ states that the samples have to be replayed in the same order as they were generated. $\delta \ll \Delta$ simply re-emphasizes $t'_i < t'_{i+1}$; otherwise, $t'_{i+1} - t'_i = \Delta \pm \delta$ will *nullify* $t'_i < t'_{i+1}$.

In the physical world, each audio sample has a pre-designated place in the music or speech or whatever it represents. Therefore, playing an audio sample at the wrong time (violation of condition $t'_i < t'_{i+1}$) is worse than *not playing the sample at all!*. Therefore, if a sample a_{i+1} is not available at the right time $t_{i+1} \pm \delta$ or $t_i + \Delta \pm \delta$, then it has to be discarded, even if it becomes available later. This stringent requirement has to be satisfied in all multimedia systems and will impact different parts of the system design in the case of the Type I, Type II, and Type III systems that we are considering.

2.14 Ideal Networking Environment for Multimedia

From our discussions so far, it is clear that multimedia means *large volume* of data and *timely handling*.

When we discuss storage and retrieval, we emphasize the *large volume* aspect more. That is why we need to understand compression (which deals with reduction of volume) and I/O devices (which store and retrieve large-volume information).

When we transport multimedia across the network, we emphasize the *timely handling*. In a network, from the source to the destination, the rate of transfer has to be guaranteed. Also, delay jitter, if any, should be very small. This is what we can conclude from the timing analysis that we discussed in the previous section. But, what we have understood so far as large volume will turn out to be *variable large volume* after compression! To support *variable large volume* one needs *isochronous* support in the network. *iso* means same and *chrono* means time. The group of bits (such as s video sample representing a frame) have to be carried across the network *together* or at the same time. Therefore, it is considered ideal to have networks with isochronous support to handle multimedia information.

2.15   Summary

In this chapter, the requirements of a multimedia system were explained quantitatively. Each medium was considered separately and its impact on volume of data to be handled by the computer system and the disk storage was highlighted. Also, the time characteristics of each medium was presented to illustrate the need for intra-media and inter-media synchronization. The discussions considered one medium at a time and then a set of media. Further information about multimedia systems can be obtained from [5, 6, 7].

This chapter also underlines *why* it is necessary to develop techniques to keep the volume of data as low as possible (also called compression in the literature). The details of *how* to achieve such compression of data and the techniques available for doing so are the subject matter of the following chapter.

REFERENCES

1. Shannon C. A Mathematical Theory of Communication, Bell Systems Technical Journal, Vol. 27, pp. 379-423, July 1948; and pp. 623-656, October 1948.

2. Nyquist H. Certain Factors Affecting Telegraph Speed, Bell Systems Technical Journal, Vol. 3, pp. 324, 1924.

3. Nyquist H. Certain Topics in Telegraph Transmission Theory, AIEE Trans., Vol. 47, pp. 617-644, 1928.

4. John G. Proakis. Digital Communications, 3rd Edition, McGraw Hill Inc., 1995.

5. Ralf Steinmetz and Klara Nahrstedt. Multimedia: Computing, Communications and Applications, Prentice-Hall, Inc., 1995.

6. Francois Fluckiger. Understanding Networked Multimedia: Applications and Technology, Prentice-Hall, Inc., 1995.

7. A. Murat Tekalp. Digital Video Processing, Prentice-Hall, Inc., 1995.

8. ISO 9592: PHIGS - Programmer's Hierarchical Interactive Graphics System, ISO Standard, 1995.

9. ISO 7942: ISO Graphics Kernel System standard, 1985.

Exercises

1. List the size of the files in your directory. Observe the relative sizes of program files and the corresponding executable files. Are they same? Are you able to edit these files using a text editor? Record your observations and comment on them.

2. Using a scanner, scan one page of your class notes into a file called class.img. Using any text editor you are familiar with, create a text file by entering your class notes through a terminal. List both the files and look at their relative sizes. What do you observe? Record your observations and comment on them.

3. Use a workstation or PC with a microphone attached to it. Using an appropriate utility for the machine, record your own voice when you read a page of your class notes. Use the same page as you used in response to the previous question. There will be a file created to store your voice. List the file. Comment on the size and compare it with the other two files you have already created. Record your observations and comment on them.

4. The file corresponding to a C++ program is 80 Kbytes long in its ASCII form in a computer system X. There are 1400 lines in the program and they are separated by an LF character. This is to be copied to a computer system Y, which codes n ASCII characters into m bytes. Moreover, the line delimiter is a CR-LF pair. The user can specify the values of n and m as a part of the copy command as shown:

copy filename -n 3 -m 2

What will be the size of the file in computer system Y?

5. An A4 page (8.5" x 11") is to be scanned in black and white. The scanner has a resolution of 75.294 dots per inch horizontally and 43.6363 dots per inch vertically. Each dot (or pixel) is represented by 8 bits. What will be the size of the scanned file?

6. A page was scanned to a resolution of 1280 x 1024 (Horizontal x Vertical). The page is pure WHITE, except for a + sign at the center. The vertical line of the + sign is 80 pixels thick and the horizontal line is 24 pixels thick. This picture is represented by four levels of grey, each level being 00, 01, 10, 11. Of these, 00 represents BLACK, 11 represents WHITE, and the others something in between. But when 01 is mixed with 10, it becomes BLACK. The horizontal line of the + sign is in 01 and the vertical line is in 10. How many 1s and 0s are there in the scanned file? What is the longest run of 1s? What is the shortest run of 0s?

7. In the scanned image obtained in Problem 6, a group of 8 bits are represented on a decimal computer (unlike normal computers which understand 0 and 1 only, the decimal computer understands 0, 1, 2, 3, 4, 5, 6, 7, 8, and 9, and works with decimal storage and arithmetic!) by their decimal equivalent. If all 8 bits are 1s, then the decimal equivalent is 255. Calculate the size of the file in terms of the number of digits, when it is stored in the decimal computer.

8. A Pentium Pro based laptop has a 1 GB disk with 400 MB free space. How many minutes of speech can be stored, if it is in uncompressed digital form with telephone quality?

9. Workstations with audio capability have the ability to record audio sampled at 64 Kbps. A child takes 4 minutes to sing "Jingle Bells...". How big a file will that song be on the computer?

10. ABC Inc. makes digital answering machines that record voice messages sampled at 8 Kbps. You are a proud owner of one of these and you leave it on when you go on travel. Your friend leaves a message for you on the machine, which is 3 minutes long. You are currently on tour, but you can login to your answering machine remotely using the telephone and pickup the message through your laptop. The telephone lines work at 14.4 Kbps. How long will it take for you to pick up the message using your laptop?

11. The entire movie *Jurassic Park* is stored on a video server and occupies 4 GB. You want to download it onto your computer in 30 minutes. What should be the link speed to accomplish this? Assume that the computers and disks on either side are fast enough and big enough, such that their operation is instantaneous.

12. If you were to get the same movie mentioned in Problem 11, through a telephone line operating at 14.4 Kbps, how long will it take to transfer the movie from the video server to your computer?

Chapter 3

Multimedia Systems Technology: Coding and Compression

3.1 Introduction

In multimedia system design, *storage* and *transport* of information play a significant role. Multimedia information is inherently voluminous and therefore requires very high storage capacity and very high bandwidth transmission capacity. For instance, the storage for a video frame with 640×480 pixel resolution is 7.3728 million bits, if we assume that 24 bits are used to encode the luminance and chrominance components of each pixel. Assuming a frame rate of 30 frames per second, the entire 7.3728 million bits should be transferred in 33.3 milliseconds, which is equivalent to a bandwidth of 221.184 million bits per second. That is, the transport of such large number of bits of information and in such a short time requires high bandwidth.

There are two approaches that are possible - one to develop technologies to provide higher bandwidth (of the order of Gigabits per second or more) and the other to find ways and means by which the number of bits to be transferred can be reduced, *without compromising the information content.* It amounts to saying that we need a transformation of a string of characters in some representation (such as ASCII) into a new string (e.g., of bits) that contains the same information but whose length must be as small as possible; i.e., *data compression.* Data compression is often referred to as coding, whereas coding is a general term encompassing any special representation of data that achieves a given goal. For example, reducing the number of bits is by itself a goal.

In 1948, Claude Shannon, the father of Information Theory, introduced

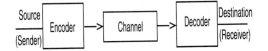

Fig. 3.1. Shannon's Communication Systems Model

a concept called *entropy* to measure the *information content* of a source[1]. Shannon proposed a communication system model (shown pictorially in Fig. 3.1) which addresses two basic issues:

- How can a communication system *efficiently transmit the information* that a source produces?

- How can a communication system achieve *reliable communication* over a noisy channel?

The first issue relates to *compression* and the second relates to *error control*. In both cases, there is a *transformation of number of bits* that represent the information produced by a source. These two aspects are also known as *source coding* and *channel coding*. Information theory is the study of efficient coding and its consequences in the form of speed of transmission and probability of error.

In this chapter we focus on source coding (compression) and standards for compression. Information coded at the source end has to be correspondingly decoded at the receiving end. Coding can be done in such a way that the *information content* is not lost; that means it can be recovered fully on decoding at the receiver. However, media such as image and video (meant primarily for human consumption) provide opportunities to encode more efficiently but with a loss.

Coding (consequently, the compression) of multimedia information is subject to certain quality[1] constraints. For example, the quality of a picture should be the same when coded and, later on, decoded. Dealing with perceptual quality it is possible for one to design a coding method that may be lossy. By lossy coding we mean that there is information loss, but the loss does not affect the perceptual quality. In practice, one or more parameters related to the source may be used in designing coding schemes that result in lossy compression. Also, the complexity and the execution time of the techniques used for coding and decoding should be minimal. These constraints

---

[1]By quality, we mean perceptual quality.

are related to the nature of the application(live or orchestrated) as well. It should be noted that all these requirements are based on the characteristics of human perception of different media. For example, for *interactive* multimedia application such as videoconferencing, the end-to-end delay should be less than 150 milliseconds. In the context of current high-speed transmission technologies, such an end-to-end delay requirement would imply that compression and decompression, if any, should be contained within 50 milliseconds. Similarly, multimedia applications that are *retrieval* based, such as on-demand video service, require that random access to single images and audio frames be possible under 500 milliseconds.

Coding and compression techniques are critical to the viability of multimedia at both the storage level and at the communication level. Some of the multimedia information has to be coded in continuous (time dependent) format and some in discrete (time independent) format. In multimedia context, the *primary motive* in coding is *compression*. By nature, the audio, image, and video sources have built-in redundancy, which make it possible to achieve compression through appropriate coding. As the image data and video data are voluminous and act as prime motivating factors for compression, our references in this chapter will often be to images even though other data types can be coded (compressed).

3.2 What is Image Compression?

Image data can be compressed without significant degradation of the visual (perceptual) quality because images contain a high degree of:

- spatial redundancy, due to correlation between neighboring pixels (this is also referred to as statistical redundancy),

- spectral redundancy, due to correlation among color components, and

- psycho-visual redundancy, due to perceptual properties of the human visual system.

The higher the redundancy, the higher the achievable compression. This is what we referred to as *source coding* earlier in the communication system of Shannon. A typical image compression system (or source encoder) consists of a transformer, quantizer, and a coder, as illustrated in Fig. 3.2.

Transformer applies a one-to-one transformation to the input image data. The output of the transformer is an image representation which is

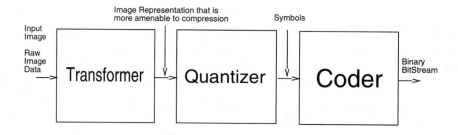

Fig. 3.2. Typical Image Compression System

more amenable to efficient compression than the raw image data. Unitary mappings such as Discrete Cosine Transform, which pack the energy of the signal to a small number of coefficients, is a popular method with image compression standards.

Quantizer generates a limited number of symbols that can be used in the representation of the compressed image. Quantization is a many-to-one mapping which is irreversible. It can be performed by scalar or vector quantizers. *Scalar quantization* refers to element-by-element quantization of data and *vector quantization* refers to quantization of a block at a time.

Coder assigns a code word, a binary bit-stream, to each symbol at the output of the quantizer. The coder may employ *fixed-length* or *variable-length* codes. Variable Length Coding (VLC), also known as entropy coding, assigns code words in such a way as to minimize the average length of the binary representation of the symbols. This is achieved by assigning shorter code words to more probable symbols, which is the fundamental principle of entropy coding.

Different image compression systems are based on different combinations of transformer, quantizer, and coder. Image compression systems can be broadly classified as:

- **Lossless:** Compression systems, which aim at minimizing the bit-rate of the compressed output without any distortion of the image. The decompressed bit-stream is identical to the original bit-stream. This method is used in cases where accuracy of the information is essential. Examples of such situations are computer programs, data, medical imaging, and so on. Lossless compression systems are also referred to as bit-preserving or reversible compression systems.

- **Lossy:** Compression systems, which aim at obtaining the best possible *fidelity* for a given bit-rate (or minimizing the bit-rate to achieve a given fidelity measure). Such systems are suited for video and audio.

The transformation and coding stages are *lossless*. However, the quantization is *lossy*.

3.3 Taxonomy of Compression Techniques

Based on the *lossless* or *lossy* compression, the encoding is broadly classified as *entropy encoding* (leading to lossless compression) and *source encoding* (leading to lossy compression).

It is interesting to note that the term *entropy encoding* refers to all those coding and compression techniques which do not take into account the nature of the information to be compressed. In other words, entropy encoding techniques simply treat all data as a sequence of bits and ignores the semantics of the information to be compressed.

On the contrary, the *source encoding* takes cognizance of the type of the original signal. For example, if the original signal is audio or video, source encoding uses their inherent characteristics in achieving better compression ratio. Normally, it is expected that source encoding will produce better compression compared to entropy encoding techniques. But, of course, the actual degree of success will depend on the semantics of the data itself and may vary from application to application. The designer of a compression system based on source encoding has the choice to render it lossless or lossy.

All of this aside, in practical systems and standards, both entropy encoding and source encoding are usually combined for better effect in compression.

Let us understand the principle behind some of the coding techniques. For an exhaustive treatment of all the techniques, the reader may want to refer to [4, 5, 6, 7].

3.4 Entropy Encoding Techniques

3.4.1 Run-length Encoding

In this technique, the sequence of image elements (or pixels in a scan line) x_1, x_2, ... ,x_n is mapped into a sequence of pairs (c_1,l_1), (c_2,l_2), ..., (c_k,l_k), where c_i represents a color (or intensity) and l_i the length of the ith run (sequence of pixels with equal intensity).

Example: Let digits 1, 2, 3 represent Red, Green, and Blue. These will correspond to c_i. Let a scan line be of length 35 consisting of

111111111111333333333332222222222211111

as x_i. Then, the run-length encoded stream will be the series of tuples (1,11), (3,10), (2,9), and (1,5), where 11,10,9,5 are the l_i.

3.4.2 Repetition Suppression

In this technique, a series of n successive occurrences of a specific character is replaced by a special character called flag, followed by a number representing the repetition count. Normal applications are suppression of 0s in a data file or a bitmap file and suppression of blanks in a text or program file.

Example: Consider a sequence of digits in a data file which looks like the following:

984000000000000000000000000000000000.

When we use the repetition sequence suppression method, the sequence will look like 984f32. The savings is obvious and is dependent upon the contents.

3.4.3 Pattern Substitution

Pattern substitution is a form of a statistical coding method. The idea here is to substitute an oft-repeated pattern by a code. If we are trying to compress the book Hound of Baskervilles, the name *Sherlock Homes* can be substituted by S*, the name *Watson* by W*, and the expression *Elementary my dear Watson* by E*. Obviously, frequent patterns will use shorter codes for better compression.

Example: Consider the lines:

This book is an exemplary example of a book on multimedia and networking. Nowhere else will you find this kind of coverage and completeness. This is truly a one-stop-shop for all that you want to know about multimedia and networking.

If we simply count, there are a total of 193 characters without counting blanks and 232 with blanks. If we group words such as a, about, all, an, and, for, is, of, on, that, this, to, and will, they occur 2, 1, 1, 1, 3, 1, 2, 2, 1, 1, 3,1, and 1 times, respectively. All of them have a blank character on either side, unless when they happen to be the first word or last word of a sentence. The sentence delimiter *period* is always followed by a blank character. The words *multimedia* and *networking* appear twice each. With all this knowledge about the text, we can develop a substitution table that will be very effective. Notice that there is no loss and the coding is reversible. Let us represent the group of words that we identified for the text under consideration by 1, 2, 3, 4, 5, 6, 7, 8, 9, +, &, =, and #. Let us also substitute multimedia by m* and networking by n*. The resulting coded string will be:

```
&    b    o    o    k    7    4    e    x    e    m    p    l    a    r    y
sp   e    x    a    m    p    l    e    8    1    b    o    o    k    9    m
*    5    n    *    .    N    o    w    h    e    r    sp   e    l    s
e    #    y    o    u    sp   f    i    n    d    &    k    i    n    d    8
c    o    v    e    r    a    g    e    5    c    o    m    p    l    e    t
e    n    e    s    s    .    &    7    t    r    u    l    y    1    o    n
e    -    s    t    o    p    -    s    h    o    p    6    3    +    y    o
u    sp   w    a    n    t    =    k    n    o    w    2    m    *    5    n
*    .
```

That is a total of 129 characters and 33.16% compression.

3.4.4 Huffman Coding

Huffman coding is based on the frequency of occurrence of a character (or an octet in the case of images). The principle is to use a lower number of bits to encode the character that occurs more frequently. The codes are stored in a codebook. The codebook may be constructed for every image or for a set of images, when applied to still or moving images. In all cases, the codebook should be transferred to the receiving end so that decoding can take place.

Example: In the sentences given in the example for *pattern substitution*, the occurrence of the alphabets are as follows:

Character: a b c d e Frequency: 15 3 2 7 18 Code: 1100 0101011 0010011 01000 1011

Character:	f	g	h	i	j
Frequency:	4	3	6	14	0
Code:	0001100	0101000	101010	00111	00000111

Character:	k	l	m	n	o
Frequency:	6	11	7	16	21
Code:	101011	1000	00010	1111	1110

Character:	p	q	r	s	t
Frequency:	5	0	7	10	15
Code:	0100111	000011000	10100	0011	001000

Character:	u	v	w	x	y
Frequency:	6	1	6	2	4
Code:	0000111	0000111	110101	0100100	0000011

Character:	z	.	sp
Frequency:	0	3	39
Code:	0000100	0000100	0111

If they are coded as per the code given in the code-book (Table above), the binary bit stream will be:

```
001000 101010 00111 0011 0111 00111 0011 0111 1100 1111
..T... ..h... ..i.. ..s. .sp. ..i.. ..s. .sp. ..a. ..n.
0111
.sp.   ....  and so on.....
```

The total size of the bit stream will be 1124 bits as compared to 1856 bits (232 x 8) of the original text; a compression of 39.44%.

3.5   Source Encoding Techniques

Source encoding is based on the content of the original signal and hence it is rightly termed as semantic-based coding. The compression that can be achieved using source coding may be very high, when compared to strict entropy coding. At the same time, it should be noted that the degree of compression is highly dependent on the data semantic. In general, source encoding may operate either in a lossless or lossy mode.

Source encoding techniques can be classified into three basic types; viz., *transform encoding*, *differential encoding*, and *vector quantization*. Each one of these methods are effective for a signal (or raw data) with certain characteristics. The methods and where they are applicable are explained in this section. Fig. 3.3 provides the bird's eye view of coding techniques.

3.5.1   Transform Encoding

In transform encoding, the *raw data* undergoes a mathematical transformation from the original form in spatial or temporal domain into an abstract domain, which is more suitable for compression. The transform process is a reversible process and the original signal can be obtained by applying the *inverse* transform. Fourier transform and Cosine transform are two popular examples. They transform the signal from the space or time domain to frequency domain.

The important point to note here is that the choice of the type of transformation depends on the type of data. For instance, in the case of images, transforming the signal from the initial time domain to the frequency domain has advantages. The reason is that the spectral representation (i.e., frequency spectrum in the frequency domain) of images captures the changes in color or luminance rapidly. When an image signal $f(x)$ (in spatial domain)

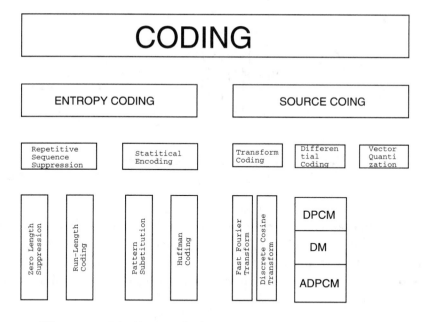

Fig. 3.3. Bird's Eye View of Coding Techniques

is transformed to $F(u)$ (in frequency domain), the DC component and the low frequency components *carry most of the information contained* in the original signal $f(x)$. Even though the signal is an infinite series in the transformed domain, the *most significant* coefficients are *only* in the first few terms. In the quantization stage, normally the less significant coefficients are dropped. Only the *first k coefficients* are actually used. The choice of k, however, depends on the application requirement. Moreover, the significant coefficients can be coded with better accuracy than the less significant ones.

Discrete Cosine Transform (DCT) is the transform encoding technique used in image compression standards such as JPEG. The coefficients (significant part of the transformed signal) retained are called *DCT coefficients*. This method is further discussed in Section 3.8.

3.5.2 Differential Encoding

In differential encoding, only the difference between the actual value of a sample and a prediction of that value is encoded. Because of this approach, differential encoding is also known as predictive encoding. Techniques such as *differential pulse code modulation*, *delta modulation*, and *adaptive pulse code modulation* belong to this class of differential encoding techniques. All

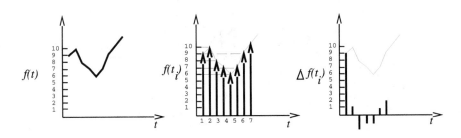

Fig. 3.4. Differential PCM Example

these methods essentially differ in the prediction part.

The differential encoding technique is well suited to signals in which successive samples do not differ much from each other, but they should be significantly different from zero values! These techniques naturally apply to motion video (where one can transmit the difference in images across successive frames) and audio signals.

Differential Pulse Code Modulation (DPCM):   In DPCM, the prediction function is simply the following:

$$f_{predicted}(t_i) = f_{actual}(t_{i-1})$$

So what needs to be encoded at every sampling instant is:

$$\Delta f(t_i) = f_{actual}(t_i) - f_{actual}(t_{i-1})$$

If successive sample values are close to each other, then only the first sample needs a larger number of bits to encode and the rest can be encoded with a relatively shorter number of bits.

Example: Consider the signal and its samples as shown in Fig. 3.4. The $f_{actual}(t_i)$ at various instances t_1, t_2, t_3, t_4, t_5, t_6, and t_7 are 9, 10, 8, 7, 6, 7, and 9. The $f_{predicted}(t_i)$ are 0, 9, 10, 8, 7, 6, and 7. Therefore, the $\Delta f(t_i)$ are +9, +1, -2, -1, -1, +1, and +2.

Delta Modulation: Delta modulation is a special case of DPCM. The prediction function is the same as DPCM. The difference is in coding the error (difference between the predicted and the actual values). Delta Modulation codes the error as a single bit or digit. It simply indicates that the 'current' sample is to be increased by a step or decreased by a step. Delta modulation is more suited to the coding of signals that do not change too rapidly with the sampling rate.

Adaptive DPCM: ADPCM is the sophisticated version of DPCM. The predicted value is extrapolated from a series of values of preceding samples using a time-varying function. That means, instead of using a constant prediction function, the estimation is made variable to be in line with the characteristics of the sampled signal.

Vector Quantization: In vector quantization, the given data stream is divided into blocks called *vectors*. These blocks can be one- or two-dimensional. Typically, when we deal with images, the blocks are usually q square block of pixels. Often, the vectors are of the same size. Consider the image presented in Fig. 3.5 and its digital representation with a resolution of 8 x 8. In the figure, there are 2 x 2 blocks that together make up the 8 x 8. Each one of the 2 x 2 blocks, will have a pattern between all 0s and all 1s, both inclusive. A table called *code book* is used to find a match for each one of the 2 x 2 blocks, which will correspond to some or all the patterns. Each entry in the code book (basically, it is a table of entries as shown in Fig. 3.5) is a 2 x 2 pattern of 0s and 1s written in a linear form by stacking the rows of the 2 x 2 matrix one after another. This is indicated as *position index* in Fig. 3.5. The code book itself may be predefined or dynamically constructed.

Using the code book, each vector in the image is coded using the best match available. As the code book is present, both at the coding and the decoding ends, only the reference to the entry is actually transferred. When there is no exact match available in the code book, the vector of the image is coded with reference to the *nearest* pattern and will appear as *distortion* in the decoded picture. Also, while coding and transmitting, one can also transfer the errors (difference between the entries in the code book and the vectors in the image) in a quantized form. Depending on the quantization level of the errors and whether or not the errors are sent along with the image, the scheme may become lossy or lossless.

Vector quantization is useful in coding (or compressing) a source whose characteristics are particularly well known. Moreover, it should be possible to construct the code book that can approximate a wide range of actual image vectors. Vector quantization is generally found to be useful in coding of speech. The reader may be interested in understanding more about optimal construction of code books and the algorithms to find out the best pattern match.

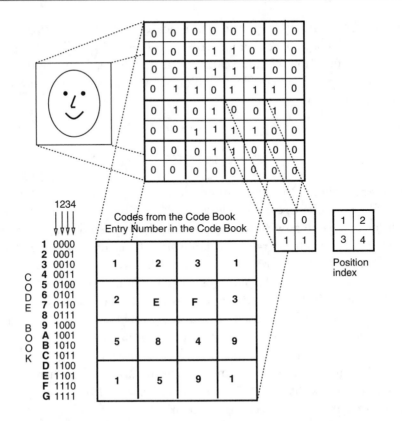

Fig. 3.5. Vector Quantization

3.6   Image Compression System

The uncompressed picture is in analog form and the compressed picture
is in digital form and there are several steps involved in compressing and
decompressing a picture. The source image data (which is in digital form) is
compressed using an encoder and reconstructed from the compressed form,
using a decoder. The *encoder* and the *decoder* are the two functional blocks of
an image compression system. This is shown in Fig. 3.6. Both the encoder

Fig. 3.6. Image Compression System

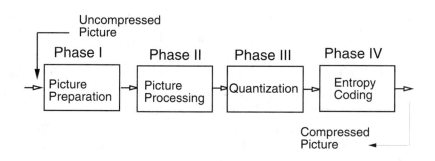

Fig. 3.7. Basic Units of an Encoder

and the decoder have different parts A generic comparison of units that together make up an encoder is shown in Fig. 3.7. These units correspond to different phases in the encoding process. The different phases together convert the analog form of the picture to a corresponding compressed digital stream at the output.

Phase I is the picture preparation phase. In this phase the uncompressed analog signal is converted to its digital counterpart through *sampling*. Each sample is then represented in digital form using the appropriate number of bits per sample. A picture is considered as consisting of a number of pixels in the X and Y axes to cover the entire screen. The picture (pixels) is also divided into *blocks* consisting of 8×8 array of pixels each. This is true for the JPEG [2] standard for still pictures or images[4]. In the case of motion video compression based on MPEG [3], motion-compensation units called Macroblocks of size 16×16 are used. This size is arrived at based on a trade-off between the coding gain provided by motion information and the cost associated with coding the motion information [5,7]. These two standards are discussed further in this chapter.

Phase II is the picture processing phase. In this phase, the actual compression takes place using a source coding or lossy algorithm. A transformation from the time domain to the frequency domain is performed. As most of the 'information' content is in the DC and low frequencies, appropriate weights are used in selecting the coefficients for inter-frame coding in this phase.

Phase III is the quantization phase. In this phase, the output of the previous stage, which are coefficients expressed as real numbers, are mapped into

---

[2] Joint Photographers Experts Group.
[3] Motion Pictures Experts Group.

integers, resulting in a reduction of precision. In the transformed domain, the coefficients are distinguished according to their significance; for example, they could be quantized using a different number of bits per coefficient.

Phase IV is the entropy encoding phase. In this phase, which is the last step in the compression process, the digital data stream which is output from the quantization phase is compressed without losses.

In some cases, depending on the content of the image, the repeated application of processing phase and quantization phase, will result in better compression. Some compression techniques realize this and gainfully employs them. Such techniques are called adaptive compression schemes, and they essentially repeat Phases II and III several times for better compression. After compression, the data looks as shown in Fig. 3.8. A preamble, the coding technique used, actual data, and possibly an error correction code are all part of a typical compressed picture.

Fig. 3.8. The Compressed Picture

At the receiving end, this information has to be *decompressed* before presentation. Decompression is the inverse of the compression process. If an application uses similar techniques resulting in same execution time for both compression and decompression, then we call that application *symmetric*; otherwise it is called *asymmetric*. Interactive applications are symmetric and presentation applications are asymmetric. Teleconferencing is an example of a symmetric application and an audio-visual tutoring program is an example of an asymmetric application. As we mentioned earlier, depending on the *picture quality* and *time constraints*, appropriate compression technique will be selected. The standards applicable for pictures provide for this option.

3.7 Compression System Standards

There are several coding and compression standards already available; some of them are in use in today's products while others are still being developed. The most important standards are:

- JPEG, standard developed jointly by ISO and ITU-TS for the compression of still images.

- MPEG 1, MPEG 2 and MPEG 4 standards developed by ISO committee IEC/JTC1/SC29/WG11 for coding combined video and audio information.

- H.261, standard developed by Study Group XV and known popularly as Video Coded for Audiovisual Services at $px64$ Kbps.

- ITU-TS H.263 for videophone applications at a bit-rate below 64 Kbps.

- ISO JBIG for compressing bilevel images.

- DVI, a de facto standard for compression from Intel that enables storage compression and real-time decompression for presentation purposes. This will not be discussed further as this standard is getting obsolete.

3.8 JPEG

JPEG is the acronym for Joint Photographic Experts Group, and is a joint collaboration between the ISO committee designated JTC1/SC2/WG10 and the CCITT SGVIII (ITU-T) to establish an international standard for continuous tone (multilevel) still images, both grey scale and color. JPEG can compress typical images from 1/10 to 1/50 of their uncompressed bit size without visibly affecting image quality. JPEG addresses several applications such as photovideotex, color facsimile, medical imaging, desktop publishing, graphic arts, newspaper wire photo transmission, and so on. In 1992, JPEG became an ISO standard and an international standard [4,11,12].

The goal of JPEG has been to develop a method for continuous tone image compression which meets the following requirements:

- Encoder should be parameterizable so that the application can set the desired compression quality tradeoff. The compression scheme should result in image fidelity.

- To be applicable to practically any kind of continuous tone digital source image; not to be restricted to certain dimensions, color spaces, pixel aspect ratio, etc. Not to be limited to classes of scene imagery with restrictions on scene content such as complexity, range of colors, etc.

- Should have tractable computational complexity, to make it possible to implement on a range of CPUs, as well as special-purpose hardware. The compression process has to be completed in real-time.

- Should be possible to implement in hardware with a viable cost for application requiring high performance

- Should have the following modes of operation:

  - *Sequential encoding:* each image is encoded in multiple scans for applications in which transmission time is long and the viewer prefers to watch the image build up in multiple coarse to clear phases.

  - *Lossless encoding:* the image is encoded to guarantee exact recovery of every source image sample value

  - *Hierarchical encoding:* the image is encoded at multiple resolutions so that the lower resolution versions may be accessed without first having to decompress the image at its full resolution

JPEG aims at a very general scheme which is picture-feature independent and technique independent. Basically, it defines a framework that can take care of all the requirements listed above. The stages of JPEG encoding are as shown in Fig. 3.9, the corresponding stages in decoding, decompression and reconstruction of the picture are shown in Fig. 3.10. The JPEG standard is general and is independent of picture size, color, and aspect ratio. JPEG considers a picture as consisting of a number of components, each with a different size. For example, brightness and color are two components of a picture.

An Aside: The *elements* specified in the JPEG standards are *encoder, decoder,* and an *interchange format.*

An *encoder* is an embodiment of an encoding process. An encoder takes as input *digital source image data* and *table specifications,* and by means of a specified set of *procedures* generates as output *compressed image data.*

A *decoder* is an embodiment of the *decoding process.* A decoder takes as input compressed image data and table specifications (same as the ones used by the encoder), and by means of a set of procedures generates as output *digital reconstructed image data.*

An *interchange format* is a compressed image data representation which includes all table specifications used in the encoding process. the interchange format is for exchange between application environments.

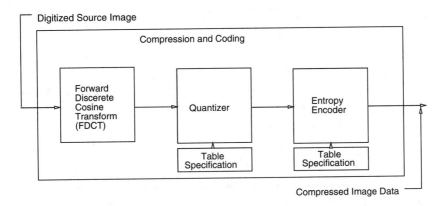

Fig. 3.9. JPEG Encoding of a Picture

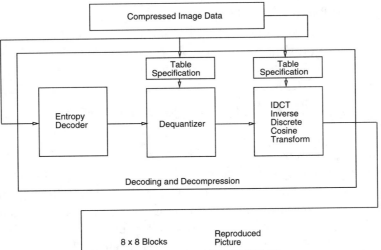

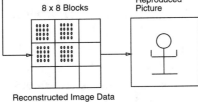

Fig. 3.10. JPEG Decoding of a Picture

3.8.1 JPEG Compression Process

The JPEG standard enables the design of two processes; viz.; image *compression* and *decompression*. In a sequential mode, each one of these processes

- JPEG Compression Process

    - Preparation of Data Blocks

    - Source Encoding step

        * Discrete Cosine Transform(DCT), also called forward DCT(FDCT)
        * Quantization

    - Entropy Encoding step

        * Run Length Coding
        * Huffman or Arithmetic Coding

- JPEG Decompression Process

    - Entropy Decoding Step

        * Huffman or Arithmetic Coding
        * Run Length Coding

    - Source Decoding Step

        * Dequantization
        * Inverse Discrete Cosine Transform(IDCT)

Table 3.1. Steps in the JPEG Process

consists of several steps as shown in Table 3.1.

JPEG may compress grey-scale and color images. As there are many ways to represent color images, the standard does not impose an initial format for the representation of color images. In general, the pictures are considered as a matrix of colored dots called pixels. Each pixel may be represented by an RGB [4] triplet, a YUV (European TV) or YIQ (North American and Japanese TV), a YC_rC_b triplet, or by many other combinations. The digitized variables which represent the image are called the *image components*. R,Y,Q or C_b are examples of image components, which are represented as matrices of values. Sometimes, these components may be sub-sampled - which is normally done in the case of color difference components. As the size of the image to be compressed is variable and the sub-sampling unknown, JPEG has foreseen the need to deal with a relatively large number of image components. The maximum number of components that JPEG can deal with is 255. In practice, regular color images use three components

---

[4]Composite signals - RGB are direct and the rest are derivatives, as explained earlier in Chapter 2.

only.

JPEG utilizes a methodology based on Discrete Cosine Transform (DCT) for compression. It is a symmetrical process with the same complexity for coding and for decoding. The reader should note that JPEG does not have an embedded encoded/compressed audio signal and is aimed at pictures or images only.

In DCT based coding, two distinct modes are possible: *sequential* and *progressive*. For sequential DCT-based mode, 8x8 sample blocks are typically input block-by-block from left-to-right, and then block-row by block-row top-to-bottom. After a block has been quantized and prepared for entropy encoding, all 64 of its quantized DCT coefficients can be immediately entropy encoded and output as a part of the compressed image data thereby minimizing the storage requirements. In this approach, the image will slowly unfold from top-to-bottom.

For the progressive DCT-based mode, 8x8 blocks are also typically encoded in the same order, but in multiple scans through the image. This is accomplished by adding an image-sized coefficient memory buffer between the quantizer and the entropy encoder. As each block is quantized, its coefficients are stored in the buffer. The DCT coefficients in the buffer are then partially encoded in each of multiple scans. This approach will make a silhouette of the image appear first and then progressively sharpen and brighten it.

Preparation of Data Blocks: As explained earlier in Chapter 2, the source image has to be converted from the analog to digital form. The source digital image in its original form is a matrix of sampled values of amplitude of signals (color or gray scale). If it is color, then there will be as many matrices as there are color components and if it is gray scale, there will be a single component. This is illustrated in Fig. 3.11. The discrete cosine transform is not applied on the entire image. Instead, in the sequential lossy mode, the image is divided into individual blocks. Each individual block is treated separately at each step of the processing chain. The blocks are small square matrices of 8×8 sampled values.

Example: Consider a color image represented by three components: the luminance Y and the two color differences U and V. The size of the image is 640 pixels per line by 480 lines, which is equivalent to computing a VGA standard. Therefore, the luminance consists of a matrix of 640 by 480 values, and each color difference component is a matrix of 320 by 240 values if we assume a 4:1:1 chrominance reduction (Fig. 3.11 and Fig. 3.9). The block preparation step will submit to the DCT process 4800 blocks of luminance and twice 1200 blocks for the color difference. Blocks may then be passed to the DCT, component after component and within each component left to right and top to bottom. This technique is called non-interleaved data ordering.

Forward Discrete Cosine Transform: In transform coding, the initial spatial or temporal domain is transformed into an abstract domain which is more suitable for compression. The process is reversible; that is, applying the inverse transformation will restore the original data.

Each 8×8 block in Fig. 3.9 can be represented by 64 point values denoted as:

$f(x,y), 0 \leq x \leq 7, 0 \leq y \leq 7$, where x and y are the two spatial domains.

That is, each 8x8 block of source image samples can be viewed as a 64 point discrete signal that is a function of the two spatial dimensions x and y. The DCT transforms these values to the frequency domain as $c = g(F_u, F_v)$ where c is the coefficient and F_u and F_v are the respective spatial frequencies for each direction using the transformation[4]:

$$\text{For } 0 \leq u \leq 7, 0 \leq v \leq 7 \; F(u,v) =$$
$$0.25 * C(u) * C(v) * \sum_{x=0}^{7} \sum_{y=0}^{7} f(x,y) * \cos(((2x+1)*u*\pi)/16) * \cos(((2y+1)*v*\pi)/16),$$
$$\text{where } C(u) = C(v) = 1/\sqrt{2} \text{ for u,v} = 0 \text{ and 1 otherwise.}$$

The output of this equation gives another set of 64 values *known as the DCT coefficients*, that is the value of a particular frequency - no longer the amplitude of the signal at the sampled position (x,y). The coefficient corresponding to vector (0,0) is called the DC coefficient and the rest are called AC coefficients. The DC coefficient generally contains a significant fraction of the total image energy. Because sample values typically vary slowly from point to point across an image, the FDCT (Forward Discrete

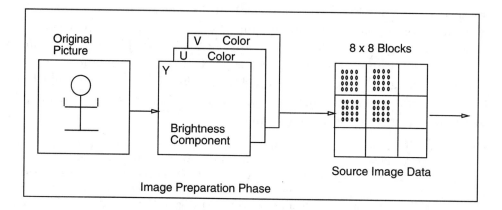

Fig. 3.11. Image Preparation Phase

Cosine Transform) processing compresses data by concentrating most of the signal in the lower values of the *(u,v)* space. For a typical 8x8 sample block from a typical source image, many, if not most, of the *(u,v)* pairs have zero or near-zero coefficients and therefore need not be encoded. At the decoder, IDCT (Inverse Discrete Cosine Transform) reverses this processing step. For each DCT-based mode of operation, the JPEG proposal specifies different codes for 8-bit and 12-bit source-image samples.

Intuition: In a block representing an image, sampled values usually vary slightly from point to point. Thus, the coefficients of the lowest frequencies will be high, but the medium and high frequencies will have a small or zero value. The energy of the signal is concentrated in the lowest spatial frequencies.

Imagine a flat monochromatic wall. Take a picture of it and divide it into 8×8 blocks. These are the *f(x,y)*. In each block, the amplitude of the signal will be nearly constant from pixel to pixel. As the value does not change much in each direction, the zero frequency will be high - as the *frequency measures the rate of change in each direction* - whereas the other frequencies will be nearly zero.

If a sharp black line is drawn on the picture, the image becomes more complex. Some of the blocks will be affected - some not all. In the affected blocks, there will be a rapid change between two consecutive values, which will entail a high coefficient for one of the highest frequencies.

In practice, continuous-tone images such as photographs do not have too many sharp lines or zeros. The transitions between areas are often smooth. Thus, the information is usually mainly contained in the low frequencies. In fact, this is the underlying assumption in JPEG. JPEG is not designed for too complex images, in particular images which look like bitonal images.

In principle, DCT introduces no loss to the source image samples; it simply transforms them to a domain in which they can be more efficiently encoded. This means that, if the FDCT and IDCT could be computed with perfect accuracy and if DCT coefficients were not quantized, the original 8x8 block could be recovered exactly. But as can be seen from the equations, the FDCT (also the IDCT) equations contain transcendental functions. Therefore, no finite time implementation can compute them with perfect accuracy. Several algorithms have been proposed to compute these values approximately. But, no single algorithm is optimal for all implementations: an algorithm that runs optimally in software, normally does not operate optimally in firmware (e.g., in a programmable DSP) or in hardware.

Because of the finite precision of DCT inputs and outputs, coefficients calculated by different algorithms or by independent implementations of the same algorithm will result in slightly different output for identical input. To enable innovation and customization, JPEG has chosen not to specify a unique FDCT/IDCT algorithm, but to address the quality issue by specifying an accuracy test to ensure against largely inaccurate coefficients that degrade image quality.

Quantization: The output from the FDCT (the 64 DCT coefficients) is uniformly quantified in conjunction with a 64 element quantization table to be specified by the application (or the user) as an input to the encoder. Each element can be an integer from 1 to 255, which specifies the step size of the quantifier for its corresponding DCT coefficient. The purpose of quantization is to achieve further compression by representing DCT coefficients with no greater precision than is necessary to achieve the desired image quality. It may be noted that *quantization* is a many-to-one mapping, and therefore is *fundamentally lossy.* It is the principal cause of lossiness in DCT-based encoders.   Quantization is defined as division of each DCT coefficient by its corresponding quantifier step size, followed by rounding to the nearest integer:

$$F^Q(u,v) = Integer\,Round \frac{F(u,v)}{Q(u,v)}$$

After quantization, the DC coefficient is treated separately from the 63 AC coefficients. The DC coefficient is a measure of the average value of the 64 image samples. Because there is usually a strong correlation between the DC coefficients of adjacent 8x8 blocks, the quantized DC coefficient is encoded as the difference from the DC term of the previous block in the encoding order, as shown in Fig. 3.12. This special treatment is worthwhile, as DC coefficients frequently contain a significant fraction of the total image energy.

Finally, all of the quantified coefficients are ordered into the "zig-zag sequence" as shown in Fig. 3.12. The ordering helps to facilitate entropy coding by placing low-frequency coefficients (which are more likely to be non-zero) before high-frequency coefficients.

The final step in DCT-based encoder is entropy coding. This step achieves additional compression losslessly by encoding the quantified DCT coefficients more compactly based on their statistical characteristics. The JPEG proposal specifies two entropy coding methods - Huffman coding and arithmetic coding. It is useful to consider entropy coding as a two-step process. The first step converts the zig-zag sequence of quantified coefficients into an intermediate sequence of symbols. The second step converts the symbols to a data stream in which the symbols no longer have identifiable boundaries. The form and definition of the intermediate symbols is dependent on both

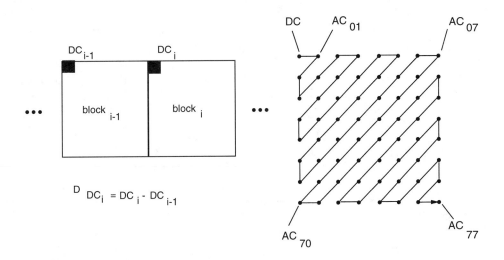

Fig. 3.12. Differential DC Coding and Zig-Zag Sequencing

the DCT-based mode of operation and the entropy coding method. Huffman coding requires that one or more sets of Huffman code tables be specified by the application. The same tables used to compress the image are needed to decompress the image. Huffman tables may be pre-defined and used within an application as defaults, or computed specifically for a given image in an initial statistics-gathering pass prior to compression. Such choices are the responsibility of JPEG applications. As such, the JPEG proposal does not endorse any Huffman tables. A comprehensive example is given in Fig. 3.13. The reader should note that the numbers given in the example are only indicative of what various matrices will look like and not from any real image.

3.8.2   Compression and Picture Quality

For color images with moderate complex scenes, all DCT-based modes of operation typically produce the levels of picture quality for the indicated ranges of compression as shown in Table. 3.2.

3.8.3   Processing at the Receiver

At the receiving end, upon decoding, de-quantization (which is the inverse function of quantization) is to be performed. That simply means that the normalization is removed by multiplying by step size, which returns the result to representation appropriate for input to the IDCT. The corresponding equation is:

$$F^{Q'}(u,v) = F^{Q}(u,v) * Q(u,v)$$

This is then fed to the IDCT that is represented by the following idealized mathematical definition for a 8x8 block:

$$f(x,y) =$$
$$0.25 * \sum_{x=0}^{7} \sum_{y=0}^{7} C(u) * C(v) * F(u,v) * \cos(((2x+1)*u*\pi)/16) * \cos(((2y+1)*v*\pi)/16)$$
$$\text{where } C(u) = C(v) = 1/\sqrt{2} \text{ for u,v} = 0 \text{ and 1 otherwise.}$$

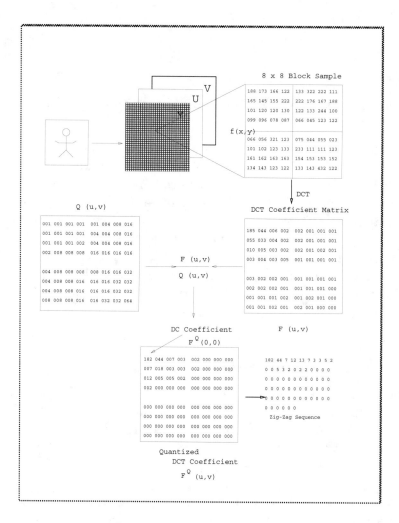

Fig. 3.13. JPEG Example

Intuitively, FDCT and IDCT behave like harmonic analyzer and harmonic synthesizer, respectively. At the decoder, the IDCT takes the 64 DCT coefficients and reconstructs a 64-point output image signal by summing the basis signals.

3.8.4 Hierarchical Mode of Operation

In hierarchical mode of operation, an image is encoded as a sequence of *frames*. These frames provide *reference reconstructed components* which are usually needed for prediction in subsequent frames. Like in the progressive DCT-based mode, hierarchical mode also offers a progressive presentation. It is useful in environments which have multi-resolution requirements. Hierarchical mode also offers the capability of progressive transmission to a final lossless stage.

Using hierarchical coding, a set of successively smaller images can be created by *down-sampling* (low-pass filtering and sub-sampling) the preceding larger image in the set. Then starting with the smallest image in the set, the image set is coded with increasing resolution. After the first stage, each lower-resolution image is scaled up to the next resolution (up-sampled) and used as a prediction for the following stage. When the set of images is stacked (as shown in Fig. 3.14), it sometimes resembles a pyramid. Just as smaller images generated as part of a hierarchical progression can be scaled up to full resolution, full-resolution images generated as part of a non-hierarchical

Compression Range	Picture Quality
0.25-0.5 bits/pixel	Moderate to good quality, sufficient for some applications
0.5-.075 bits/pixel	Good to very good quality, sufficient for many applications
0.75-1.5 bit/pixel	Excellent Quality, sufficient for most applications
1.5-2.0 bits/pixel	Usually indistinguishable from the original picture, sufficient for the most demanding applications

Table 3.2. Compression Range versus Picture Quality [4]

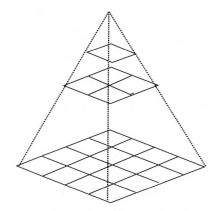

Fig. 3.14. Hierarchical Multi-Resolution Encoding

progression can be scaled down to smaller sizes. These scalings are done at the decoder and are not restricted to powers of 2.

3.8.5 Multiple-Component Images

In the JPEG standard, a source image may contain 1 to 255 image components, also referred to as color or spectral bands or channels. Each component consists of a rectangular array of samples. All samples are defined to be an unsigned integer with precision P bits, with any value in the range $[0, 2^P\text{-}1]$. All samples of all components within the same source image must have the same precision P, the value of which can be 8 or 12 for DCT-based codes and 2 to 16 for predictive codes, respectively. The multicomponent source image model is shown in Fig. 3.15.

The component C_i has sample dimensions $x_i \times y_i$. As the formats in which some image components are sampled may differ (compared to other components), in the JPEG source model, each component can have different dimensions. The dimensions must have a mutual integral relationship defined by H_i and V_i, the relative horizontal and vertical sampling factors, which must be specified for each component. Overall, image dimensions X and Y are defined as the maximum x_i and y_i for all components in the image, and can be any number up to 2^{16}. H and V are allowed only the integer values 1 through 4. The encoded parameters are X, Y, and the H_is and V_is for each component. The decoder reconstructs the dimensions x_i and y_i for each component, according to the following ceiling function:

$$x_i = \text{X} * H_i/H_{max}$$

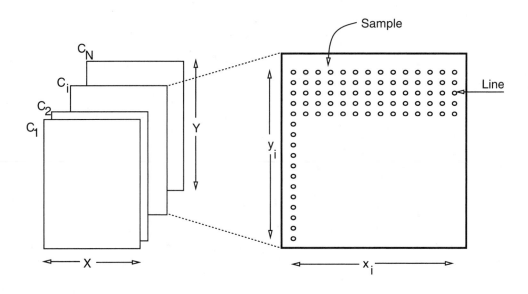

Fig. 3.15. JPEG Source Image Model

$$y_i = \text{Y} * V_i/V_{max}$$

Example: In the example discussed so far, the $C_i s$ are Y, U, and V, the corresponding H_i and V_i are $(H_Y = 4, V_Y = 4), (H_u = 2, V_U = 2)$, and $(H_V = 2, V_V = 2)$ for Y, U, and V, respectively. The resolution of each component Y, U, and V can be assumed to be $(X_Y = 512, Y_Y = 512), (X_U = 256, Y_U = 512)$, and $(X_V = 256, Y_V = 512)$.

3.8.6   Encoding Order and Interleaving for Multi-Component Images

In practice, many applications need to pipeline the process of displaying multi-component images in parallel with the process of decompression. For many systems, this is only feasible if the components are interleaved together within the compressed data stream. The JPEG proposal defines the concept of a *data unit*, which is a single sample in the case of predictive codecs and an 8x8 block of samples in the case of DCT-based codecs. When two or more components are interleaved, each component C_i is partitioned into rectangular regions of x_i by y_i data units, as shown in Fig. 3.15. Regions are ordered within a component from left-to-right and top-to-bottom, and within a region, data units are ordered from left-to-right and top-to-bottom. The JPEG proposal defines the term Minimum Coded Unit *(MCU)* to be the

	C_1						C_2						C_3			C_4		
	0	1	2	3	4	5	0	1	2	3	4	5	0	1	2	0	1	2
0	A	B	E	F	I	J	a	b	c	d	e	f	0	2	4	*	+	=
1	C	D	G	H	K	L	g	h	i	j	k	l	1	3	5	#	$	%
2	M	N	Q	R	U	V	m	n	o	p	q	r	6	8	0	@	!	&
3	O	P	S	T	W	X	s	t	u	v	w	x	7	9	1	^	-	)
4	Y	Z																
5																		

MCU_1 = ABCD ab 01 *

MCU_2 = EFGH cd 23 +

MCU_3 = IJKL ef 45 =

MCU_4 = MNOPgh 67 #

Fig. 3.16. Interleaved Data Ordering Example

smallest group of interleaved data units. In the example given in Fig. 3.16, MCU_1 consists of data units taken from the top-left most region of C_i, followed by data units from the same region of C_2, and likewise for C_3 and C_4. MCU_2 continues the pattern as shown in Fig. 3.16. Thus the interleaved data is an ordered sequence of *MCUs*, and the number of data units contained in an *MCU* is determined by the number of components interleaved and their relative sampling factors. The maximum number of components which can be interleaved is 4, and the maximum number of data units in an *MCU* is 10.

3.8.7 Using Multiple Tables

When multiple components and interleaving are involved, JPEG codes must control the use of a proper data table for each component. It should be ensured that the same quantization table with the same entropy coding table

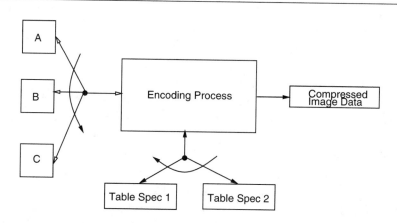

Fig. 3.17. Table Switching Control

be used to encode all samples within a component. JPEG decoders can store up to four different quantization tables and the same entropy coding table must be used to encode all samples within a component. Therefore, it is necessary to switch between tables during decompression of a scan containing multiple interleaved components, as the tables cannot be loaded during decompression of a scan. Fig. 3.17 illustrates the task switching control that must be managed in conjunction with multiple component interleaving for the encoder side.

3.8.8 Some Remarks on JPEG

Most importantly, an interchange format syntax is specified which ensures that a JPEG compressed image can be exchanged successfully between different application environments. The applications have the freedom to specify default or referenced table, as appropriate.

In essence, JPEG is a standard to be strictly followed for Image Exchange and efficient hardware, software, and hybrid implementations are available [14]. While a multimedia system designer cannot afford to change the JPEG process, the designer can certainly fine-tune the implementation.

3.9 JBIG

Images can be broadly classified into two categories: *bi-tonal* and *continuous-tone* images. A regular printed text without any gray-scale characters is an ideal example of a bi-tonal image. JBIG concentrates on bi-tonal images while JPEG concentrates on continuous-tone images. Bi-tonal images are also called *bi-level* images (that is, an image that has only colors like black and white). ITU-T Recommendations T.4 and T.30 are coding standards for Group 3 facsimile machines. Compression algorithm of the Group 3 standard was lain down in 1990 for use with switched telephone networks. The coding standard recommendation T.6 for Group 4 facsimile machines was published in 1984. While T.6 provides better resolution, it requires line speeds of the order of 56 Kbps or 64 Kbps to operate.

JBIG (Joint Bi-level Image Group) is an advanced compression scheme utilizing lossless, predictive methods [6,8,9]. The JBIG compression algorithm is defined by ISO/IEC Standard 11544:1993. The JBIG specification defines the compression scheme, not the file format. The JBIG Alliance is sponsoring the JBIG Interchange Recommendation, which provides a well-defined method for storing JBIG-compressed data in industry standard TIFF (Tagged Image File Format)-formated files.

JBIG is an advanced lossless compression algorithm originally developed for facsimile transmission. The efficiency of the algorithm derives from arithmetic encoding, a mathematically complex concept based on image contexts. Because JBIG stores data in independent bit-planes, JBIG efficiently compresses both bi-tonal and gray-scale data.

The main characteristics of JBIG are:

- Compatible progressive/sequential coding. This means that a progressively coded image can be decoded sequentially, and the other way around.

- JBIG will be a lossless image compression standard: all bits in the images before and after compression and decompression will be exactly the same.

JBIG specifies the number of bits per pixel in the image. Its allowable range is 1 through 255, but starting at 8 or so, compression will be more efficient using other algorithms. On the other hand, medical images such as chest X-rays are often stored with 12 bits per pixel while no distortion is allowed, so JBIG can certainly be of use in this area. To limit the number of bit changes between adjacent decimal values (e.g., 127 and 128), it is wise to use Gray coding before compressing multi-level images with JBIG. JBIG then compresses the image on a bit-plane basis, so the rest of this text assumes bi-level pixels.

Progressive coding is a way to send an image gradually to a receiver instead of all at once. JBIG uses discrete steps of detail by successively doubling the resolution. Compatibility between progressive and sequential coding is achieved by dividing an image into stripes. Each stripe is a horizontal bar with a user-definable height. Each stripe is separately coded and transmitted, and the user can define in which order stripes, resolutions, and bit-planes are intermixed in the coded data. A progressive coded image can be decoded sequentially by decoding each stripe, beginning by the one at the top of the image, to its full resolution, and then proceeding to the next stripe. Progressive decoding can be done by decoding only a specific resolution layer from all stripes.

After dividing an image into bit-planes, resolution layers, and stripes, eventually a number of small bi-level bitmaps are left to compress. Compression is done using a Q-coder.

The Q-coder codes bi-level pixels as symbols using the probability of occurrence of these symbols in a certain context. JBIG defines two kinds of context: one for the lowest resolution layer (the base layer), and one for all other layers (differential layers). Differential layer contexts contain pixels in the layer to be coded, and in the corresponding lower resolution layer.

For each combination of pixel values in a context, the probability distribution of black and white pixels can be different. In an all-white context, the probability of coding a white pixel will be much greater than that of coding a black pixel. The Q-coder assigns, just like a Huffman coder, more bits to less probable symbols, and so achieves compression. The Q-coder can, unlike a Huffman coder, assign one output code-bit to more than one input symbol, and thus is able to compress bi-level pixels without explicit clustering, as would be necessary using a Huffman coder.

Maximum compression will be achieved when all probabilities (one set for each combination of pixel values in the context) follow the probabilities of the pixels. The Q-coder therefore continuously adapts these probabilities to the symbols it sees.

3.10 MPEG

The MPEG system layer has the basic task of combining one or more audio and video compressed bit-streams into a *single bit-stream*. It defines the data stream syntax that provides for timing control and the interleaving and synchronization of audio and video bit-streams. From the systems perspective, MPEG bit-stream consists of a *system layer* and *compression layers*. The system layer basically provides an envelope for the compression layers. The compression layers contain the data to be given to the decoders, whereas the system layer provides the control for *demultiplexing* the interleaved compression layers. A typical MPEG system block diagram is shown in Fig. 3.18.

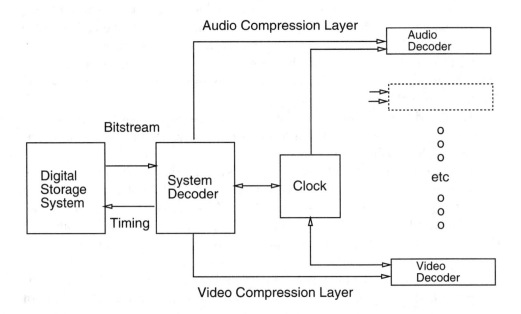

Fig. 3.18. MPEG System Structure

The MPEG bit-stream consists of a sequence of packs that are in turn subdivided into packets, as shown in Fig. 3.22. Each pack consists of a unique 32-bit byte aligned pack start code and header, followed by one or more packets of data. Each packet consists of a packet start code (another unique 32-bit byte aligned code) and header, followed by a packet data (compressed audio or video data). The system decoder parses this bit-stream and feeds the separated audio and video to the appropriate decoders along with timing information.

The MPEG system uses an idealized decoder called System Target Decoder (STD), which interprets the pack and packet headers to deliver the elementary bit-streams to the appropriate audio or video decoder. In STD the bits for an access unit (a picture or an audio access unit) are removed from the buffer instantaneously at a time dictated by a Decoding Time Stamp (DTS) in the bit-stream. The bit-stream also contains another type of time stamp, the Presentation Time Stamp (PTS). Buffer overflow or underflow is controlled by the DTS; synchronization between audio and video decoding is controlled by the PTS.

3.10.1 MPEG Audio Compression

MPEG audio coding supports 32, 44.1, and 48 KHz. At 16 bits per sample the uncompressed audio would require about 1.5 Mbps. After compression, the bit-rates for monophonic channels are between 32 and 192 Kbps; the bit-rates for stereophonic channels are between 128 and 384 Kbps.

The MPEG audio system first segments the audio into windows of 384 samples wide and uses a filter bank to decompose each window into 32 sub-bands, each with a width of approximately 750 Hz (for a sample of 48 KHz). As is typical of sub-band coding, each sub-band is decimated such that the sampling rate per sub-band is 1.5 KHz and there are 12 samples per window. An FFT (Fast Fourier Transform) of the audio input is used to compute a global masking threshold for each sub-band, and from this a uniform quantizer is chosen that provides the least audible distortion at the required bit-rate. For more information on MPEG audio coding, the reader is referred to [3].

3.10.2 MPEG Video Compression

MPEG is a generic compression standard that addresses video compression, audio compression, and the issue of audio-video synchronization for sequences (movie or VCR output). MPEG compresses the video and audio signals at about 1.5 Mbps per channel. The MPEG system addresses the issue of synchronization and multiplexing of multiple compressed audio and video list streams. The motivation for the MPEG standard comes from the need to handle full-motion video for storage and retrieval with random access. MPEG is designed to compress across multiple frames and therefore can yield compression ratios of 50:1 to 200:1 instead of 20:1 or 25:1 in JPEG. Its algorithm is asymmetrical; that is, it requires more computational complexity (hardware) to compress than to decompress it. This is useful for applications where the signal is produced at one source but is distributed to many, or compressed once and decompressed several times.

At this point, the reader should recall that JPEG deals with a (single) still image (picture) and the compression was an effort to reduce the *spatial redundancy* in the source. In the case of motion video, we are dealing with a stream of (single) still images (pictures) that are available from the source at a constant rate. A sequence of video frames inherently carries a lot of redundant information. Therefore, MPEG compression concentrates on reducing the *temporal redundancy across the frames* in addition to the *spatial redundancy* within a frame. The MPEG standard incorporates a special concept called "group of pictures" (GOP) to deal with temporal redundancy and to allow random access to be stored MPEG-coded videos.

There are three types of pictures that are considered in MPEG; viz.; Intra pictures (I-Frames), predicted pictures (P-Frames) and bi-directional (interpolated) pictures (B-Frames). The I-Frame is the first frame of each *GOP*. The Intra pictures (I-Frames) provide reference points for random access and are subjected to moderate compression. From the compression point of view, I-pictures are equivalent to *images* and can be DCT encoded using a JPEG-like algorithm. In P- and B-pictures, the motion-compensated prediction errors are DCT coded. Only forward prediction is used in the P-pictures, which are always encoded relative to the preceding I- or P-pictures. The prediction of the B-pictures can be forward, backward, or bidirectional relative to other I- or P-pictures. In addition to these three, there is a fourth type of picture called D-pictures, containing only the DC component of each block. They are mainly useful in browsing at very low bit-rates. The number of I, P, and B frames in a *GOP* is application dependent. For example, it depends on the access time requirement and the bit-rate requirement.

Example: In Fig. 3.19 the relationship between the different pictures and what their relative roles are is shown. The example introduces an intra-coded picture every 8 frames and the sequence of I, B, P is IBBBPBBBI. Note that the first frame is an I-frame. In MPEG, the order in which the pictures are processed is not necessarily the same as their time sequential order. The pictures in the example can be coded as 1,5,2,3,4,9,6,7,8 or 1,2,3,5,4,9,6,7,8, since the the prediction for P- and B-pictures should be based on pictures that are already transmitted.

Prediction pictures are coded with reference to a past picture (intra(I) or predicted(P)) and can, in general, be used as a reference for future predicted pictures. Interpolated pictures or B-pictures achieve the highest amount of compression and require both a past and future reference frame. In addition, bi-directional pictures (B-Pictures) are never used as a reference. In all cases, when a picture is coded with respect to a reference, *motion compensation* [5] is used to improve the coding efficiency. Fig. 3.20 expands on the example and shows how they act as inter-frame coding and the relative sizes of the compression information process. As in the example, an intra coded picture every 8 frames and the sequence of I, B, P is IBBBPBBBI. Motion compensation is the basic philosophy behind the coding of B and P frames.

---

[5]A technique used to compress video.

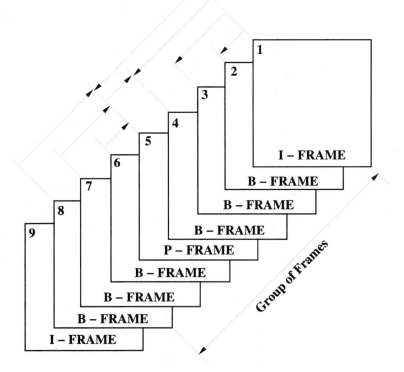

Fig. 3.19. Group of Frames

3.10.3 Motion Compensation

There are two techniques that are employed in motion compensation: prediction and interpolation. Motion-compensated prediction assumes that the current picture can be modeled as a transformation of the picture at some previous time. This means that the signal amplitude and the direction of displacement need not be the same everywhere in the picture. Motion-compensated interpolation is a multi-resolution technique; a sub-signal with low temporal resolution (typically 1/2 to 1/3 the frame rate) is coded and the full resolution signal is obtained by interpolation of the low-resolution signal and addition of a correction term. The signal to be reconstructed by interpolation is obtained by adding a correction term to a combination of a past and future reference [3,5,7].

3.10.4   Motion Representation

MPEG uses a *Macro block* consisting of 16×16 pixels. There is always a trade-off between coding gain provided by the motion information and the cost associated with coding the motion information. The choice of 16×16 blocks for the motion compensation unit is based on such a trade-off. In a bi-directionally coded picture, each 16×16 macro block can be of type Intra, Forward-Predicted, Backward-Predicted, or Average.

3.10.5   Motion Estimation

The extraction of motion information from a video sequence is called motion estimation. If we use the block matching technique, the motion vector is obtained by minimizing a cost function measuring the mismatch between a block and each predictor candidate. The search range V of the possible

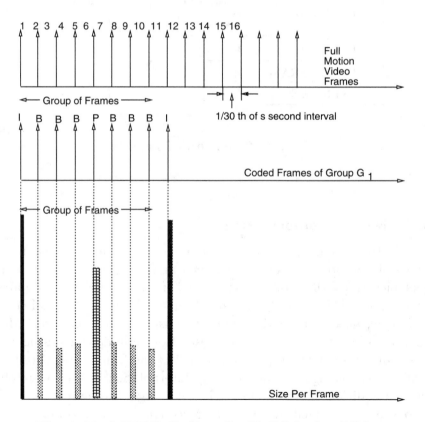

Fig. 3.20. MPEG Coding for Full-Motion Video

Sequence Layer	Random Access Unit: Context
Group of Pictures Layer	Random Access Unit: Video Coding
Picture Layer	Primary Coding Unit
Slice Layer	Re-synchronization Unit
Macro Block Layer	Motion Compensation Unit
Block Layer	DCT Unit

Table 3.3. Six Layers of the MPEG Video

motion vectors and the selection of the cost function are left to the implementation. Exhaustive searches, where all the possible motion vectors are considered, are known to give good results, but at the expense of a very large complexity of computation for large ranges.

3.10.6 Layered Structure, Syntax, and Bit-stream

The MPEG syntax allows for provision of many application-specific features without penalizing other applications. For example, random access and easy accessibility require many access points implying groups of pictures of short duration (e.g., 6 pictures, 1/5 second) and coded with a fixed amount of bits (to make edit-ability possible). Similarly, in order to provide robustness in the case of broadcast over noisy channel, the predictors are frequently reset and each intra and predicted picture is segmented into many slices. The composition of an MPEG video bit-stream contains six layers, as given in Table. 3.3.

Each layer supports a definite function: either a signal processing function (DCT, motion compensation) or a logical function (Re-synchronization, Random Access Point). The MPEG syntax defines a MPEG bit-stream as any sequence of binary digits.

3.10.7 MPEG System

The MPEG standard is a three-part standard; viz., video coding, audio coding, and system coding. The MPEG system coding part specifies the system multiplexer and encoder to produce a MPEG stream from the encoded video and audio streams with a system reference clock as the base.

That is, the MPEG stream is the synchronization of elementary streams and carries enough information in the data fields to do the following tasks:

- Parsing the multiplexed stream after a random access.

- Managing coded information buffers in the decoders.

- Identifying the absolute time of the coded information.

The most important task of the system coding process is the actual multiplexing. It includes the coordination of input data streams and output data streams, the adjustment of clocks, and buffer management. The system's semantic rules impose some requirements on the decoders and allow freedom in the implementation of the encoding process. Fig. 3.21 shows the schematic of such an encoder at the functional level. The video encoder receives the uncoded digitized picture in units called Video Presentation Units (VPUs) at discrete time intervals; similarly, at discrete time intervals, the audio encoder receives uncoded digitized blocks of audio samples in units called Audio Presentation Units (APUs). The video and audio encoders encode digital video and audio, producing coded pictures called Video Access Units (VAUs) and Audio Access units (AAUs). These outputs are referred to as elementary streams. The system encoder and multiplexer produces a multiplexed stream that contains the elementary streams and some additional information to help in handling synchronization and timing. MPEG supports audio from 32 Kbps to 384 Kbps in single channel or in two stereo channels.

Timing and Synchronization: The audio and video sample rates at the encoder are significantly different from one another, and may or may not have an exact and fixed relationship to one another. Also, the duration of a block of audio samples or APUs is generally not the same as the duration of a video picture. There is a single, common system clock in the encoder, and this clock is used to create time stamps that indicate the correct presentation and decoding timing of audio and video, as well as to create time stamps that indicate the instantaneous values of the system clock itself at sampled intervals. The time stamps that indicate the presentation time of audio and video are called Presentation Time Stamps (PTS); those that indicate the decoding time are called Decoding Time Stamps (DTS); and those that indicate the value of the system clock are called the System Clock Reference (SCR). It is the presence of the common system clock in the encoder, the

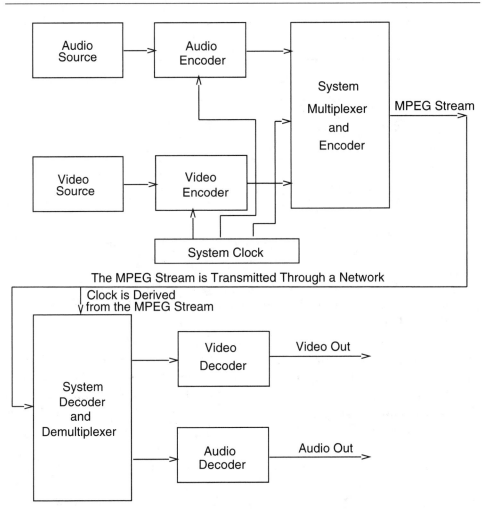

Fig. 3.21. MPEG Data Stream Generation Model

time stamps that are created from it, the recreation of the clock in the decoder, and the correct use of the time stamps that provide the facility to synchronize properly the operation of the decoder.

The MPEG system embodies a timing model in which all digitized pictures and audio samples that enter the encoder are presented exactly once each, after a constant end to end delay, at the output of the decoder. As such, the sample rates, i.e., the video picture rate and the audio sample rate, are precisely the same at the decoder as they are at the encoder. Constant delay, as envisaged in the MPEG system, is required for correct synchro-

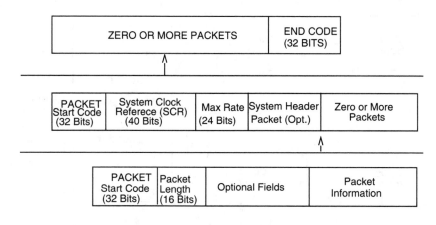

Fig. 3.22. MPEG Bit-stream Layering

nization; however, some deviations are possible due to the variable delays at the encoding buffer during the transmission through the network and at the decoding buffer.

To achieve synchronization in multimedia systems that decode multiple video and audio signals originating from a storage or transmission medium, there must be a 'time master' in the decoding system. MPEG does not specify which entity is the time master. The time master can be any of the decoders, the information stream source, or an external time base. All other entities in the system (decoders and information sources) must slave their timing to the time master. For example, if a decoder is taken as the time master, the time when it presents a presentation unit is considered to be the correct time for the other entities. If the information stream source is the time master, the SCR values indicate the correct time at the moment these values are received. The decoders then use this information to pace their decoding and presentation timing.

MPEG Stream: The most important task of MPEG stream generation process is multiplexing. It includes a combination of input data streams and output data streams, the adjustment of clocks, and the buffer management. The MPEG stream syntax consists of three coding layers: stream layer, pack layer, and packet layer, as shown schematically in Fig. 3.22. Of these three layers, it is the packet layer which actually carries the information from the elementary streams; each packet carries information from exactly one elementary stream. Zero or more packets are grouped together to form a pack, which carries the SCR value. The decoder gets the information necessary for its resource reservation from this multiplexed stream. The maximal data rate is included in the first pack at the beginning of each MPEG stream. Though MPEG does not specify directly the method of multiplexing the elementary streams such as VAUs and AAUs, MPEG does lay down some constraints that must be followed by an encoder and multiplexer in order to produce a *valid* MPEG data stream. For example, the individual stream buffers must not overflow or underflow. That is, the sizes of the individual stream buffers impose limits on the behavior of the multiplexer. Decoding the MPEG data stream starting at the beginning of the stream is straightforward since there are no ambiguous bit patterns. But starting the decoding operation at random points requires locating pack or packet start codes within the data stream.

MPEG Decoding Process: The MPEG standard defines the decoding process - not the decoder. There are many ways to implement a decoder, and the standard does not recommend a particular way. The decoder structure given in Fig. 3.23 is a typical decoder structure with a buffer at the input of the decoder. The bit-stream is demultiplexed into overhead information such as motion information, quantizer step-size, macroblock type, and quantized DCT coefficients. The quantized DCT coefficients are dequantized, and are input to the Inverse Discrete Cosine Transform (IDCT). The reconstructed waveform from the IDCT is added to the result of the prediction. Because of the particular nature of the bidirectional prediction, two reference pictures are used to form the predictor.

3.10.8   MPEG-2, MPEG-3, MPEG-4

MPEG standard is an optimal solution for a target data rate of about 1.5 Mbps. The optimality is with respect to perceptual quality and not necessarily performance. To address the high-quality video requirement (with a target rate of about 40 Mbps), MPEG-2 video standard has been developed. MPEG-2 builds upon MPEG standard (also referred to as MPEG-1 standard) and supports interlaced video formats and HDTV. MPEG-3 was originally started for HDTV and, after the development of MPEG-2 which addresses this issue, MPEG-3 has been dropped. MPEG-4 looks at the other end of the spectrum; low bit-rate coding of audiovisual programs. It is expected to be used in mobile telephony systems.

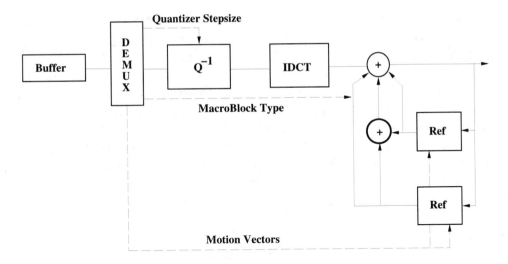

Fig. 3.23. MPEG Decoding Process

3.11 H.261 Standard

CCITT Recommendation H.261 is a video compression standard developed to facilitate videoconferencing and videophone services over the Integrated Services Digital Network (ISDN) at $px64$ *Kbps, p = 1,...30* [6,13]. For example (when $p=1$), one 64 Kbps may be appropriate for low-quality videophone service, where the video signal can be transmitted at a rate of 48 Kbps and the remaining 16 Kbps is used for audio signal. videoconferencing services generally require higher image quality, which can be achieved with $p \geq 6$, that is, 384 Kbps or higher. Note that the maximum available bit-rate over an ISDN channel is 1.92 MBPS *(p = 30)*, which is sufficient to obtain VHS quality images.

H.261 has two important features:

- It specifies a maximum coding delay of 150 milliseconds, because it is mainly intended for bidirectional video communication. It has been estimated that delays exceeding 150 milliseconds do not give the viewer the impression of direct visual feedback.

- It is amenable to low-cost VLSI implementation, which is important for widespread commercialization.

To permit a single recommendation for use in and between regions using 625 and 525 line TV standards, the H.261 input picture is specified in Common Intermediate Format (CIF). For lower bit-rates a smaller format QCIF, which is one quarter of the CIF, has been adopted. The number of active pels per line has luminance and chrominance are 360 and 180 (352 and 176 visible) for CIF and 180 and 90 (176 and 88 visible) for QCIF, respectively. The number of active lines per picture has luminance and chrominance 288 and 144 for CIF and 144 and 72 for QCIF, respectively. The temporal rates are adjustable for 30, 15, 10, 7.5, for both CIF and QCIF. If we consider 30 frames per second, the raw data rate for CIF will be 37.3 Mbps and for QCIF 9.35, respectively. It may be noted that even with QCIF images at 10 frames per second, 48:1 compression is required for videophone services over a 64 Kbps channel. CIF images may be used when $p \geq 6$, that is, for videoconferencing applications. Methods for converting from CIF to QCIF, or vice versa, is not specified by the recommendation.

3.12   H.263

H.263 is a low bit-rate video standard for teleconferencing applications that has both MPEG-1 and MPEG-2 features [6,7]. It operates at 64 Kbps. The video coding of H.263 is based on that of H.261. In fact, H.263 is an extension of H.261 and describes a hybrid DPCM/DCT video coding method. Both H.261 and H.263 use techniques such as DCT, motion compensation, variable-length coding, and scalar quantization. Both use the concept of macroblock structure.

The idea of PB frame in H.263 is interesting. The PB frame consists of two pictures being coded as one unit. The name PB is derived from the MPEG terminology of P-pictures and B-pictures. Thus, a PB frame consists of one P-picture that is predicted from the last decoded P-picture and one B-picture that is predicted from both the last decoded P-picture and the P-picture currently being decoded. This last picture is called a B-picture because parts of it may be bi-directionally predicted from the past and future P-picture.

It has been shown that the H.263 system typically outperforms H.261 by 2.5 to 1. That means, for a given picture quality, the H.261 bit-rate is approximately 2.5 times that of H.263 codec.

3.13   Summary

In this chapter, we described the image compression system and explained some of the key coding and compression techniques. The concepts relating to coding, compression, and transformation of digital samples of analog signals to their frequency domain equivalents were discussed at length. The two popular coding standards, called JPEG and MPEG, were explained in some detail. JPEG is aimed at still pictures and MPEG is aimed at motion pictures. Other standards, such as H.261, H.263, and JBIG, were discussed to enable the reader to understand the purpose and positioning of different standards. It may be pointed out that this chapter is one of the *key* chapters in the entire book, as it explains the nature of the one dominant media in all multimedia systems, viz., the video. Further information about multimedia systems can be obtained from [10, 11, 12].

REFERENCES

1. C. Shannon A Mathematical Theory of Communication, Bell Systems Technical Journal, Vol. 27, pp. 379-423, July 1948; and pp. 623-656, October 1948.

2. John G. Proakis. Digital Communications, 3rd Edition, McGraw Hill Inc., 1995.

3. D. Pan. An Overview of the MPEG Audio Compression Algorithm, In SPIE. Digital Video Compression on Personal Computers: Algorithms and Technologies, Vol.2187, pp. 260-273, 1994.

4. Gregory K. Wallace. The JPEG Still Picture Compression Standard, Communications of the ACM, Vol.34, No.4, pp.31-44, April 1991.

5. Didier Le Gall. MPEG: A Video Compression Standard for Multimedia Applications, Communications of the ACM, Vol.34, No.4, pp. 46-58, April 1991.

6. Richard Schaphorst. videoconferencing and Video-telephony: Technology and Standards, Artech House Inc., 1996.

7. Joan L. Mitchell, William B. Pennebaker, Chad E. Fogg, and Didier J. Legall (Eds.). MPEG Video Compression Standard, Chapman & Hall, 1997.

8. www.jbig.org

9. ISO/IEC JTC1/SC2/WG9. Progressive Bi-level Image Compression, Revision 4.1, CD 11544, September 16, 1991

10. W.B. Pennebaker, J.L. Mitchell, G.G. Langdon, and R.B. Arps. An Overview of the Basic Principles of the Q-Coder Adaptive Binary Arithmetic Coder, IBM Journal of Research and Development, Vol.32, No.6, November 1988, pp. 771-726.

11. Ralf Steinmetz and Klara Nahrstedt. Multimedia: Computing, Communications and Applications, Prentice-Hall, Inc., 1995.

12. Francois Fluckiger. Understanding Networked Multimedia: Applications and Technology, Prentice-Hall, Inc., 1995.

13. A. Murat Tekalp. Digital Video Processing, Prentice-Hall, Inc., 1995.

14. William B. Pennebaker and Joan L. Mitchell. JPEG : Still Image Data Compression Standard, Van Nostrand Reinhold, 1992.

Exercises

1. Find the digitized values of the samples of the signal given in Fig. 3.24. Each sample is 8 bits.

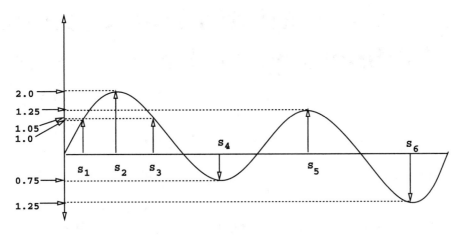

Fig. 3.24. Signal for Exercise 1 in Chapter 3

2. Calculate the Fourier Transform of the digital samples from the previous exercise.

3. An 8x8 pixel formation has elements with values that are inverse of $(r + s)^2$, where r and s are row and column numbers. Compute the value of the pixel matrix.

4. Find the FDCT of the pixel matrix from the previous exercise.

5. The weights to be associated with each FDCT coefficient from the previous exercise are inversely proportional to the position value. Encode the values as per this weightage, keeping the order of the coefficients the same as the order in the pixel matrix (left-to-right and top-to-bottom). Use run-length coding for coding the resulting string.

6. Repeat the previous exercise, using the zig-zag pattern. Use run-length coding for coding the resulting string.

7. Scan your picture after disabling compression in the scanner. Now compress the picture using the JPEG standard. Scan the picture again with compression enabled in the scanner. Compare.

8. Obtain an MPEG Trace from the Internet. Find out the order in which I, P, and B frames appear in that trace.

9. Find out the sizes of the I, P, and B frames from any MPEG trace. Calculate the maximum and minimum size for all three types of frames.

Chapter 4

Multimedia Systems Technology: I/O and Devices

4.1 I/O Problem

Storage and access have been essential parts of large volume data handling in computer applications. The amount of information to be stored (and retrieved) has been growing larger and larger over the years. When such a trend is noticed with respect to the applications, the technology developers responded by providing increased storage capacity and faster controllers to move data in and out. But large volume I/O poses new challenges for the designer. Let us consider the following scenarios.

- When we make a note for ourselves on one of the windows (perhaps the mail window) on a workstation screen, it is easily traceable and definitely locatable.

- If you have a gigabit disk space on the system and a ten-level directory structure with an average number of 100 files per directory or subdirectory, and if you store a file bearing the note, describe what your condition will be while trying to retrieve it after a month, when you have totally forgotten some access clues.

When you increase the storage capacity, and at the same time increase the amount of information to be stored per file and also store several files, both storage and retrieval become harder. Moreover, if the information to be stored is continuous data, the problem becomes a lot more complex. It is at this point that designers start raising the following questions:

- What is the optimal unit of storage?

- How large can storage be?

- What are the factors that influence the net transfer rates?

- How can net transfer rates be improved?

These questions are well posed, but not precise, in the sense that they do not have a unique answer. Perhaps we can find answers which are close. Let us look at some examples to better appreciate the I/O problem.

Example: A text file of size 10 KB is to be stored. The file is always retrieved in units of 1 KB at a time. Disk capacity on a certain system is 200 MB and the transfer rate of the controller is 5 Mbps. How long does it take to read the file? How long does it take to write the file?

In order to answer the question, we need some more information. What is the basic unit of storage on the disk? The basic unit of storage will decide how many reads or writes are to be issued. Assume that it is 1 KB. If disk is the source of information, what is the destination? Let us say it is the primary memory. What is the interconnection between the disk and the primary memory? In what units does the interconnection mechanism transfer? How much time does it take per unit of transfer? This information is required because the file has to be transferred using these fundamental steps. Let us assume that the system has a 32-bit bus and transfers at 100 Mbps[1] rate. Now, we have all that we want to calculate the read and write times.

PerBlockReadTime = Time to transfer from Disk to Bus (T_1) + Time to transfer through the Bus to memory(T_2). PerBlockWriteTime = Time to transfer a unit of information from memory through the Bus (T_2) + Time to transfer from Bus to Disk (T_1). T_1 = Number of Bytes per Block * Transfer time per Byte (t_1).

t_1 = (1/Disk transfer rate).

$t_1 = (1/5*10^6) = 2 * 10^{-7}$.

$T_1 = (1 * 10^3) * (2 * 10^{-7}) = 200 * 10^{-6}$ Seconds.

t_2 = (1/Bus transfer rate/8bits).

$t_2 = (1/(100*10^6/8bits)) = 1.25 * 10^{-9}$ Seconds.

$T_2 = (1 * 10^3) * (1.25 * 10^{-9}) = 1.25 * 10^{-6}$ Seconds.

N = (10 KB / 1 KB) = 10 (Number of Blocks).

PerBlockReadTime = PerBlockWriteTime = $(200 * 10^{-6}) + (1.25 * 10^{-6})$ Seconds.

FileReadTime = $10 * [(200 * 10^{-6}) + (1.25 * 10^{-6})] = 2.0125$ milliseconds.

This assumes that the mechanical operations such as head positioning and the disk rotating are such that the right point-of-start is available for reading and does not require any time. For the disk capacity that we have assumed, these figures combined would be of the order of 20 milliseconds for each read or write operation, which renders the net FileReadTime 100 times more than the actual transfer time. Actually, with this time taken into account, the FileReadTime = 202.0125 milliseconds. If we record the entire file *contiguously* on the disk, then we need to spend only 20 milliseconds as opposed to 200 milliseconds, resulting in significant improvement.

---

[1]Whenever 'B' is used, we refer to a Byte and 'b' is used when we refer to a bit.

This example, albeit simple, illustrates a very important point: the positioning of the file in one piece or in multiple pieces on the disk has a direct bearing on performance of the I/O. If we view this in the context of multimedia information, the impact is significant. The reason is that multimedia information, especially video, comes from a MPEG source at a rate of approximately 1.5 Mbps (for MPEG 1 video), and if we are recording the lecture on this chapter for 60 minutes, we are recording a single file of 700 MB. Based on our example, it will take 2 minutes and 20 seconds.

In addition to these, in the operating system environment, the corresponding file systems and device drivers should be so scheduled that the actual transfers can be effected. In current operating systems, I/O streaming from device to device without OS intervention is not easy and one that will require radical changes in an OS suited for multimedia, which, in fact, is the subject matter of discussion in a later chapter. In this chapter, we introduce the problem and describe one solution for the storage part alone. The optical storage technology which has large capacity (in GB) holds promise for the future.

4.2 High-Performance I/O

It is important to know the interplay of various factors that are influencing I/O. We highlighted one aspect of the problem, namely, contiguous store as opposed to scattered store, through our discourse in the earlier section. We will describe the interplay and options in the larger context of multimedia system design in this section. There are four different factors influencing the I/O performance. They are data, data storage, data transfer, and operating system support for these.

Data: The data that come in from the external world can be text, digitized voice, motion video, image, or graphics. Of these, text, image and graphics are different from voice and video. The reason is that voice and video are *continuous media* and hence generate continuous data. They are of high volume also, as we discussed in Chapter 2. There is a direct and proportional relationship between how much is handled and how long it takes. To improve the situation at this level, the only way is to reduce the information to be handled. That is why compression is necessary for multimedia.

Data Storage: The strategy adopted for data storage will depend on the storage technology, storage design, and the nature of data itself. Any storage has the following parameters:

- Storage capacity.

- Standard operations of Read and Write.

- Unit of transfer for Read or Write.

- Physical organization of storage units.

- ReadWrite heads, Cylinders per Disc, Tracks per Cylinder, and Sectors per Track.

- Read time and seek time.

Storage design refers to the organization of several independent drives in one disk drive as a composite unit. This essentially enables parallel reading and writing operations. Any storage design has to match the physical characteristics of the disk to the nature of the information to be stored. The disk storage subsystem should be designed to match the I/O requirements. In the example that we discussed earlier in this chapter, if the file was stored on a disk subsystem which allows 4-way parallelism, and the reads and writes were issued for 4 KB instead of 1 KB, the time to transfer the entire file will come down to about 0.5 milliseconds; an improvement of a factor of 4. As we still need data sequentially, it is assumed that the 4 KB are buffered appropriately by the controller or the application.

Data Transfer: The problem of data transfer has two sides: one depends on how data are generated and are written to the disk and the other in what sequence it is retrieved. In the case of multimedia data, the data are generated sequentially and are written as generated. In the same way, the data are read for display in the same order. It may be noted that the so called random access applies only to higher level units of video data, and is referred to variedly as clips, scenes, etc. If multimedia data are generated at 1.2 Mbps rate and recording can be accomplished at 0.3 Mbps rate, with 4-way parallelism, then we will store them in a 4-way interleaved form, so that for reading or writing, one can realize the full I/O transfer potential.

Operating System Support: Operating system support refers to the scheduling of the corresponding processes whenever we initiate I/O. As the operations are time-critical, the strategies that have to be adopted vary from the conventional ones. Also, as the data are read from disk, if they have to be moved to devices such as network interface units, direct transfers without having to copy into operating system space will lead to tremendous amount of performance gains. These issues are further discussed in a later chapter.

4.3   RAID Technology

RAID is the acronym for Redundant Array of Inexpensive Disks. RAID is a new technology that provides a potential alternative to mass storage combined with high throughput and reliability [1,2,3]. By definition, RAID has three attributes:

- It is a set of disk drives viewed by the user as one or more logical drives.

- Data is distributed across the set of drives in a pre-defined manner.

- Redundant capacity or data reconstruction capability is added, in order to recover data in the event of a disk failure.

RAID technology uses an array of multiple disks where data is spread across the drives to achieve fault-tolerance, large storage capacity, and performance improvement through overlapped I/O. The I/O (read or write) across multiple disk spindles are done in parallel by distributing across drives. Data is spread across the drives in units of 512 bytes called segments. Multiple segments form a block. This process, called *data striping*, causes data to be split across multiple spindles so that different sections of a single I/O request are served in parallel by multiple disks. There are *eight*[2] discrete levels of RAID functionally defined so far. They are :

Level 0	-	Disk Striping
Level 1	-	Disk Mirroring
Level 2	-	Bit Interleaving and Header Error Correction (HEC) Parity
Level 3	-	Bit Interleaving and XOR Parity
Level 4	-	Block Interleaving with XOR Parity
Level 5	-	Block Interleaving with Parity Distribution
Level 6	-	Fault tolerant system
Level 7	-	Heterogeneous system

4.3.1   RAID Level 0 - Disk Striping

RAID Level 0 is based on distribution of data across multiple drives connected to a single disk controller as shown in Fig. 4.1. Data is recorded in such a way that successive segments are recorded on successive drives (That

---

[2]Originally there were only 0 - 5; later, 6 and 7 were added.

means a minimum of two drives are required). The disk block sizes normally range from 1 to 64 KB. By distributing data across drives, data striping provides a high transfer rate for applications that read or write blocks of data. The data being written to disk is broken into segments and directed to different drives in a pre-determined order. For example, for a segment

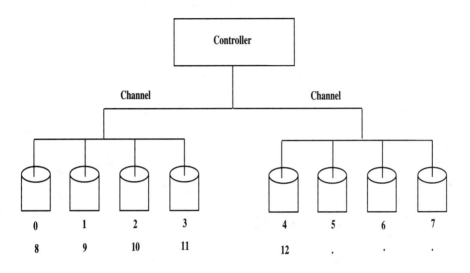

Fig. 4.1. Disk Striping for RAID Level 0

size of 512 bytes each and a block size of 4 KB, we have 8 segments to be written for every block I/O. When the I/O is actually scheduled, the first segment is written to the first drive, the second segment is written to the second drive, and so on. When a segment is written to the last drive, the process is repeated, beginning with the first drive. If there are two drives, then the block I/O results in 4 actual I/Os. If there are four drives, then the block I/O results in 2 actual I/Os and so on.

Performance improvement is achieved because of overlapping of disk reads and writes. The actual performance achieved depends on the design of the controller and how it manages disk reads and writes. The controller must be able to start a transfer to the disk buffer of one drive and then go on to the next without waiting for confirmation from the physical media for successful completion of a disk write. Basically, controller should be intelligent enough to remember the multiple and related state information for each block I/O requested and actual (physical I/O) initiated.

4.3.2   RAID Level 1 - Disk Mirroring

RAID Level 1 focuses on fault tolerance in addition to striping. Here not only is data striped across multiple physical drives (as in RAID Level 0), but also mirrored on two disks so that copies of files are written on two separate drives, resulting in complete redundancy. This is shown in Fig. 4.2.

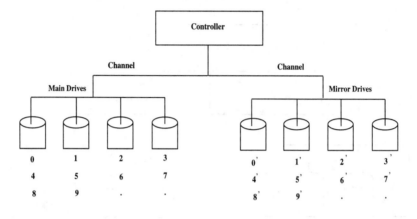

Fig. 4.2. Disk Layout in RAID Level 1

As data is written to both the main disk and the mirror disk, writes take almost twice as long; however, reads can be speeded up by overlapping seeks! This is because while the main drive is seeking a block of data, the mirror drive can start the seek for the next required block, resulting in less seek latency. The major drawback of this model is that by mirroring all information, the cost per megabyte is effectively doubled as the disk storage space required is doubled.

4.3.3   RAID Level 2 - Bit Interleaving and HEC Parity

As in RAID 0, data is distributed across several drives in smaller units and with fine coordination. Typically, RAID 2 disk subsystems contain multiple drives connected to a disk controller, with either single or multiple channels. Data, written in smaller units (often one bit at a time), is interleaved across multiple drives. The disk organization for bit interleaving consisting of seven data drives and one parity drive will look similar to Fig. 4.1.

In addition to data drives, in RAID 2, a Hamming error correction code (initially developed for dynamic random access memory) is also recorded on an additional drive(s), to be used for data reconstruction in the event of a disk failure. This can be viewed as a parity drive. This allows error recovery without the inefficiency of a complete RAID 1 duplication.

In RAID 2, the drive spindles must be synchronized as a single I/O operation accesses all drives. In this configuration, rotational latency (the delay time from when a read/write head is on track and when the requested data passes under it) is generally the same as a single drive. As data bits are read in parallel, performance of RAID 2 for large data transfers can be excellent (transfer rate is the sum of the data disks).

However, this is not necessarily the case for small data transfers. With the disks operating completely in parallel, small transfer requests have the same performance characteristics as a single disk. Also, as all disks in a group must be accessed for any transfer and hence the performance is determined by the speed of the slowest disk. For these reasons, RAID 2 is used where data integrity is the prime concern.

4.3.4   RAID Level 3 - Bit Interleaving with XOR Parity

RAID 3 introduces parity to the model by interleaving the data at a bit level across several drives similar to data striping. For a group of disks, there is a single drive dedicated to storing the parity information generated using XOR for disks in that group. When a disk fault is detected, the parity disk can be used to reconstruct the affected information.

However, RAID 3 still suffers from one of the major drawbacks inherent in the previous architectures–it is still required that all disks in a group are accessed with any transfer. Thus, the slowest drive determines the performance of the I/O system as a whole. Also, concurrent access implies that the drive spindles must be synchronized. Furthermore, with a large number of transfers within a group, the parity drive may become a throughput bottleneck.

4.3.5   RAID Level 4 - Block Interleaving with XOR Parity

This level is very similar to RAID 3 except that striping is done at block level across several drives. As in RAID 2 the speed of reads can be greatly increased while, on the other hand, write accesses suffer from having to update the parity data at each write occurrence. XOR is used to generate parity data. For small transfers, however, faster individual disk accesses are possible. As with RAID 3, only one drive in the array stores redundant information and hence can be quite cost effective.

4.3.6   RAID Level 5 - Block Interleaving with Parity Distribution

In RAID 5 architecture, parity is distributed across various drives. With this, the need for a parity drive for each disk array is alleviated - thereby removing a potential bottleneck. On the other hand, with a greater number of concurrent disk accesses that are likely to be made, there is an increased degree of overhead (to track the location of the parity addresses) present. Generally, higher performance is witnessed if most I/O occurs randomly and in small chunks. Such an I/O distribution suggests that this model is perhaps the most useful in database applications. In fact, the actual increase in I/O throughput increases relatively little throughout RAID 2-5 as the overhead incurred in updating a parity drive is considerable. Thus, most RAID systems were used as file or database server, where reliability and availability are the key concerns.

4.3.7   RAID Level 6 - Fault-Tolerant System

RAID 6 is an improvement over RAID 5 model through the addition error recovery information. Conceptually, the disks are considered to be in a matrix formation and the parity is generated for rows and for columns of disks in the matrix. The multi-dimensional level of parity is computed and distributed among the disks in the matrix. Recovery of lost data is now possible in the event of two disks failing simultaneously. The additional overhead in this dual-level redundancy compared to RAID 5 is substantial.

The RAID 6 specification has been refined further by implementing additional extensions to this definition. To minimize potential exposure to a scenario where three drives fail (which would render data on a RAID 6 system inoperable), global disk sparing and dynamic drive reconstruction have been added to the model. Using the parity method described previously, a failed disk can be recovered to a spare disk before a second failure is likely to occur. Using dual parity for the reconstruction process, data reconstruction can be completed successfully even if non-recoverable read errors are encountered during the recovery process.

Indeed, RAID 6 has become a common feature in many systems, though the advent of the RAID 7 architecture may lead to its eventual abandonment as RAID 7 borrows from and improves upon this specification. Many of these individual refinements of RAID 6 were fully incorporated into the RAID 7 design.

4.3.8   RAID Level 7 - Heterogeneous System

RAID 7 is the most recent development in the RAID taxonomy. RAID 7 architecture allows each individual drive to access data as fast as possible by incorporating a few crucial features. Each I/O device is, firstly, connected to a high-speed data bus which possesses a central cache store capable of supporting multiple host I/O paths. Secondly, a real-time process-oriented operating system is embedded into this disk array architecture. This embedded operating system frees the drives by allowing each drive head to move independently of the other drive heads. This is a substantial improvement over previous RAID constraints, where all disk heads had to move in parallel. Indeed all of the RAID 7 parity generation, check control logic, microprocessor control logic, bus control logic, the high-speed bus and cache control logic, and the resource drive control logic, are all tied together and managed by this embedded operating system. Each read/write to the parity drive is managed, scheduled, and executed in an optimized asynchronous manner. The operating system enabled in the disk array architecture is designed to support multiple host interfaces, in comparison to the other RAID architectures' support of only one.

The ability to reconstruct data in the event of dependent drive failure is also increased. The independent structure of the RAID 7 architecture with separate device cache, separate device control, and embedded OS permits the optional addition of a secondary, tertiary, and beyond parity calculation, which can be configured to protect for up to four simultaneous disk failures.

The ease of upgrading to a RAID 7 architecture from a previous configuration is another significant supplement introduced. Previously, being forced to use only one type of drive had proven to be an encumbrance when chaining multiple RAID systems together or when moving on to a completely new platform. Most RAID systems allow only the use of similar drives, but RAID 7 has the ability to handle a heterogeneous mix of drive types and sizes. This allows drives of different capacities, different access times, different transfer speeds, and different form factors to interconnect – allowing expandability to suit the future requirements of the system. A similar feature afforded by the asynchronous architecture is the ability to support multiple standby drives for 'hot swapping', vastly improving maintenance and repair times.

But, perhaps the most striking change in structure is the use of dynamic mapping. In the traditional storage architecture, a block of data, once created, is written to a fixed memory location on disk. Any update or alteration of that data must be rewritten to that same physical location on the disk. Removing this constraint frees the system from the write performance penalty inherent in other RAID architectures. Dynamic mapping is a process by which updated data is not written back to its original location in memory. Log structured files permit updates to be written to new locations within the array. When an update occurs, the parity information for the changed data is computed and data and parity are written to the new locations within the array group. Thus, only a single write is required to support update operations and a background task operates to collect free space left by update operations. This effectively eliminates the additional disk accesses (and potential for a bottleneck) required for updating parity during write operations and allows disks to be accessed independently.

4.3.9   Future of RAID Technology

With the growth in the speed of computers and communications in response to the demands for speed and reliability, the RAID theme has begun to attract significant attention as a potential mass storage solution for the future. Eventually, a RAID architecture may be an essential part of any computer system. This model has the demands for speed progressed from its foundation as an area of academic research into the forefront of industry standards, where it is positioned to become the standard for disk drive architecture in the foreseeable future.

4.4   Optical Storage Technology

Of the storage technologies that are available as computer peripherals, the optical medium is the most popular in the multimedia context. Their popularity is attributable to compact size, high-density recording, easy handling, and low cost per MB. This technology started as a support technology for digital audio recording for music, because of its high fidelity in reproduction compared to audio cassettes. Over a period of time, it has become the mainstay of storage for multimedia information. We, therefore, consider it appropriate to devote the rest of this chapter to introducing the CD technology to the reader and revisiting the other I/O issues later in the book.

4.5   Compact Disc: A Historical Perspective

Compact Discs started with CD-DA (Compact Disc-Digital Audio) or standard music CDs. CD-DA became CD-ROM when people realized that it was possible to store lots of computer data on a 12 cm optical disc (650

MB). CD-ROM drives are simply another kind of digital storage media for computers, albeit read-only. They behave just like hard disks and floppy drives.

CD-I (Compact Disc-Interactive) demonstrates the use of the optical disc in conjunction with a computer to provide a home entertainment system that can deliver music, graphics, text, animation, and video. Unlike a CD-ROM drive, a CD-I player is a stand-alone system requiring no external computer. It plugs directly into a TV and stereo system and comes with a remote control to allow the user to interact with software programs stored on discs. It looks and feels much like a CD player, except that it can store images as well as music and the user can interactively control what happens. In fact, one can play all the standard music CDs on a CD-I player since the formats are compatible.

CD-ROM/XA (eXtended Architecture) is an extension of a conventional CD-ROM drive with some of the compressed audio capabilities found in a CD-I player (called ADPCM). This allows interleaving of audio and video, so that an XA drive can play audio and display pictures (or other things) simultaneously. There is special hardware in an XA drive controller to handle the audio playback.

One can say that CD-ROM, CD-ROM/XA, and CD-I discs are normally "mastered" as opposed to burned. That means that one master copy is made and then hundreds, thousands, or millions are pressed from the master. This process is much cheaper than burning for quantities above a few dozen or so. Generally, disc pressing plants can handle all of these formats as the underlying technology is the same; the only difference is in the data and disc format.

Photo-CD from Kodak is for recording photographs as digital pictures on compact disc. This raises the question of *writing* on a read-only device. Until recently there was no way for anyone but the producer of one of these discs to store his/her own content on the disc - that is, to write to it. But a technology called WORM (Write Once Read Many), based on an optical disc, can be written to but only once. One can write data on it, but once written the data can not be erased, although it can then be used like a CD-ROM disc, i.e., read only forever. The reason that WORM technology was critical for Photo-CD is obvious - the content of these discs is not determined by the manufacturer but by the publisher. For Photo-CD, each disc will be different - a roll or few rolls of film per disc from a customer. Kodak and Philips wanted Photo-CD discs to be playable on both computer peripherals for desktop publishing uses, and on a consumer device for home viewing.

For the former, CD-ROM/XA was chosen as a carrier; for the latter CD-I was chosen, which was already designed as a consumer electronics device.

Although a WORM disc can only be written to once, it is not necessary to write, or burn, the entire disc all at once. One can write the disc initially with, say, a few hundred megabytes of data, and then go back later and write some more data onto it. Of course, each write must be to an unrecorded part of the disc; once a spot on the disc is written, it can not be re-written. Each write operation is referred to as a "session," and a drive or a disc that supports this multiple write operation is called "multisession." Originally, all WORMs were single-session only. That is, the user could not go back and add data to a WORM disc once it was written, even if it was not full. For Photo-CD, the motivation was to enable the user to be able to add more pictures to an existing disc as additional rolls of film were processed. So the extension of WORM technology to multisession was developed and adopted for the Bridge disc format. This required hardware changes to CD-ROM/XA drives and that is why there are a fair number of single-session XA drives on the market and multisession ones appearing more and more.

A single session drive can read a multisession disc, but it can only read the contents of the first session that was burned. Incidentally, all Philips CD-I players are multisession, although all current CD-I discs have only a single session on them. Table 4.1 describes the relevant standards.

4.6   CD-ROM

Compact Disc Read Only Memory (CD-ROM) is physically identical to a Digital Audio Compact Disc used in a CD player, but the bits recorded on it are interpreted as computer data instead of music. One has to buy a CD-ROM drive and attach it to a computer in order to use CD-ROMs. A CD-ROM has several advantages over other forms of data storage, and a few disadvantages. As mentioned earlier, a CD-ROM can hold about 650 megabytes of data, the equivalent of thousands of floppy discs. CD-ROMs are not damaged by magnetic fields or the x-rays. The data on a CD-ROM can be accessed much faster than on a tape, but CD-ROMs are 10 to 20 times slower than hard discs [4,5]. Also, one cannot write to a CD-ROM.

Why are CD-ROM drives so slow?   Compact discs were originally designed for music. In order to fit as much music as possible on the disc, the data is recorded at the same linear density near the outer edge of the disc as near the center, so there is more information in the outside tracks than in

---

Standards for CDs

Red Book is the common name of the Compact Disc Digital Audio Standard. When a disc conforms to the red book standard, it will usually have *digital audio* printed below the "disc" logo. Most music CDs conform to this standard.

Yellow Book is the standard for CD-ROM. When a disc conforms to the yellow book, it will usually say *data storage* beneath the "disc" logo.

Green Book is the CD-I (compact disc interactive) standard.

Orange Book is the standard for write-once compact discs.

Blue Book is the standard for LaserDisc.

Table 4.1. Standards for Compact Discs

the inside tracks. In order to deliver a steady rate of data, the linear velocity of the disc moving under the head is constant, so the angular velocity of the disc changes (decreases) when the head moves from the center toward the outside tracks. This does not matter when is no big deal playing music, but for random access to a CD-ROM, the need to accelerate and decelerate the disc is the biggest obstacle to making it faster. Most magnetic discs spin at a constant angular velocity, so the data density decreases toward the outside of the disk, but seeks are faster. There are other reasons as to why CD-ROMs are slow: Optical disc heads tend to be heavier than magnetic disk heads, so they have more inertia and take longer to stabilize onto a new track. Many CD-ROMs contain too much data to make effective use of RAM caches.

CD-ROM Capacity: The capacity of a CD-ROM depends on the drive. Almost all CD-ROM drives will handle up to 620 megabytes without any problems. Many newer drives can read discs with over 700 megabytes. ISO-9660 is an international standard, which all systems support, that defines a file system for CD-ROMs.

4.7   Compact Disc

4.7.1   Structure

A CD-ROM disc is 120 mm (about 4.72 inches) in diameter, 1.2 mm thick, and has a hole 15 mm across in the center. The information, represented by a spiral of small pits, is moulded on to one surface. The surface is coated with a reflective metal layer, which is then coated with a protective lacquer. The plain (top) view and cross-sectional view of a CD-ROM are shown in Fig. 4.3.

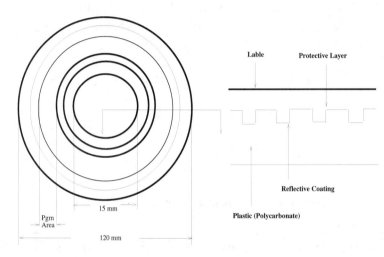

Fig. 4.3. Plain (Top) View and Cross-Sectional View of a CD-ROM

The program area consists of spiral pattern of *pits.* The pits are 0 - 12 μm deep and about 0.6 μm wide. The neighboring turns of the spiral pattern of pits are 1.6 μm apart. This spacing corresponds to a track density of 16,000 tracks per inch. Spaces between the pits, called *lands,* run from 0.9 to 3.3 μm long. These are shown in Fig. 4.4.

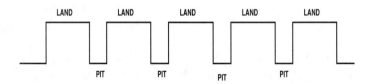

Fig. 4.4. Pits and Lands

4.7.2   Information Storage

Information is stored according to the principle shown in Fig. 4.5. The length of pits is always a multiple of $0.3\ \mu m$. The transition for bit to land and from land to bit corresponds to the coding of a 1 in the digital data stream. A 0 is coded as no transition. Fig. 4.5 shows a digital data stream as a sequence of pits and lands.

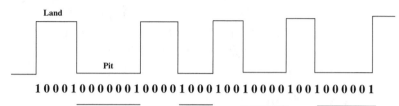

Fig. 4.5. Digital Data Stream Recorded as Pits and Lands

4.7.3   Recording Process

Getting data converted for its digital form into pits and lands of an optical disc is accomplished through a process known as *mastering*. In this process, the waveform carrying the encoded information is transferred to a modulator. The modulator controls a powerful short-wavelength laser beam as it passes through a lens, forming a spot on the photoresist coating of a glass master disc.

The lens moves radially while the master disc spins, so that the information is laid out in the spiral track characteristic of CD-ROM. When the photoresist is developed, it turns the exposed region into pits. The developed master has exactly the *surface profile* which each usable CD-ROM disc should have copied, either by electroplating or photopolymer replication, onto one or more physical negatives. These "stampers" are used to form the actual disc sold to users. The transfer is actually done through injection moulding, etching, or cold embossing.

4.7.4   User Data and CD-ROM Recorded Data

Contrary to what one might think, pits and lands do not correspond to 1s and 0s of user data. In fact, there will never be two 1s without at least two 0s in between. The reason for this is the bit resolution, which is limited to a certain size because of the wavelength of the laser light and the numerical aperture of the objective lens used in the drive. Adjacent transitions too

	Data Bits	Channel Bits
0	00000000	01001000100000
1	00000001	10000100000000
2	00000010	10010000100000
3	00000011	10001000100000
4	00000100	01000100000000

Table 4.2. Sample of a 8-to-14 Conversion Table

close together cannot be read. These considerations, together with the need for self-clocking, have led to a 14-bit modulation symbol: 14 bits are the minimum that can represent the 8 user data bits in a CD-ROM. The actual conversion of 8 user-bit bytes to 14 channel-bit modulation codes is done in a lookup table, a sample of which is given in Table 4.2.

This 14-channel bit modulation symbol solves the minimum run-length problem for bits within a symbol but still leaves a problem at the concatenation points of the 14-bit symbols: a 1 at the end of one symbol could be too close to a 1 at the beginning of the next. This is solved by placing 3 *merge* channel-bits between symbols.

So now each 8-bit user data byte is represented by a total of 17 channel bits. A set of 24 of these 17 bit symbols is combined with a *sync pattern* (another 24 channel bits with 3 merge bits), a control and display symbol, and 8 error correction symbols to form a *frame*, which is the basic unit of informal storage on a CD.

Thus, a frame carrying 24 bytes (192 bits) of error data is represented by 588 channel bits as shown in Table 4.3. Then channel bits are actually instructions to the master recorder, in the sense that a bit will be started when a one channel bit is received, continued while the channel bits are 0s, and ended when the next one channel bit is received. Fig. 4.6 shows the stages the user data goes through in order to become bits.

Frames are grouped together in *blocks*, with 98 frames forming a block. Blocks occur 75 times per second, with each one carrying 2352 bytes (98×24) of user data in the CD standard or 2048 bytes in CD-ROM standard (2352

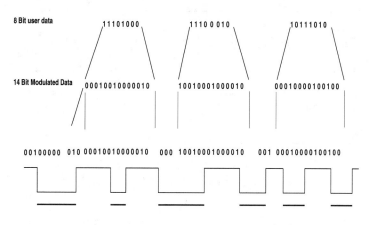

Fig. 4.6. From Bytes to Pits

bytes less the error correction, sync, and address bytes - see Fig. 4.7). This results in a sustained user data rate for CD-ROM of 1.2288 Mb per second.

4.7.5 Storage Capacity

Because the amount of data per track is not constant across the disc, addresses are expressed in the manner used in CD; that is, in units of 0 to 59 minutes, 0 - 59 seconds, and 0 - 74 blocks. This information is carried at the beginning of each block.

The 60-minute limit for CD-ROM is not required by the standard - it can, as does CD, hold up to 74 minutes of sequential data - rather, it comes from the layout of the disc. Since the data spiral starts at the inside and runs towards the outside, the last 14 minutes of playing time in CD occupy the outer 5 mm of the disc. This just happens to be the hardest area to make well and keep clean.

Sync Pattern	24	+	3 channel bits
Control and Display	1	*	(14 + 3) channel bits
Data	24	*	(14 + 3) channel bits
Error Correction	8	*	(14 + 3) channel bits
Total	588		channel bits

Table 4.3. Composite of a frame

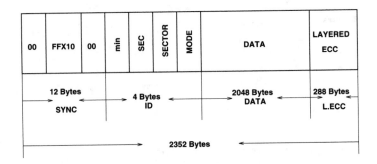

Fig. 4.7. One CD-ROM Block

At 60 minutes, the total number of blocks available per CD-ROM disc is 270,000. At 2048 bytes per block, this yields a total user capacity per disc of 552,960,000 bytes (553 MB). If 74 minutes are used, the numbers become 333,000 blocks and 681,984,000 bytes (682 MB)

4.8 CD-ROM/XA

CD-ROM/XA is an extension to the Yellow Book Standard. A track on a CD-ROM/XA disc can contain computer data, compressed audio data, and video/picture data. Many CD-ROM drives do not support CD-ROM/XA. CD-ROM/XA extends CD-ROM by adding some of the CD-I disc features (such as using Mode 2 tracks with interleaved compressed audio and other data). Thus, CD-ROM/XA (eXtended Architecture) is often called the "Bridge" format between CD-ROM and CD-I; CD-ROM/XA applications still require specific code for each target platform.

4.9 Photo-CD

The Photo-CDs are written according to the Orange Book Part II "Hybrid Disc" specifications. This will allow photographs to be written to the disc in several different sessions. Additionally, the disc will use the CD-Bridge disc format to allow the disc to be readable by both CD-I and CD-ROM/XA players.

The photographs written to the disc in the first session will use the ISO 9660 format. These photographs will be readable with the existing CD-ROM/XA players connected to a computer running software written for the Photo-CD picture structure. Additionally, the photographs will be displayable on CD-I Players and Photo-CD Players connected to a TV set.

Photographs written to disc after the first session will be displayable on CD-I Players and Photo-CD players. New software and/or firmware will be needed to read photographs recorded on later sessions with existing CD-ROM/XA players.

4.10 HDCD

HDCD is the Philips and Sony specification for reading information for a 3.3 GB CD-ROM. This quad-speed CD, using a 635-nm red laser, is designed to have a track pitch of 0.85 microns data rate of 5.6 Mbps. The specified use is an improved version of EFM (8-to-14 modulation) encoding and cross interleaved Reed-Solomon error correction (CIRC). The storage capacity allows the CD to store a complete 130 minutes of a MPEG -2 compressed movie for a broadcast-quality playback at 5.6 Mbps.

4.11 ECMA 168 Standard

ECMA 168 (European Computer Manufacturers Association) is a volume and file format standard for write-once CD and CD-ROM. It was approved as a European standard by the ECMA General Assembly in June of 1992. It provides for full Orange Book functionality, including multisession recording, track-at-once recording, and packet recording. When used with an Orange Book writer, this will allow a write-once CD to be used more like a general-purpose storage peripheral than is possible by using ISO 9660. ECMA 168 also incorporates the functionality of Rock Ridge: the ability to use Unix-style filenames, Unix permissions, and deep directory hierarchies. Much thought was put into character set issues, and ECMA 168 accommodates multiple-byte character sets such as ISO 10646. Although ECMA 168 is not upward-compatible with ISO 9660, it is possible to write a "conformant disc" containing both sets of volume and file structures. If such a disc is Yellow Book compatible (a CD-ROM or a CD-WO written disc-at-once), it could be read on either an ISO 9660 system or an ECMA 167 system.

Hopefully this will encourage developers to support both standards. A new international standard on CD-ROM/CD-WO format is under way.

4.12 CDs and Standards

- The Red Book defines CD-Audio.

- The Yellow Book defines CD-ROM; Mode-1 is for computer data and

Mode-2 is for compressed audio data and video/picture data. CD-ROM/XA is an extension to Yellow Book and defines a new type of track. CD-ROM Mode 2, XA Format, is used for computer data, compressed audio data, and video/picture data. A CD-ROM/XA track may interleave Mode 2 compressed audio and Mode 2 data sectors. Additional hardware is needed to separate these when playing the disc. The hardware is programmed to separate the audio from the data, decompress the audio, and play it out through the audio jacks. Simultaneously, the hardware transfers the data to the computer.

- The Green Book is for Compact Disc Interactive (CD-I).

- The Orange Book defines the Recordable Compact Disc Standard. Part I of the Orange Book defines CD-MO (Magneto Optical,) which consists of optional Pre-Mastered (read-only) area and a recordable (re-writable) user area. Part II of the Orange Book defines CD-WO (Write Once). Orange Book Part II also defines a second type of CD-WO disc called a "Hybrid Disc". This disc consists of a pre-recorded area and a recordable area. The pre-recorded area is a READ-ONLY area where the information is manufactured onto the disc. (This area is written per the Red, Yellow, and Green Book specifications, and can be played on any CD-player.) The recordable areas are where additional recordings can be made in one or, more sessions. Only the first session on the disc is readable by today's CD-players; additional software will be needed to read the additional sessions. A TOC (Table of Contents) is written during each recording session. A disc will have multiple TOCs, one for each recording session.

- Photo-CD is an example of a "Hybrid Disc".

- The CD-Bridge Disc defines a way to add additional information in a CD-ROM/XA track in order to allow the track to be played on a CD-I player. The result is a disc that can be played on both a CD-I player connected to a TV set and on a CD-ROM/XA player connected to a computer.

An example of a CD-Bridge Disc is the new Photo-CD disc. The Photo-CD disc will be playable on CD-I players, Kodak's Photo-CD players, and in computers using CD-ROM/XA drives.

4.13 Summary

In this chapter we introduced the I/O problem in a multimedia system. An example, which progressively introduced the concepts from very simple notions such as data transfer in a computer system, was used for illustration. The different dimensions of this problem (namely, the nature of data, opportunities for parallism in disk subsystem design, recording formats, and their impact on performance, etc.) were discussed. The core technologies of the 1990's for storage, RAID, and CD-ROM and their variations were explained. The standards that are being followed in the optical storage media and their compatibilities were explained. The use of CD-ROMs in multimedia has generated a wide range of new developments, which in turn started a new round of standardizing efforts. New standards beyond the current CD-I, storage bulk, and Photo-CD are expected. In fact, efforts are afoot to define a universal CD standard to cover most of the multimedia requirements.

REFERENCES

1. Patterson, D; Garth, G; Katz R. A Case for the Redundant Arrays of Inexpensive Disks (RAID). University of California, Berkeley, Report No UCB/SCD/87/391, 1987.

2. Flynn, Michael. Computer Architecture: Pipelined and Parallel Processor Design, Jones and Bartlett Publishers, Inc., London UK, 1995.

3. Prabhat K. Andleigh and Kiran Thakrar. Multimedia Systems Design, Prentice-Hall, Inc., 1995.

4. S Schwerin. CD-ROM Standards: The Book, Information Today Inc., August 1986.

5. ANSI/NISO/ISO 9660-1990. Volume and File Structure of CD-ROM for Information Exchange, Transaction Pub., May 1993.

Exercises

1. For CD-quality audio, estimate the amount of storage required.

2. Compute the storage requirement for HDTV.

3. A digital video file is 40 MB in size. The disk subsystem has four drives and the controller is designed to support read and write onto each drive, concurrently. The digital video file is stored using 'disk striping' concept. The block size of 8 KB is used for each I/O operation. Compute the performance improvement in reading the complete file (in strictly sequential form) when compared to a disk subsystem with a single drive. Express the performance improvement as a percentage of the number of physical I/O operations to be performed in each case.

4. Repeat the previous exercise for block sizes 1 Kb, 2 Kb, 4 Kb and 16 Kb. Plot the curve *performance improvement* (*Y*-axis versus *block size* (*X*-axis).

5. If you were to record HDTV-quality video and CD-quality audio for a 15-minute show, what strategy do you propose for disc storage? Assume that synchronization information is 'automatically' available.

Chapter 5

Multimedia Systems Technology: Networking

5.1 Introduction

Networking was originally conceived to interconnect heterogeneous computers that are spread out over a large geographic area. In the 1960's and early
1970's, hardware sharing was the only aim. The major applications which
were acting as driving forces for the development of networking technology
were logging onto a computer system from a remote location and accessing
files stored in a remote computer system. The late 1970's and early 1980's
saw a significant change in the nature of applications. Software sharing and
information sharing became popular. All along, there was always some form
of electronic mail but only among the privileged.

Two simultaneous developments were noticeable: one was the growth in
number and complexity of the applications and the other was the growth in
technology resulting in powerful computer systems that were small and af-
fordable. Many organizations purchased several computers to support their
functioning. A natural consequence was a need for networking covering computers in small geographical areas as well as across countries and continents.
This led to the development of several networking mechanisms during the
1970's and 1980's such as Ethernet, Token Ring, etc., to support local area
networking and X.25 for wide area networking. Many organizations and
institutions established local area networks to enable information flow and
information integration.

The 1980's witnessed a large number of networks spread out across the
globe. There was an urgent need to have global standards that could be
followed for building networks and also interconnecting them. The International Standards Organization (ISO) defined the OSI (Open Systems Inter-

connection) architecture with all the functionalities for networking. There was a parallel (and commercially successful) effort by a group of people who nurtured a suite of protocols, which later came to be known as TCP/IP architecture or more popularly the Internet architecture. The result was that by the dawn of the 1990s, the INTERNET (the network of networks) started growing rapidly.

Around the same time, the digitalization of continuous media became popular due to developments in integrated circuits technology as well as digital signal processing technology. As a result, continuous media such as voice and video were available in digital form. New applications that use multiple media as an integral part of their interface to users started becoming available. This new change increased the number of bits to be transported as a part of applications from *kilobits* range to *hundreds of megabits* range. Added to such large volumes, the different media required stringent time-based synchronization. As a consequence, networks had to be designed such that a large number of bits could be transported in a short period of time and without delays. As a result, new technologies started emerging: fiber-optics-based carrier technology became popular for high-speed applications. While fiber technology was positioned as *the* answer to gigabit networking, the traditional Ethernet technology based on copper was revived with a new name - *Gigabit Ethernet*. At the time of writing this book, both camps were optimistic about their share of future networking!

Let us look at a simple calculation. If we design a network to operate at 10 Mbps, and if we use such a network to transport 100 Mbits, then we will use the network for 10 seconds continuously to accomplish our goal. This is an obvious response based on simple arithmetic. *The implicit assumption is that the data are generated at a 10 Mbps rate for 10 seconds.* Supposing this assumption is not true for an application and all the 100 Mbits are available instantaneously. Then, by design, we are introducing a 9 second delay in the application. If such a delay is not acceptable to the application, then the only way is to increase the bandwidth to 100 Mbps. While doing so, the network becomes inherently capable of handling more traffic for *every* second. From the network designer's viewpoint, it turns out to be a problem of utilization of the extra capacity or bandwidth. The obvious solution is to *share* the bandwidth across several applications.

Sharing has been the key to several aspects of computer systems design, and networking is no exception. For *sharing* to be efficient, one should know *a priori* the requirements of all users of a network. This is referred to as *workload*, and defining workload precisely has been a hard problem for over two decades. *Sharing* also raises the following questions:

- What is to be shared? (presumably bandwidth)

- What are the user requirements?

- What is the pattern of the requirement?

- What is the unit of sharing?

- Is sharing to happen in time? or space?

- Should sharing be deterministic or probabilistic?

- Should sharing be guaranteed or best-effort?

Several digital technologies were developed in the 1980's. The first one was an extension of the existing telephone network to carry all types of digital information. This was called Integrated Services Digital Network (ISDN). Simultaneously, there were developments such as Fiber Distributed Data Interface (FDDI) to replace the local area networks and Distributed Queue Dual Bus (DQDB) to establish metropolitan area networks. The network service providers saw a large demand for high-capacity links over long distances and started providing a new service called Frame Relay service, which in a sense can be seen as a substitute for leased lines.

ATM technology was expected to become the ubiquitous technology in networking in the early and mid-1990's. ATM can interface to fiber optic carrier technology at the SONET/SDH [1] level and can seamlessly integrate the local area networks and wide area networks. In the late 1990's, it is becoming increasingly certain that Gigabit Ethernet will be equally well positioned. Ethernets are, in fact, reemerging as a major force in local area networks, with a speed of 100 megabits per second and a promise of ramping up to gigabits. There are switches that can switch at a gigabit rate between Ethernets.

Today, a lot of the research and development in the world concentrates on ATM-based networking solutions. ATM[2] addresses the networking-related technology and the corresponding protocols. ATM networks capable of running at 622 Mbps (OC12) are commercially available. On the other hand, Internet is predominantly based on leased lines interconnecting IP routers.

---

[1] Synchronous Optical Network/Synchronous Digital Hierarchy.
[2] Standards specified by ATM Forum.

It is important to know how the ATM and the Internet are going to be glued together to provide the network subsystems that will carry the multimedia information. Needless to say that the multitude of technologies and the associated protocols have necessitated standardization, which is the harbinger of global communication. To address the problem of the magnitude that is being tackled by the computer and communication community, we need standards in architecture, protocols, technology, and the computing environment. OSI[3] and TCP/IP[4] address the standards in the architecture and protocol area. The OSI model provides an excellent conceptual framework and helps one to understand the key issues and developments in networking technology. TCP/IP architecture, on the other hand, *is the Internet itself.* In this chapter, we will study the architecture of computer networks and various networking technologies.

5.2   OSI Architecture

To reduce the complexity of the network design, the network is modeled as a series of layers or levels so that the architectural details can be specified. Fig. 5.1 shows the layering of the Open Systems Interconnection (OSI) architecture [1, 2]. The OSI reference model has *seven* layers; viz., Physical, Datalink, Network, Transport, Session, Presentation, and Application Layers. Each layer provides a set of services to the layer above. Services of all the layers combine together to provide the total networking environment. The functions of each one of the layers are briefly described below.

Physical layer is concerned with the transmission and reception of unstructured bit stream over any physical medium. It deals with the mechanical aspects and signal voltage levels. Some examples of physical layer are RS-232-C, X.21, and X.21bis.

Datalink layer ensures reliable transfer of data across the physical media. It also provides access control to the media in the case of local area networks. Some examples of data link layer are HDLC, LLC, and SDLC.

Network layer provides the upper layers with independence from the switching technology. It is responsible for establishing, maintaining, and terminating connections. More importantly, the network layer is responsible for routing. Some examples of network layer are X.25 and IP.

Transport layer is responsible for the reliable and transparent transfer of data between end points, takes care of end-to-end flow control and, end-to-

---

[3]Standards specified by the International Standards Organization.
[4]Standards specified by the Internet Engineering Task Force.

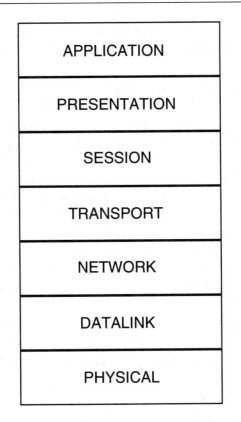

| APPLICATION |
| PRESENTATION |
| SESSION |
| TRANSPORT |
| NETWORK |
| DATALINK |
| PHYSICAL |

Fig. 5.1. OSI Architecture

end error recovery. Some examples are TP Class 4 and TCP.

Session layer provides a means for establishing, managing, and terminating connections (services) between processes. It may also provide checkpoints, synchronization, and restart of services.

Presentation layer performs a transformation on the data to provide a standardized interface to applications. It helps to resolve the syntactic differences when the internal representation of data differs from machine to machine.

Application layer provides services that can be used by user applications. Some of these services are FTAM (File Transfer Access and Management) and CASE (Common Application Service Elements). These services provide communication facilities between application processes. Some examples are FTAM, X.400, and X.500.

The layered approach solves the communication problem by dividing it into smaller problems to be tackled independently. The machine-dependent features are separated out to make implementation easy.

5.3   Internet Standard - TCP/IP

The need, potential, and importance of Internet Technology were first realized by some U.S. government agencies. These agencies funded a number of research programs to develop the technology for DARPA [5]. The DARPA technology includes a set of network standards that specify the details of how computers communicate as well as a set of conventions for interconnecting networks and routing traffic. This technology has been officially named the TCP/IP Internet Protocol Suite, where TCP and IP refer to two of its main standards [3, 4]. The idea was to allow processes running on a computer present in one network to communicate with processes running on a computer present in a physically different network by providing a direct logical connection between them.

TCP, which is used in conjunction with the TCP/IP Internet protocol suite, forms one of the layers of this four-layer protocol architecture. At the highest level, the users invoke application programs that access services available across an internet. An application interacts with the transport-level protocol (TCP) to send or receive data. Each application program chooses the size of transport needed, which can be either a sequence of individual messages or a continuous stream of bytes. The application program passes data in the required form to the transport level for delivery.

The primary responsibility of the transport layer is to provide communication from one system to another system. Such communication is often referred to as *end-to-end* communication. The transport layer regulates the flow of information, ensures error-free transfer of data, and in-sequence delivery. For achieving this, the transport layer uses the technique of the receiver acknowledging receipt of data and retransmitting in case packets are lost. Note that, in general, multiple application programs can access the Internet at the same time and this will require proper multiplexing of connections on the physical links. TCP fits into the layered protocol architecture just above a basic Internet Protocol (IP) layer, which provides a way for TCP to send and receive variable-length segments of data across the Internet.

The Internet Protocol(IP) is designed for use in interconnected systems of packet-switched computer communication networks. The Internet proto-

---

[5]Defence Advance Research Projects Agency.

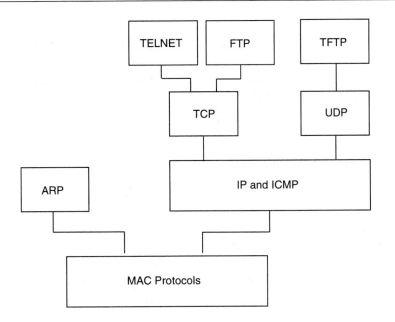

Fig. 5.2. Protocol Relationships

col suite is shown in Fig. 5.2. The IP basically runs over any Media Access Control protocol (MAC). Above IP, there are two options; viz., TCP and UDP (User Datagram Protocol). The UDP has less overhead compared to TCP, but does not guarantee transfers. The Trivial File Transfer Protocol (TFTP) runs on UDP. Popular Internet applications, such as TELNET and FTP, run on TCP. IP provides for transmitting blocks of data called datagrams from sources to destinations, where sources and destinations are hosts identified by fixed-length addresses. IP also provides for fragmentation and reassembly of long datagrams, if necessary, for transmission through *small packet* networks. IP interfaces on one side to the high-level host-to-host protocols (such as TCP)and on the other side to the local network protocol (such as Ethernet, Token Ring, X.25, etc.). IP being a connection-less[6] protocol, the user of IP (TCP) has to take care of reliable, error-free, flow-controlled and in-sequence delivery of packets. There are a number of support protocols that help IP manage the subnetwork. The most important among these are the *Address Resolution Protocol (ARP)*, *Reverse Address Resolution Protocol (RARP)*, and *Internet Control Message Protocol (ICMP)*.

---

[6]At the IP level, there is no end-to-end connection maintained between the sender and the receiver.

The TCP/IP architecture is extremely important as it is used in the Internet. Many of the applications such as WWW, MBone, Electronic mail, FTP, TELNET and so on, are used world-wide by billions of users. New multimedia-based applications, such as netvideo, are becoming increasingly popular. Multimedia applications are expected to be the standard way of using computers in the near future.

5.4   Network Components

A network consists of several components that are interconnected. Each component has a well-defined role to play. But the components themselves can be classified broadly into two categories: those which are end systems and those which are required to establish the network itself. An appreciation of different network components will enable the reader to appreciate the discussions on different networks better. Also, the terminologies need some understanding. The network components are:

- *Personal Computer:* This is the computer connected by the user (also known as PC). From a simple personal computer to a multimedia PC that is capable of handling all media, many varieties of PCs are available which are generally synonymous with the DOS operating system or Windows software. However, in the academic environments, use of a variety of Unix, called Linux, is becoming popular.

- *Workstation:* Normally a larger computer system compared to a PC. The term 'workstation' was originally associated with the RISC architecture machines, but currently it is being used to refer to high-end PCs as well. The workstations are either UNIX-based or Window-based.

- *Client:* The term 'client' refers to either a PC or a workstation in its physical form. It can also be used to refer to a software running on a PC or workstation.

- *Server:* This is typically a high-end PC or RISC architecture based machine which is configured liberally in terms of memory and disk space. Normally, a server serves a number of clients by providing special software or services. Also, a group of clients are attached to a server for better management. Servers can be more than one, in any given network. They can optionally interoperate, for special services such as files. NFS is a good example. Windows NT server, SQL server,

NFS server, File server, and Compute server are a few manifestations that one normally comes across.

- *Network Interface Unit:* The hardware required to attach the client or the server to a network is called the Network Interface Unit or NIU. Each access method will require a different NIU (for example, Ethernet NIU, Token Ring NIU, etc.).

- *Transceiver:* The hardware that is capable of both sending and receiving is called a transceiver. They are normally part of the NIU. In some designs, they can be separate from NIU. When they are part of NIU, the distance from the network to the workstation is small and when they are separate units, the distance is large.

- *Attachment Unit:* When the transceiver is not part of the NIU, an attachment unit is used for interfacing the external transceiver and the NIU itself.

- *Repeater:* The bits transmitted over a medium suffer attenuation with distance. In order to strengthen the signals, repeaters are used. In the case of Ethernet, repeaters also provide an opportunity to have star and tree topologies as opposed to the original bus-only topology. They are active devices.

- *Hub:* A generic reference for a point of confluence in a network. Hub is the same as the repeater. It is also common to refer to radial lines from workstations and servers to a repeater as a hub-and-spoke configuration. The hubs can be chained to one another to form a star, tree, ring, or any hybrid topology.

- *DTE:* Data Terminal Equipment is a generic terminology to refer to equipment at the premises of the user. A DTE connects to a DCE.

- *DCE:* Data Communication Equipment is at the exchange connected to the DTE. Typically, the protocols to connect a DTE to a DCE over a medium is defined as a standard. For example, the X.25 protocol is an interface protocol defined between a DTE and a DCE.

- *Switch:* A place where a number of cables converge from different locations, and there is an opportunity to steer the electric signals from one cable to another. The process of doing this is called switching. *What, when, how, how long,* and *where* to switch make the switch design interesting and challenging. Each switch supports a protocol and a data format. Usually, the switches are known by the protocols they support.

- *Ether Switch:* A switch that supports Ethernet protocol.

- *X.25 Switch:* A switch that supports X.25 protocol.

- *ISDN Switch:* A switch that supports ISDN protocol.

- *IP Switch:* A switch that supports IP protocol.

- *ATM Switch:* A switch that supports ATM protocol.

- *Frame Relay Switch:* A switch that supports Frame Relay protocol. Normally, this is just referred to as Frame Relay only. The word 'Relay' carries the meaning switch with it in this case.

- *Connection-oriented:* Each network has a characteristic mode of operation. A mode of operation refers to the way the communication is maintained by the network from the source to the receiver. When the mode of operation is connection-oriented, the network finds a path between the source and the destination and assigns it to support a 'session' (which is a logical sequence of exchanges of information between the source and the destination). This mode implies that resources are dedicated.

- *Connectionless:* In a connectionless mode of operation, each packet is viewed as an independent unit of information from a source to a destination. The task of finding out where the destination is and how to reach it is repeated for every unit of information that is exchanged.

- *Packets, Datagrams, Frames, and Cells:* These are units in which information is typically transferred. Packets are used in LANs, X.25, and IP networks. Datagrams are the generic name associated with a packet in a connectionless network. Frame is used in the case of an ISDN network or a Frame Relay network. It is also used in the case of some carriers, such as SONET, to refer to a unit of information exchanged between them. Cell is a very small-sized packet and is used with the ATM network.

Fig. 5.3 shows how all these components can be part of a network.

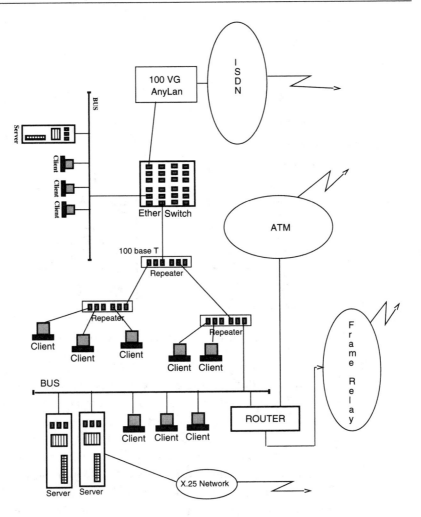

Fig. 5.3. An Illustrative Network

5.5 Local Area Networks (LAN)

Traditionally, a LAN (Local Area Network) is characterized by a limited physical span, speed of the order of megabits per second, and single-party ownership. In the late 1970's, LANs started with the popular Ethernet protocol running at 10 megabits per second on a shared bus operating in a broadcast mode [5, 6]. The Ethernet protocol was based on self-regulation by stations in accessing the shared medium. This is also referred to as distributed access control.

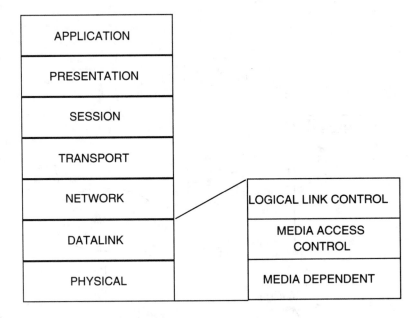

Fig. 5.4. LAN Architecture

The key to the popularity (or should we say growth) of LAN is the availability of a low-cost interface. The cost to connect any equipment to a LAN must be an order of magnitude less than the cost of the equipment. A LAN standard has made it possible to meet this requirement through a high-volume market. When it became apparent that no single standard would satisfy differing requirements, the CSMA/CD [7] access method along with Token Bus and Token Ring[8] methods have been standardized as the media access control technology. The LAN architecture which essentially reflects this idea, is shown in Fig. 5.4 along with its correspondence to OSI. The bottom two layers of OSI are split into three layers, viz., physical media dependent layer, media access control layer, and logical link control layer. The reason is that the physical medium itself is a shared medium, in the case of LANs.

Networks, in general, can be divided into two categories - those using point-to-point connection and those using broadcast channels. Broadcast systems have a single communication channel shared by all the machines

---

[7]Carrier Sense Multiple Access - Xollision Detection, which is explained later in this chapter.

[8]Explained later in this chapter.

in the network. Packets sent by any machine are received by all others. An address field within the packet specifies for whom it is intended. The key issue in any broadcast network is how to determine who gets to use the channel when there is competition for it. An important consideration during the determination of use of channel is " fair sharing"- "Does every channel get an equal opportunity to transmit its data onto the channel?" One estimator of fair sharing is "delay time", which evaluates the mean delay a station should experience before it can transmit its data. Again, several factors may have to be considered to determine how fair sharing is to be implemented - equality may be tilted to favor certain stations on size of data, relative importance of the stations, etc. Finally, during an evaluation of the efficiency of MAC protocols, a key factor is a study of the variation of load *versus* waiting time.

The key parameters in any MAC technique are "where" and "how". "Where" refers to whether control is exercised in a centralized or distributed fashion. In a centralized scheme, a controller (or station) is designated as having the authority to grant access to the network. A station wishing to transmit must wait until it receives permission from the controller. In a decentralized network, the stations collectively perform a MAC function to dynamically determine the order in which stations transmit. "How" is constrained by topology and is a trade-off among competing factors such as cost, performance, and complexity. In general, access control techniques may be classified as *synchronous* and *asynchronous*. With synchronous techniques, a specific capacity is dedicated to a connection and as such may not be efficient in LANs because the needs of stations are generally unpredictable. It is preferable to allocate capacity in an asynchronous, dynamic fashion in response to immediate needs. The asynchronous approach can be further divided into three categories:

- *Round Robin:* Each station, in turn, is given an opportunity to transmit and when it is finished must relinquish its turn and the right to transmit passes to the next station in logical sequence. Control of turns may be centralized or distributed. Token Ring is an example of this scheme.

- *Reservation:* Typically, time on the medium is divided into slots, much as with synchronous time-division multiplexing(TDM). To transmit, a station reserves future slots for an extended or indefinite period. Shared satellite channel is an example of this scheme.

- *Contention:* No control is exercised to determine whose turn it is to transmit. These methods are likely to lead to collisions and may require retransmissions. CSMA/CD is an example of this scheme.

5.5.1 CSMA/CD: Ethernet

CSMA/CD is most commonly seen in bus topologies. A transmission from any station propagates the length of the medium and can be received by all other stations. The intended destination station will recognize its address as the packets go by, and copy them. There is no centralized communication control strategy, and each station that is attached must incorporate the framing and access control logic. From a communication point of view, the network is a passive transmission medium with no processing. Each station has to assess for itself the network conditions and decide on the *opportunity to transmit*. CSMA/CD stations follow the steps enumerated *(MAC Protocol)* below, in order to transmit.

1. If the medium is idle, transmit. Otherwise, go to step2.

2. If the medium is busy, continue to listen until the medium is sensed idle and then transmit (after waiting for recovery time due to hysteresis).

3. If a collision is detected during the transmission, transmit a brief *Jamming Signal* to indicate to all stations that there has been a collision and then cease transmission.

4. After transmitting the jamming signal, wait a random amount of time and then attempt transmission again. (Go to step 1).

It is essential to use packets long enough to allow collision detection before the end of transmission. Thus, the slot time[9] determines the minimum MAC frame length and also the retransmission algorithm. Consider that if a collision occurs and the two stations involved back off an equal amount of time and retransmit, there will be a collision again. To avoid this, each station backs off a random amount of time, forming a uniform probability distribution. A collision generates additional traffic (due to retransmission), and it is important not to clog the network with retransmissions, which can lead to more collisions. So when a station experiences repeated collisions, it should back off for a longer period of time to compensate for the extra load on the network.

In the truncated binary exponential back-off algorithm, the back-off delay is an integral number of slot times, R. The number of slot times to delay before the nth retransmission is a uniformly distributed random integer in

---

[9]Slot time is defined to be larger than the sum of the physical layer round-trip time and the MAC layer jam time. This time depends on the details of the physical layer.

the range $(0 < r < 2^k)$; $k = min(n, 10)$. After P attempts (user defined), the MAC entity assumes that some problem exists and reports failure to the logical link control layer.

Algorithm:
   while $n < Backoff - limit$
   $k := min(n, 10)$
   $r := random(0, 2^k)$
   $delay := r * slot - time.$

The unfortunate effect of the above algorithm is the Last-in/First-out effect, i.e., stations with no or few collisions will have a chance to transmit before stations that waited longer.

The IEEE 802.3 standard defines the CSMA/CD medium access control (MAC) protocol for bus topology [7]. It is also applicable to the tree topology. The standard defines a variety of physical layer transmission medium and data rate options.

CSMA/CD performs well when the network load is less, progressively drops off at moderate loads, and performs poorly at high loads. The primary reason is that the collisions start increasing as the loads increase and the network tends to get overloaded due to the retransmissions. Every Ethernet network is a collision domain (the number of stations competing for the same bandwidth). The design of a network has to ensure that the collision domain is kept to the minimum. This will ensure that the network continues to operate in the *low load* condition. Ethernet switches provide the designer with the opportunity to design such networks, but still the performance is not deterministic.

5.5.2 Token Ring

Token Ring protocol is a MAC protocol that adopts the round robin strategy for resource sharing. The main motivation for employing Token Ring networks is that a ring is fair and has a known upper bound on channel access. Also, a Token Ring system consists of a collection of ring interfaces connected by point-to-point links, which involve a well-understood and field-proven technology. In a Token Ring, a special bit pattern called the token circulates around the ring whenever all stations are idle. When a station wants to transmit a frame, it is required to seize the token, i.e., change the token from an idle token to a busy token. The station then transmits the

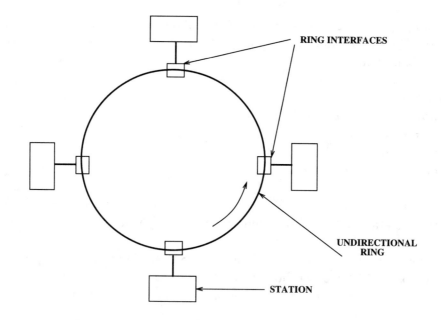

Fig. 5.5. Token Ring and Station Interface

frame immediately on the ring. There is now no free token on the ring, and therefore other stations wishing to transmit must wait. The transmitting station will insert a new free token on the ring after it has finished transmission. Now the next free station downstream will be able to seize the token and transmit.

A ring consists of a collection of point-to-point links. Each bit arriving at an interface is copied into a 1-bit buffer and copied out into the ring again. While in the buffer, the bit can be inspected and possibly modified before being written out. The copying step introduces a 1-bit delay at each interface. A ring and its interfaces are shown in Fig. 5.5.

Ring interfaces have two operating modes - *listen* and *transmit*. In listen mode, the input bits are simply copied to the output with a 1-bit delay. In transmit mode, the interface breaks the connection between input and output, entering its own data onto the ring. To switch from the listen mode to the transmit mode in 1-bit time, the interface usually needs to buffer a couple of frames itself rather than fetch them from the station. When all stations are idle, the token frame has a bit pattern indicating a "free" token. A station wishing to transmit must wait until it detects a token passing by. It then changes the token from "free" to "busy". The station then transmits frames immediately following the busy token. As bits that have propagated around the ring come back, they are removed from the ring by the sender. The sending station is responsible for discarding this from the ring. If it fails to does so, "orphan" frames are produced, which may persistently circulate. This is a frequent problem that must be addressed. This is illustrated in Fig. 5.6.

The broad issues that are addressed by the IEEE 802.5 Token Ring standards are highlighted below[8]:

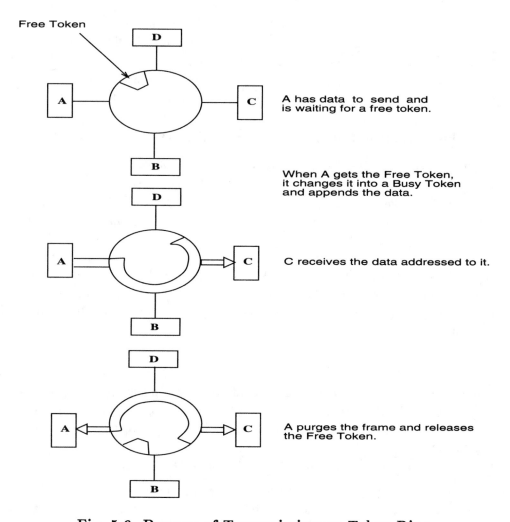

Fig. 5.6. Process of Transmission on Token Ring

- *Contention-Free Access:* The Token Ring network aims at providing contention-free access and preventing collisions. The standard must clearly define how this is to be achieved.

- *Ring Maintenance:* Several problems are likely to occur in the ring, and an elaborate method is required for the maintenance of Token Rings. Some of the important ones include lost tokens, persistently circulating tokens or frames, handling of breaks in links, and presence of garbled frames.

- *Fair Sharing of Resources:* As has been explained earlier, every station must get equal opportunity to transmit its data. Also, there must be some provision for 'priorities'; that is enabling some stations to take precedence over others, if it is so desired.

Performance of Token Ring networks are deterministic. When a token ring and CSMA/CD LAN are compared, at low loads the Token Ring performance is marginally poor and it becomes appreciably better under heavy loads. Since the bandwidth allocation policy is deterministic, it is possible to use it for continuous media such as voice and perhaps video.

5.6 Fiber Distributed Data Interface (FDDI)

The experience with Token Ring networks encouraged designers to adopt the scheme for larger and faster networks. The deterministic and fair sharing aspects of a token-based system was quite attractive. Around the same time, the fiber technology matured to a level where 100 Mbps was possible. A fiber-based ring system, called FDDI, became popular. An FDDI ring consists of stations connected in series by medium segments that form a closed loop, as shown in Fig. 5.7. Data is transmitted serially as a symbol stream from one attached station to its downstream neighbor. Each station, in turn, regenerates and repeats each symbol, passing the symbol to the next station.

5.6.1 Ring Scheduling

The fundamental concepts of FDDI include the use of a timed-token protocol (TTP). The TTP defines the rules for acquiring access to the ring. The timed token protocol guarantees that the token appears at a station within twice the target token rotation time (TTRT). The MAC standard specifies the rules by which the TTRT is negotiated by the attached stations.

Asynchronous Services: Asynchronous ring transmission pertains to ring traffic and services that are not extremely delay sensitive. (This is not to be confused with the asynchronous transmission of data on low-speed lines

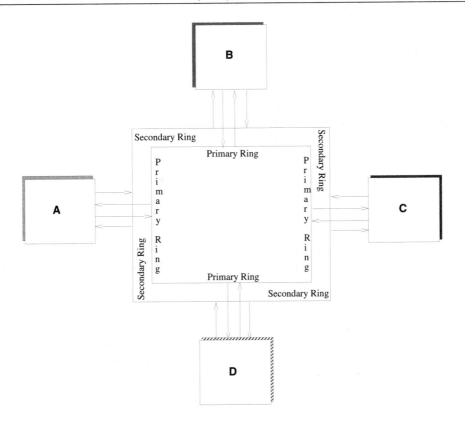

Fig. 5.7. Stations on a FDDI Ring

used by devices such as ASCII terminals.) These are provided in FDDI using the asynchronous transmission to pass data around the ring. Asynchronous transmission is a method of communication in which information is sent when the token holding rules allow transmission. Asynchronous services are designed for bandwidth-intensive applications such as datagram traffic. Asynchronous frames are designed to be transmitted during the time when the station does not require the bandwidth that synchronous service guarantees.

Synchronous Services: These are provided in FDDI, whereby each station is guaranteed a portion of the 100 Mbps FDDI bandwidth. This percentage is negotiated using a synchronous bandwidth allocation function defined by SMT. Synchronous frames are sent at any time as long as the bandwidth negotiated via the synchronous bandwidth allocation is not exceeded. This service is useful for frames that require guaranteed delivery within a time period of two times TTRT. Such frames include compressed audio and video, among other things.

5.6.2   Ring Operation

FDDI ring operation includes connection establishment, ring initialization, steady-state operation, and ring maintenance. Timers are used to regulate these operations. Each station on the FDDI ring uses three timers to regulate its operation. These timers are administered locally by the individual stations. These are the token rotation timer (TRT), the token holding timer (THT), and the valid transmission timer (TVX).

Token Rotation Timer: TRT is used to time the duration of operations in a station. This timer is critical to the successful operation of the FDDI network. It controls ring scheduling during normal operation and fault recovery times when the ring is not operational. TRT is initialized to different values, depending on the state of the ring. During steady-state operation, TRT expires when the target token rotation time (TTRT) has been exceeded.

Token Holding Timer: THT controls the length of time that a station can initiate asynchronous frames. A station holding the token can begin asynchronous transmissions if THT has not expired. THT is initialized with the value corresponding to the difference between the arrival of the token and TTRT.

Valid Transmission Timer: TVX times the period between valid transmissions on the ring. TVX detects excessive ring noise, token loss, and other faults. When the station receives a valid frame or token, the valid transmission timer resets. If TVX expires, then the station will start a ring initialization sequence to restore the ring to proper operation.

Timers regulate activity on the ring. For example, the TRT times the receipt of tokens. This time is initialized to a given value depending on the target token rotation time established by negotiation between active stations on the ring. Stations bid for the right to set the TTRT, initialize the ring, and start circulating the token. To transmit, a station captures the token, stops the repeat process, and sends asynchronous or synchronous frames until none is left to send or the appropriate timer expires. Then the station releases the token onto the ring for use by another station. A transmitting station is responsible for removing (stripping) all frames that it sends. This process leaves frame fragments on the ring that are removed by the next transmitting station or by the cumulative action of repeat filters in many stations.

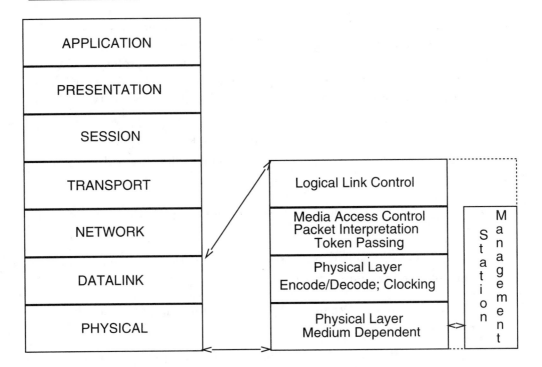

Fig. 5.8. FDDI Protocol Architecture

5.6.3 FDDI Protocol Architecture

The structure of FDDI protocol follows the layering concept laid down by OSI architecture. It spans the bottom two layers of the OSI seven-layer model, as illustrated in Fig. 5.8. FDDI standards [9, 10] subdivide this OSI physical layer into two sublayers: Physical Layer Medium Dependent (PMD) and Physical Layer Protocol (PHY). These two sublayers separate the physical medium and the transmission details into two distinct parts.

PMD: The function of PMD is transmission of data between stations by first converting the data bits into a series of signals, and then transmitting these signals over the cable linking the two stations. The PMD standards deal with all the areas that are associated with physically transmitting the data, such as optical and electrical transmitters and receivers, fiber-optic or copper cable, media interface connectors, and optical bypass relay (optional in optical PMDs). The PMD standards ensure that transmitters, cables, and receivers will interoperate when the specified parameters are properly implemented. The PMD and SMF-PMD (Single-Mode Fiber-PMD) are standards today, with the LCF-PMD (Low-Cost Fiber-PMD) under development by ANSI. The fiber medium is described by the following characteristics: operating wavelength, core and cladding diameters, index profile, and mode capacity (multi-mode or single-mode). The TP-PMD (Twisted Pair-PMD) is also under development by ANSI for shielded and unshielded twisted pair copper media.

PHY: The Physical Layer Protocol (PHY) standard defines those portions of the physical layer that are media independent. The Physical Layer Protocol defines:

- clock and data recovery (recovers the clock signal from the incoming data),

- encode/decode process (converts data from the MAC into a format suitable for transmission over the FDDI ring),

- symbols (smallest signaling entities used for communication between stations),

- elasticity buffer (accounts for clock tolerances between stations),

- smoothing function (prevents frames from being lost due to shortened preambles), and

- repeated filter (prevents the propagation of code violations and invalid line states).

The PHY standard establishes rules for transmission of symbols on the FDDI ring. It provides the method for clock generation and recovery, and data encoding/decoding. The PHY performs the encoding in two stages: first is through a 4B/5B encoder and the second is through a NRZ/NRZI [10] encoder. The basic unit of information in FDDI is the symbol. There are three types of symbols: data symbols that represent hexadecimal data, line state symbols that are used for PHY-level signaling, and control indicator symbols that show the status of a frame. The elasticity buffer accounts for clock differences between stations, which could otherwise result in loss of frames. The smoothing function of the PHY inserts and deletes symbols at the beginning of a frame to ensure proper reception of the frame by the downstream neighbor. The repeat filter function prevents the propagation

---

[10]Non Return to Zero.

of code violations and invalid line states, which assist in isolating errors to a single link.

MAC: The FDDI MAC standard defines the fair and equal access to the ring through the use of the *timed token protocol*. Communication between attached devices is achieved using frames and tokens. When stations join the ring, the ring is initialized by a bidding process that results in an agreement for a guaranteed service time. The right to transmit data is controlled by a token, which is generated by the winner of the bidding process. The token is passed from one station to another on the FDDI ring. It is a unique symbol sequence that circulates around the ring and is divided into several fields. Each field contains a number of FDDI symbols that define the start of token, token type, and end of token. A station on the ring captures the token when it wants to transmit data. The station then transmits for as long as the token holding rules allow, and reissues the token onto the ring. It reissues the token when it has sent all of its frames, or exhausted its available transmission time. When the frame returns to the sending station, that station removes the frame from the ring via a process called stripping.

In summary, we see that the characteristics of a token-based mechanism have been well exploited by FDDI. The delay to access the ring is strictly bounded (deterministic) and, by appropriate handling of timer mechanisms, an average bit-rate can be guaranteed for each station.

FDDI-II is an enhancement over FDDI to cope with multimedia traffic. In FDDI-II, the total bandwidth is divided into 16 wide-band channels of 6.144 Mbps. These may be further subdivided into any multiples of 8 Kbps. When a station establishes a connection, it can pick on a channel speed and the network will handle it as if it is a circuit-switched constant bit-rate channel. This mode essentially provides isochronous support, which is ideal for multimedia. At this point, the reader may recall our discussions in Chapter 2 on ideal environments for multimedia.

5.7 X.25

X.25 technology was invented in the 1970's, as the first packet switched network built along the lines of a telephone network. The telephone exchanges were conceptually replaced by X.25 switches, so that machines connected on two ports on two different X.25 switches can communicate. Similar to telephone numbers, X.25 ports had numbers that were associated with ports and hence the machines connected to the ports. The protocol architecture was such that it was a connection-oriented network. The protocol architecture had a number of features that took care of the poor quality transmission lines that were available in the 1970s. From today's standard, the X.25 protocol will appear to be very 'heavy'. During the heydays of X.25, only moderate data rates of the order of 64 Kbps was available (Some switches were built for 8 Mbps operations but were not sustained). The concepts of QoS, bandwidth guarantee, and delay jitter were not part of X.25 design. In fact, the main applications were telnet and ftp. Today, it appears that X.25 has only historical, and perhaps nostalgic, value. ISDN was the next level of technology, which provided what X.25 did for data and in addition carried voice. ISDN was all digital.

5.8   Integrated Services Digital Network (ISDN)

The principles of ISDN, as laid down by the standards, are as the following:

- The main feature of the ISDN concept is the support of a wide range of voice and non-voice applications in the same network. A key element of service integration for ISDN is the provision of a range of services using a limited set of connection types and multi-purpose user-network interface arrangements.

- ISDNs support a variety of applications, including both switched and non-switched connections. Switched connections in ISDN include both circuit-switched and packet-switched connections and their concatenations.

- As far as possible, new services introduced into ISDN should be arranged to be compatible with 64 Kbps switched digital connections.

- ISDN will contain intelligence for the purpose of providing service features, maintenance, and network management functions. This intelligence may not be sufficient for some new services and may have to be supplemented by additional intelligence within the network or possibly compatible intelligence in the user terminals.

- A layered protocol structure should be used for the specification of the access to an ISDN. Access from a user to ISDN resources may vary depending upon the services required and upon the status of implementation of national ISDNs.

- It is recognized that ISDNs may be implemented in a variety of configurations according to specific national situations.

5.8.1 Evolution of ISDN

During the 1981-84 CCITT study period, ISDN was first addressed. The complete output of this work is in the I-series recommendations of the Red Book. The ISDN Recommendations were then updated and made more complete during the 1985-88 study period, and these include description of many services. These updated ISDN recommendations are in the Blue Book version of the I-Series Recommendations published early in 1989. In 1986, the first ISDN features were introduced in the United States. Since then, significant progress has been made in the growth of the number of customers actively using *basic* and *primary rate* interface lines of ISDN.

The key service offered by ISDN since its inception has continued to be voice, although many other services have been added. ISDN data transmission services allow users to connect their computers (called ISDN terminals) to any other computer (with ISDN interface) across the globe. A new communication service that became widespread with ISDN is videotex, which is interactive access to a remote database by a person at a terminal. Another popular ISDN service is teletex, which is essentially a form of electronic mail for home and business. In addition to the above-mentioned services, there are also potential services requiring low bandwidth. These go by the name of telemetry or alarm services. The goal of ISDN has been to integrate all these services and make them as commonplace as the telephone.

The first step to ISDN was to define and standardize the user-to-ISDN interface. The next step was to slowly start replacing existing end offices with ISDN exchanges that support the ISDN interface. At this point, those ISDN users connected to an ISDN exchange can use ISDN services on calls to other ISDN users even though these calls use the existing networks. The ISDN concept has moved towards maturity over the past decade. Eventually the existing transmission and switching networks will be replaced by an integrated one, but this will not occur until well into the twenty-first century. Multimedia applications such as video conferencing are already possible using ISDN. Compression standards H.261 and H.263 have played a significant role in this regard.

5.8.2 ISDN Architecture

The key idea behind the ISDN architecture is that of the digital bit pipe, a conceptual pipe between the customer and the carrier through which the bits flow. The digital pipe can support multiple independent channels by *time division multiplexing* of the bit stream. Two principal standards for the bit pipe were developed: a low bandwidth standard for home use, and a higher bandwidth standard for business use that supports multiple channels that are identical to the home use channel. Furthermore, businesses may have multiple bit pipes if they need additional capacity beyond what the standard business pipes can provide.

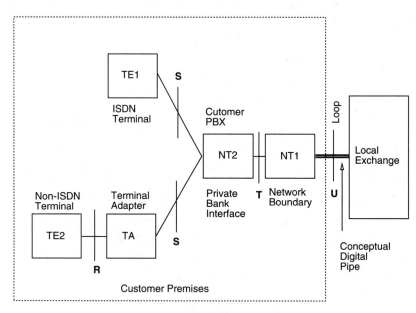

Fig. 5.9. B-ISDN Reference Points

In the normal configuration for home or small business use, the carrier places a network terminating device (NT1) on the customer's premises and then connects it to the ISDN exchange in the carrier's office, several kilometers away, using the twisted pair. The NT1 box has a connector on it, into which a passive bus cable can be inserted. Up to eight ISDN terminal devices can be connected to this cable. From the customer's point of view, the network boundary is the connector on NT1. NT1 also contains logic for contention resolution, so that if several devices try to access the bus at the same time, it can determine which one would win. In terms of the OSI model, NT1 is primarily a physical layer device.

For large businesses, the above-mentioned model is inadequate as it is common to have more telephone conversations going on simultaneously than the bus can handle. In the configuration for business use (shown in Fig. 5.9), we have a device called a Private Branch Exchange (PBX) which in turn can connect to NT1 and provide the interface for telephones, terminals, and other equipment with the help of a terminal adapter. An ISDN PBX is not very different conceptually from an ISDN exchange, although it is usually smaller and cannot handle as many conversations at the same time. Calls between two terminals within the company, usually 4-digit extension numbers, are connected inside the PBX without the carrier's ISDN exchange being aware. An ISDN PBX can directly interface to ISDN terminals and telephones, but the world is still full of non-ISDN devices (e.g., RS-232-C). To accommodate such devices, the customer can install one or more terminal adapters that speak RS-232-C to the terminal and ISDN to the PBX. Thus, at the customer's premises we essentially have five different types of devices: NT1 (Network Boundary), NT2 (Customer PBX), TE1 (ISDN Terminal), TE2 (Non-ISDN Terminal) and TA (Terminal Adaptor).

CCITT has defined four reference points (R,S,T, and U) between the various devices. The U reference point is the connection between the ISDN exchange in the carrier's office and NT1. Today it is implemented in the form of a two-wire copper twisted pair, but might soon be replaced by fiber optics. The T reference point is what the connector on NT1 provides to the customer. The S reference point is the interface between the ISDN PBX and the ISDN terminals. The R reference point is the connection between the terminal adapter and non-ISDN terminals. Many different kinds of interfaces will be used at point R.

5.8.3   ISDN Channels

The digital pipe between the provider's office and the ISDN subscriber will be used to carry a number of communication channels. The capacity of the pipe, and therefore the number of channels carried, may vary from user to user. The transmission structures are constructed from the following types of channels.

- A - 4 KHz analog telephone channel

- B - 64 Kbps digital PCM channel for voice or data

- C - 8 or 16 Kbps digital channel

- D - 16 or 64 Kbps digital channel for out-of-band signaling

- E - 64 Kbps digital channel for internal ISDN signaling

- H - 384, 1536, or 1920 Kbps digital channel

B-Channel: The B-channel is the basic user channel.   It can be used to carry data, digitized voice, or a mixture of lower-rate traffic including digital data and digitized voice encoded at a fraction of 64 Kbps.   In the case of mixed traffic, all traffic of the B-channel must be destined to the same end point; that is, the elemental unit of circuit switching is the B-channel.   If a B-channel consists of two or more subchannels, all subchannels must be carried over the same circuit between the same subscribers. Three kinds of connections can be setup over a B-channel:

- *Packet Switched:* The user is connected to a packet-switching mode and data are exchanged with other users via X.25.

- *Circuit Switched:* This connection is equivalent to switched digital service. The user places a call and a circuit-switched connection is established with another network user.

- *Semipermanent:* This connection to another user is setup by prior arrangement and does not require a call establishment protocol.

In addition to the above, the B-channel can also be used for facsimile and slow-scan video.

D-Channel: The D-channel serves two purposes. First it carries signaling information to a control circuit-switched call on associated B-channels at the user interface. The D-channel is used to setup calls on all of the B-channels at the customer's interface. This technique is known as "common channel signaling", as the D-channel is common for providing controls for all the other channels. This allows the other channels to be used more efficiently. Secondly, in addition to its use for control signaling, the D-channel may be used for packet switching or low-speed telemetry when no signaling information is waiting. The D-channel is divided into three logical subchannels: the *s-subchannel* for signaling (e.g., call setup), the *t-subchannel* for telemetry (e.g., smoke detectors) and the *p-subchannel* for low-bandwidth packet data.

H-Channel: The H-channel is provided for user information at higher bit-rates. The user may use such a channel as a high-speed trunk or may sub-divide the channel according to the user's own time division multiplexing (TDM) scheme. Examples of applications include fast facsimile, video high-speed data, high-quality audio, and multiplexed information streams at lower data rates.

5.8.4 Transmission Structures

The channel types are grouped into transmission structures that are offered as a package to the user.

Basic Access: Basic access consists of two full-duplex 64 Kbps B-channels and a full-duplex D-channel. The total bit-rate, by simple arithmetic, is 144 Kbps. However, framing synchronization and other overhead bits bring the total bit-rate on a basic access link to 192 Kbps. The basic service is intended to meet the services of most individual users. It allows the simultaneous use of voice and several data applications, such as packet-switched access, facsimile, and teletex. These services could be accessed through a multi-function terminal or several separate terminals. In either case, a single interface is provided. Most existing twisted-pair local loops can support this interface.

In some cases, one or both of the B-channels remain unused. This results in either a B + D or D interface. However, to simplify the network implementation, the data at the interface remains at 192 Kbps.

Primary Access: Primary access is intended for users with greater capacity requirements, such as offices with a digital PBX or a LAN. Because of differences in the digital transmission hierarchies used in different countries, it was not possible to get a single data rate. The United States, Canada, and Japan make use of a transmission structure based on 1.544 Mbps; this corresponds to the T1 transmission facility. In Europe, 2.048 Mbps is the standard rate. Both of these data rates are provided as a primary interface service. The channel structure for 1.544 Mbps is 23B + D, while that for the 2.048 Mbps is 30B + D. Again, it is possible for a customer with lesser requirements to employ fewer B-channels than provided. Also a customer with high-data rate requirements may be provided with more than one physical interface. In this, a single D-channel on one of the interfaces suffice for all signaling purposes and all other interfaces may consist solely of B-channels. The primary rate interface is intended for use at the T reference point for businesses with a PBX.

Hybrid Access: The Hybrid configuration is intended to allow ordinary analog telephones to be combined with a C-channel to produce something vaguely reminiscent of the basic rate.

5.8.5 Protocol Architecture

The development of standards for ISDN includes development of protocols for interaction between ISDN users and the network and for interaction between two ISDN users. To a great extent, these ISDN protocols have been fitted within the OSI framework. A subtle difference is to be noted at this point. While the term interface refers to the boundary between two layers in OSI , the ISDN interface in a CCITT sense refers to the peer protocols among the lower layers. Examples of these protocols are:

- *Multiple related protocols:* ISDN allows the use of a protocol on the D-channel to setup, maintain, and terminate a connection on a B-channel.

- *Multimedia calls:* ISDN allows a call to be setup that permits information flow consisting of multiple media types, such as voice, data, facsimile, and control signals.

- *Multipoint connections:* Conference calls.

As a network , ISDN is essentially unconcerned with user layers 4 through 7, which are end-to-end layers employed by the user for exchange of information. Network access is concerned with layers 1 through 3. The physical interface for basic access and primary access corresponds to the OSI layer 1. Above layer 1, the protocol structure differs for B- and D-channels.

For the D-channel, Link Access Procedure on D-channel (LAPD) is the data link layer standard. This standard is based on the high-level data link control (HDLC) modified to meet ISDN requirements. All transmission on the D-channel is in the form of LAPD frames that are exchanged between the user equipment and the ISDN switching element. This supports the three applications, namely control signaling, packet switching, and telemetry. For control signaling, a call control protocol has been defined at the network layer. This protocol establishes, maintains, and terminates connections on B-channels. To provide packet-switching services to the subscriber, X.25 level 3 protocol is used and X.25 packets are transmitted in LAPD frames.

The X.25 level 3 protocol is used to establish virtual circuits on the D-channels to other users and to exchange packetized data.

The B-channel, as mentioned earlier, offers circuit switching, packet-switching, and semipermanent circuit services. For circuit switching, a circuit is setup on a B-channel on demand using the D-channel protocols. The semipermanent circuit is a B-channel circuit that is set by a prior agreement between the connected users and the network. With either circuit-switched connections or semipermanent circuits, the connected stations 'experience' a direct full-duplex link with one another. In the case of packet-switching, a circuit-switched connection is setup on a B-channel between the user and a packet-switched node using the D-channel protocol. Once the circuit has been setup on the B-channel, the user employs X.25 layers 2 and 3 to establish a virtual circuit to another user over that channel and to exchange packetized data.

5.8.6   ISDN Operation

One of the distinguishing features of ISDN is that user information and signaling are kept logically separate. In ISDN parlance, the user information lies in the user-plane (U-plane) and the signaling lies in the control-plane (C-plane). ISDN is, in effect, composed of two subnets: a switched information subnet (above the dotted line in Fig. 5.10) and a signaling subnet (below the dotted line in Fig. 5.10). The signaling protocols are layered in accordance with the OSI reference model. There is a network layer call control protocol, specified in ITU-T standard Q.931, which defines the call control messages and procedures. There is also a link layer protocol defined in Q.921 which makes sure that the call control messages are reliably passed, without errors, between the terminal and the call control process in the serving local switch.

The basic call setup procedure is indicated in Fig. 5.11. As a development of PSTN, the ISDN is intrinsically circuit switched but for many data applications packet-switching is more appropriate. X.25, however, does not fit the ISDN model of keeping user information and signaling separate. Nor is it necessary to include X.25's heavyweight error correction protocols in the comparatively error-free digital environment. Frame Relay is designed to bridge this gap.

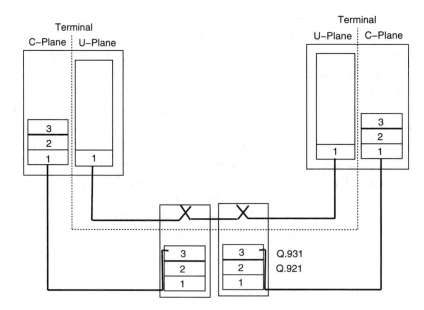

Fig. 5.10. ISDN - Separation of User and Signaling Information

5.9   Frame Relay

Frame Relay is a simple connection-oriented, virtual circuit packet service. Frame Relay provides both switched virtual connections (SVCs) and permanent virtual circuits (PVCs), and follows the ISDN principle of keeping user data and signaling information separate.

An ISDN Frame Relay SVC would be setup in exactly the same way as an ordinary circuit-mode connection using ISDN common-channel signaling protocols. The difference is that in the data transfer, or *conversation phase,* the user's information is switched through simple packet-switches (known as frame relays) as shown in Fig. 5.12, rather than circuit-mode cross-points.

From the user's point of view, Frame Relay is a multiplexed interface to a packet-switched network. This means that at the customer premises (the DTE interface), there is a single electrical interface but it gives the appearance to be many distinct interfaces to specific systems. As an interface between user and network equipment, Frame Relay provides a means for statistically multiplexing many logical data conversations (referred to as virtual circuits) over a single physical transmission link. The design approach of frame relay focuses on eliminating some of the problems of earlier protocols, such as X.25, in dealing with errors. The network switches performed error checking operations on all traffic. This included retransmissions in case of errors and messages to the user in the case of failed retransmission. The premise of Frame Relay is that modern communication systems, which are relatively error free, do not require the extensive and resource-consuming operations that are required of older networks for error correction. In the event that a rare error occurs, instead of tasking the network and network components with the correction, Frame Relay assumes that end-user machines will handle the detection and resolution of errors. The idea is to notify the user about actual or potential congestion problems, and for the user to respond accordingly. Frame Relay assumes that the user machine supports end-to-end acknowledgment of traffic, which in the past was the network's responsibility.

Frame Relay services provide *bandwidth on demand*. For example, a user may use 64 Kbps for an application at a given point in time and may use 128 Kbps for a different application at another instant. Frame Relay allows the user to obtain dynamic allocation of bandwidth capacity.

The main approaches used are:

- *Circuit-switching using TDM:* In the Time Division Multiplexing (TDM) approach, time slots are reserved for each user device. This method

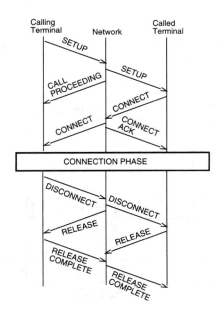

Fig. 5.11. Call Control using ISDN Signaling

is fast and uses no error checking. Consequently, it is well suited for voice and video traffic but not for bursty traffic, because resources are committed even during times when user data is not available.

- *Unchanelized T1:* This is a modification of the TDM approach that uses proprietary schemes for using traffic in a non-slotted manner.

- *Statistical time division multiplexing (STDM):* This corresponds to the X.25 standard. Here each user is identified by a logical channel number (LCN) and is provided with a virtual circuit to other users. The advantage of X.25 is that up to 4095 users can share an individual physical port.

Frame Relay is a compromise between circuit-switching and STDM. Frame Relay's statistical multiplexing provides more flexible and efficient utilization of available bandwidth. It can be used without TDM techniques, or on top of channels provided by TDM systems. Each user is assigned a LCN and provided with a Permanent Virtual Circuit (PVC) or a Switched Virtual Call (SVC). The Frame Relay identification tag is called a Data Link Connection Identifier (DLCI). The variable slots are ideally suited for bursty

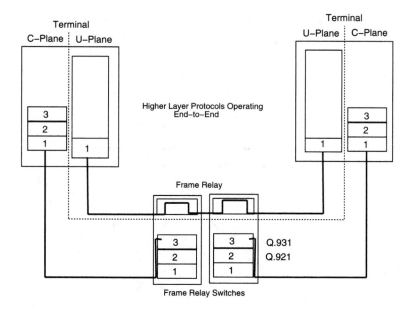

Fig. 5.12. Frame Relay as an ISDN Bearer Service

traffic, providing low delay and high throughput. Frame Relay is a product of the 'digital age', exploiting the much lower error rates and higher transmission speeds of modern digital systems. Frame Relay has its roots in the Integrated Digital Services Network (ISDN).

5.9.1 Frame Relay Data Transfer Protocol

In Frame Relay, information is transferred in variable-length frames. In addition to the user's information there is a header and a trailer, each of two octets. The header contains a ten-bit label agreed between the terminal and the network at call setup time (or at subscription time in case of a PVC) which uniquely identifies the virtual call. This label is known as the Data Link Connection Identifier (DLCI).

Terminals can support many simultaneous virtual calls to different destinations, or even a mixture of SVCs and PVCs, using the DLCI to identify which virtual connection each frame belongs to. DLCI values 16 to 991 are available to identify the SVCs and PVCs. Other DLCI values are reserved for specific purposes. For example, DLCI=0 is used to carry call-control signaling, and DLCIs 992 to 1007 are used to carry link-layer management information.

HDLC flags (the bit pattern 01111110) are used to indicate the beginning and end of each frame, and as interframe channel fill, with zero-bit insertion and deletion used to avoid flag simulation in the user information field. This is exactly as in X.25. The minimum amount of user information that a frame may contain is one octet, and the default maximum size of the information field is 260 octets. However, most implementations support up to 1600 octets to minimize the need to segment and reassemble LAN packets for transport over a Frame Relay network.

The trailer contains a two-octet Frame Check Sequence (FCS) calculated in the same way as for an X.25 frame.

A link layer protocol has been defined for frame mode bearer services. Usually referred to as LAPF or Q.922, it is based on Q.921 (the link layer protocol used to carry user signaling.) The data transfer protocol used in Frame Relaying is a (small) subset of LAPF, known as the data link core protocol.

The LAPF core protocol provides for the bi-directional transport of frames between terminals and preserves the frame sequence. It includes the detection of frame errors, but not error correction nor does the network operate flow control. It is left to the higher-layer protocols operating directly

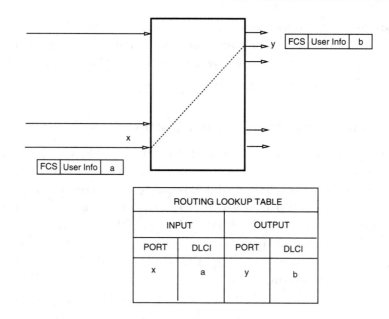

Fig. 5.13. Principle of Frame Relaying

between the terminals to look after error correction and flow control. There is thus very little processing of frames by the network nodes, and frames can pass through the network quickly and transparently.

Fig. 5.13 illustrates the principle of Frame Relaying. Consider that we have a Frame Relay terminal connected to port x and that we have a single virtual connection established. The DLCI is shown as a. The terminal sends a sequence of frames into the network. When the Frame Relay switch receives a frame, it does a few checks. First it looks for transmission errors using the 2-octet frame check sequence contained in the trailer. If the frame has any transmission errors, it is simply discarded. If not, a few other checks are done: is the frame too long? too short? has the DLCI=a been allocated? Again, if an error is found, the frame is simply discarded.

The Frame Relay switch then looks in the routing look-up table to see which outgoing link it must be transmitted on. Looking at the routing table for port x, the switch finds that frames with DLCI=a should be routed out on port y and should be given the new label DLCI=b on the outgoing link. Because the DLCI has changed, it is necessary to recalculate the frame check sequence.

At call setup time, entries in routing lookup tables were made in all Frame

Relay switches en route, exactly as shown. One of the merits of Frame Relay is that the two directions of transmission are treated independently and can be configured to have different throughput. Additional virtual connections would be assigned different DLCIs, and the switches would process and route them independently.

5.9.2 Frame Relay and Congestion

One of the greatest merits of a simple data transfer protocol is that it provides a high degree of transparency to the higher-layer protocols that are carried. This contrasts with X.25, where the scope for destructive interference with higher-layer protocols often causes problems and can seriously impair performance and throughput.

The absence of flow control leaves the network open to congestion. Congestion ultimately means throwing frames away. This causes higher-layer protocols to retransmit lost frames, which further feeds the congestion, leading to the possible collapse of the network. Congestion management is therefore an important issue to the network designer and network operator if these serious congestion effects are to be controlled and, preferably, avoided.

Congestion management includes dimensioning the network so that it can carry the expected traffic. It also includes implementing real-time controls in the network, which attempt to minimize the likelihood of congestion arising, recover gracefully from any congestion that does actually occur, and spread the effects of congestion fairly across all users. Congestion management is not standardized but is rather left to the network operators and differs from one network to another, depending on the capabilities and features designed into the switches, the network topology and dimensioning rules used, the services actually delivered to the users, and the control the network operator has over the Customer Premises Equipment.

Two of the bits in the frame header, the forward explicit congestion notification (FECN) and backward explicit congestion notification (BECN) bits, are used to carry congestion indications to user terminals. When the onset of congestion is detected by a Frame Relay switch (typically by a transmission queue length exceeding a preset threshold), it sets the FECN and BECN bits in the headers of all frames currently passing through the switch, which can then be used by higher-layer protocols to make the transmitting terminal reduce its sending rate (typically by reducing window size).

Alternatively, a congested switch can send congestion notification to switches at the edge of the network 'in bulk' using a consolidated link layer management (CLLM) message. The CLLM is sent on a Layer 2 management connection (DLCI = 1007) and contains a list of the DLCIs of virtual connections that are currently affected by congestion. The edge node can then take appropriate action to temporarily throttle the input of frames to the network, using either FECN/BECN or further CLLM messages to notify congestion to the relevant terminals.

In addition to these explicit indications of congestion the terminal can sense congestion from the loss of frames or a significant increase in cross-network delay. This is referred to as 'implicit' congestion notification.

In addition to the the explicit congestion notification bits, a third bit, designated the discard enable (DE) bit, can be set by the user or the network to indicate that the associated frame should, in the event of congestion, be discarded in preference to frames in which the DE bit is not set.

5.9.3   Quality of Service

The Frame Relay standards specify more than a dozen parameters which characterize service quality, some relating to the demand the user will place on the network, and others specifying the performance targets the network operator is expected to meet.

The key parameters that characterize the Frame Relay service are *committed information rate (CIR)*, sometimes also known as throughput, the *committed burst size (Bc)*, and the *excess burst size (Be)*, all defined in relation to an *averaging period Tc*, normally calculated as Bc/CIR. They are negotiated at call setup time in the SETUP message requesting the connection (or set at subscription time for a Permanent Virtual Circuit). The relationship between them is indicated in Fig. 5.14.

The precise meaning of these parameters is open to a bit of interpretation. *Bc* is usually regarded as the maximum amount of data the network is prepared to accept during *Tc* with any real guarantee of delivery; *CIR* is the corresponding data rate. *Be* is usually taken to indicate the maximum amount of data during an interval *Tc*, over and above *Bc*, that the network will accept; this 'excess' data is usually carried on a 'best efforts' basis.

These service parameters are policed at the point of entry to the network, and they can be set independently for each direction of transmission to cater efficiently for applications that send more information in one direction than the other, such as interactive screen-based applications.

In the 'guaranteed' region, the network operator aims to offer a high-level of assurance that frames will be delivered and dimensions the network accordingly. In the 'discard eligible' region, the network will accept the traffic but set the DE bit; in the event that congestion is encountered, this frame will be discarded before frames in which the DE bit is not set. In the 'discard on entry' region, the frames are discarded on entry as a means of protecting the network from traffic levels likely to cause congestion.

In practice, *CIR* on a 2048 Kbps access circuit would typically be selectable up to a maximum of 1024 Kbps for each virtual circuit in steps of 16 Kbps.

5.9.4   Frame Relay Data Transmission Service

Frame Relay services can be broadly classified into two kinds:

- ISDN-based services where Frame Relay acts as an ISDN bearer service (I.233).

- Non-ISDN services.

The Non-ISDN services, which were the original use for which Frame Relays were envisaged, are known as the Frame Relay Data Transmission Service, (also referred to as X.36). In these services, the ISDN dependencies

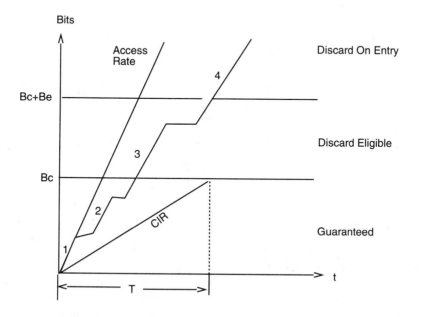

Fig. 5.14. Frame Relay - QoS Parameters

have been removed. With the profusion of high-speed LANs such as the Ethernet, Frame Relays were designed for the interconnection of LANs over public high-speed data networks.

Using Frame Relays to interconnect the LANs of a corporation can provide complete any-to-any connectivity through a single access circuit, using multiple Virtual Circuits. This greatly reduces the physical complexity of the routers. For example, consider the internetworking of LANs as in Fig. 5.15, which shows that LANs at four different locations are intercon-

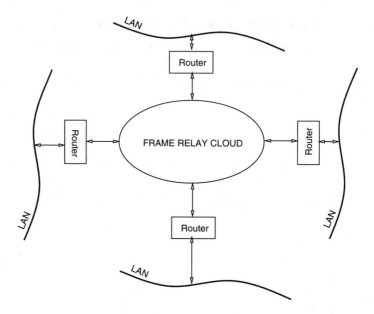

Fig. 5.15. Internetworking using Frame Relays

nected through the Frame Relay interface at each site, thereby enabling a number of simultaneous connections between them. In the same situation, leased lines cannot provide complete any-to-any connectivity. Also, while using Frame Relays, each router need to have only one access link. It is also possible to carry multiple LAN protocols over Frame Relay.

5.10   Era of High-Speed Networking

Due to the increased demand for communication services of all kinds (e.g., audio, video, and data), Broadband Integrated Services Digital Network (B-ISDN) has become necessary. The existing telecommunication networks, whether circuit switched or packet switched, are oriented towards particular applications. Thus, we have different networks for different media such as audio, video, and data applications operating in parallel and independently. While each of these networks is suitable for the application it is designed for, they are not very efficient for supporting other applications. The advantages of an integrated communication system which can accommodate diverse services with varying bandwidth requirements, has been recognized for a long time. The performance requirements for one service, such as data transfer, turns out to be different from that of another service such as audio transfer. Data transfer is bursty, loss sensitive, and delay insensitive. On the other hand, audio is continuous, delay sensitive, and limited-loss insensitive. The concept of ISDN was to have a single network catering to the demands of data as well as audio. With the advent of multimedia applications, high-resolution video is also a potential candidate for transfer over computer networks. ISDN was extended to B-ISDN, which caters to the demand of audio, video, and data transfer [35]. Foreseeable multimedia applications include video telephony, video conferencing, and multimedia mail. The bandwidth needed for these applications are of the order of hundreds of Mbps. These applications are also characterized by low delay requirements and bursty nature.

The industry is investigating fiber-optic cross-country links with gigabit per second speeds, and would like to carry digital information in an integrated way. Both real-time traffic such as audio and high-resolution video (which can tolerate some loss but not delay), as well as non-real-time traffic such as computer data or file transfer (which may be able to tolerate some delay but not loss), are being considered. The emerging multimedia networks are envisioned to carry traffic from a wide range of services catering to different media, which have diverse traffic flow characteristics and performance requirements [32, 33, 34].

The problem with carrying traffic with different characteristics on the same carrier in an integrated fashion is that the peak bandwidth requirement of some of these traffic sources may be quite high, but the duration for which the data is actually transmitted may be quite small. In other words, the data comes in bursts and must be transmitted at the peak rate of the burst, but the average arrival time between bursts may be quite large. The traffic characteristics of multimedia traffic are shown in Fig. 5.16. For such bursty connections, it would be a considerable waste of bandwidth to reserve time slots to cater to their peak bandwidth rate for all times, while on the average only 1 in 10 time slots may actually get used. It would be nice if these available time slots could be used for another pending connection. Synchronous mode of transfer becomes inefficient as the peak bandwidth of the link, peak transfer rate of the traffic, and overall burstiness of the traffic expressed as a ratio of peak/average go up. Asynchronous Transfer Mode (ATM) was conceived to overcome this inefficiency. At present, Fast Ethernet (100 Mbps) at LAN level and ATM at LAN as well as WAN levels seem to hold promise for the future. It must also be noted that there are other developments such as ISO Ethernet and 100 VG AnyLan, which are attracting the attention of the researchers and developers all over the world over.

5.11   Fast Ethernet

The Fast Ethernet is a new IEEE Local Area Network standard completed in 1995 by the IEEE 802.3 Working Group that produced the original Ethernet specifications. Fast Ethernet is officially known as 100Base-T. Fast Ethernet runs at 100 Mbps, supports star topology (as opposed to the bus topology of the earlier Ethernet), runs on twisted pairs (Unshielded or Shielded, called

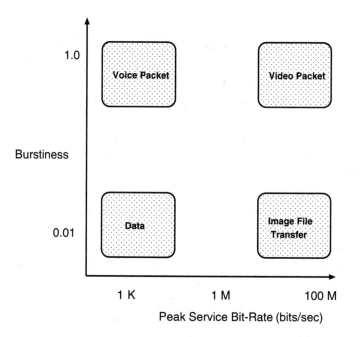

Fig. 5.16. Multimedia Traffic Characteristics

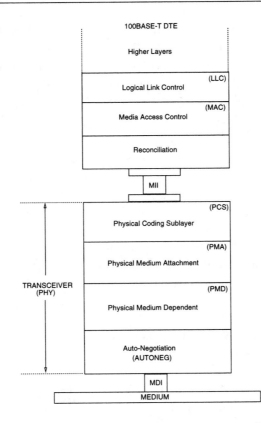

Fig. 5.17. Fast Ethernet Protocol Architecture

UTP or STP) and fiber, has a collision diameter of 412 meters (as opposed to the 300 meters of the original Ethernet), operates on full-duplex mode, and supports a link distance of 100 meters. A significant enhancement is that the AUI (Attachment Unit Interface) is replaced by the Media Independent Interface (MII). The architecture of the Fast Ethernet is illustrated in Fig. 5.17.

5.12 ISO-Ethernet

ISO-Ethernet means Isochronous Ethernet, and it is an attempt at defining a multimedia workstation. It can be described as time division multiplexing of pure 10 Mbps Ethernet and multiple ISDN channels totaling to an aggregate capacity of 6.144 Mbps (which is equivalent to 4 T1s or 3 E1s[11]).

---

[11]E1 is a 2 Mbps line equivalent of T1 in Europe.

ISO-Ethernet is a standard adopted by the IEEE 802.9 Working Group. ISO-Ethernet integrates traditional Ethernet with wide area switched digital services. It is suited for organizations whose local area networks and ISDN terminals in different locations are interconnected using public switched data communications (such as ISDN, T1 switched, or T1 leased) and where the traffic between the LANs are heavy. The official name of the standard is IEEE Std 802.9a.

ISO-Ethernet has three components:

- A new ISO-Ethernet signaling standard that mixes 10 Mbps Ethernet and the equivalent of 48 bi-directional ISDN B-channels into a single cable.

- New clients that combine Ethernet-style data with ISDN isochronous voice, video, and data communications.

- New hubs that perform the combined functions of an Ethernet hub and a digital PBX. Digital PBX is the digital version of the analog telephone exchange.

Typical ISO-Ethernet architecture is illustrated in Fig. 5.18. The ISO-Ethernet standard simultaneously conveys two types of data: one that is 10 Mbps with collision detection completely analogous to 10Base-T, and the other equivalent as 48 isochronous 64 Kbps ISDN B-channels in each direction. Both these data types can be mixed onto a common signaling interface. An 802.9a link supports both Ethernet and ISDN simultaneously at both ends. The standard supports Auto-Negotiation, which can be used to connect an 802.9a device to a pure 10base-T interface, when necessary.

The goal of 802.9a is to ultimately integrate voice, video, and data services into common desktop platforms using common available switching hardware.

5.13   100VG AnyLan

100VG AnyLan is a standard adopted by the IEEE 802.12 Committee for supporting *Demand-Priority Access Method* on LANs. It connects both Ethernet and Token Ring stations. Contrary to the normal belief, 100VG Any-Lan is not a LAN architecture; it is a circuit-switched architecture. The key concepts of 100VG AnyLan are:

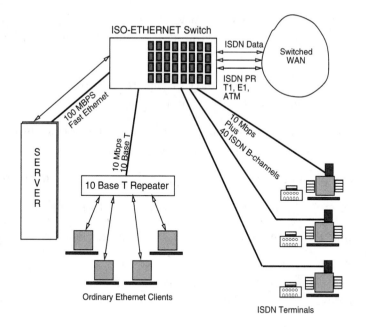

Fig. 5.18. ISO-Ethernet Architecture

- Each station is connected in a star pattern to a fast circuit-switching hub.

- Multiple-pair (four twisted pairs) UTP cables run from the hub to each workstation, each at 25 Mbps, thus delivering an aggregate of 100 Mbps. During control and signaling, two pairs are used in each direction so there is a full-duplex path available from workstation to hub. During the data transfer phase, all four pairs are used in one direction, essentially in a half-duplex mode.

- The LAN frame formats (either Ethernet or Token Ring) are preserved. Only the MAC part changes. There is no mapping between Ethernet headers and Token Ring headers, so stations in the two networks cannot communicate, although they are in a common 100VG AnyLan.

The protocol operates as follows:

1. When a station wants to transmit, it places a REQUEST condition onto its link. The REQUEST condition is a repetition of a simple 16-bit pattern endlessly.

2. When the hub decides to service the station, it signals the station to start transmission. At this point, the hub has no knowledge of the destination.

3. The hub receives the first part of the frame into an elastic buffer and determines the destination station.

4. The hub signals the destination station that data is about to arrive, using another 16-bit pattern endlessly.

5. The destination station signals the hub that it is ready to receive.

6. During steps 3, 4, and 5, the hub continues to receive data.

7. The hub commences the transmission to the destination on all four pairs.

8. Both stations and the hub go back to idle, when the transmission completes.

The advantages of 100VG AnyLan are that there are no collisions, as the hub controls which station sends at any time. Stations can be assigned priority, and access delays can be controlled deterministically. That is why the standard is called the Demand-Priority Access Method. The performance problems due to propagation delays can be controlled by limiting the distance between the hub and the stations, but the hub can turn out to be bottleneck.

5.14   Synchronous versus Asynchronous Transfer

The *Asynchronous Transfer Mode (ATM)* [11, 12] was chosen as the multiplexing and switching technique for B-ISDN. The term *asynchronous* in this context pertains to the multiplexed transmission of cells, a unit of data bytes. In ATM terminology, fixed-size packets are called *cells*. Cells allocated to a particular connection may exhibit an irregular recurrence pattern as they are filled according to actual demand. *Synchronous Transfer Mode (STM)* is used by telecommunication networks to transfer packetized voice and data across long distances. It is a circuit-switched networking mechanism, where a connection is established between two end points before data transfer commences, and is torn down when the two end points have completed their transfer. Thus, the end points allocate the connection bandwidth for the entire duration, even when they are not actually transmitting the data. Data

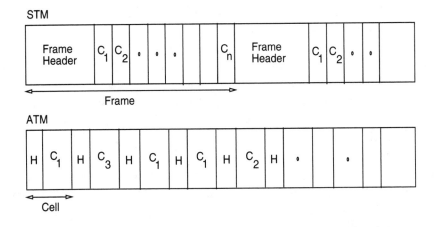

Fig. 5.19. Transmission Cycles of STM versus ATM

are transported across an STM network by dividing the bandwidth of the STM links into a fundamental unit of transmission called *time slots*. These time slots are organized into a cycle containing a fixed number of time slots and are labeled from 1 to N. The cycle repeats periodically every T time period, with the time slots in the cycle always in the same position with the same label. There can be up to M different cycles labeled from 1 to M, all repeating with the time period T, and all arriving within the time period T. The parameters N, T, and M are determined by standards committees, and are different for Europe and America. Fig. 5.19 depicts the transmission cycle for a STM network with N = n and M = 1.

On a given STM link, a connection between two end points is assigned a fixed time slot number between 1 and N, on a fixed cycle between 1 and M, and data from that connection are always carried in that time slot number on the assigned cycle. If there are intermediate nodes, it is possible that a different time slot number on a different cycle is assigned on each STM link in the route for that connection. However, there is always one known time slot reserved *a priori* on each link throughout the route. In other words, once a time slot is assigned to a connection, it remains allocated for that connection's sole use throughout the lifetime of that connection. The disadvantage of the STM technique is that the number of connections that can be simultaneously supported is given by the number $N \times M$. Furthermore, when some of the stations which have reserved the bandwidth are not using the same one at some time, that bandwidth (or time slot) is wasted. This is the main drawback with the STM network, and motivated the development of statistical time multiplexing which overcomes this wastage and ATM is the technology based on the concept of statistical multiplexing.

Statistical multiplexing is the most common scheme for multiplexing information in a channel. Here, the packets of all traffic streams are merged into a single queue and transmitted on a first-come/first-serve basis. It can be proved analytically that the statistical multiplexing scheme has a smaller average delay per packet than either TDM[12] (STM) or FDM[13]. The physical link is multiplexed among the logical links (virtual channels) on a demand basis [13]. If a large number of sources are very bursty, all of them may still be assigned to the same link in the hope that statistically the bursts will not occur at the same time. If some of them do burst simultaneously, the burst can be buffered up and put in subsequently available free time slots. Statistical multiplexing allows the sum of the peak bandwidth requirement of all connections on a link to exceed the aggregate available bandwidth of the link under certain conditions of discipline. This was impossible on an STM network, and it is the main distinction of an ATM network.

5.14.1 Why Asynchronous Transfer Mode for Multimedia?

To support packet-switching function at very high-speeds, hardware solutions are mandatory. Since fixed-sized cells are easier to handle than variable-sized cells, the ATM technique has emerged as a leading contender for high-speed packet switching. ATM is a switching and multiplexing technique which is totally independent of the underlying transmission technology and the transmission medium. The main idea is to carry the *connection identifier* along with the data in every time slot, and keep the size of the time slot small enough so that if data in a time slot gets dropped en route due to congestion, the loss is minimized. The fixed size of the cells arose out of the motivation from the telecommunications companies to sustain the same transmitted voice quality as in STM networks, in spite of losing some cells on ATM networks. Fig. 5.19 also depicts the transmission cycle for an ATM network wherein the reader can see the demand-based assignment for source c1. The performance expected of an ATM network by the multimedia services are shown in Fig. 5.20. At one extreme, the *compressed video* is loss sensitive and delay sensitive and at the other extreme, *data* is loss insensitive and delay insensitive. The term *insensitive* in this context has to be understood as recovery being available at the application level.

---

[12]Time Division Multiplexing.
[13]Frequency Division Multiplexing.

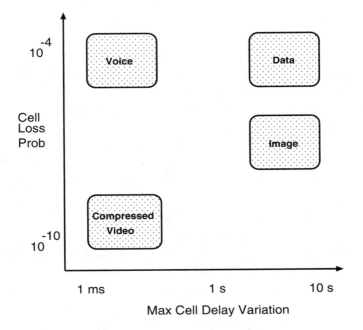

Fig. 5.20. Performance Requirements in an ATM Context

5.14.2 A Word on Modern Traffic

Multimedia applications require that the data be received *on time*. A traditional application such as telnet or ftp might slow down when the traffic is heavy, but a video conference may have to be abandoned if the images of the persons involved in the conference are not received on time! Timely delivery is an important concern of a network supporting multimedia applications. Therefore, the network service provider has to give an assurance to all the clients using multimedia applications that a certain Quality of Service will be guaranteed for the application. In general, two different types of traffic go through a computer network: Elastic Traffic and Real-Time Traffic.

Elastic traffic is nothing more than traditional best-effort message delivery, which has been the basis of datagram and internetworking. This traffic is characterized as 'elastic' because it adapts to changing network conditions without losing its usefulness. For example, a traditional file transfer protocol tacitly assumes that the file being downloaded does not change frequently with time. So the usefulness of the downloaded file is independent of the time it takes to download it. It must be noted that there are interactive applications that are elastic, e.g., telnet. A telnet session may be extremely slow, but the usefulness of the session is independent of the time it takes to complete the session.

Real-time traffic contrasts markedly with elastic traffic. It primarily supports applications, such as audio and video, that have traditionally used dedicated bandwidth that is often circuit-switched. Such traffic has some ability to adapt to network conditions, but only within narrow parameters. For example, one may stretch silent periods in an audio transmission without impact on intelligibility, but stretched syllables and dropped phonemes can change the meanings of words. Similarly, the network may delay video traffic a certain amount, but if delayed beyond that point the frame content becomes useless - the next frame then turns out to be the frame of interest. An interesting aspect of real-time traffic routing is that if the network has too much load, it is probably more efficient to drop those frames that could not be delivered on time rather than deliver them after they have become useless. This type of service is called 'predictive service'. When providing predictive service, the network seeks to forward the traffic without loss but drops any traffic not forwarded within the delay bounds. The obvious example of this kind of traffic is 'freeze frame' video or lower-quality audio. If such a dropping of frames is not permitted, the type of service is called 'guaranteed service'.

As real-time traffic has to be transported within certain time bounds, the traditional best-effort delivery system has to be modified to include the notion of Quality of Service (QoS). In other words, the network should assure some QoS to the application.

5.15 Asynchronous Transfer Mode (ATM) Network

ATM is designed for switching small fixed-length cells in hardware over gitabit/sec links across very large distances [14, 15]. Thus, its place in the protocol stack concept is somewhere around the data link layer. However, it does not cleanly fit in the OSI layered model, because within the ATM network itself end-to-end connection, flow control, and routing are all done at the ATM layer. So there are a few aspects of traditional higher-layer functions present in it. What is perhaps more relevant is how all this will interact with current networks, and with applications which want to use the ATM services directly. A convenient model for an ATM interface is to consider it as another communications port in the system. Thus, from a system software point of view, it can be treated like any other data link layer port. For instance, in IP networks connected via gateways to ATM backbones,

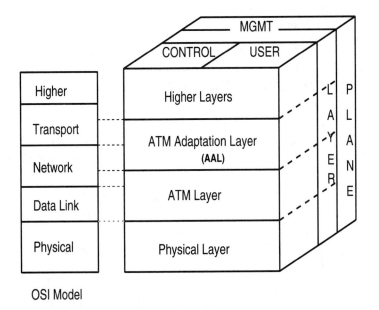

Fig. 5.21. Protocol Reference Model for the ATM Network

the model would be no different than it presently is for a virtual circuit connection carried over an STM link except that an IP packet over an ATM network would get fragmented into cells at the transmitting User Network Interface (UNI) and reassembled into the IP packet at the destination UNI [16].

5.15.1 ATM Protocol Architecture

The protocol architecture of ATM and its comparison to OSI are shown in Fig. 5.21. Interestingly enough, ATM has two dimensional hierarchies: one for the protocols, (similar to OSI), and the other for management. The management part is divided into three planes: *user, control, and management.* The User plane is concerned with functions such as transfer of user information, flow control, and recovery from error. The Control plane deals with signaling aspects, call control, connection control, and other aspects pertaining to connection establishment and connection release. The Management plane is divided into two subplanes - plane management and layer management. Plane management defines management functions relating to the whole system. Layer management is responsible for operation and maintenance at each layer.

5.15.2 ATM Physical Layer

The ATM physical layer is divided into two sublayers - Physical Medium sublayer (PM) and Transmission Convergence sublayer (TC).

Physical Medium sublayer: The physical medium sublayer includes only physical-medium-dependent functions. It provides bit transmission capability including bit alignment, line coding, and electrical/optical conversion. The functions of bit timing (generation and extraction of waveforms which are suitable for the medium) and insertion and extraction of bit timing information are the additional responsibilities.

Transmission Convergence sublayer: Transmission frame adaptation function is responsible for adapting the cell flow according to the payload structure of the transmission system. In the receiving process, this amounts to extracting the cell flow from the received information. The transmission frame may be cell equivalent or SDH (Synchronous Digital Hierarchy) equivalent. ITU-T recommendations specify for *SDH-based interfaces* at two speeds - one at 155.52 Mbps and the other at 622.08 Mbps (4×155.52). The *cell-based interface* consists of a continuous stream of cells, each of length 53 bytes. Physical layer operation and management information is conveyed in specific OAM cells, which are identified using specific bit patterns. One way to generate these OAM cells is to automatically generate an ATM OAM cell after every 26 normal cells. The other mechanism is to insert OAM cells on demand.

Cell delineation: Cell delineation is a mechanism to recover the cell boundaries. To protect the cell delineation from malicious attacks, the cell information is encoded before transmission and decoded on reception. Fig. 5.22 shows the finite state diagram of the cell delineation process.

Header error control generation/verification: Checksum is computed for the first four octets of the header at the sending side and is appended as the fifth octet. It is checked at the receiver, and the cell is accepted or discarded based on the outcome of the above check.

Cell rate decoupling: In the sending direction, the cell rate decoupling mechanism inserts idle cells in order to adapt the rate of ATM cells to the payload capacity of the transmission system. In the receiving side, this mechanism suppresses all the idle cells. The bit pattern that is followed for idle cells is 01101010

The physical layer specification is not explicitly a part of the ATM definition. The T1S1 (ANSI committee) standardized SONET as the preferred physical layer, and the STS classifications refer to the speeds of the SONET

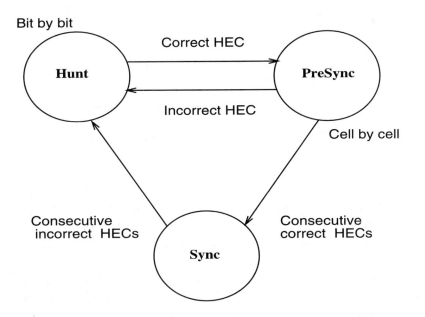

Fig. 5.22. Finite State Diagram of the Cell Delineation Process

link. STS-3c is 155.5 Mbit/sec. STS-12 is 622 Mbit/sec, and STS-48 is 2.4 Gbit/sec. It standardizes transmission around the bit-rate of 51.84 Mbit/sec, which is also called STS-1, and multiples of this bit-rate comprise higher bit rate streams. Thus, STS-3 is 3 times STS-1, STS-12 is 12 times STS-1, and so on. STS-3c is of particular interest as this is the lowest bit-rate expected to carry the ATM traffic, and is also referred to as STM-1 (Synchronous Transport Module-Level 1).

The SDH specifies how payload data is framed and transported syn-chronously across fiber-optic transmission links without requiring all the links and nodes to have the same synchronized clock for data transmis-sion and recovery (i.e., both the clock frequency and phase are allowed to have variations or be plesiochronous). The intention being that products from multiple vendors (across geographical and administrative boundaries) should be able to plug-and-play in a standard way, and hence B-ISDN can be called a true international network. The fundamental clock frequency around which the SDH or SONET framing is done is 8 Khz or 125 μsec.

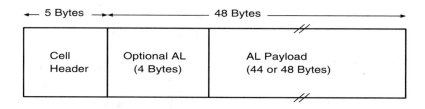

Fig. 5.23. Format of an ATM Cell

5.15.3 ATM Layer

An ATM cell, as specified by the T1S1 subcommittee, consists of 53 bytes. Five bytes comprise the header, and 48 bytes are payload. The format of the ATM cell is as shown in Fig. 5.23. The contents of the header are shown in Fig. 5.24.

A user basically interacts with well-defined and well-controlled interfaces called *User Network Interfaces (UNI)*, and sends data into the network based on certain agreed-upon requirements that are specified to the network at the connection setup time. The network will then try to ensure that the connection guarantees these requirements, and that the quality of service parameters for that connection remain satisfied for the entire duration of the connection. Typically, an ATM network will require a network management

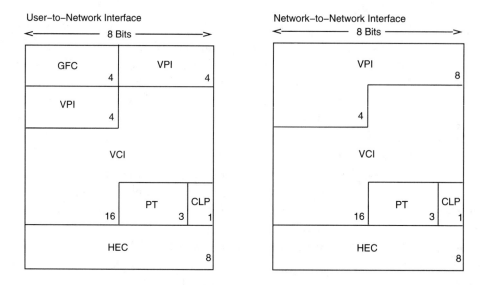

Fig. 5.24. Format of an ATM Cell Header

agent or proxy to be running as every UNI communicates and exchanges administrative messages with the user attachments at the UNI for connection setup, connection release, and flow control of the payload using some standard signaling protocol.

Payload Type (PT) field in the header is used for identifying the contents of the payload. If it is 00, it indicates user information. ATM cells can be lost from time to time due to buffer overflows, physical layer impairments, or errors in the cell routing field. *Cell Loss Priority (CLP)* field is used to tag a priority with the cells. If it is 1, then the cell can be discarded. If CLP is 0 (high priority), then the network has to take care of this cell so that it is not lost. Synchronization cells belonging to CBR[14] traffic will generally have a CLP bit set to 0. At the switching nodes, a small portion of the buffer area can be reserved for high-priority cells and the rest to low-priority cells [17, 18].

The 48 bytes of payload may optionally contain a 4-byte ATM adaptation layer and 44 bytes of actual data, or all 48 bytes may be data. The actual length of the payload may be deduced from the VCI or VPI identifier. This enables fragmentation and reassembly of cells into larger packets at the source and destination, respectively. The control field may also contain a bit to specify whether this is a flow control cell or an ordinary cell as indicated by the GFC (Generic Flow Control) bits.

ATM is a connection-oriented protocol and, as such, VCI/VPI is a connection identifier in every cell header which explicitly associates a cell with a given virtual channel on a physical link. The connection identifier consists of two subfields: the Virtual Channel Identifier (VCI) and the Virtual Path Identifier (VPI). Together they are used in multiplexing, switching, and demultiplexing a cell through the network. VCIs and VPIs are not addresses. They are explicitly assigned at each segment (link between ATM nodes) of a connection when a connection is established, and remain for the duration of the connection. Using the VCI/VPI, the ATM layer can asynchronously interleave (multiplex) cells from multiple connections [19].

Let us look at the need for two connection identifiers; viz., VCI and VPI. The Virtual Path concept originated with concerns over the cost of controlling B-ISDN networks. The idea was to group connections sharing common paths through the network into identifiable units (paths). Network management actions would then be applied to the smaller number of groups of connections (paths) instead of a larger number of individual connections

---

[14]Constant Bit-Rate traffic, typical of audio and video.

(VCI). Management here includes call setup, routing, failure management, bandwidth allocation, etc. For example, use of Virtual Paths in an ATM network reduces the load on the control mechanisms because the functions needed to setup a path through the network are performed only once for all subsequent Virtual Channels using that path. Changing the path mapping of a single Virtual Path can effect a route change for every Virtual Channel using that path.

There is no end-to-end reliable delivery service at the ATM layer. However, QoS can be built at this level as is done in the existing provision of CBR and VBR [15] services. The ATM layer does not do any retransmissions and there are no end-to-end acknowledgments for what has been received. Reliable delivery service can be implemented as a layer on top of the basic connection-oriented ATM layer, where acknowledgment of received data and retransmission of missing data can be done for connections requiring reliable delivery.

Functions of the ATM layer are as follows:

- *Cell multiplex and demultiplex*
  In the transmit direction, cells from different streams (different VP's and VC's) are multiplexed into one resulting stream by the cell multiplexing function. At the receiving side, the cell demultiplexing function splits the arriving cell stream into individual cell flows appropriate to VP's and VC's.

- *Cell VPI/VCI translation*
  At the intermediate switches or nodes, the values of VPI and VCI are translated. At the VP switches, the incoming VP value is changed to an outgoing VP value. At the VC switches, both the VP and VC value are changed.

- *Cell header generation/extraction*
  In the transmit direction, after receiving the cell information field from the AAL (ATM Adaptation Layer, on top of the ATM Layer), the cell header generation adds appropriate cell headers except for the HEC. VPI/VCI could be obtained from the translation of a Service Access Point (SAP) identifier. At the receiving side, the cell header extraction takes place and the AAL payload alone is passed to the AAL layer. Also, the VPI/VCI value can be changed into a SAP identifier.

---

[15]Variable Bit Rate.

- *Flow control in ATM*

    Unlike the reactive end-to-end flow control mechanisms of TCP in internetworking, the gigabits-per-second capacity of the ATM network generates a different set of requirements for flow control. If flow control was based on end-to-end feedback, then by the time the flow control message was received at the source, the source would have already transmitted over several million bytes of data into the ATM pipe, worsening the congestion. By the time the source reacted to the flow control message, the congestion condition might have disappeared altogether, unnecessarily throttling the source. The time constant of end-to-end feedback in ATM networks (actually feedback_delay x link_bandwidth product) may be so large that solely relying on the user attachments to keep up with the dynamics of the network is impractical. The congestion conditions in ATM networks are expected to be extremely dynamic, requiring fast hardware mechanisms for relaxing the network to steady state and necessitating the network itself to be actively involved in quickly achieving this steady state. Thus, a simplistic approach of end-to-end closed loop reactive control to congestion conditions is not considered suitable for ATM networks. The actual method is not yet standardized.

The ATM standards specify that all ATM cells be *delivered in order*. Any switch and adaptation equipment design must take this into consideration. An ATM cell may encounter congestion and suffer variable delay due to buffering within the ATM switches, and may even be dropped either due to congestion control or header checksum error. However, in an ATM connection, the cells belonging to a particular connection (i.e., cells with the same VCI label) arrive in order at the destination. This is so because there is no store and forwarding in the network, cells travel over a single virtual circuit path, the ATM switches do not switch the cells in the same VCI out of order, and no retransmission is done at any point in the ATM network.

Connectionless services are also supported on ATM networks, but these are implemented as a higher-layer service layered over the ATM layer. Thus, cells in a connectionless service may arrive out-of-order because there might be multiple VCIs over multiple paths setup to deliver the connectionless datagrams and cells may arrive over different paths in different order. Thus, the fragmentation and reassembly mechanism which implements the connectionless datagrams, and which is layered on top of the basic connection-oriented service of the ATM layer, must carry sequence numbers in the adap-

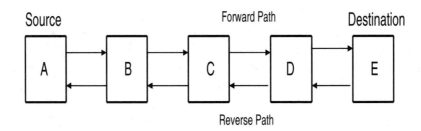

Fig. 5.25. An Illustration of a Connection Setup

tation layer in each cell and correct any reordering of the cells at reassembly time.

5.15.4 Connections using an ATM Network

As in STM networks, where a packet may undergo a time slot interchange between two intermediate nodes in a route, the VCI label in an ATM cell may also undergo a VCI label interchange at intermediate nodes in the route. Otherwise, the connections in the ATM network look similar to that of STM networks.

Consider a set of five nodes connected as shown in Fig. 5.25. Each node has a 4 tuple <InLink, InVCI, OutLink, OutVCI> defined in a routing table. Before transferring data, a connection must be established between source and destination and QoS parameters negotiated with the network. Initially when A is trying to establish connection with E, it sends a control cell to B, using some routing strategy, indicating the buffer requirements and other QoS parameters. A has a tuple like <0, 3, 1, ?> which means that InLink and OutLink are known. A has the input VCI as 3. It will get transformed into an OutVCI. The OutVCI will correspond to InVCI of node B. This information will enter in A's table in the reverse path of connection establishment. When this cell comes to B, B enters in its internal table a tuple having InLink, OutLink, and InVCI. OutVCI will be left empty. This process goes on until the cell reaches E, where OutVCI will be empty. At all these intermediate nodes, buffers are reserved at minimum/average level and other QoS parameters are negotiated. If any of the nodes cannot provide the required QoS, the connection is rejected. The InVCI of E is passed back to D, which updates its table. (OutVCI of D is InVCI of E). Also, the results of QoS negotiation at E is passed to D. Thus, the information flows from downstream nodes to upstream nodes until it reaches A.

5.15.5   ATM Adaptation Layer

The ATM Adaptation Layer (AAL) is between the ATM layer and the higher-layers. Its basic function is the enhanced adaptation of the services provided by the ATM layer to the requirements of the higher-layer. The functions performed by AAL are:

- Segmentation and reassembly of packets

- Handling of cell delay variation

- Handling of lost and misinserted cells

- Source clock frequency recovery at the receiver

- Monitoring of the AAL protocol control unit for bit errors as well as handling them

- Monitoring of the user information field for bit errors and possible corrective actions

ATM Adaptation Layer is divided into two sublayers:

1. *Segmentation and Reassembly (SAR) sublayer:* The essential functions of the SAR sublayer at the transmitting side is the segmentation of higher-layer PDU's into a suitable size for the information field of the ATM cell (48 bytes) and at the receiving side is reassembly of the ATM cells into suitable higher-level PDU's.

2. *Convergence sublayer (CS):* In order for ATM to support many kinds of services with different traffic characteristics and system requirements, it is necessary to adapt the different classes of applications to the ATM layer. This function is performed by the AAL CS, which is service dependent.

Four types of AAL were originally recommended by CCITT as shown in Fig. 5.26. Two of these have now been merged into one. Later, a fifth type of AAL will be added.

AAL1 Supports connection-oriented services that require constant bit-rates and have specific timing and delay requirements. A typical example is constant bit-rate services like audio streams.

Service Classes

	Class A	Class B	Class C	Class D
Timing Relation between Source & Destination	Required		Not Required	
Bit Rate	Constant	Variable		
Connection Mode	Connection Oriented			Connection less
AAL Types	AAL1	AAL2	AAL 3/4, 5	AAL 3/4

Fig. 5.26. AAL Classification by CCITT

AAL2 Supports connection-oriented services that do not require constant bit-rates. In other words, variable bit-rate applications like some video streams.

AAL3/4 This AAL is intended for both connectionless and connection-oriented variable bit-rate services. Originally two distinct adaptation layers AAL3 and 4, they have now been merged into a single AAL named AAL3/4 for historical reasons.

AAL5 Supports connection-oriented variable bit-rate data services. It is a substantially leaner AAL compared with AAL3/4, at the expense of error recovery and built-in retransmission. This trade-off provides a smaller bandwidth overhead, simpler processing requirements, and reduced implementation complexity. Some organizations have proposed AAL5 for use with both connection-oriented and connectionless services.

AAL is organized around a concept called service classes. The purpose of this classification is to convert and aggregate different traffic into standard formats to support different user applications. The classes are explained below:

- *Class A:* Constant Bit-Rate (CBR), Connection-oriented, Timing relationship between source and destination is required, e.g., CBR for video.

- *Class B:* Variable Bit-Rate (VBR), Connection-oriented, Timing relationship between source and destination is required, e.g., VBR for video and voice.

- *Class C:* Variable Bit-Rate (VBR), Connection-oriented, Timing relationship between source and destination is not required, e.g., Bursty data services.

- *Class D:* Variable Bit-Rate (VBR), Connectionless, Timing relationship between source and destination is not required, e.g., Bursty datagram services.

- *Class X:* Traffic type and timing requirements are defined by the user (unrestricted).

At the moment, the following mapping between AAL's and classes applies:

Class A: AAL 1
Class B: AAL 2
Class C: AAL 3/4
Class D: AAL 5

AAL1 SAR Protocol Data Unit (PDU) consists of 48 bytes. It has a 4-bit sequence number, a 4-bit sequence number protection, and data payload. The sequence number makes it possible to detect the loss or misinserted cells. The functions performed by the convergence sublayer include forward error correction of data, clock recovery by monitoring buffer filling, and handling of lost/misinserted of cells. The user plane of AAL1 will exchange information with the control plane and the management plane. The following information is transferred to the management plane:

- Errors in the transmission of user information

- Cells which have been lost

- Received AAL protocol control information is not correct

- Timing/sync information is not correct

AAL2 is used for VBR services with a timing relation between the source and destination. AAL payload consists of sequence number, information type, length of payload, and CRC. SAR accepts CS-PDU's with variable length and it may be that a SAR PDU cannot be fully filled. The CS may perform clock recovery for VBR audio and video services. This can be achieved by the insertion of a time stamp or a real-time synchronization word in the CS PDU. The handling of lost or misinserted cells is also performed by the CS. If necessary, this sublayer may also provide forward error correction capabilities for audio and video services.

AAL3/4 is for VBR services in connection-oriented and connectionless modes. Two modes of service for AAL3 are defined. The message mode service can be used for framed data transfer (for high-level data link control frames), and the streaming mode service may be suitable for the transfer of low-speed data with low delay requirements. In the streaming mode, one or more fixed-size AAL SDU's are transported in one CS PDU. Two peer-to-peer operations are offered by both service modes - assured operations where retransmission of missing or errored AAL SDU's are present, and non-assured operation where lost or errored AAL SDU's will not be corrected by retransmission.

Let us look at the SAR sublayer for AAL3/4 in detail. CS PDU's can have variable length. SAR sublayer generates SAR PDU's containing up to 44 bytes of CS PDU's. SAR PDU for AAL 3 consists of segment type, sequence number, payload, length indicator, and CRC code. AAL4 being a connectionless service, a *Multiplexing Identifier* is also present in the SAR PDU. SAR PDU's with an identical MID belong to a particular PDU. The MID field assists in the interleaving of ATM SDU's from different CS PDU's and reassembly of these CS PDU's. Segment type can be the beginning of message, continuation of message, end of message, or single segment message. Error detection is a second function of the SAR sublayer. This includes detecting bit errors as well as detecting lost/misdelivered cells. The third function of the SAR sublayer is one of the concurrent multiplexing/demultiplexing of CS-PDU's from multiple AAL connections over a single ATM layer connection.

AAL5 is composed of a common part convergence sublayer (CPCS) and a service-specific part convergence sublayer (SSCS) as shown in Fig. 5.27. The CPCS is further composed of a convergence sublayer (CS) and a segmentation and reassembly (SAR) sublayer. SAR sublayer segments higher-layer

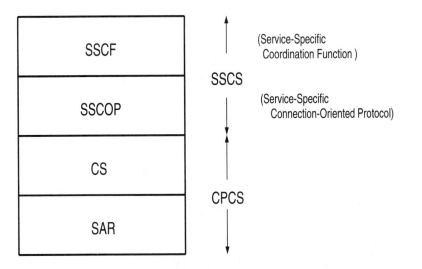

Fig. 5.27. Signaling ATM Adaptation Layer (AAL5)

PDU into 48-byte chunks that are fed into the ATM layer to generate 53-byte cells. The payload type in the last cell is marked to indicate that this is the last cell in a packet. The receiver may assume that the next cell received on that VCI is the beginning of a new packet. CS provides services such as padding and CRC checking. It takes an SSCS PDU, adds padding if needed, and then adds an 8-byte trailer such that the total length of the resultant PDU is a multiple of 48. The trailer consist of 2 bytes reserved, 2 bytes of packet length, and 4 bytes of CRC.

SSCS is service dependent and may provide services such as assured data transmission based on retransmissions. One example is the SAAL (Signaling ATM Adaptation Layer) developed for signaling as shown in Fig. 5.27. SS-COP (Service-Specific Connection-Oriented Protocol) is a general-purpose data transfer layer providing, among other things, assured data transfer. SSCF is a coordination function that maps SSCOP services into those primitives needed specifically for signaling (by Q.2931). Different SSCFs may be prescribed for different services using the same SSCOP. The SSCS may be null as well (e.g., IP-over-ATM).

5.15.6   Key Issues in ATM Networks

Unlike STM networks, ATM networks must rely on considerable user-supplied information about the *traffic profile* in order to provide the connection with the desired quality of service. There are some sources of traffic which are easier to describe than others, and herein lies the cost/performance challenge for best bandwidth utilization in an ATM interface.

An ATM network can support many types of services, such as connection-oriented as well as connectionless. It can support services which may fall in any of the four categories (loss sensitive, delay sensitive), (loss insensitive, delay sensitive), (loss sensitive, delay insensitive), and (loss insensitive, delay insensitive). It can further reserve and allocate a fixed bandwidth for a connection carrying a continuous bit stream for isochronous traffic (repeating in time such as 8 khz voice samples), allocate a bandwidth range for a variable bit stream for isochronous traffic (variable frequency such as interactive compressed video), as well as allocate no specific amount of bandwidth and rely on statistical sharing among bursty sources. It may also provide multiple priorities within any of the above categories. The services can span the entire gamut from interactive such as telephony and on-line data retrieval, to distributed such as video and stereo Hi-Fi broadcasts and multicasts for conferencing and database updates.

Typically, the ATM network may not permit 100% loading of any link bandwidth, and in fact user-available bandwidth may not be allowed to exceed more than 80% of the peak bandwidth of the link. The UNI may start policing and/or denying new connection requests on the link if utilization exceeds this amount. Some of the key issues that must be dealt with carefully in an ATM network are characterizing the traffic source, routing, call admission strategies, and congestion control strategies. We discuss them in the following subsections.

5.15.7   Traffic Source Characterization

Traffic that is carried in an ATM network can be classified as *continuous bit-rate (CBR) and variable bit-rate (VBR)* [20]. One type of characterization used in the modeling studies of ATM networks is the *two-state ON/OFF model*. In this model, a source is active for some period of time, referred to as a busy period. A busy period is followed by a silence period, where nothing is transmitted. The two periods alternate continuously. This model captures the basic idea of VBR that may be either active or inactive. It also implies that there is no correlation between the successive interarrival times.

Usually the specified behavior is a worst-case or a worst-case plus average case (i.e., at worst, this application will generate 100 Mbits/s of data for a maximum burst of 2 seconds and its average over any 10-second interval will be no more than 50 Mbit/s). Of course, the specified behavior may closely match the way the actual traffic was going to behave. But by knowing precisely how the traffic is going to behave, it is possible to allocate resources inside the network such that guarantees about availability of bandwidth and maximum delays can be given [21, 22]. Several traffic parameters have been proposed for resource management. The important ones are:

- mean bit-rate, peak bit-rate, and variance of bit-rate

- burst length and burst frequency

- cell loss rate and cell loss priority

These parameters exist in three forms: actual, measured, or estimated and are declared (by the customer) before the connection starts. Quantifying the values of these parameters and specifying the accurate traffic model is still in the research stage. In fact, all these issues and some possible solutions are the subject matter of the rest of the book.

5.15.8 Cell Routing in ATM Networks

The VPI and VCI fields of the ATM header are used for cell routing. Multi-stage interconnection networks have been proposed as switch fabrics in high-speed networks. The self-routing capability of these switches require that its output port address be known before a cell can be forwarded through the switch. However this information is not carried within the cell. Accordingly, based on the VPI, a table lookup needs to be performed to determine the output ports of available cells. As this operation takes place every time a cell arrives at an input port, efficient methods for table lookup needs to be developed to handle the incoming traffic. The identifier of the path can be used as an index in these routing tables. These aspects are discussed in more detail in Section 5.15.11. A path from source to destination must be decided at the connection request time. Most algorithms determine route by choosing the shortest or least expensive path. In traditional networks, cost was mainly defined as the mean end-to-end delay. In case of ATM, however, it may be preferable to sacrifice delay for other objectives such as jitter, probability of rejecting connection requests, and loosing cells.

5.15.9 Call Admission in ATM Networks

Each node has the option of accepting a virtual circuit request based on the declared traffic parameters as given by the customer. *Acceptance* is given if the resulting traffic mix will not cause the node to not achieve its quality of service goals. The acceptance process is performed by every node in a virtual circuit. If a downstream node refuses to accept a connection, an alternate route might be tried [23, 24, 25].

Since a connection has to be established before any transmission occurs, a process that checks the requirements of the connection while taking into account the current state of network is needed. Call admission procedures decide whether a new connection request should be accepted or rejected. The establishment of a connection over a path from its source to destination would mean that all nodes along the path can provide the requested QoS to the connection without degrading the QoS agreed upon for connection already established in the network.

The decision to accept or reject a new connection request requires the analysis of network resources along the connection's route. The exact solution may not be feasible to obtain in real-time. Methods proposed in the literature use queuing theory to decompose a given path into individual transmission links and analyze each link in isolation to approximately obtain the performance metrics of link to be used in decision making. Another method used is to calculate the incremental bandwidth needed by a connection request, given the source characteristics of the new connection together with the amount of bandwidth already allocated to the connections. Then if the total bandwidth computed including the new connection is less than some predefined fraction of the link capacities, then the connection request is accepted or rejected. The problem is that traffic characteristics of sources may change as the traffic stream goes through a number of nodes. Traffic from a virtual channel may become more bursty at downstream nodes than at upstream nodes.

5.15.10   Congestion Control in ATM Networks

Call admission may not be sufficient to control network congestion as users may deviate from their negotiated terms. It may not be possible for a user to accurately specify its source characteristics. The users equipment may malfunction or users may purposefully use more bandwidth than specified. Hence, congestion control is required to ensure that QoS is met for each connection. Reactive congestion control schemes are used in existing networks, and preventive schemes are attempted in ATM networks. These schemes use *policing functions* to protect the network against congestion by forcing the traffic to conform to the parameters negotiated at the call connection phase [26]. The most popular one is the leaky bucket scheme. Here, a counter is incremented each time a cell is generated by the source and decremented periodically at a suitable leaky rate. A cell arriving at a time when the counter has reached a given threshold is considered to be in violation of the negotiated terms. Depending upon the implementation, the violating cell is dropped, buffered, or marked as being in violation and sent to the network. Allowing marked cells to enter the network increases the utilization of the network resources. Leaky rate can be set to monitor the average or peak bandwidth. The threshold value cannot be set easily and its value has a major impact on QoS offered to the cell. Another mechanism for congestion control includes jumping window, moving window, and exponential weighted moving average.

Another mechanism to reduce congestion is to enforce discipline at the source nodes itself by forcing one's traffic to conform to a certain specified behavior. This can be achieved using a traffic shaper which uses the information about the policing and charging functions in order to change the traffic characteristics of the customer's stream to get the lowest charge or the smallest cell loss. For example, an IP router attached to an ATM network might delay some cells slightly in order to reduce the peak rate and rate variance without affecting throughput.

5.15.11 ATM Switches

A general architecture of an ATM switch is shown in Fig. 5.28. Input Port Controllers (IPC) and Output Port Controllers (OPC) are present at the input and output ports, respectively. The functionality of an IPC is also depicted in Fig. 5.28. It consists of one table called a VCI table, which maps an input VCI (VCI_i) to an output VCI (VCI_o) and an output port address (Po). Before cells are released to the switching fabric, the VCI is replaced by the output VCI and the output port address is appended for self routing. Each ATM switch has a switch controller that performs different switch management function including updating tables in the IPC's. The main tasks performed by an ATM switch are *VPI/VCI translation and cell transport* from input to the concerned output. We can distinguish between two types of ATM switches - VPI switches and VCI switches. VPI switches perform VPI translation only, whereas VCI switches perform both VPI and VCI translations. A switch can act as either a VPI or VCI switch.

Several interconnection networks for fast packet-switching have been widely investigated in literature [27, 28, 29]. Each design has some merits and demerits related to efficiency, complexity, modularity, and cost. Fast

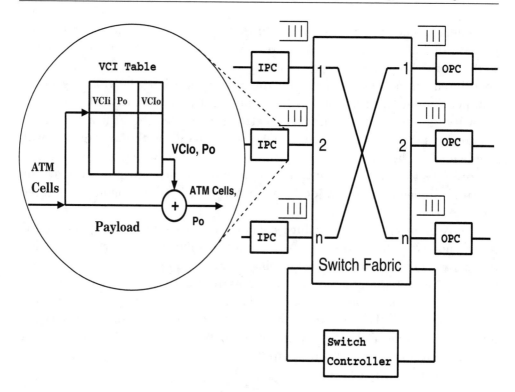

Fig. 5.28. A General Architecture of an ATM Switch

packet switches can be classified based on several aspects, including:

1. Design and structure of the switch fabric

2. Type of switching service they provide internally (blocking/non-blocking)

3. Location of the queues (input, shared, or output queues)

Structure of Switch Fabric: Some of the popular structures for switch fabric are:

1. Fabric with shared medium (ring/bus)

2. Multistage Interconnection Networks (MIN's)

3. Crossbar-based fabrics

4. Disjoint path fabrics (trees, multiple rings/buses)

Broadcasting can be performed easily using shared medium switches. They are less complex to build than others like multistage interconnection networks. The drawback of shared medium switches is that the number of ports it can support is limited. Multistage interconnection networks allow for self routing and their modular architecture is easily scalable. They require complex fault-detection procedures and they have poor broadcasting capabilities. Most of modern fast packet switches are based on MIN's. Some of the well-known interconnection networks are Omega, Shuffle Exchange, Cube, and Flip. These networks have been considered for packet-switching techniques to obtain high throughput because several cells can be switched simultaneously and in parallel. The principal characteristics of these networks are that they consist of log_2N stages and $N/2$ switch elements per stage and the switching elements have a *self-routing property* for cell movements from any input to any output.

While multistage interconnection networks are capable of switching cells simultaneously and in parallel, they are blocking networks in the sense that cells can collide with each other and may be lost. There are two forms of blocking - internal link blocking and output port blocking. The *internal link blocking* refers to a case where cells are lost due to contention for a particular link inside the switch fabric. The *output port blocking* occurs when two or more cells are contending for the same output port. Internal link blocking and output port blocking in an 8×8 shuffle exchange network (Delta) are shown in Figs. 5.29 and 5.30, respectively. Crossbar-based fabrics are internally non-blocking in nature. Their main disadvantage stems out of the fact that for a $N \times N$ switch, the number of crosspoints are N^2. Disjoint path fabrics like trees are internally blocking, but the number of crosspoints are much less than N^2.

Type of Switching Service: The second classification is based on the type of switching service provided internally. There are two types of switching services:

- Non-blocking or contention free within the switch fabric

- Blocking switch fabric where not all inputs can reach free outputs

There are several techniques to get around internal blocking. Some of them are

- Increasing the internal link speeds relative to the external speeds

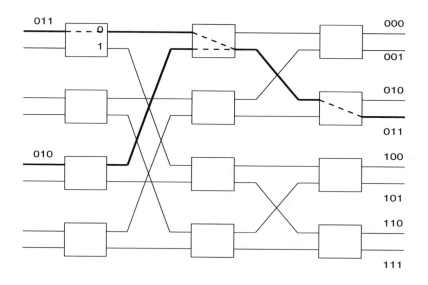

Fig. 5.29. Internal Link Blocking in a Delta Switch

- Placing buffers in every switch element

- Using a handshaking mechanism between stages or backpressure mechanism to delay the transfer of blocked cells

- Using multiple networks in parallel to provide multiple paths from any input to any output or multiple links for each switch connection

- Using a sorting network and shuffle exchange to sort and arrange output port requests in a manner that will not cause internal blocking.

Location of Queues: To deal with output port blocking, queues are used to buffer contending cells. The third classification is based on the location of the queues [30, 31]. There can be three types of queuing; viz., *input queuing, output queuing,* and *shared queuing.* The location of the queue is one of the critical factors in determining the performance of the switch fabric. Switch fabrics which employ input queuing suffer in maximum throughput due to a phenomenon called Head of Line (HOL) blocking. This is due to the input ports, which fail to receive acknowledgment, retaining the cell in their input queue and retrying in the next cycle; this prevents other cells in the queue from getting routed. Techniques such as switch expansion, windowing, or channel grouping have been used to reduce HOL blocking. Compared to input queuing architectures, switch fabrics with output queuing generally show severe implementation problems. Multistage networks still provide a good answer for larger-size switches with shared queuing.

Requirement of an ATM Switch Fabric: Some of the desirable requirements of an ATM switch fabric are:

- Capability to support multicasting

- Non-blocking switch fabric with as little buffer as possible.

One of the important requirements of ATM switch fabrics is to support *multicasting*. Multicasting switches have the capability of sending cells from one switch input to many switch outputs. Video conferencing is one application that requires such facility. Starlite and Turner's broadcast packet switches are examples of switch architectures that are able to multicast packets. Two approaches to switching cells can be applied in ATM networks.

1. Self-routing switching elements: When using self-routing switching elements, the VPI/VCI translation only has to be performed at the input of the switching network. After the translation, the cell is extended

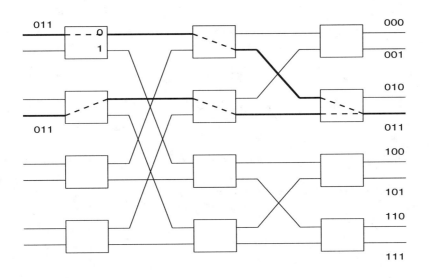

Fig. 5.30. Output Port Blocking in a Delta Switch

by a switching network internal header. This header precedes the cell header. In a network with k stages, the internal header is subdivided into k subfields. Subfield i contains the destination output port number of the switching element in stage i.

2. Table-controlled switching elements: When using the table-controlled principle, the VPI/VCI of the cell header will be translated in each switching element into a new one. Therefore, the cell length need not be altered. During the connection setup phase, the contents of the tables are updated. Each table entry consists of the new VPI/VCI and the number of the appropriate output in the switch.

5.16 Summary

In this chapter we discussed the basic network architectures, different standards and technologies available for local area networks, emergence of broadband ISDN networks, and high-speed networks such as FDDI and ATM. Among the techniques proposed for the B-ISDN transfer mode, the ATM concept is considered to be the most promising technique because of its flexibility and efficiency. The ATM networks use optical fibers and provide huge bandwidths with low error rates. We explained how ATM networks can be used to transmit multimedia traffic with diverse traffic flow characteristics. The ATM protocol reference model in general and the physical layer, ATM layer, and ATM adaptation layer were described. We also briefly discussed some of the key issues like traffic source characterization, routing, call admission, and congestion control.

REFERENCES

1. A.S. Tanenbaum. Computer Networks (2nd Ed.), Prentice-Hall, Inc., 1988.

2. Agrawala Ashok and Bijendra N. Jain. OSI: Its Architecture and Protocols, Mc-Graw Hill Publishing Company.

3. Douglas Comer. Internetworking with TCP/IP: Vol I, Prentice-Hall, Inc., Englewood Cliffs, NJ, 1988.

4. Douglas E. Comer and David L. Stevens. Internetworking With TCP/IP : Client-Server Programming and Applications, Prentice-Hall, Inc., 1993.

5. William Stallings. Networking Standards : A Guide to OSI, ISDN, LAN, and MAN Standards, Addison-Wesley Publishing Company, 1993.

6. William Stallings. ISDN and Broadband ISDN With Frame Relay and ATM, Prentice-Hall, Inc., 1995.

7. IEEE 802.3 CSMA/CD MAC Standard, IEEE Press, New York, 1984.

8. IEEE 802.5 Token Ring MAC Standard, IEEE Press, New York, 1984.

9. Raj Jain. FDDI Handbook: High-Speed Networking Using Fiber and other Media, Reading, MA: Addison-Wesley Publishing Company, 1994.

10. Shah Amit and G. Ramakrishnan FDDI: A High-Speed Network, Enlglewood Cliffs, NJ: Prentice-Hall, Inc., 1994.

11. Steven E. Minzer. Broadband ISDN and Asynchronous Transfer Mode(ATM), IEEE Communications, Vol.27, No.9, pp. 17-24, September 1989.

12. Ulyss Black. Asynchronous Transfer Mode, Prentice-Hall, Inc., 1995.

13. Hiroshi Saito, M. Kawarasaki, and Hiroshi Yamada. An Analysis of Statistical Multiplexing in an ATM Transport Network, IEEE Journal on Selected Areas in Communication, Vol.9, No.3, pp. 359-367, April 1991.

14. Handel Rainer and Huber Manfred. Integrated Broadband Networks - An Introduction to ATM Based Networks, Reading, MA: Addison Wesley, 1993.

15. Jean-Yves Le Boudec. The Asynchronous Transfer Mode: A Tutorial. Computer Networks and ISDN Systems, Vol.24, pp. 279-309, 1992.

16. H Jonathan Chao, Dipak Ghosal, Debanjan Saha, and Satish K Tripathi. IP on ATM Local Area Networks, IEEE Transactions on Communications, pp. 52-59, August 1994.

17. Hans Kroner and Gerard Hebuterne. Priority Management in ATM Switching Nodes, IEEE Journal on Selected Areas in Communication, Vol.9, No.3, pp. 418-427, April 1991.

18. Arthur Y.M. Lin and John A.Silvester. Priority Queuing Strategies and Buffer Allocation Protocols for Traffic Control at an ATM Integrated Broadband Switching Systems, IEEE Journal on Selected Areas in Communication, Vol.9, No. 9, pp. 1524-1536, December 1991.

19. Ken Ichi Sato, Satoru Ohta, and Kuo Tokizawa. Broadband ATM Network Architecture Based on Virtual Paths, IEEE Transactions on Communications, Vol.38, No.8, pp. 1212-1222, August 1990.

20. Mitsuru Nomura, Tetsurou Fijii, and Naohisa Ohta. Basic Characteristics of Variable Rate Video Coding in ATM Environment, IEEE Journal on Selected Areas in Communication, Vol. 7, No. 5, pp. 752-760, June 1989.

21. Jaime Jungok Bae and Tatsuya Suda. Survey of Traffic Control Schemes and Protocols in ATM Networks, Proceedings of IEEE, Vol. 79, No. 2, pp. 170-189, February 1991.

22. Peter Newman. Traffic Management for ATM Local Area Networks, IEEE Transactions on Communications, pp. 44-50, 1994.

23. Zbigniew Dziong and Jean Choquette. Admission Control and Routing in ATM Networks. Computer Networks and ISDN Systems, Vol. 20, pp. 189-196, 1990.

24. David Yates, James Kurose, Don Towsley, and Michael G. Hluchyj. On per-session end-to-end delay distributions and the call admission problem for real-time applications with QoS requirements, Proceedings of ACM SIGCOMM'93, Ithaca, N.Y, pp. 2-12, September 1993.

25. H. Saito and K. Shiomoto. Dynamic Call Admission Control in ATM Networks, IEEE Journal on Selected Areas in Communication, Vol. 9, No. 7, pp. 982-989, September 1991.

26. K. Sriram. Methodologies for Bandwidth Allocation, Transmission Scheduling, and Congestion avoidance in Broadband ATM Networks, Computer Networks and ISDN Systems, Vol. 26, pp. 43-59, 1993.

27. Richard G Bubenik and Jonathan S Turner. Performance of a Broadcast Packet Switch, IEEE Transactions on Communications, Vol. 37, No. 1, pp. 60-69, January 1989.

28. C. Fayet, A. Jacqeus, and G Pujolle. High-Speed Switching for ATM: The BSS, Computer Networks and ISDN Systems, Vol. 26, pp. 1225-1234, 1994.

29. Hamid Ahmadi and Wolfgang Denzel. A Survey of Modern High Performance Switching Techniques, IEEE Journal on Selected Areas in Communication, Vol. 7, No. 7, pp. 1091-1103, September 1989.

30. Hosein F. Badran and H.T.Mouftah. ATM Switch Architectures with Input-Output Buffering: Effect of Input Traffic Correlation, Contention Resolution Policies, Buffer Allocation Strategies and Delay in Backpressure Signal, Computer Networks and ISDN Systems, Vol. 26, pp.1187-1213, 1994.

31. Enrico Del Re and Romano Fantacci. Performance Evaluation of Input and Output Queuing Techniques in ATM Switching Systems, IEEE Transactions on Communications, Vol. 41, No. 10, pp. 1565-1575, October 1993.

32. S. Radhakrishnan and S. V. Raghavan. Network Support for Distributed Multimedia - Issues and Trends, Proceedings of SEACOMM'94, International Conference on Communications and Computer Networks, October 1994.

33. Domenico Ferrari. Client Requirements for Real-Time Communication Services, IEEE Communication Magazine, Vol. 28, No. 11, pp. 65-72, November 1990.

34. Gillian M. Woodruff and Rungroj Kositpaiboon. Multimedia Traffic Management Principles for Guaranteed ATM Network Performance, IEEE Journal on Selected Areas in Communication, Vol. 8, No. 3, pp. 437-446, April 1990.

35. J. S. Turner. New Directions in Communications (or Which Way to the Information Age?), IEEE Communications Magazine, Vol. 24, No. 10, pp. 8-15, October 1986.

Exercises

1. Draw the configuration diagram of two 10 Base T Ethernet LANs interconnected using ISDN.

2. Draw the configuration diagram of two 10 Base T Ethernet LANs interconnected using Frame Relay.

3. Draw the configuration diagram of two 10 Base T Ethernet LANs interconnected using an ether switch.

4. Calculate the bandwidth required to support 10 telephones on PCs connected to an Ethernet. All the telephones are digital and produce voice at a 8 Kbps rate.

5. Calculate the bandwidth required to support 10 telephone conversations over an Ethernet. All the telephones are digital and produce voice at a 8 Kbps rate.

6. Design a multimedia system, based on an ATM network and TCP/IP protocol suite. Show what is managed by the network and what needs to be managed outside.

7. Imagine that you are a traveling salesman of ATM adapters. You are in Timbactoo where the only type of ATM connection available is with AAL5. You need to setup your video conference with your headquarters in New York. How will you go about it?

Chapter 6

Multimedia Systems Architecture

6.1 Multimedia Applications

Many computer applications today make use of multimedia for effective communication with the users of these applications. Examples span a wide spectrum from multimedia-based games to scientific computing. In a practical application such as Tour Planner, incorporating voice annotation along with video in response to a query is quite common. Also, the encyclopedia, which is available today in multimedia form, is able to mimic the sound made by gadgets and species that are historic (and some are non-existent today) for the benefit of the reader. These examples and several others of similar nature follow the steps given below in order to become full-fledged multimedia systems:

- Collect the appropriate information for the application.

- Digitize the information, if it is not already in digital form.

- Organize the information in the form of a database so that it can be retrieved and combined as required whenever queries are to be answered.

- Use standard support software which is capable of handling audio, video, and a combination of these, for the purpose of organizing the multimedia information. Normally, these are part of Authoring Tools.

- Use standard support software and techniques to store different media in the disk with their synchronization information intact. (These are also part of Authoring Tools).

220

- Respond to the user queries using appropriate application packages with built-in multimedia presentation capabilities.

There are many tools available to support the steps mentioned above to develop multimedia applications [1]. Some popular tools are the Authoring Tools and Presentation Tools. Mediascript, OS/2 Pro, IconAuthor, Tool-Box, Authorware Professional, and Info Designer 2, are some examples of Authoring Tools. There are many tools available to make multimedia presentations with computers that are capable of handling audio and video. Some examples are PowerPoint, FreeLance Graphics, Harward Graphics, etc. Hardware such as sound blaster cards and video adapters, conforming to coding and compression standards, are increasingly common in multimedia systems. Such special hardware are supported by tools for authoring as mentioned earlier; noteworthy examples are Movieworks and Composer.

When we discuss multimedia applications, there are two distinct types of applications that are to be considered. The distinction mainly arises from the fact that one class of application deals with information 'captured' (in real-time) from the external world, and the other class deals with information that is 'stored'. Basically, these two classes of multimedia applications are based on the *longevity* of the information that they handle. The class of applications wherein the information pertaining to different media is captured online from the external world is called 'live' and the other class is called 'orchestrated'. We referred to these two classes of applications in Chapters 1 and 2. At this point, let us recall some of the discussions we had earlier in Chapter 1 about multimedia applications. The multimedia information that is captured from the actual scene during a teleconference is an example of 'live' information. It will be presented during the session and will be lost unless stored on a disk. Once stored, the information becomes 'orchestrated' information; in simple terms, that means the information is available for repeated use or even processing. Applications such as multimedia database systems deal with 'orchestrated' information. Applications such as multimedia teleconferencing deal with 'live' information. Applications such as multimedia presentation use both 'orchestrated' and 'live' information.

In essence, multimedia applications deal with *live* or *orchestrated* media information and require software tools that are capable of capturing, storing, manipulating, and displaying such information. When we consider a *multimedia system* comprising the computer system, the underlying network, and the software, an appropriate framework will be required in order to comprehensively describe the *functional* requirements and possibly the *performance* requirements of the system. Such a definition will have to be flexible enough to accommodate:

- different types of application software that support some (or all) of the facilities required by the applications,

- system software that integrates a variety of computing elements (or computer systems),

- a network that brings together the distributed computing resources to present a seamless unified computing environment, and

- a variety of information storage servers that may be located all around.

Before we attempt such a comprehensive description, it would be worthwhile to understand the components of a multimedia system.

6.2 Components of a Multimedia System

A multimedia system has several components such as sensors, user interfaces, databases, domain-specific applications, protocol systems, network, and the computing environment. The multimedia applications are often described using a client-server paradigm because it naturally brings out the relationship between the *source* of multimedia information and the *destination* (point of usage). If we consider a multimedia application which helps a tourist to plan a tour of a city, the information for *planning a route* comes from a server (and possibly computation of a route takes place there too) and the result is displayed on a screen on the user's (or client's) system.

From the networking viewpoint, the components of a multimedia system are the client, the server, and the communication network. The client is an active element in the multimedia system supporting one or more windows that carry the multimedia information. The server is an active element in the multimedia system that provides a predefined set of services that are accessible through the network. The communication subsystem interconnects, either directly or indirectly, the server and the client.

From the systems viewpoint, a typical multimedia application generates information belonging to different media types (such as data, voice, video, image, or graphics) in the form of one or more streams of objects. The objects can be viewed as composed of packets, in turn. At the point of generation of the multimedia information, an *implicit relationship* across the streams (belonging to different media types) will be *naturally* built in.

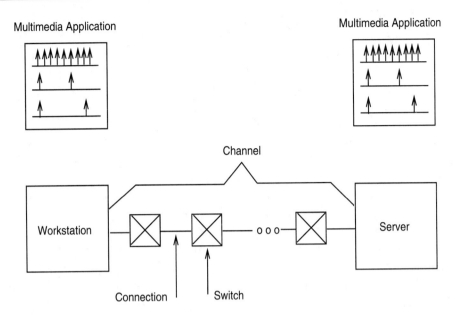

Fig. 6.1. End-To-End Connection in a Multimedia System

In a multimedia system, the multimedia information generated by the application is transferred from client to server and vice-versa, through the communication subsystem consisting of one or more connections and switches. While the information passes through various connections and switches, the *inherent delay* associated with connections and switches will distort the *implicit relationship* across the streams. Hence, the goal in every multimedia system design is to *preserve this inter-stream relationship* across media from the source to the destination, within certain bounds. Such a view of a multimedia system is shown in Fig. 6.1. When we describe the architecture of multimedia systems in general, the architecture should be capable of describing various multimedia applications and systems.

6.3 Architecture of a Multimedia System

The word *architecture* means[1]:

- The art of making plans for a system

---

[1] From Marriem Websters Dictionary, which deals with *architecture* in the context of building construction.

- The work of an architect

- The style or styles of building a system

- The system built following a specific style.

Given this definition of the word *architecture*, we need to state the perspective adopted here, so that the architecture that we define is versatile enough to express the variations as seen from *that* perspective. As has been the basis of this book, we will view the multimedia system architecture from the network viewpoint. That means the architecture and the taxonomy that we use for describing the multimedia system will absorb all variations with respect to the network and protocols.

In general, an architecture has two dimensions: functional description and performance description. Whereas the functional part of the architecture is described through a block schematic with appropriate annotations, the performance part is described through a model of the system. In this chapter, we will discuss both.

The architecture of a multimedia system for the purpose of discussions here is shown schematically in Fig. 6.2. The architecture is a four-layer hierarchy. In line with the concepts developed in conventional layered systems such as the OSI [2] or Internet models, each layer in the multimedia architecture hierarchy performs a specific function and supports the functions performed by the layer above. The functions of each layer are explained below:

Network Subsystem (Layer 1):   This is the bottom layer as shown in Fig. 6.2. This layer takes care of functionalities up to layer 3 of the conventional OSI model. The network-specific functions will depend on the technology used in this layer. Some possible technologies are FDDI, ATM, etc. Essentially, this layer provides a possible connection through the network subsystem with a specified bandwidth and error probability as supported by the underlying technology.

End-to-End QoS Control (Layer 2):   This layer maintains the connection between the source and the destination. The connection can be conceptually viewed as a single connection, but physically it may consist of several connections through the network subsystem. Each connection is managed to ensure that the *quality of service* or QoS is maintained between the source and the

---

[2]Open Systems Interconnection.

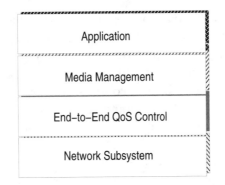

Fig. 6.2. Architecture of a Multimedia System

destination, as negotiated with the application at the time of admitting a connection.

Media Management (Layer 3): This layer provides 'generic' services to applications in so far as the media management is concerned. One of the primary functions performed by this layer is to maintain the synchronization across media. At start, the applications will be able to specify the type of media and the number of streams in each type of media. Then onwards, it will be the responsibility of this layer to ensure that the synchronization is maintained during the lifetime of the application.

Application (Layer 4): This is the uppermost layer in the architecture and directly interfaces with the user. The applications will interface with the operating systems environment, if required. For instance, if storage-media-specific library functions are required by an application, then the application will interface with the operating system.

The architecture described in Fig. 6.2 is called **RT³ architecture**, as it pertains to Real-Time information handling. Especially in a multimedia application such as *teleconferencing*, Real-Time movement of multimedia information is an absolute necessity.

Let us use the RT architecture to describe some of the multimedia systems that are published in the literature. The primary aim is to see how their architectures map onto RT architecture.

MHEG: MHEG⁴ provides a specification for documents which includes time and user interaction [2]. MHEG views the multimedia application based

---

[3] Also after the authors, Raghavan and Tripathi! A coincidence.

[4] Multimedia and Hypermedia Information Coding Expert Group.

on *object orientation* and does not assume any granularity of the single composite object. A composite object can relate to a single user interaction or an entire presentation. The application has to decide on the granularity. But the MHEG view of the media world enables one to construct applications that can deal with objects, object compositions, and virtual views. All of these functions are essentially confined to layer 3; viz., the media management layer in the RT architecture.

Movieworks: Movieworks is essentially an authoring tool for movies [3]. Movieworks allows the user to create and edit objects in text, sound, and paint. It also allows the user to integrate the objects into a scene and add special effects such as scaling, transitions, and animation. All of these are essentially functions at Layer 4 of the RT architecture.

Firefly System: Firefly systems allow the user to generate consistent presentation schedules for interactive multimedia documents with media such as audio and video along with user inter-actions, wherever necessary. The support provided at the media level is an off-line version of the media management layer and, as such, these functionalities are part of Layer 4 of the RT architecture.

In summary, the RT architecture captures the essence of a multimedia system. Its simple view of a multimedia system is best summarized in Fig. 6.3. The figure illustrates the interaction between four different systems that are running the same application. Two users are interacting with systems that play the role of servers. In the RT architecture, the network subsystem has been abstracted out and shown separately. The systems on which the users are located are opening QoS-based connections with the servers. On the top of the QoS managed connection, the systems have media management and temporal adjustments with synchronization to take care of any delays and any variations in delay. On the top of these layers, application-specific media manipulation takes place. While most of the manipulations of events have predictable intervals, some manipulations involving user interaction will be non-deterministic.

So far, we have successfully explained existing multimedia systems in terms of the RT architecture. We have basically suggested that the media-specific needs are confined to a particular layer in our architecture and the application uses it as is required. Another interesting point to note about the RT architecture is that the bottom two layers are network oriented and the top two layers are media-manipulation oriented.

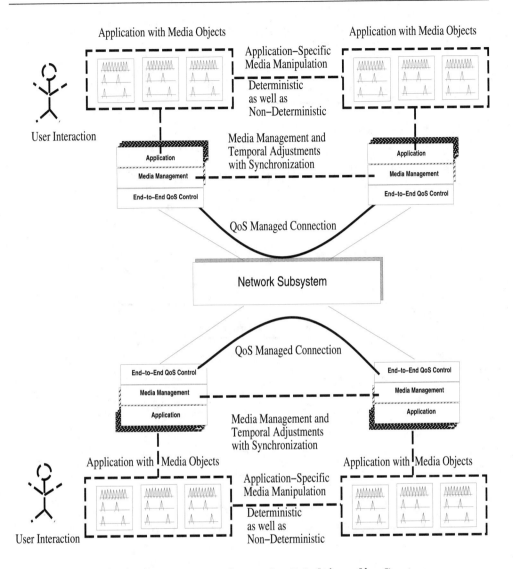

Fig. 6.3. RT Based View of a Multimedia System

Example: We digress here for a discussion on media when they are part of the application. Let us consider a multimedia presentation application. This is, by definition, an orchestrated application, i.e., all the multimedia information is stored somewhere in the system. Let us further assume that this presentation application deals with one image stream and one audio stream. When viewed by the user at the receiving end, the user will see an image sequence annotated by voice. The annotations by voice relate to specific images. In line with the description of different media in Chapter 2, we can say that in

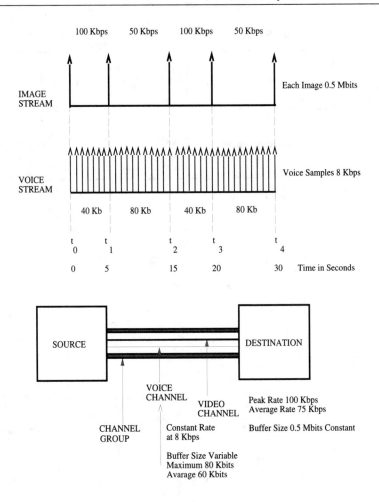

Fig. 6.4. Example Multimedia Application

this application we are considering two *media streams* with *synchronization* requirement. In Fig. 6.4, we show this application for five images and voice for them.

Fig. 6.4 describes the media handled by the application and its impact at the system level. For example, the image stream requires 100 Kbps bandwidth during the first five seconds (first interval t_0 to t_1), 50 Kbps during the next 10 seconds (second interval t_1 to t_2), 100 Kbps during the subsequent interval (third interval t_2 to t_3), and 50 Kbps again during the last interval (fourth interval t_3 to t_4). This amounts to a *peak rate* of 100 Kbps and an *average rate* of 75 Kbps. But the buffer requirement is constant at 0.5 Mbits.

On the other hand, the voice stream has constant data rate at 8 Kbps besides variable buffer requirement; maximum buffer size of 80 Kbits and an average of 60 Kbits. These data are to be related to the two resources in the system; viz., bandwidth and buffers. In both cases, if we operate at peak rate, we have instances where the bandwidth will go underutilized. For our example, if we allocate bandwidth at peak rate for the entire duration of 30 seconds, the channel utilization will be 66.66% if we assume that the first image is transferred before the start. There will be no delay. On the contrary, if we allocate a channel at average rate for the 30-second duration, the channel utilization is 100%. But, the second image and the fourth image will be delivered after a delay of 2.5 seconds each. If we had a voice channel at 8 kbps, then the synchronization between the image that is being displayed and the voice will be totally lost at two instances. This example underlines the need for *media management*. Also, if we assume that the source and destination are at two different points on a network, the Quality of Service as contracted by the network with the application should be ensured during the lifetime of the application. This underlines the need for *End-to-End QoS Control*. The reader may want to study this example once again to understand the effect of peak and average allocation of buffers for voice.

6.4 Multimedia Systems Taxonomy

So far, we have described the RT architecture and illustrated, through an example, the importance of the layers. This essentially means that we can describe any application through this architecture. In order to show that RT architecture leads naturally to the description of a multimedia system taxonomy, we will introduce a few definitions. It may be recalled that our definition of a multimedia system included the hardware, the software, the network, the application environment, and the application.

When we view the multimedia system in the context of a network, the essential abstraction of a multimedia application compared to a normal computer application is that the multimedia application deals with a large number of bits, with an additional constraint that these bits have to be delivered in a time-synchronized manner.

6.4.1 Definitions

Bits: Bit is the basic unit of information. Bit has a value 0 or 1.

Byte: Byte is a group of 8 bits. Byte is also refered to as an *octet*.

Packet: Packet is a group of bytes or octets. Normally, a packet has the data enveloped by header and trailer bits. When the size of a packet is very small, it is also referred to as a Cell.

Objects: Objects are a composition of packets or cells. Objects have a special meaning for each media. For example, a video frame which is generated every 1/30th of a second can be called an object.

Media: Digital data, voice, video, image, and graphics are all examples of media. Voice, video, and graphics with animation are all examples of *continuous* media, while others are called *discrete* media.

Stream: A sequence of objects (or packets or cells) is called a stream. Normally, a stream has some statistical properties and can be characterized by a distribution or an appropriate generative function. Media are represented as a stream. A stream can also be viewed as a time-ordered series of events. The presence of a media object, packet, or cell in a stream is referred to as *an event* while discussing the relationship across different streams. In short, stream is a time-ordered sequence of events.

An application will contain at least two streams, of which at least one will be a continuous medium. An application is described by a *StreamList*.

StreamRelation: StreamRelation refers to the synchronization requirement across streams for a given application. In our example in Fig. 6.4, if the rates of either voice or video channel or both are below the peak rate, the synchronization instants (or StreamRelation) will slip off. In real systems, it is unavoidable and is specified as an interval within which the events corresponding to the two streams should occur at the receiving end.

6.4.2   Description of the Multimedia Application

Multimedia applications are characterized by the presence of multiple media streams, the timing relationship across the streams called synchronization, and a certain quality of service from the high-speed network subsystem. Therefore, the behavior exhibited by a multimedia application can be described using the 3-tuple:

$$MMA = (QoS_{app}, StreamList, StreamRelation)$$
where
$$QoS_{app} = (B_{app}, D_{app}, J_{app}, PLP_{app});$$
B_{app} is the Bandwidth,

D_{app} is the Delay,

J_{app} is the Delay Jitter Bound

PLP_{app} is the Packet Loss Probability.

Examples of *StreamList* can be a combination of different media such as voice, video, etc. In the description of a multimedia application, *Stream-List* specifies the list of multimedia streams used in that application and is described as:

$$StreamList = (S_1, S_2, \ldots, S_k)$$

Where the S_i belongs to either Data, Voice, Video, Image, or Graphics and

$$S_i = (s_i^1, s_i^2, \ldots)$$

each stream consists of units of information which can be appropriately grouped for that stream. For example, if the stream under consideration S_1 is video, then each s_i^l will refer to a motion sequence or frame sequence. The actual choice will depend on the requirement for describing the stream for that application. It may be noted that different applications may choose to use different units of information, for reasons peculiar to the applications themselves. While the possible types of descriptions for a given stream will remain the same, which one is actually used for a particular application will depend on the application and the purpose of description.

$$s_i^l = S_i(t_l) \wedge t_l - t_{l-1} = \delta \wedge l \geq 0$$

s_i^l refers to the occurrence of a unit of information at time t_l. It is the instantaneous value of the stream S_i. Also, it should be noted that in a given stream, different units of information occur in a sequence, as emphasized by the relation that $t_l - t_{l-1}$ should be a non-zero value.

StreamRelation states the synchronization requirement between streams.

$$\forall \, (s_i^{l_1} \epsilon S_i) \, \wedge \, (s_j^{l_2} \epsilon S_j), \; s_i^{l_1} \theta s_j^{l_2} \text{ iff } l_1 = l_2$$

states that if we consider any two elements from S_i and S_j, they can be synchronized if and only if their times of occurrence coincide. The following relationship says that:

$$S_i \Theta S_j \implies \exists \, (l_1 \& l_2), s.t. \; s_i^{l_1} \theta s_j^{l_2} \text{ iff } l_1 = l_2$$

$$S_i \Theta S_j \; \forall \; t_i \epsilon \; \mathcal{T}, \; \text{iff} \; \forall t_{l_k} \epsilon \; \mathcal{T}, \; s_i^{l_k} \theta s_j^{l_k}$$

where θ and Θ are synchronization relations (expressed as probability distribution functions of delay) with respect to events in streams and across streams, respectively. For example, if two streams S_i and S_j are said to be synchronized, then there exists a time instant when the respective units of information occur simultaneously. Though we have used the time interval δ as a constant for brevity of notation, in general δ can be a random variable.

Example: Let us consider once again our simple multimedia application. Based on the description above, the application in Fig. 6.4 can be described as:

$MMA = (QoS_{app}, StreamList, StreamRelation)$

where

$QoS_{app} = (100 \text{ Kbps}, 0, 0, 0)$

$StreamList = (\text{Image } (S_1), \text{Voice } (S_2))$

where $S_1 = (s_1^0, s_1^1, s_1^2, s_1^3, s_1^4)$

$s_1^0 = S_1(t_0) = 0.5$ Mbits at 0th second

$s_1^1 = S_1(t_1) = 0.5$ Mbits at 5th second

$s_1^2 = S_1(t_2) = 0.5$ Mbits at 15th second

$s_1^3 = S_1(t_3) = 0.5$ Mbits at 20th second

$s_1^4 = S_1(t_4) = 0.5$ Mbits at 30th second

$t_1 - t_0 = 5$, $t_2 - t_1 = 10$, $t_3 - t_2 = 5$, $t_4 - t_3 = 10$

$StreamRelation$: For our example, we will assume that the time instants in the two streams are represented as t_0, t_1, t_2, t_3, t_4, and $t_0', t_1', t_2', t_3', t_4'$. Then,

$$s_1^{t_1} \theta s_2^{t_2}$$

where θ is a function of delay. For example, θ can be a probability distribution function. In our example, the function is null and hence will generate $zero$ as a value. If we define $\theta = f(D)$, then the value returned will be d and $t_1 \; t' - 1 \le d$. In addition, if jitter is defined as a function and generates a value j, then, $d - j \le t_1 \; t' - 1 \le d + j$.

$$S_i \Theta S_j \; since \; \exists \; s_1^{t_1} \theta s_2^{t_1'}$$

How is StreamList Useful? It is the StreamList that enumerates all the media types that are part of a given application.

How is StreamRelation Useful? StreamRelation specifies the behavior of D and J across streams, thereby describing the synchronization function.

6.4.3 Some Basic Questions About Multimedia Systems

So far, we have successfully described a multimedia application capturing the two most important features that distinguish multimedia applications from the 'routine' computer applications. These two features are:

- Media types and their composition.

- Relationship between the media (synchronization).

This is the description at Layer 4 of the RT architecture. There are certain implications of this description that the reader should be aware of at this juncture. Let us understand them by raising a few questions.

- What is QoS?

- How do we recognize it?

- How do we quantify it?

- Will QoS be always guaranteed by the system?

- Are guarantees deterministic or probabilistic?

- How will the system know the QoS of an application?

- How will the receiver know the synchronization information?

- Is QoS important from the Application Viewpoint or is it important from the Network Service Provider's Viewpoint?

- How does one translate the multimedia application description to a system-level description?

Even risking some repetition of ideas and definitions, we recount some of these ideas here because we need to understand clearly the interplay of functions and parameters between multimedia applications and systems that support multimedia.

What is QoS? QoS is an acronym that expands to Quality of Service. QoS is a collection of parameters that relate to a sequence as seen at the source and as seen at the destination. For example, the four parameters of Bandwidth, Delay, Delay Jitter, and Packet or Cell Loss Probability are currently considered vital for representing the *fate* of a sequence as it leaves the source and as it gets to the destination. *Bandwidth* refers to the capacity of the transfer mechanism that is available between source and destination. The transfer mechanism can range from a simple straight electrical connection to a complex set of connections dynamically pieced together between a given source and destination. *Delay* is the time a unit of information (packet, cell, or bits) spends in the transmission system, from the point of departure from the source to the point of arrival at the destination [4]. When we consider a sequence of objects (units of information), each one may suffer a variable amount of delay through the system. *Jitter* specifies the variation in delay. The *Loss Probability* (Cell or Packet) refers to the ratio of units of information that the application can afford to lose. This essentially helps the service provider manage the operations internally in a network.

How do we recognize QoS? The QoS is related to the StreamList and StreamRelation that we discussed earlier. Theoretically, QoS is derivable from the StreamList and StreamRelation that has been defined. That means, if we are given the multimedia application description, we can derive the QoS. But in practice, it is a much harder problem.

Will QoS be always guaranteed by the system? In the RT architecture, the Media Management Layer understands the StreamList and StreamRelation from the application and interfaces with the End-to-End QoS Control Layer. It is the responsibility of the QoS Control Layer to make sure that the QoS guaranteed is actually provided. It should be noted that there are two types of guarantees: *hard* and *soft*. While giving hard guarantee, the QoS Control Layer makes sure that all the required resources are reserved by the system well ahead of the start of the application. In the case of soft guarantee, the QoS Control Layer makes sure that the QoS values are maintained as best as possible.

How will the system know the QoS of an application? This is a hard problem. Theoretically, the system can derive QoS from the description of the multimedia application. But in practice it is hard. Here is a reason why. Consider, for example, the QoS parameter Delay. This consists of the propagation delay, transmission time, queuing delays, and protocol overheads. Of these, the queuing delay depends on *what else the system wants to do at that point*, which is difficult to quantify. This is also referred to as cross traffic. Also, the application requirement of bandwidth is not constant through the lifetime of the application. Therefore, contracting a fixed bandwidth may not be desirable. In view of all these, the application requests a peak or average bandwidth.

How will the receiver know the synchronization information? The receiver can know the synchronization information only through a protocol at layer 3 of the RT architecture. This protocol will take parameters from the application, in turn. For example, at the time of placing a call through the network, the application will invoke a service at the Media Management level with synchronization (and hence QoS) as one of the parameters. The Media

Management layer will interact with its counterpart at the destination and agree if the conditions in the network subsystem are conducive for processing the call.

Is QoS important from the Application Viewpoint or is it important from the Network Service Provider's Viewpoint?   Both. While the application is concerned with QoS from synchronization and response viewpoints, the network service provider is concerned with it from the network utilization point of view. They are basically two sides of the same coin.

How does one translate the multimedia application description to a system-level description?   It is hard. But we have illustrated this process with our example in Fig. 6.4, with a few simplifying assumptions.

6.4.4   Description of a Multimedia System

It is interesting to see how one can define a multimedia system from relatively simple notions. In this section, we develop a *taxonomy* that will help us describe the multimedia systems and their components. The approach adopted here has *four* parts. They are:

- Description of the basic elements of multimedia information.

- Description of the basic elements of the endsystems.

- Description of the basic elements of the network subsystem.

- Integration of all the components to define a total system.

The description of the elements corresponding to the four parts are shown in separate tables (Tables 6.1 to 6.4).

Table 6.1 describes the stream starting with the simple notion such as a bit. This definition of a stream was given in the previous section. Each medium is shown as a stream, which is basically a function of packets or cells. The functions f_d, f_v, ..., f_G, listed in Table 6.1, can be distribution functions or more complex and comprehensive descriptions of the respective streams. The arrows in Fig. 6.5 represent packets, cells, or objects of the corresponding stream. The streams view of media and the applications have been described in Chapter 2. We have also described the multimedia application as consisting of a series of multimedia formations, which are a combination of StreamList and StreamRelation.

b	Bits	1
B	Bytes	8
P	Packets	p
S	Streams	$f(P)$
S_d	Data Stream	$f_d(P)$
S_v	Voice Stream	$f_v(P)$
S_V	Video Stream	$f_V(P)$
S_I	Image Stream	$f_I(P)$
S_G	Graphics Stream	$f_G(P)$

Table 6.1. Basic Elements of a Multimedia System - Level I

When we look at the endsystems, the media are associated with windows, especially in the case of workstations or PCs. A workstation basically contains multiple media or correspondingly multiple windows. Table 6.2 describes an ordinary workstation and a multimedia workstation along these lines. All five media that we have been considering are represented as a set $\Re$. The set $\Re^2$ gives the combinations of media to designate a workstation

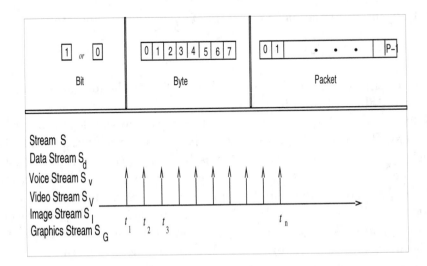

Fig. 6.5. Relationship between Level 1 Elements

W	Window	$(\Re^1, t)$
		$0 < t \leq T$
WS	Workstation	$(n * W)$
MMW	Multimedia Window	$(\Re^2, t)$
		$0 < t \leq T$
$MMWS$	Multimedia Workstation	$((n * W), (m * MMW))$
		$\Re = (S_d, S_v, S_V, S_I, S_G)$
		$\Re^1 = Powerset\ of\ \Re - \emptyset$
		$\Re^2 = \Re^1 - (S_d, S_v, S_V, S_I, S_G)$

Table 6.2. Basic Elements of a Multimedia System - Level II

as a multimedia workstation.

The two endsystems are connected by a single physical medium if they are on the same network and are connected by one more connection than the number of switches in between. Both the switch and the physical connection are represented in Table 6.3 as a delay element. This is exemplified in the notations used as a delay associated with each stream, subject to an upper bound. The notion of a channel is introduced here in order to connect two endsystems. Channel is a logical entity and is realized using the physical entities *connections* and *switches* alternately, such that there are N switches and $N + 1$ connections.

Each channel, so formed, may carry any one of the media. Depending on the media carried by the channel, the channels are called data channel, voice channel, etc. An application will use one or more of these channels. From the application viewpoint, this was what was referred to as StreamList. The collection of various media channels that are part of the same application (and, hence, the application StreamList) are together referred to as a Channel Group. Note the symbol $\otimes$ is used in Table 6.4 to represent the fact that the media is tied to a channel.

Once the channel groups are identified, synchronous channel groups are defined using the symbol $\triangle$. This, in fact, is the StreamRelation or synchronization. Since the ultimate communication is always between two endsystems, the two ends of the synchronous channel group, identified by SCG^- and SCG^+, are attached to the workstation end and server end, respec-

sw	Switch	$(\ (S_d, S_v, S_V, S_I, S_G),\ t_d)$ $0 < t_d \le T_{Delay}^{Upperbound}$
$conn$	Connection	$(Cap,\ t_p)$ $0 < t_p \le T_{Proptime}^{Upperbound}$
ch	Channel	$N * (conn \vert sw) \vert conn$

Table 6.3. Basic Elements of a Multimedia System - Level III

tively. An active multimedia workstation will have one or more of SCG^-, and an active server will have one or more of SCG^+. Finally, a multimedia system will have one or more servers and clients (workstations). These are described systematically in Table 6.4, culminating in the definition of a multimedia system.

Example 1: Let us try to apply the description technique that we have learned to a multimedia system that deals with database queries. A simple verbal description of such a system would be that it consists of a number of client stations and a few server systems, and that queries are generated by the clients and are processed and answered by the servers. From the systems point of view, we have already described the client-server system using our taxonomy. That additional information that needs to be provided is the nature of queries and replies. A generic way of describing those would be again in terms of the basic elements that describe the media. An example of such a description is given in Table 6.5. When prefixed to the client-server system, describe the database system that deals with multimedia databases.

Example 2: To describe a multimedia presentation system, we need to describe the nature of the script or presentation that will act as input or media description to the client-server system. If we assume that the proposed multimedia presentation system has the same characteristics as given in our example described in Fig. 6.4, then the media description will be $(n_I S_I, n_v S_v)$.

6.5 Issues in Multimedia System Design

Having described the multimedia system from application down to the system level, let us understand what it means to design such a system. By multimedia system design, we mean the design of the network subsystem [5]. We will therefore be concentrating on issues that relate to design for

DC	Data Channel	$(\mathrm{ch} \otimes S_d)$
vc	Voice Channel	$(\mathrm{ch} \otimes S_v)$
VC	Video Channel	$(\mathrm{ch} \otimes S_V)$
IC	Image Channel	$(\mathrm{ch} \otimes S_I)$
GC	Graphics Channel	$(\mathrm{ch} \otimes S_G)$
CG	Channel Group	$(n_d * DC \oplus n_v * vc \oplus n_V * VC \oplus$ $n_I * IC \oplus n_G * GC)$
SCG	Synchronous Channel Group	$(CG, \triangle)$
SCG^-	WS End of Connection	
SCG^+	Server End of Connection	
AWS	Active Workstation	$(WS, n_{aws} * SCG^-)$
$AMMWS$	Active Multimedia WS	$(MMWS, n_{ammws} * SCG^-)$
$Server$	Multimedia Server	$(n_{server} * SCG^+)$
MMS	Multimedia System	$(N_a * AMMWS, N_s * Server)$

Table 6.4. Basic Elements of a Multimedia System - Level IV

Q	Query	$n_d^q * S_d + n_v^q * S_v + n_V^q * S_V) + n_I^q * S_I + n_G^q * S_G$
R	Response	$n_d^r * S_d + n_v^r * S_v + n_V^r * S_V) + n_I^r * S_I + n_G^r * S_G$

Table 6.5. Database Query Response System

networks that are sensitive to multimedia traffic.

In general, communication can be classified as follows:

- Point-to-Point,

- Point-to-Multipoint, and

- Multipoint-to-Multipoint.

These classifications are based on the fact that there are one or multiple sources and/or destinations. The functional requirements for any of these communications are:

- Identify the destinations

- Find the route to the destinations

- Transfer data.

Connection establishment refers to the process of finding a route to the destination(s). A connection has to be established prior to the start of data transmission. It is referred to as *unicast* if it is Point-to-Point and *multicast* if it is Point-to-Multipoint.

Unique address (e.g., IP address) is used to identify a destination. In multimedia applications, during route finding, the QoS to be guaranteed is considered *while selecting the network service provider(s)* from the source to the destination. By *selecting a route and reserving resources along the route,* a multimedia call is said to be admitted into the network. This is referred to as *'Call Admission Control'.*

In a network, many applications will be trying to establish connections at the same time. All the applications that have calls admitted will essentially start sharing the resources such as bandwidth, buffers at switches, and so on. When units of information (in the form of packets or cells) start flowing through the network, it may so happen that at one or more intermediate switches (which happen to lie in the preferred route of some applications) *queuing delays will start increasing.* Such an occurrence is an indication of a temporary overload condition referred to as *congestion.* The network design should be capable of avoiding such situations or at least identifying the condition as soon as it arises and taking some corrective action. In many cases, these conditions may affect the QoS guarantees.

Since QoS guarantees must be satisfied for multimedia applications, it is essential to monitor and control the connection after call admission, that is, during data transfer. Traffic characteristics from the source can be continuously monitored, and any violation can be regulated by regulating or shaping the traffic at the source. This process of forcing the traffic to abide by the demanded QoS values is known as *'traffic policing'.* In many designs, it is combined with *Traffic Shaping,* which is a preventive measure.

Well-behaved streams (that is shaped output) do not mean that all the QoS parameters will be satisfied through the network. This is because the end-to-end behavior experienced by an application largely depends on the delays incurred at the intermediate switches. Hence, in order to guarantee the end-to-end (delay) QoS parameter, it is essential that the media streams are

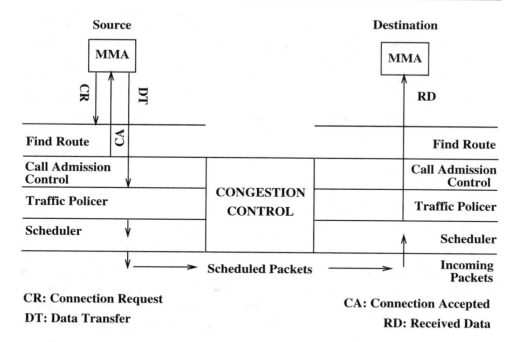

Fig. 6.6. Interaction Among Different Network Functions

'*scheduled*' using a certain service discipline at all the intermediate switches during the lifetime of the connection.

These issues and their interactions are shown in Fig. 6.6.

6.5.1 Congestion Control

The unpredictable statistical fluctuation of traffic flows is the main cause for congestion in high-speed networks. Both *reactive* and *preventive* congestion control mechanisms are attempted in design. Reactive congestion control refers to the regulation of traffic flow at the access points, when congestion occurs in the network. For achieving this, a feedback mechanism with adequate lead time to react is required. Hence, reactive congestion control mechanisms may not be considered desirable for broadband multimedia applications. On the contrary, the *preventive congestion control* mechanism tries to prevent the network from reaching an unacceptable level of congestion. This approach is best suited for connection-oriented networks such as ATM networks, because the decision to admit a new connection can be made based on the knowledge of the state of the proposed route of the new connection.

Congestion control for high-speed networks can be viewed as a collection of three independent functions; viz., admission control and resource reservation, traffic enforcement (policing and shaping), and scheduling. Admission control determines whether to accept or reject a new connection at the time of call setup. This decision is based on the traffic characteristics of the new connection and the current network load. A new connection is admitted if and only if the required resources are available and it is ensured that such an addition will not cause overuse of network resources, i.e., will not aggravate congestion further.

6.5.2   Admission Control

There are several admission control policies discussed in the literature. Based on the performance metrics, they can be classified as algorithms that use link-level performance measures and algorithms that use connection-level performance measures. The link-level performance measures are based on the statistical behavior of cells on a link. Since cells on a link over high-speed networks (such as ATM networks) are statistically multiplexed from many connections, it is difficult to distinguish from which sources cells are generated. Even though global performance objectives can be achieved using link-level performance measures, individual connections may experience a higher loss rate and queuing delay than desired. As satisfactory link-level performance does not guarantee satisfactory user-level performance, it may not be possible to satisfy user-level QoS using link-level performance measures. Connection-level performance measures give the performance for individual connections and are better suited to manage QoS.

6.5.3   Traffic Policing

Multimedia information covers a wide spectrum of traffic characteristics ranging from low bit-rates to broadband bit-rates suitable for video transmission. Also, these heterogeneous traffic sources differ widely in the degree of burstiness, correlations, and expected QoS from the network. Access control is required to enforce and maintain a specific QoS for each traffic. Access control algorithms enforce specific QoS by either 'bit or cell dropping' mechanisms or 'feedback preventive control' mechanisms. In the bit dropping method, the cells or packets that violate the negotiated traffic call admission parameters (QoS) are dropped. The feedback preventive control uses a control signal that is a function of the buffer occupancy level to control the source coder sampling rate. Frequent decisions to drop increase the cell or packet loss probability.

In networks where packets or cells are transferred without flow control between the user and network, and when the network operates based on the asynchronous multiplexing principle, a need to control the individual cell or packet streams arises automatically. The control must be enforced during the entire duration of the call in order to ensure an acceptable quality of service for all ongoing calls that are sharing the network resources. Such a control is exercised by introducing *policing* and (or) *shaping*.

6.5.4   Traffic Analysis and Prediction

Ideally, performance evaluation should be based on measurements taken directly from an actual, fully operating multimedia network. Since such a network does not exist yet, two other approaches to performance evaluation have been used by network analysts. The first (and most common) approach is based on a presumed traffic model that encapsulates some of the stochastic characteristics of the actual input stream(s). Such a model can be used in subsequent queuing analysis or simulations of buffers at nodes. The second approach is based on traces of actual traffic streams. These traces can be used as traffic inputs to simulations (i.e., *trace-driven simulations*). Indeed, this latter approach relies heavily on the availability of such traces. Whatever assumptions are used to characterize the arrival process of the traffic will have a significant impact on the predicted performance. Therefore, it is necessary when studying the performance to use traffic models that capture the most important characteristics of the actual traffic.

Another strategy is to build models at a functional level, and use them to predict the traffic by appropriately combining the models with values measured from actual networks. For instance, the functional behavior of an orchestrated multimedia presentation describes the events that happen in time domain. These events specify the objects to be part of the presentation in different media streams that make up the presentation. This functional behavior of an orchestrated presentation, represented by its synchronization characteristics, can be effectively used for understanding the performance behavior of the application. For characterizing the performance behavior, we need to describe the multimedia application in terms of tangible system-related parameters such as the QoS discussed earlier.

6.5.5   Buffer Management

A traffic model of an application, which is based on the functional behavior, is represented as a sequence of objects to be presented at different time instants with an associated duration of presentation. Such a sequence gives an implicit description of the traffic associated with the orchestrated presentation. But the actual traffic generated by an application also *depends on the object retrieval schedule* adopted by the client. The retrieval schedule basically determines the time instant(s) at which the client wants to receive the object(s). This schedule depends on the buffering that can be done at the client side. In a similar manner, the QoS requirements of a client carrying out the application depends on the size of different media objects to be presented, the duration available for retrieving them, and the buffering strategies adopted by the client.

6.5.6   Scheduling

The heart of a quality of service architecture is the multiplexing policy used at the switching nodes. Multiplexing is the allocation of link capacity to competing connections. The manner in which multiplexing is performed has a profound effect on the end-to-end performance of the system. Since each connection might have different traffic characteristics and service requirements, it is important that the multiplexing discipline treats them differently, in accordance with their negotiated quality of service. However, this flexibility should not compromise the integrity of the scheme; that is, a few connections should not be able to degrade service to other connections to the extent that the performance guarantees are violated. Also, the scheme should lend itself to analysis since performance guarantees are to be given. Finally, it should be simple enough for implementation in high-speed switches.

6.6   Summary

In this chapter, we learned about the multimedia applications and described a formal method of describing them. Through a simple orchestrated example, we highlighted the process of describing the media types and compositions in a typical multimedia application. Most importantly, we introduced a simple and elegant architecture which can form the basis for a multimedia system, called the RT architecture. The RT architecture is influenced by the hierarchical abstraction propound by OSI for describing complex interacting systems. We also introduced a taxonomy for the classification and description of multimedia systems and components and showed through examples that the requirements of multimedia applications can, in practice, be converted to concrete Quality of Service parameters at system level. Finally, we briefly mentioned a series of issues that will require greater attention in the design of future network-based systems that will carry multimedia traffic.

REFERENCES

1. Arch C. Luther. Authoring Interactive Multimedia, Academic Press, January 1994.

2. Colaitis F and Bertrand F. The MHEG Standard, Principles and Examples of Applications, Proceedings of Eurographics Symposium held at Graz, Springer-Verlag (Vienna), 1994.

3. www.movieworks.com

4. K. Nahrstedt and J.M. Smith. The QoS Broker, IEEE Multimedia, Vol.2, No.1, pp. 53-67, May 1995.

5. K. Nahrstedt and R. Steinmetz. Resource Management in Networked Multimedia Systems, IEEE Computer, May 1995.

Exercises

1. Look at any Authoring Tool that you have access to and describe the tool as a multimedia application, along the lines described in this chapter.

2. What do you think will be the QoS requirement of the Authoring Tool that you are using? If you were to convert the contents of this chapter using that tool, can you estimate the QoS parameters? How does it compare with your earlier assessment, when you estimated QoS without a specific application motivation? Explain the differences, if any.

3. I am using a SUN server with two SUNSparc stations. My application is directory query with voice input and text cum image output. Describe the sytem based on the taxonomy suggested in this chapter.

4. Discuss the possible services that can be provided by the Media Management layer in the RT architecture. Hint: Study the session layer services in OSI.

5. Describe the end-to-end connection for the following scenario:

   - Two end systems.
   - Three swiches.
   - Four connections.
   - Four windows each, on end systems.
   - Each window deals with Data, Voice, Video, and Image, in that order.
   - All are CBR traffic with rates of 1, 10, 100, and 20 packets per second.

   The application can tolerate 10% delay. Links are all of equal capacity, (200 packets per second). Packets are all of constant size. What is the time within which a scheduling decision has to be taken in a switch? Can the system support the application if the tolerance is reduced to 5%?

6. Certain workstation has a microphone, scanner, and a camera attached to it. The microphone output is 8 Kbps digital voice. The scanner scans any picture to a resolution of 300 dots per inch. The camera produces MPEG 1 stream as output. If a videoconference is setup between three such workstations, describe the entire system using the texonomy described in the chapter.

Chapter 7

Multimedia Systems Design: Traffic Analysis

7.1 Multimedia System Design

Multimedia system design is the process of building a system with the technologies and the architecture discussed so far, in order to support a multimedia application. Each multimedia application handles one or more media information or traffic. For example, an application which deals with retrieval and display of movies on a multimedia workstation is said to generate traffic that consists of video frames and voice samples. There are two levels of description for an application - one at the functional level and the other at the frames or samples level (can be called cell or packet level as well). To describe the application (example introduced earlier) at the functional level, we say that the application deals with a movie (at the source end) and displays on the full screen as a single window (at the display end). Obviously, the number of frames presented, the rate at which they are available from the source, and a host of other characteristics will depend on the actual movie being handled. That means, the load to be handled by the system is application dependent and hence is bound to vary from application to application. But when we discuss the design of a multimedia system, we consider the technologies and the load to be handled by the system simultaneously. In order to use load as a common measure or description across *all possible* applications, researchers analyze the traffic (or load) generated by the existing or known applications. The redeeming feature is that the media are *quantifiable, describable,* and hence *predictable.* In the first part of this chapter, we introduce the notion of functional description of a multimedia application and discuss how we can decompose it hierarchically to a level where one can associate what an application wants to do to system parameters such as a series of cells or packets. In the second part of this chapter, we discuss how the media can be quantified and described with the help of various traffic models. The traffic models and descriptions are important, as integrating different media in a network raises a number of issues, some of which were outlined at the end of the previous chapter.

7.2   Functional Description of a Multimedia Application

In Chapter 6, we described the RT architecture and the taxonomy for the classification and description of multimedia systems. We described a client workstation and a server, starting from a bit, by progressively building structures in a hierarchical form. It was also illustrated through examples how one can describe a multimedia application, such as a database system. The description assumed that we know the functions associated with each media stream. Only a system-level description was considered in the description presented in the previous chapter. Also, while mapping from one level to another, it was assumed (for the sake of simplicity) that only one element from the next level was possible. But, in general, it can be a sequence that is controlled by probabilities. There is still a gap in our description. Basically, the question that remains unanswered is the following:

How does one translate the application-level description to a system-level description?

By application-level description or functional description, we refer to statements of the following types:

- Multimedia presentation system with one voice, one video, and two image streams.

- Multimedia teleconferencing system where 10 users are using the system, each one opening a voice channel and a video channel. Half of them are using stored graphics for demonstration.

Such descriptions are at application level, and can be specified by the user easily. As we mentioned earlier for the design, we need system parameters such as cell or packet sequences, buffers, quality of service, and so on. The rest of this chapter is devoted to answering this question using an orchestrated multimedia application as an example.

The functional behavior of an application describes the activities in the time domain. Each one of these activities specifies presentation of objects in various media streams composing the presentation. As the functional behavior is represented in the time domain, the synchronization characteristics across media are automatically present, and the designer can use this to derive the system-related parameters. We refer to these as operational behavior. We consider two aspects of the operational behavior: the traffic generated by the application and the QoS requirements. In order to derive the operational behavior from the functional behavior, we need a translator to perform the function.

It turns out that it is possible to systematically decompose the user-level specifications until we reach a physical unit of information that can be carried across the network. Such decomposition has been achieved using specific symbols at each level. For example, there will be a symbol set at the user level (let us call it S_u) and there will be a symbol set at system level (let us call it S_s). Assuming that we can map directly in one step, it is equivalent to mapping a symbol from S_u to one or more symbols in S_s. Context-free grammar can be used for such representation. If there are three such functions possible at user level, viz., play, rewind, and fast forward, they will be used by a user in a certain sequence. While a sequence such as rewind, play, fast forward, play, rewind, play makes sense, a sequence such as rewind, fast forward, rewind, fast forward, rewind, fast forward, rewind, fast forward does not seem to make any sense. This can be written as the production rules of the grammar associated with the symbol set.

Grammar-based approaches have been used in workload characterization [1,2]. From simple user-level descriptions such as login and logout, the behavior of users in a single server environment, multi-server environment, and web client behavior have been successfully described. To control the application of the rules to the symbol set, certain attributes are associated with the symbols themselves. Also, to control the sequence of application of the production rules, probabilities are associated with the production rules. In the sequel, we describe a methodology based on Probabilistic Attributed Context Free Grammar (PACFG) for describing a hierarchical system and illustrate its use for translating the functional behavior of a multimedia application into an operational behavior specification. Such a translator is shown in Fig. 7.1. The material described here is based on [3].

7.3 Description of Hierarchical Systems

Let us consider a hierarchical system with n levels. At each level, let us assume that the system supports a number of operations. The topmost level is similar to the functional behavior at the application level and the bottom-most level is similar to the operational behavior at system level. We illustrate the use of the CFG (Context-Free Grammar) to represent such a hierarchical system. At each level of the hierarchy, we first identify the set of operations. This forms the alphabet or symbol set at that level. Each of these operations is represented by a nonterminal. Operations (nonterminals) in the nth level of the hierarchy expand into one or more operations (a string of nonterminals) in the $(n-1)^{th}$ level. Production rules are used for representing this expansion. At level n, the number of classes of operations is represented by K_n.

Each nonterminal has two attributes, s and e. They represent the start and end times of the nonterminal, respectively. The duration of an operation is described by the difference between the start and end times.

The grammar for mapping from the nth level to the $(n-1)^{th}$ level is given in Table 7.1. The function f characterizes the duration of an operation. Whenever an operation at a certain level is expanded, function g characterizes the interarrival time between arrivals of the next (lower) level of operations; function h characterizes the idle time between the operations. g is used to generate operations which occur in parallel, and h is used to generate operations that occur in a sequence. The ϵ move terminates the expansion.

In the grammar, the nonterminal $A_{n,i}$ and $A_{n,i}^+$ are of the same type but $A_{n,i}^+$ is used to represent the remaining duration of the nonterminal $A_{n,i}$ after it has produced $A_{n-1,j}$. To decide on the operations in a lower level (to which an operation in a given level expands to), a set of probabilities are used. There are K_{n+1} rules for expansion, and a rule that allows $A_{n,i}$ to go to ϵ. Each of the K_{n+1} rules have probabilities associated with them, and a rule is selected based on these probabilities.

The distribution functions are essentially used to determine when the expansion of a nonterminal has to be stopped, that is, when the ϵ rule has to be applied. A proposed end time for a nonterminal is generated using

Fig. 7.1. Functional-to-Operational Behavior

$A_{n,i} \rightarrow A_{n-1,j} A_{n,i}^{+}$	$A_{n-1,j}.\text{s} = A_{n,i}.\text{s}$ $A_{n-1,j}.\text{e} = A_{n,i}.\text{s} +$ $f_{n-1,j}(\lambda_{n-1,j})$ $A_{n,i}^{+}.\text{s} = A_{n1,j}.\text{s} +$ $g_{n,i}(\mu_{n,i})$ $A_{n,i}.\text{e} = A_{n,i}.\text{s} +$ $f_{n,i}(\lambda_{n,i})$ $A_{n,i}^{+}.\text{e} = A_{n,i}.\text{e}$	Select next rule based on probabilities $A_{n,i}.\text{e} > A_{n,i}.\text{s}$ (parallelism)
$A_{n,i} \rightarrow A_{n-1,j} A_{n,i}^{+}$	$A_{n-1,j}.\text{s} = A_{n,i}.\text{s}$ $A_{n-1,j}.\text{e} = A_{n,i}.\text{s} +$ $f_{n-1,j}(\lambda_{n-1,j})$ $A_{n,i}^{+}.\text{s} = A_{n-1,j}.\text{e} +$ $h_{n,i}(\mu_{n,i})$ $A_{n,i}.\text{e} = A_{n,i}.\text{s} +$ $f_{n,i}(\lambda_{n,i})$ $A_{n,i}^{+}.\text{e} = A_{n,i}.\text{e}$	$A_{n,i}.\text{e} > A_{n,i}.\text{s}$ (sequential)
$A_{n,i} \rightarrow \epsilon$		$A_{n,i}.\text{e} \leq A_{n,i}.\text{s}$ or Nonterminal for idle time

Table 7.1. Generative Grammar for Hierarchical Systems

the distribution function; as it expands, with the operations at the lower level and when the end time is reached, the ϵ rule is applied. The method described hitherto can be used to illustrate the translation from a functional behavior description of a multimedia application to the operational behavior description.

7.4 Functional-to-Operational Behavior Translation

One of the key elements in the translation of the functional behavior into operational behavior is our ability to represent synchronization. Representing the synchronization characteristics of a multimedia application can be viewed at three levels: window level, object level, and frame level. At the window level or the user interface level, the synchronization represents the sequence of windows that are created at specific time instances for a specified duration, demarcated by the start and termination of its display. At the object level, the synchronization represents a sequence of objects to be presented at specific time instances for a specified duration. At the frame level, the synchronization consists of composite multimedia objects (e.g., a video clipping for a few minutes) with frames to be presented at a regular interval of time.

From the *functional behavior model* (as represented by the synchronization characteristics) to the *operational behavior*, there is a hierarchy of levels, implying that we need multiple levels of translations. Each media object may translate into a series of frames (their nature to be decided by the coding and compression schemes in use) and each frame may translate into a series of cells or packets. Thus, we see that for every application, there may be multiple media streams which can be described as a sequence of window symbols where each window is a sequence of object symbols and each object is a sequence of frame symbols. Based on the sequence of objects and frames to be presented, we can describe the traffic that will be generated and derive the QoS requirements. This situation is akin to generating sentences in a language guided by a set of symbols and a grammar (expressed as the rule set or productions), possibly with some attributes and probabilities.

We use the Probabilistic Attributed Context Free Grammar (PACFG)[4]-based description to describe the hierarchy in a multimedia application. The basic idea here is that the productions specify the sequence of windows, objects, and frames to be presented along with their start and end times. The attribute functions (which are part of the semantic rules) describe the way in which the start time and the duration of a presentation can be identified. The probability associated with the productions represent the stochastic behavior of the application.

7.5   PACFG-Based Model for Multimedia Presentation

A multimedia presentation application is an example of an orchestrated application, wherein the information to be presented is stored in the system. The media (that are part of the application) and the synchronization information are stored as per some convention. In the example considered here, it is assumed that the user interacting with the application may manipulate the media streams. It is further assumed that the network service provider may alter the media stream flow as a result of changes in the network conditions. This is because it is assumed that the QoS negotiated is in a range and not necessarily in one particular value.

Attributed Context Free Grammar is a 4-tuple $G_A = \{G, A, R, D\}$, with

G as the regular grammar $G = \{S, V_N, V_T\}$. Here, S is the start symbol, V_N is a set of non terminals, and V_T is a set of terminal symbols. A represents a set of attributes, R represents a set of rules, and D represents an interpretation. In Probabilistic Attributed Context Free Grammar (PACFG), a probability is associated with the production rules defined in the grammar. The PACFG representation, describing the presentation sequence of a multimedia presentation, will be of the form:

$$\{SS, V_N, V_T\}$$
$$V_N = \{W, O, F, P, C, T, t, \tau, D, d, \delta\}$$
$$V_T = \{w, o, f, U_w, U_o, U_f, N_w, N_o, N_f, a, b, c\}$$

The symbols used and their explanations are summarized in Table 7.2. We associate an attribute $Val \in \Re$, the set of real numbers, with the terminal symbols $a, b,$ and c in the production rules discussed later.

The production rules defined as part of the PACFG in Table 7.3 describe the operational behavior of an orchestrated multimedia presentation. The multimedia presentation is represented by a sequence of windows (W), objects (O), frames (F), packets (P), and channel throughput (C), as described by the rule PR I. At the window level, the multimedia presentation is viewed as different media streams to be presented at different time instances and for different durations. The rule PR II describes the sequence of windows to be displayed on the user screen, time instance of creation, and duration of the display of the window. Each window has a series of objects to be displayed; hence, at the object level, the presentation is viewed as an object sequence for different windows. Production rule PR III describes the sequence of objects to be displayed, time instance of display, and duration of the display. The objects themselves may be composed of a series of frames. Production rule IV describes this frame sequence of an object (in case the object is composed of a sequence of frames) along with the associated time instance of display and duration of display. Each object or frame, as the case may be, is translated into a series of packets at the network level. Translation into a series of packets also depends on other factors such as the coding scheme used, buffer design strategy, the object retrieval schedule adopted by the client, etc. The production rules for nonterminal P (representing cells or packets generated) and nonterminal C (representing the communication channel throughput required) are based on traffic characterization and QoS estimation.

Symbol	Type	Explanation
SS	start symbol	represents synchronization sequence
W	nonterminal	sequence of windows created
O	nonterminal	sequence of objects in the windows
F	nonterminal	sequence of object frames
P	nonterminal	sequence of packets
C	nonterminal	communication channel throughput
T	set of nonterminals	time instant of creation of windows
t	set of nonterminals	time instant of presentation of objects
τ	set of nonterminals	time instant of presentation of frames
D	set of nonterminals	duration associated with windows
d	set of nonterminals	duration associated with objects
δ	set of nonterminals	duration associated with frames
w	set of terminals	window identifiers
o	set of terminals	object identifiers
f	set of terminals	frame identifiers
U_w	set of terminals	user inputs manipulating the windows
U_o	set of terminals	user inputs manipulating the objects
U_f	set of terminals	user inputs manipulating the frames
N_w	set of terminals	network manipulating the windows
N_o	set of terminals	network manipulating the objects
N_f	set of terminals	network manipulating the frames
a, b, c	set of terminals	constants $(0 \leq$ a,b,c $\leq$ Finish Time Of Presentation)
ε	terminal	null input
p_{U_w}, p_{N_w}	variable	probability of modification of window presentation due to user and network behavior
p_{U_o}, p_{N_o}	variable	probability of modification of object presentation due to user and network behavior
p_{U_f}, p_{N_f}	variable	probability of modification of frame presentation due to user and network behavior
x	variable	$1 \leq$ x $\leq$ Number of windows in the presentation
y	variable	$1 \leq$ y $\leq$ Object identifier
z	variable	$1 \leq$ z $\leq$ Frame identifier
i, j, k	variable	time instants of presentation of windows, objects, and frames $(0 \leq$ i, j, k $\leq$ Finish Time Of Presentation)

Table 7.2. Symbols Used

No.	Productions		
PR I	SS	$\rightarrow$	$WOFPC\|\varepsilon$
PR II	W	$\rightarrow$	$(T_i(w_x D_x)^*)^*\|\varepsilon$
PR III	O	$\rightarrow$	$(t_j(o_{xy}d_{xy})^*)^*\|\varepsilon$
PR IV	F	$\rightarrow$	$(\tau_k(f_{xyz}\delta_{xyz})^*)^*\|\varepsilon$
PR V	P	$\rightarrow$	?
PR VI	C	$\rightarrow$	?

Table 7.3. Production Rules

Table 7.4 gives the set of production rules for identifying the time instant and duration of display of windows, objects, and frames. PR V specifies the time instance of creation of a window and the probabilities of its modification by either user input or network behavior. The time instance of creation of a window is described by the function $funct_1$. For an orchestrated presentation, $funct_1$ can work on the stored temporal relationships for the particular window to determine the time instance(s) of creation of the window. Functions $funct_2$ and $funct_3$ describe the modification of the time instance of creation of a window due to user interaction or network behavior. $funct_2$ and $funct_3$ may be modeled based on actual measurements, as these are useful in prediction and hence in buffer design and QoS estimation. As an example, the network connection setup time can be used as the time instance of creation of a window. p_{U_w} and p_{N_w} associate a probability with the productions, describing the probability of modification of the presentation of windows due to user interaction and network behavior respectively. In a similar manner, PR VI and VII specify the time instant of presentation of objects and frames, and their probable modification by dynamic user and network interactions.

PR VIII specifies the duration of a window presentation and its modification by user input and network behavior. This production rule incorporates three functions ($funct_{10}$, $funct_{11}$, and $funct_{12}$) which describe the duration associated with the window. $funct_{10}$ can work on stored temporal relationships for orchestrated presentations. $funct_{11}$ and $funct_{12}$ describe the modification of the duration by user interaction or network behavior with a probability of p_{U_w} and p_{N_w}. These can be modeled based on actual measurements. In a similar manner, PR IX and X specify the duration of presentation of objects and frames, and their probable modifications by user

No.	Productions			Semantic Rule
PR I	SS	$\rightarrow$	$WOFPC\vert\varepsilon$	
PR II	W	$\rightarrow$	$(T_i(w_x D_x)^*)^*\vert\varepsilon$	
PR III	O	$\rightarrow$	$(t_j(o_{xy}d_{xy})^*)^*\vert\varepsilon$	
PR IV	F	$\rightarrow$	$(\tau_k(f_{xyz}\delta_{xyz})^*)^*\vert\varepsilon$	
PR V	T_i	$\xrightarrow{(1-p_{U_w}\cdot p_{N_w})}$	a	$\text{Val}(a) = funct_1()$
		$\xrightarrow{p_{U_w}}$	b	$\text{Val}(b) = funct_2(U_w)$
		$\xrightarrow{p_{N_w}}$	c	$\text{Val}(c) = funct_3(N_w)$
PR VI	t_j	$\xrightarrow{(1-p_{U_o}\cdot p_{N_o})}$	a	$\text{Val}(a) = funct_4()$
		$\xrightarrow{p_{U_o}}$	b	$\text{Val}(b) = funct_5(U_o)$
		$\xrightarrow{p_{N_o}}$	c	$\text{Val}(c) = funct_6(N_o)$
PR VII	τ_k	$\xrightarrow{(1-p_{U_f}\cdot p_{N_f})}$	a	$\text{Val}(a) = funct_7()$
		$\xrightarrow{p_{U_f}}$	b	$\text{Val}(b) = funct_8(U_f)$
		$\xrightarrow{p_{N_f}}$	c	$\text{Val}(c) = funct_9(N_f)$
PR VIII	D_x	$\xrightarrow{(1-p_{U_w}\cdot p_{N_w})}$	a	$\text{Val}(a) = funct_{10}()$
		$\xrightarrow{p_{U_w}}$	b	$\text{Val}(b) = funct_{11}(U_w)$
		$\xrightarrow{p_{N_w}}$	c	$\text{Val}(c) = funct_{12}(N_w)$
PR IX	d_{xy}	$\xrightarrow{(1-p_{U_o}\cdot p_{N_o})}$	a	$\text{Val}(a) = funct_{13}()$
		$\xrightarrow{p_{U_o}}$	b	$\text{Val}(b) = funct_{14}(U_w)$
		$\xrightarrow{p_{N_o}}$	c	$\text{Val}(c) = funct_{15}(N_w)$
PR X	δ_{xyz}	$\xrightarrow{(1-p_{U_f}\cdot p_{N_f})}$	a	$\text{Val}(a) = funct_{16}()$
		$\xrightarrow{p_{U_f}}$	b	$\text{Val}(b) = funct_{17}(U_w)$
		$\xrightarrow{p_{N_f}}$	c	$\text{Val}(c) = funct_{18}(N_w)$

Table 7.4. Full Set of Production Rules

interactions and network behavior.

The production rules given above have an associated set of functions to describe the time instances and durations of presentation of windows, objects, and frames. For orchestrated presentations, these functions work on the stored temporal relationships. One such technique for storing temporal relationships is the Dynamic Timed Petri Net or DTPN-based representation [5]. The functions used to describe the time instances and durations of presentation can work on the DTPN-based multimedia representation to generate the required grammar.

The PACFG rules given above can specify the temporal relations in a multimedia stream by describing the time instance of occurrence of an event and its duration. Given any two distinct events occurring in time, there are thirteen ways in which they can be related [6]. These relations describe how the events are related in time according to their start time and end time. The thirteen relations can be represented by a total of seven cases since the six others are inverses, with the equality relation having no inverse. Fig. 7.2 shows these relations using a timeline representation. The Fig. also shows the DTPN representation and the event strings generated by the PACFG production rules for each relation. Here, a null object is assumed to be played out for a time duration depending on the type of temporal relationship, in order to preserve the synchronization characteristics. Hence, the PACFG described thus far can represent all possible temporal relations.

Traffic Prediction Example: We now apply the traffic source model for the example of orchestrated presentation given in Fig. 7.3. By applying the PACFG rules at the window level for this example, we see that there are four streams of information : A, V, I_1, and I_2. They have the same start time t_1 and the duration of the presentation of all the windows will be $t_7 - t_1$. Hence, the sequence generated at the window level for this example is as follows:

$< t_1, A, (t_7 - t_1), V, (t_7 - t_1), I_1, (t_7 - t_1), I_2, (t_7 - t_1) >$.

By applying the PACFG rules at the object level for this example, we see that audio and video streams have objects to be played out at every time tick starting from t_1 to t_7. Image stream I_1 has objects to be played out at every three time ticks, and the stream I_2 has objects to be played out only at the start and the end. Hence, the sequence generated at the object level is as follows:

$< t_1, a_1, (t_2 - t_1), v_1, (t_2 - t_1), x_1, (t_4 - t_1), y_1, (t_7 - t_1) >$
$< t_2, a_2, (t_3 - t_2), v_2, (t_3 - t_2) >$
$< t_3, a_3, (t_4 - t_3), v_3, (t_4 - t_3) >$
$< t_4, a_4, (t_5 - t_4), v_4, (t_5 - t_4), x_2, (t_7 - t_4) >$

and so on.

When we apply the production rules at the frame level, the frame interval can vary depending on the coding as well as the compression schemes in use. Assuming a frame interval of τ_i for the video object v_1, the sequence generated at the frame level is as follows:

$< t_1, f_{v_1}, (\tau_2 - t_1) >, < \tau_2, f_{v_2}, (\tau_3 - \tau_2) >, ...$

At this point, the description of parameters that relate directly to physical resources comes into the picture. For effecting the final level of the mapping, we use multimedia traffic characterization at the cell or packet

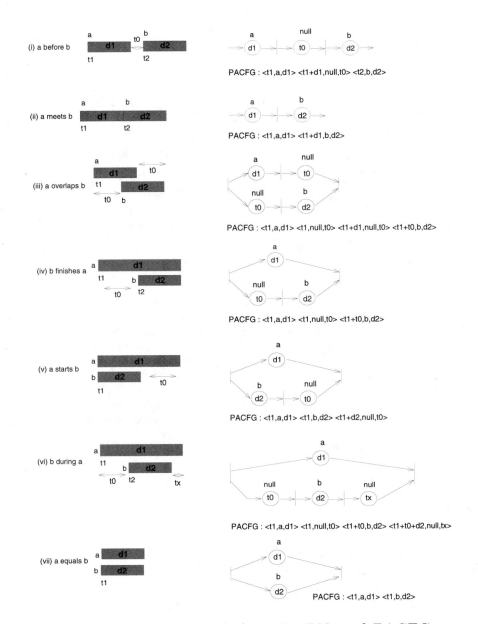

Fig. 7.2. Temporal Relations, DTPN, and PACFG

level.

7.6   Need for Traffic Characterization

Let us now recapitulate our observations about multimedia traffic and the importance of characterizing the same. In multimedia networks, traffic characterization and performance evaluation of networks are essential to providing guaranteed QoS requirements to all traffic streams. They also impact the optimization and dimensioning of the network resources (i.e., buffer space

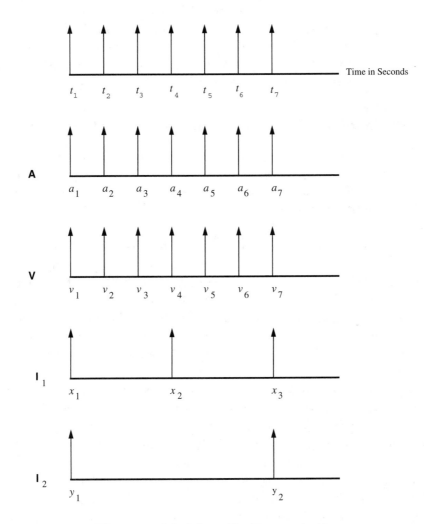

Fig. 7.3. Multimedia Presentation

and bandwidth). Ideally, traffic characterization should be based on measurements taken directly from an actual, fully operating network such as an ATM network. Two approaches have been used by network analysts. The first (and most common) approach is based on a presumed traffic model that encapsulates some of the stochastic characteristics of the actual input stream(s). Such a model can be used in subsequent queuing analysis or simulations of buffers at network nodes. The second approach is based on traces of actual traffic streams. These traces can be used as traffic inputs to simulations (i.e., *trace-driven simulations*). Indeed, this latter approach relies heavily on the availability of such traces. Whatever assumptions are used to characterize the arrival process of the traffic will have a significant impact on the predicted performance. Therefore, while studying the performance, it is necessary to use traffic models that capture the most important (with regard to queuing performance) characteristics of the actual traffic.

7.7 Description of Multimedia Traffic at the Cell Level [7]

One important feature of the multimedia traffic at the cell or packet level that has a significant impact on performance is traffic correlation. The complexity of the traffic in a multimedia network (B-ISDN) is a natural consequence of integrating, over a single communication channel, a diverse range of traffic sources (i.e., video, voice, and data) that significantly differ in their traffic patterns as well as their performance requirements. This heterogeneous traffic mix cannot be adequately approximated by a simple Poisson process. Specifically, bursty traffic patterns generated by data sources and VBR real-time applications (e.g., compressed video and audio) exhibit certain degrees of correlations between arrivals that preclude the use of renewal processes to model these patterns, not to mention a Poisson process. Even if the traffic generated by a single source was approximated by a renewal process, the aggregate traffic of the superposition of several sources is a complex non-renewal process which is modulated (i.e., controlled) by the number of active sources at each instant. Correlations between arrivals have been found to cause a considerable degradation in the network performance (as measured by cell loss rate and delay jitter), which cannot be predicted by a Poisson model. This situation was investigated for the case of multiplexed voice packets using the *index of dispersion for intervals* (IDI).

The superposition process of a *finite* number of voice sources deviates asymptotically from a Poisson process. A similar result applies as well to video traffic.

7.8 Multimedia Traffic Models

To capture the effect of correlations between cell arrivals in bursty streams and to accommodate the variability of arrival rates in VBR sources, a number of traffic models have been developed recently. These models have been used either as part of an analytical queuing model or to drive discrete-event simulations of buffer systems. In the following, we describe some of these models that are relevant to multimedia system design.

7.8.1 MMPP Model

The Markov Modulated Poisson Process (MMPP) is a doubly stochastic Poisson process whose arrival rate is a random variable which is modulated (i.e., controlled) by the state of a continuous-time Markov chain. A 4-state MMPP was used to approximate the *aggregate* arrival rate of several voice sources. More complicated traffic mixes can be modeled using the *superposition* principle of MMPPs: *"The superposition of two MMPP processes (with possibly different parameters) is another MMPP (with expanded state space)"*. The major advantage of the MMPP model is that it captures some of the important correlations between cell arrivals, while remaining analytically tractable. However, and like any queuing approach, its computational complexity is proportional to the buffer size, which makes this model computationally impractical for systems with large buffers. The MMPP was mainly used to model voice and data traffic sources. It is still questionable whether it is an appropriate model for VBR video traffic. Modeling a heterogeneous traffic mix using MMPP is also an open issue.

7.8.2 ON/OFF Models

These models capture the alternating active/idle behavior of a typical data source. A voice source with a silence detector can also be characterized using an ON/OFF model. In its basic form, an ON/OFF source alternates between burst (active) and silence (idle) periods. A burst consists of a random number of consecutive cells. For this reason, this model is often referred to as packet-train model. Commonly, the number of cells in a burst is assumed to follow a geometric distribution. No cell arrivals occur during idle periods.

7.8.3 Fluid Models

In stochastic fluid models, a traffic source is viewed as a stream of fluid which is characterized by a flow rate. The notion of discrete arrivals of individual packets is lost as packets are assumed to be infinitesimally small. The fluid approach has been found appropriate to model the traffic in high-speed ATM-based networks for several reasons. First, the burst level of the traffic in ATM networks is well captured in fluid models. Second, the granularity of the traffic, which resulted from the standardization of small fixed-length ATM cells along with high transmission speeds (on the order of hundreds of megabits and above), makes the impact of individual cells insignificant. This provides a strong justification for the separation of time scales, which is the basis of the fluid approach. Third, the computational complexity in fluid analysis is, unlike queuing analysis, independent of the buffer size, which makes the fluid approach particularly useful for systems with large buffers.

A two-buffer system with complete preemptive priority for one buffer, i.e., the multiplexer dedicates up to its full capacity to the high-priority buffer with the low-priority buffer being served only when the high-priority buffer is empty, has been analyzed.

In its simplest from, a traffic source in the fluid approach alternates between ON (burst) and OFF (silence) periods whose durations are random with some probability distribution (often exponentially distributed). During ON periods, infinitesimally small units of information arrive at a constant rate, similar to the flow of liquid. ON periods (also OFF periods) are independent and identically distributed. For N independent voice sources (or ON/OFF sources, in general), the aggregate arrival process is modeled as an $(N+1)$-state *Markov-modulated fluid flow* (**MMFF**) process, where each state represents the number of simultaneously active sources. In addition to modeling ON/OFF sources, a fluid model was also proposed to analyze VBR video traffic from videophones.

Although the fluid analysis is tractable, its numerical solution has two major computational problems: one is the possibility of 'state explosion' resulting from a large state space, and the second is the inherent *numerical instability* that results when trying to obtain solutions for finite (or partitioned) buffers.

7.8.4   Time-Series Models

These models are particularly suitable for compressed video streams. The VBR output of a video compressor consists of a sequence of frames generated at a fixed rate (e.g., 30 frames/sec in the NTSC standard). Therefore, interframe times are constant for the whole video stream. Because of the natural visual similarities between successive images in a typical video stream, frame sizes (within a range of consecutive frames) are highly correlated. Only scene changes (and other visual discontinuities) can cause an abrupt change in the frame size. The strong correlations in the VBR sequence, along with the constant interarrival times between successive frames, suggest that VBR traffic streams can be adequately modeled using time-series analysis and, particularly, autoregressive models.

The class of linear autoregressive models has the following general form:

$$X_n = a_0 + \sum_{r=1}^{p} a_r X_{n-r} + \epsilon_n, \;\; n > 0 \tag{7.1}$$

where X_n can be the size of a frame or part of a frame such as a slice (horizontal strip in an image), and $\{\epsilon_n\}$ is a sequence of *iid* random variables, called the *residuals*, which are used to explain the randomness in the empirical data. Equation 7.1 describes an autoregressive model of order p, i.e., *AR(p)*. An *AR(1)* model was used to approximate the frame size sequence taken from a videophone that generates a VBR stream based on a conditional replenishment compression scheme. Although this model cannot capture accurately the behavior of many empirically observed video sources, its main advantage is simplicity. Higher-order autoregressive models have been used to match the first two moments and the autocorrelation function (*acf*) of a measured VBR stream. A sophisticated *ARMA* process was used to model the number of ATM cells generated by a video codec (coder/decoder). With the growing complexity of video compression schemes, more complicated models, such as *Autoregressive Integrated Moving Average (ARIMA)* processes, are being considered. Fractal ARIMA models were first used to characterize Ethernet traffic. Later, these models were found appropriate for certain types of VBR video. The use of ARIMA models, in general, was motivated by empirical evidence of nonstationarity (or near-nonstationarity) in the arrival process of VBR video streams. A major disadvantage of a fractal ARIMA model is the large number of parameters that are needed to describe the model (i.e., the model is nonparsimonious).

7.8.5   TES Model

Correlated random variates can be generated using the Transform-Expand-Sample (TES) technique. This technique is used to generate synthetic traffic streams to be used in trace-driven simulations. The main characteristic of this technique is that it captures both the marginal probability distribution and the autocorrelation structure of an arbitrary empirical record of data. For a given set of parameters, the *acf* of a TES-based stream has a closed-form analytical expression. Therefore, by systematically searching in the parameter space and numerically computing the resulting *acf* of the model, one is able to approximately match the *acf* of a given VBR sequence. The TES approach was used to evaluate the performance of a multiplexer whose input consists of a number of VBR video streams taken from an entertainment movie. A disadvantage of the TES model is that it requires the availability of the empirical data. It is not possible to use the parameters of the model that were obtained for a given trace to characterize other traces. Moreover, the TES model cannot capture negative correlations that are observed in MPEG streams.

7.9   A Note on Fluid Models for Video

While the fluid assumption is quite acceptable in the cases of data and voice streams, it is unlikely that this assumption is appropriate for VBR compressed video stream. Certain fluid models are applicable *only* to certain types of video (i.e., videophones) and based on certain compression schemes (i.e., the conditional replenishment scheme). In fact, it is quite improbable that a single traffic model can adequately characterize all sorts of compressed video streams due to two reasons. First, different types of video are quite different with regard to their scene dynamics (e.g., videophones depict much less scene activity than video movies, which in turn depict less activity than commercial advertisements). Second, the existence of various compression algorithms result in traffic streams with different patterns, i.e., the same (uncompressed) video source can be compressed in different ways, resulting in different traffic patterns.

7.10   Summary

In this chapter, we described the characterization of performance behavior of an orchestrated presentation from its functional behavior specification using PACFG model for *translating* the functional behavior specification into a sequence of viewing windows, objects, and frames to be presented. We also discussed the need for traffic analysis and described different traffic models that are available for adoption in evaluation of systems that carry multimedia traffic.

REFERENCES

1. Q. Dulz and S. Hofman. Grammar-based Workload Modeling of Communication Systems, Proc. of Intl. Conference on Modeling Techniques and Tools For Computer Performance Evaluation, Tunis, 1991.

2. S.V. Raghavan, D. Vasuki Ammaiyar, and G. Harring. Generative Networkload Models For A Single Server Environment, Proceedings of ACM SIGMETRICS'94, Nashville, Tennessee, pp. 118-127, May 1994.

3. S.V. Raghavan, B. Prabhakaran, and S.K. Tripathi. Synchronization Representation and Traffic Source Modeling in Orchestrated Presentation, IEEE Journal of Selected Areas in Communication, Vol. 14, No.1, Special Issue on Multimedia Synchronization, January 1996.

4. K. S. Fu. Syntactic Methods in Pattern Recognition, Academic Press, 1974.

5. S.V. Raghavan and B.Prabhakaran. Synchronization Models for Multimedia Presentation with User Participation, Vol. 2, No. 2, pp. 53-62, ACM/Springer - Verlag Multimedia Systems, August 1994.

6. J.F. Allen. Maintaining Knowledge About Temporal Intervals, Vol. 26, No. 11, pp. 832-843, November 1983.

7. George Kesidis. ATM Network Performance, Kluwer Academic Pub., June 1996.

Exercises

1. Write a program for plotting the departure process in a M/M/1 queue.

2. Modify the program written in response to the earlier question, to handle bursty traffic following the ON-OFF model.

3. Obtain the MPEG data for Star Wars from the Internet and try fitting it to the models described in this chapter. Which model describes the movie better?

4. Write a PACFG for a three-level hierarchy that has five symbols at each level.

5. Describe an MPEG stream using PACFG. What is your start symbol? How many levels do you want to assume? Justify.

Chapter 8

Multimedia Systems Design: Buffer Design

8.1 Introduction to Buffer Design

In the previous chapter, we discussed the *functional behavior* of a multimedia presentation application, using the PACFG model for describing the sequence of objects to be presented at different time instants with an associated duration of presentation. Such a sequence gives an implicit description of the traffic associated with the application. The traffic generated by an application also depends on the object retrieval schedule adopted by the application. The retrieval schedule determines the time instant(s) at which the client should receive the object(s). One can view the opportunity to schedule as an opportunity to design buffer requirements. The schedule can impact the QoS requirements as well. As shown in Fig. 8.1, the PACFG model first translates the application-level functional specification into windows, objects, and frames; applies the traffic models as appropriate; and then incorporates the client buffering strategies to describe the traffic and the QoS requirements associated with the application. In this chapter, we discuss the strategies that can be adopted by a client for buffering multimedia objects and then derive the buffer requirements and the QoS requirements for a multimedia application.

A Short Note on Buffers: Buffers can be viewed as spatial representations of time. If we consider a sequence of cells or packets, buffer plays an important role in smoothing the traffic. In general, the flow of information is from a server to a client. In any application, there is always a preset movement of media streams as the application progresses with its execution. There is always a window that is available for the designer to plan the movement of further bits. At any point during execution, the number of bits in transit

266

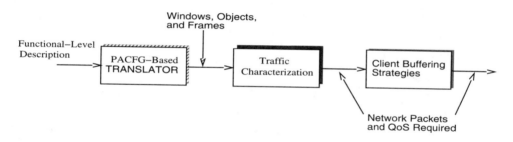

Fig. 8.1. Client Buffering and Performance Behavior

equals the buffer size at the client plus the bits equivalent of the channel, in between the server and the client. Buffer management strategies essentially balance these three all the time. The strategies can be fixed (nonadaptive) or dynamic (adaptive).

8.2 Buffering Strategies at the Receiver

At the receiving end, it is essential that the object be available before the display on the output medium. The receiver can adopt either the minimum buffering strategy (**minbuf**) or the maximum buffering strategy (**maxbuf**)[1]. The **minbuf** strategy tries to minimize the buffer requirements by buffering at most one unit of information[1]. While this mode of object retrieval minimizes the buffering requirements on the client side, it makes more demands from the network in terms of throughput and delay guarantees for delivering the objects in time. The **maxbuf** strategy buffers up to a certain limit (B_{max}) for each media stream on the receiving side, before the display. This implies that more than one unit of information may be buffered by the receiver. This mode of object retrieval eases the demand to a certain extent on the network, in terms of throughput and delay guarantees.

The buffering strategy adopted by the receiver impacts the object delivery schedule at the sender, and hence the sender traffic description. With **minbuf**, the delivery time of a unit of information is the display time of the previous unit. For example, object O_i will be delivered from the sender at t_{i-1} just after the presentation time instant t_{i-1} of the object O_{i-1}. Assuming Z_{O_i} represents the size of a unit of multimedia information at time t_i in bits, the minimum throughput that will be required from the network with **minbuf** strategy is:

---

[1]Unit of information may be an object or a frame.

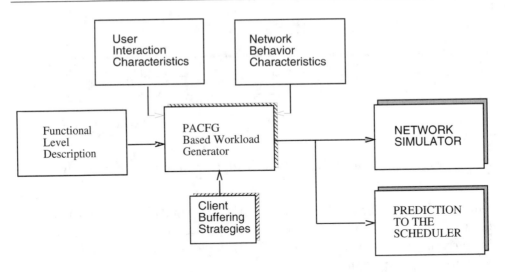

Fig. 8.2. Traffic Source Model

$$C_{min}^{minbuf} \geq \frac{Z_{O_i}}{t_i - t_{i-1}}$$

The delivery time instant of the first unit of information is t_x seconds before the start of the display, where $t_x = Z_{O_i}/C_{min}^{minbuf}$.

With maximum buffering strategy **maxbuf**, the delivery schedule at the sender is such that B_{max} bits will be delivered from the server every Γ seconds, where $\Gamma = B_{max}/C$, and C is the throughput offered by the network for the multimedia stream under discussion. For the application, the network should be able to guarantee a minimum throughput, so that the objects can be retrieved in time. With the **maxbuf** strategy, the minimum throughput, C_{min}^{maxbuf}, required for a multimedia stream is:

$$C_{min}^{maxbuf} \geq \frac{(\sum_{i=1}^{n} Z_{O_i} - B_{max})}{Stream Display Duration}$$

Here, the summation of Z_{O_i} represents the total size of all the objects that will be presented in the stream.

8.3 PACFG-Based Traffic Source Model

The PACFG approach discussed in Chapter 7 describes the sequence of the time instances and duration of presentation of windows, objects, and frames

PR V a.	P	$\rightarrow$	$(t_{i-1}(p_{il}s_{il})^*)^*\|\varepsilon$	B_{minbuf} & $p_{il} = Z_{o_i}/z$
b.		$\rightarrow$	$(\tau_{k-1}(p_{kl}s_{kl})^*)^*\|\varepsilon$	B_{minbuf} & $p_{kl} = Z_{f_k}/z$
c.		$\rightarrow$	$(\Gamma_i(p_l s_l)^*)^*\|\varepsilon$	B_{maxbuf} & $p_l = B_{max}/z$
				$\Gamma_i = B_{max}/C$

Table 8.1. Productions for Nonterminal P

in a multimedia application, such as orchestrated multimedia presentation. This sequence, along with the object delivery schedule for the buffering strategy adopted by the client, describes the traffic generated from the orchestrated presentation server. Fig. 8.2 shows a block diagram of the traffic source model based on a PACFG description. The model makes use of the functional-level description of the application to identify the sequence of objects to be delivered from the server. It takes into account the dynamic interactions from the user and the network. The client buffering strategies influence the output of the model as it changes the rate of flow of objects. As suggested in the figure, the output from the PACFG model can be used with a simulator or scheduler. When we use the model with the scheduler, we are using the predictive nature of the model.

The PACFG production rules translate the functional behavior of an orchestrated presentation into its operational behavior expressed as a sequence of windows, objects, and frames along with the associated temporal constraints. For translation of objects or frames into a series of packets at the network level, the production rules at the network level should incorporate the client buffering strategies as well. Table 8.1 shows the production rules for the nonterminal P, which represents the sequence of packets generated at the orchestrated presentation server.

Rules V (a) and (b) describe the traffic generated using the minimum buffering strategy B_{minbuf}. Production V (a) describes the packet sequence generated for an object with presentation time t_i (this object is delivered by the source at t_{i-1}). Rule V (b) describes the sequence for a frame with a frame interval time of τ time units. Here, Z_O (or Z_f) represents the size of an object (or a frame), z represents the maximum allowable packet size of the network, p represents the number of packets that are generated by the application at various time instances, s represents the size of each packet, and C represents the network throughput offered for the particular media stream. The packet sequence generated using the B_{maxbuf} strategy is described by

Rule V (c). This sequence reflects the fact that in B_{maxbuf} strategy, B_{max} bits are made available by the application to the network every Γ seconds ($\Gamma = B_{max}/C$ seconds).

The generation of the sequence of viewing windows, objects, and frames to be presented for an orchestrated presentation from its functional behavior using the PACFG model was discussed earlier. However, for translating this generated sequence into the traffic that can be generated by the application, we need to know the presentation characteristics such as the size of the objects, presentation duration, buffering at the client, and the network packet size. The characteristics such as the object size and the presentation duration, in the normal case, would be stored in the multimedia database. The PACFG representation can work on this database to generate the cell or packet sequence, to decide on a buffering strategy, or both. We make a few assumptions regarding the presentation characteristics, and apply the PACFG model to a synthetic multimedia application to illustrate the effect on buffer design at the client and on the QoS.

Example: Consider a video window V. We can assume 20 frames per second for the objects v_1, v_2, v_3 while the objects v_4, v_5, v_6, v_7 can be a slow-motion video clipping at 5 frames/second. Assume a frame size of 1 Mbits for objects v_1, v_2, v_3, a frame size of 2 Mbits for objects v_4, v_5, v_6, v_7, and a uniform time interval of 10 seconds for presentation of all the video objects ($v_1, v_2, ..$). For the image stream (I_1), we consider that the objects are color images with 1024 * 1024 pixels and 24 bits per pixel of color information. (Each object has a size of 24 Mbits). For the network, let us also assume a packet size of 100 bits.

We can apply the PACFG given in Table 8.1 to compute the traffic generated from the orchestrated presentation server. For the video stream V, objects v_1 to v_3 have a frame interarrival time of 0.05 seconds and the objects v_4 to v_7 have a frame interarrival time of 0.2 seconds. Using the **minbuf** strategy, delivery of the first frame of v_1 will start 0.05 seconds before the start of the presentation. Fig. 8.3 shows the traffic generated for the video stream when objects v_1, v_2, v_3 are being presented using the minimum buffering strategy **minbuf**. As shown in the figure, 10^4 packets will be generated every 0.05 seconds. Fig. 8.3 also shows the traffic generated for the video stream when objects v_4, v_5, v_6, v_7 are being presented using the minimum buffering strategy. In this case, the delivery of the first frame will start 0.2 seconds before the presentation and $2 * 10^4$ packets will be generated every 0.2 seconds. For the **maxbuf** strategy, let us assume a maximum buffer space (B_{max}) of 200 Mbits for the video stream. The minimum throughput needed from the network (C_{min}^{maxbuf}) will be 10 Mbps. With these assumptions, $2 * 10^6$ packets will be generated by the server every $\Gamma = B_{max}/C = 20$ seconds. The initial chunk will be delivered 20 seconds before the presentation. Fig. 8.4 also shows the traffic generated for the video stream V in Fig. 8.6 with maximum buffering strategy **maxbuf**. It should be noted that the origin in the X-axis corresponds to the presentation start time. The **minbuf** and the **maxbuf** strategies are shown as B1 and B2 in Fig. 8.3, respectively.

The traffic description of the image stream (I_1) is shown in Fig. 8.5. With the **minbuf** strategy, $24 * 10^4$ packets will be generated by the server every 30 seconds. For the **maxbuf**

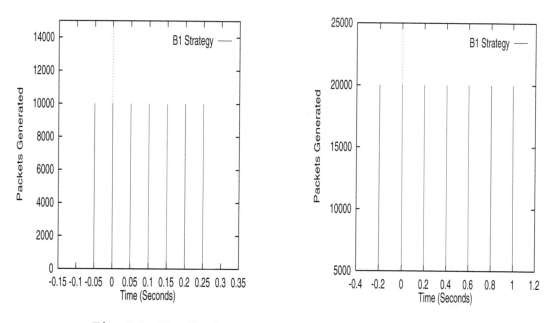

Fig. 8.3. Traffic for Stream V with minbuf Strategy

strategy, let us assume B_{max} to be 32 Mbits. C_{min}^{maxbuf} will be 0.66 Mbps. With these assumptions, $32 * 10^4$ packets will be generated by the server twice (48 seconds before presentation and at the start time) and $8 * 10^3$ packets will be generated once (48 seconds after presentation start time).

In a similar manner, we can generate traffic descriptions for other streams such as Audio (A) and Image (I_2) in the orchestrated presentation example of Fig. 8.6.

8.4 Estimation of QoS Requirements

The operational behavior of an orchestrated presentation in terms of the QoS required is specified by a set of parameters such as throughput, delay, delay jitter, and packet loss probabilities. Let us consider the example orchestrated presentation as shown in Fig. 8.6. Objects a_1, v_1, x_1, and y_1 have to be presented to the user at the time instant t_1. To achieve this, the presentation can be started either after the retrieval of the multimedia objects from the server is completed or during the retrieval. Objects such as still images (x_1 and y_1) have to be retrieved completely before presentation. However, presentation of objects such as video objects $v_1, v_2, ...$, which can be considered as video clippings for a time interval, can be started as the frames composing the objects are being retrieved. In either case, the objects

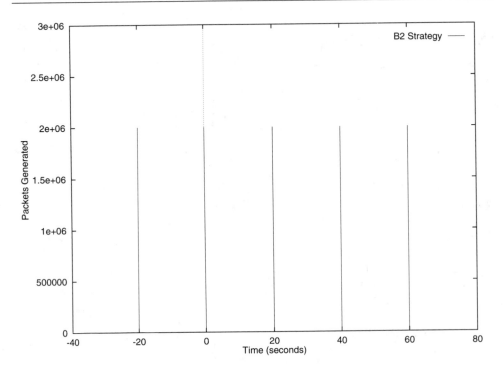

Fig. 8.4. Traffic for Stream V with maxbuf Strategy

have to be buffered on the client system, either wholly or partially. The client can adopt either the **minbuf** strategy of minimum buffering or the **maxbuf** strategy of maximum buffering, as discussed in Section 8.2. Depending on the type of presentation (the number of concurrent objects to be presented, the type of objects, and duration of presentation), the buffer space requirements on the client system will vary. Based on the buffering strategy adopted, the QoS requirements of the application are going to vary.

The **minbuf** strategy minimizes the buffer space requirements of the client, and the QoS derived based on this strategy gives the *preferred* values for the client. The QoS requirements derived based on the **maxbuf** strategy specify the *acceptable* values for the client. The preferred and acceptable values denote the maximum and minimum values of the QoS spectrum, as shown in Fig. 8.7. The guaranteed QoS, arrived at after negotiation with the network service provider, will be somewhere in this spectrum. Based on the modifications made to the application by the user (e.g., slowing down the speed of presentation or dropping a medium), the acceptable and preferred QoS may reduce. In contrast to this, if another medium is included or the presentation is speeded up, the acceptable and preferred QoS may move up.

In a distributed orchestrated presentation, multimedia objects composing the presentation are retrieved from the server. The retrieval of objects does not impose any real-time demands from the network service provider. Hence, for orchestrated presentations, it is sufficient if the network service provider guarantees the required throughput. In this section, we will discuss how the preferred throughput requirement of an orchestrated multimedia presentation application can be computed for one time interval in the lifetime of the application.

Object Retrieval minbuf Strategy: For objects like still images, we can determine the average throughput required by the application with the B1 buffering strategy, assuming that at most one object in each multimedia stream is buffered by the application on the client system before the presentation. Let us consider a multimedia stream with an object O_i at a playout time instant t_i and let the object size be Z_{O_i}. Since only one object is assumed to be buffered before the playout time instant for the stream, the retrieval of objects can start only after the immediately preceding playout time instant t_{i-1}, and has to be completed before t_i. Hence, the preferred throughput C_{app}^{pref} for objects such as still images, that should be retrieved

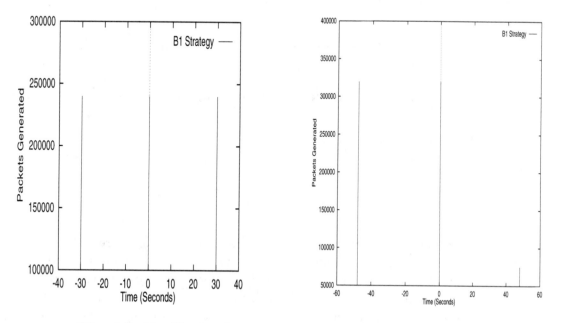

Fig. 8.5. Traffic for Stream I_1 with minbuf and maxbuf

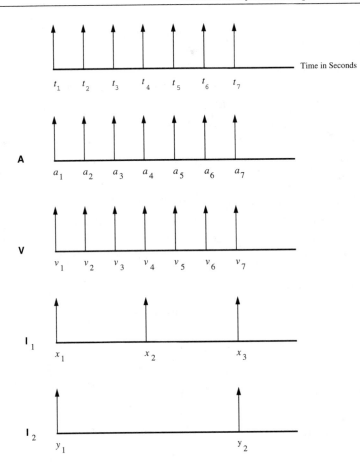

Fig. 8.6. An Example of Multimedia Presentation

fully before presentation, is :

$$C_{app}^{pref}[t_{i-1}, t_i] \geq \frac{Z_{O_i}}{t_i - t_{i-1}}$$

For objects like video which consist of a set of frames to be presented at regular intervals, buffering the whole object can lead to very high demands on the system buffer resources. To avoid the high demands on buffer resources, the application following the **minbuf** strategy can buffer at most one frame of the video object. The rest of the frames composing the video object can be retrieved as the presentation is started. If τ_i is the presenta-

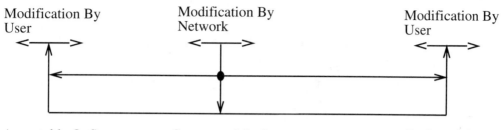

Fig. 8.7. QoS Spectrum

tion time of frame i, then the preferred throughput is :

$$C_{app}^{pref}[\tau_{i-1}, \tau_i] \geq \frac{Z_{f_i}}{\tau_i - \tau_{i-1}}$$

where Z_{f_i} denotes the size of the ith video frame.

Throughput For An Application Lifetime: The discussions in the above subsection basically help in computing the preferred QoS parameters required by a multimedia stream for one time interval. The throughput required by a communication channel during the lifetime of a multimedia application can be determined by applying the computations for one time interval. For an orchestrated presentation, the required information (like the size of the object) can be stored along with the temporal relationships. Hence, the QoS required for orchestrated multimedia applications during its lifetime can be estimated from the stored information.

For calculating the *acceptable* QoS parameters, we should find out the minimum values that are required by the application. A minimum value of throughput (C_{app}^{acc}) implies that the application will be following the **maxbuf** buffering strategy of buffering more than one object (in the stream for which throughput is being calculated) before its presentation. When more than one object in a stream is buffered by the application, the start of the presentation is delayed by the time required for retrieving B_{max} bits using the acceptable throughput of C_{app}^{acc}. If B_{max} is the maximum buffer space available and $\sum_{i=1}^{n} Z_{O_i}$ is the total size of all objects to be retrieved, then the acceptable throughput is :

$$C_{app}^{acc} \geq \frac{(\sum_{i=1}^{n} Z_{O_i} - B_{max})}{t_{final} - t_{initial}}$$

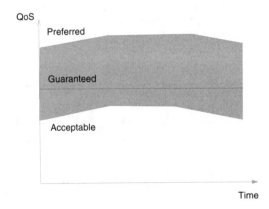

Fig. 8.8. QoS During Application Lifetime

PR VI a.	C	$\rightarrow$	$(t_{i-1,i}C)^*\|\varepsilon$	B_{minbuf} & $C = Z_{O_i}/(t_i - t_{i-1})$
b.	C	$\rightarrow$	$(\tau_{i-1,i}C)^*\|\varepsilon$	B_{minbuf} & $C = Z_{f_i}/(\tau_i - \tau_{i-1})$
c.		$\rightarrow$	$(t_{initial,final}C)^*\|\varepsilon$	B_{maxbuf} & $C = \dfrac{(\sum_{i=1}^{n} Z_{O_i} - B_{max})}{(t_{final} - t_{initial})}$

Table 8.2. Productions for Required Throughput C

The QoS scale in the lifetime of presentation of the multimedia stream will look as shown in Fig. 8.8.

The PACFG description of an orchestrated presentation discussed earlier shows that the sequence of presentation of windows, objects, and frames, the time instants of their presentation, and their durations of presentations can be modeled for each application. Based on the PACFG description and based on the buffering strategy adopted, the production rules can be written. Table 8.2 summarizes the production rules for the nonterminal C which represents the communication channel throughput required by the orchestrated presentation from the network service provider. Rule VI (a) specifies the preferred channel throughput with a **minbuf** buffering strategy, assuming that the time interval for retrieving the object O_i is $(t_i - t_{i-1})$. Rule VI (b) specifies the preferred throughput (with **minbuf** strategy) for video objects with a frame presentation duration of $(\tau_i - \tau_{i-1})$. Rule VI (c) specifies the acceptable throughput with the **maxbuf** buffering strategy.

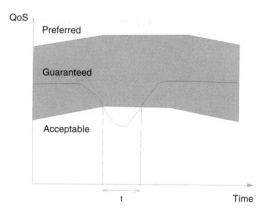

Fig. 8.9. Dynamic QoS Modification by the Network Service Provider

8.5 Interaction With Network Service Provider

Once the required QoS parameters are determined by the multimedia application, the application has to interact with the network service provider to establish the network channels with the required QoS parameters. The network service provider evaluates the application's request for establishing communication channels and provides a (positive or negative) reply [3,4]. In case the network is not able to support the requested QoS parameters, the application has the option of abandoning the request, retrying later with the same requirements, or working with the QoS parameters returned by the network as possible values. If the guarantees are soft, then the network service provider may modify the offered QoS parameters dynamically, depending on the load. The application carrying out the multimedia presentation should then be able to handle the dynamic modification of the QoS parameters. Fig. 8.9 shows an example where modification of QoS is made dynamically by the network service provider during an application lifetime. During the time interval t, the guaranteed QoS falls below the acceptable limit. When the modification falls within the "safe" range (between the preferred and acceptable QoS), then the multimedia presentation can proceed smoothly. Otherwise, the application has to use other options for continuing the presentation such as employing more buffers, slowing down the speed of presentation, or dropping a medium from presentation. Some of these options can be employed only with the concurrence of the user going through the presentation.

Options For Handling QoS Degradation in Orchestrated Presentations: When the guaranteed QoS falls below the safe range, the application has different options for continuing the presentation. If the available buffer space is lower than the required one, then the application has no other option but to slow down the speed of presentation (i.e., when C_{net} offered by the network is less than C_{app}^{acc}). Slowing down the speed of presentation has to be done with the consent of the user going through the presentation. The factor by which the presentation has to be slowed down can be determined as follows: Assume that C_{app} is the throughput requested from the network service provider. Let C_{net} ($C_{net} < C_{app}$) be the average throughput that can be guaranteed by the network. A total of s bits have to be retrieved in the time interval $(t_{i+1} - t_i)$. With the offered throughput of C_{net}, the application can retrieve only $(C_{net}*(t_{i+1}-t_i))$ bits in the interval. Hence, the time delay for complete retrieval is :

$$t_{delay} = [s - C_{net} * (t_{i+1} - t_i)]/C_{net}.$$

And the scaling factor for slowing down the presentation is :

$$ScalingFactor = t_{delay}/(t_{i+1} - t_i).$$

If the modified presentation with the speed scaled down by the given factor is acceptable to the user, then the application can proceed with the presentation. It should be noted that slowing down the speed of the presentation affects other synchronized multimedia streams, as well. Also in the case of audio stream, the slowed down presentation may not make much sense and the application can stop the audio presentation in consultation with the user.

8.6   Interaction with the User

In an orchestrated presentation, the user can interact by giving inputs such as skip event(s), reverse presentation, navigate in time, scaling the speed of presentation, scaling the spatial requirements, handling spatial clash, freeze, and restart of a presentation. In the example of Fig. 8.6, consider a skip event operation on the image stream I_1 when the event x_1 is being presented and other events a_1, v_1, y_1 are being presented in parallel. The skip event modifies the synchronization sequence by changing the next set of objects to be delivered. In this example, the next set of objects to be delivered will be $\{a_4, v_4, x_2, y_1\}$. A similar discussion holds for user inputs like reverse presentation and navigate in time.

A set of algorithms have been proposed in [2], outlining the operations to be carried out for skip, reverse presentation, and navigate in time. Operations such as skip, reverse presentation, and navigate in time modify the sequence of objects being presented and hence the instantaneous QoS requirements.

User input, like scaling the speed of presentation, modifies the time duration of presentation. Scaling the spatial requirements of the presentation modifies the size of the multimedia object being presented. If the source of the object can employ some compression techniques to adopt to the modified spatial requirement, the size of the object to be communicated can also be suitably modified. Operations like scaling the speed of presentation and scaling the spatial requirements alter the QoS requirements of a stream by modifying the preferred and acceptable limits. If the guaranteed QoS is below the acceptable limit, then the application has to renegotiate its QoS requirements at time t.

8.7 QoS Computation and Buffer Design

For computation of QoS, however, we need to know the details regarding the size of the multimedia objects. We can assume that these details are stored along with the temporal relationships governing the presentation sequence. For the video window V of Fig. 8.6, we can consider the assumptions made in Section 8.3 for computing the QoS requirements of the video stream.

Example: The preferred QoS requirement of the application is 20 Mbps for the time interval 0 to 30 seconds and 10 Mbps for the interval 30 to 70 seconds, based on the above assumptions. For calculating the acceptable QoS, let us assume the maximum buffer space (B_{max}) available as 400 Mbits. The acceptable QoS will be 8.58 Mbps, and hence the retrieval of the 400 Mbits has to be started 46.66 seconds before the start of the presentation.

8.8 Summary

In this chapter, we discussed the buffer design and the QoS estimation for a multimedia application. The PACFG-based approach, apart from giving a compact representation, can help in developing syntax-driven traffic generators. This model reflects both the temporal interdependencies and stochastic effects (due to user and network interactions) in traffic generation. A single traffic source model may not describe all types of multimedia applications.

Hence, the PACFG traffic source model can be used for describing the traffic generated by orchestrated multimedia applications, as the traffic generated by them reflects directly the functional behavior of the application. *lex* and *yacc*[2] based tools can be used for developing the traffic generators for a variety of multimedia applications.

The QoS requirements depend on the size of the objects, the time instant of presentation of the objects, and their duration of presentation. The QoS requirements of a multimedia application have an upper and lower bound corresponding to the preferred and acceptable QoS values. With these bounds, the multimedia application can negotiate its QoS requirements with the network service provider. Dynamic modification of QoS by the network service provider and the participating user can also be handled by keeping the estimated QoS requirements in mind.

REFERENCES

1. S.V. Raghavan, B.Prabhakaran, and S.K. Tripathi. QoS Negotiation and Buffer Design, Journal of High Speed Networks, Vol. 2, 1996.

2. S.V. Raghavan, B. Prabhakaran, and S.K. Tripathi. Quality of Service Negotiation For Orchestrated Multimedia Presentation, Proceedings of High Performance Networking Conference HPN 94, Grenoble, France, June 1994.

3. Domenico Ferrari. Client Requirements for Real-Time Communication Services, IEEE Communication Magazine, Vol. 28, No. 11, pp. 65-72, 1990.

4. Domenico Ferrari, Jean Ramaekers, and Giorgio Ventre. Client-Network Interactions in Quality of Service Communication Environments, Fourth IFIP Conference on High Performance Networking, Liege, Belgium, pp. E1.1-E1.14, December 1992.

Exercises

1. Calculate the buffer requirements for a videophone call, when minbuf or maxbuf are used. Which one do you recommend?

2. For a video conference on an ISDN line, write the PACFG rules. Assume any traffic model.

3. For an on-line automatic product presentation, estimate the buffer requirement when the user rewinds three times (once every time that 25% of the program is played). Assume an minbuf strategy. If the program is stored as a MPEG stream, what will the requirement be? Assume the I:P:B ratio as 1:4:1.

---

[2]Unix utilities.

Chapter 9

Multimedia Systems Design: Traffic Shaping

9.1 Introduction

Multimedia applications comprised of a heterogeneous mix of video, voice, and data are characterized by stringent QoS requirements in terms of throughput, delay, delay jitter, and loss guarantees. The heterogeneity of the sources necessitates effective control schemes to meet the diverse Quality of Service (QoS) requirements of each application. These schemes include admission control at connection setup, traffic enforcement and shaping at the edges of the network, and multiclass scheduling schemes at the intermediate switches. One of the key factors in QoS management in modern high-speed networks is congestion control. The latency effects of gigabit speeds render the conventional feedback techniques for control ineffective. Thus, the responsibility of preventing congestion lies with the admission control and traffic enforcement schemes.

A survey of some of the admission control, resource reservation, and scheduling schemes proposed for integrated broadband networks in the recent past, and the related issues, can be found in [1]. Admission control restricts the number of connections that can be supported by the network. It is performed using an algorithm which expects that the user provides an estimate of the traffic parameters and abides by the negotiated values. Resource reservation schemes manage the allocation of the resources at each of the nodes so that per-node QoS requirements can be met for each connection. Scheduling policies provide sharing of bandwidth among the various classes and the various streams within each class so that the individual requirements can be satisfied.

In a packet network that implements resource sharing, admission control,

281

and scheduling schemes by themselves are not sufficient to provide guarantees. This is due to the fact that users may, inadvertently or otherwise, attempt to exceed the rates specified at the time of connection establishment. The QoS negotiated at the time of admission control may be exceeded due to the burstiness in the multimedia sources. This is especially so, when the QoS was negotiated for the average rate. When bursts appear at peak rate, scheduling and the consequent resource allocation become unbalanced. It is therefore necessary to have a constant watch over the traffic associated with each application. Traffic policing schemes proposed in the literature include Leaky Bucket (LB), Jumping Window (JW), Moving Window (MW), Exponential Weighted Moving Average (EWMA), and associated variations. A performance comparison among these schemes from the point of view of violation probability, sensitivity to overloads, dynamic reaction time, and worst-case traffic admitted into the network can be found in [2]. It has been shown that the LB and the EWMA are the most promising mechanisms to cope with short-term fluctuations and hence are suited for policing bursty traffic. Several improvements of the LB have been proposed for increasing utilization in an ATM environment [3,4,5]. Traffic enforcement schemes police the source streams to check that their characteristics conform to the declared values throughout the life of the connection. The various schemes have been studied from the point of view of their capability to smooth the burstiness in the source. Traffic Shaping, on the other hand, smoothes the input stream so that the characteristics are amenable to the scheduling mechanisms to provide the required QoS guarantees. The former checks for the conformance to the declared values, whereas the latter shapes it to be more agreeable to the scheduling policies.

Traffic shapers have been mainly studied hitherto from the point of view of their effectiveness in smoothing the burstiness. The Leaky Bucket scheme, to cite an example, is a mean rate policer smoothing at the token generation rate. Studies on bursty sources show that burstiness promotes statistical multiplexing at the cost of possible congestion. Smoothing, on the other hand, helps in providing guarantees at the cost of utilization. Thus, the need for a flexible scheme which can provide a reasonable compromise between utilization and performance is imminent. Recent studies [6,7] have also questioned the suitability of LB for policing real-time traffic. LB, in its attempt to enforce smoothness, often introduces excessive access delays thereby making it incapable of regulating real-time traffic. A policy which is less stringent on short-term burstiness while bounding long-term behavior with a LB-bound would be better suited for time-critical traffic.

We discuss two new traffic shapers which can adjust the burstiness of the input traffic to obtain reasonable bandwidth utilization while maintaining statistical service guarantees. One employs multirate shaping, and the other uses a window-based shaping policy which captures the essence of the LB scheme, permits short-term burstiness in a more flexible manner, and is inherently peak rate enforced. The decision to admit an arriving packet is based on the temporal image of the past data maintained in a shift register. The material in this chapter is based on [8,9,10].

9.2 Burstiness and Bandwidth Allocation

Traffic sources in multimedia applications can be generally classified into five categories, viz., data, voice, video, image, and graphics. But we confine our discussion to data, voice, and video. Data sources are generally bursty in nature, whereas voice and video sources are naturally continuous and bursty if compression and coding techniques are used. Recall that continuous sources are said to generate constant bit-rate (CBR) traffic and bursty sources are said to generate variable bit-rate (VBR) traffic. A CBR source needs peak rate allocation of bandwidth for congestion-free transmission. For a VBR source, average rate of transmission λ_a can be a small fraction of the peak rate λ_p. Thus, a peak rate allocation would result in gross underutilization of the system resources. With peak rate allotment, providing performance guarantees is easy. On the other extreme, average allotment may lead to buffer overflows and consequent losses/delays. No meaningful guarantees can be offered in such cases. An effective bandwidth λ_{eff}, whose value lies between the average and the peak rates, is to be determined for the various sources [11,12]. An allocation corresponding to the effective bandwidth optimizes the network utilization and performance guarantees. An allocation nearer to the peak rate allows providing probabilistic guarantees. In the extreme, with peak rate allotment, the guarantees can be deterministic.

In order to provide guaranteed services, resources, buffer, and bandwidth resources have to be reserved *a priori* so that the promised quality of service is not violated due to system overloading. The resource reservation algorithm at a multiplexing node takes into account the traffic envelopes[1] and the service envelopes[2] of all the connections passing though the node in order to determine how many resources to reserve for a particular connection, or whether to reject a connection when sufficient resources are not available.

---

[1] Peak and average rates, burst lengths, and duration.
[2] Maximum tolerable delay, desired delay jitter, etc.

Besides traffic and service envelopes, resource reservation also depends on the multiplexing schemes used at the switching nodes. Hence, in order to design and develop an effective quality of service (QoS) architecture, we need to understand the interaction between the traffic characteristics and service requirements of different virtual channels, each carrying a media stream.

A generalized packet stream is said to be $< n_1, T_1; n_2, T_2; ..; n_k, T_k >$ smooth, if over any time window of duration T_i the number of packets $\leq n_i$ where k denotes the number of windows for characterizing the smoothness of the stream. A larger k can provide a more flexible description of the stream.

9.3   Traffic Shapers

One of the most important components in a QoS architecture is the characteristics of the traffic source associated with each connection. The resource reservation algorithm at a multiplexing node needs to analyze the traffic envelopes associated with all the connections passing through the node in order to determine the service quality that can be offered to individual connections. Since the number of connections passing through a node may run into hundreds or even thousands, it is important that the traffic envelopes are succinct and simple for easy management. Unfortunately, traffic generated by most multimedia applications is very bursty and often difficult to model and specify. To alleviate this problem, traffic generated by a source is passed through a traffic shaper which shapes the traffic to a form that is simple to specify and easy to analyze. Besides shaping, a shaper (or regulator) also polices traffic so that a source may not violate the traffic envelope negotiated at the time of connection setup and degrade the service quality of other users. If the traffic generated by a source does not conform to the traffic envelope enforced by the shaper, the shaper can either drop the violating cells, tag them as lower-priority traffic, or hold them in a reshaping buffer. In the rest of the discussion, we assume that the shaper exercises the third option. In our model, traffic generated by a source (autonomous device) is first fed into a shaper buffer. From the shaper buffer, the data is passed through a regulator and is released into the system/network in the form of fixed-size cells satisfying the traffic envelope. The shape of the traffic envelope is determined by the shaping mechanism and the shaper parameters.

By introducing a shaper at the edge of the network, we get better control on the traffic entering the network. From the perspective of the network, the traffic generated of the shaper is really the traffic entering the network. In the rest of the chapter, our objective is to study different shaping mechanisms and characterize the traffic envelope they enforce on a source. These traffic envelopes are used later to model the traffic arrival into the network.

9.3.1 Leaky Bucket Scheme

A Leaky Bucket shaper consists of a token counter and a timer. The counter is incremented by one at each t units of time and can reach a maximum value b. A cell is admitted into the system/network if and only if the counter is positive. Each time a cell is admitted, the counter is decremented by one. The traffic generated by a Leaky Bucket regulator consists of a burst of up to b cells followed by a steady stream of cells with a minimum intercell time of t. The major attraction of Leaky Bucket is its simplicity. A Leaky Bucket regulator can be implemented with two counters: one to implement the token counter and the other to implement the timer.

Leaky Bucket [2] and its variant schemes are described in [3,4,5]. In a generalized model of the Leaky Bucket shown in Fig. 9.1, tokens are generated at a fixed rate as long as the token buffer of size b is not full. When a packet arrives from the source, it is released into the network only if there is at least one token in the token buffer. This scheme enforces the token arrival rate λ_t on the input stream. Clearly, λ_t should be greater than the average arrival rate λ_a for stability and less than the peak arrival rate λ_p for achieving bandwidth utilization. An input data buffer of size d permits statistical variations. An arriving packet finding the input buffer full is said to be a violating packet and can be dropped or tagged for a preferential

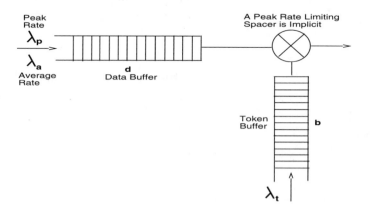

Fig. 9.1. A Generalized Leaky Bucket Scheme

treatment at the switching nodes.

A peak rate limiting spacer is an integral part of the Leaky Bucket mechanism. When a burst of data arrives at the input and not enough tokens are present, the packets are not instantaneously released into the network. Successive packets are delayed by τ and the transmission time at negotiated peak rate λ_p, where $\tau = 1/\lambda_p$. We will use LBP to designate the Leaky Bucket with peak rate policer. For the Leaky Bucket parameters defined above, maximum burst size at the output is $b' = b/(1 - \lambda_t/\lambda_p)$. This includes the new tokens that arrive during the transmission of the first b packets. The output of the Leaky Bucket is characterized as follows:

1. **Maximum burst size**: For the LBP, maximum burst size at the output is $b' = b/(1 - \lambda_t/\lambda_p)$ and is obtained as follows. If we assume the largest burst starts at t_1, the token buffer should be full at t_1. This would be possible only if the source generated an input burst after a prolonged OFF period of b/λ_t, where b is the token buffer size. Since the burst service is not instantaneous due to peak rate policer, more tokens may arrive during the consumption of the existing tokens. Since tokens are removed at λ_p and arrive at λ_t, the instantaneous token count in TB will be $b(t) = b + (\lambda_t - \lambda_p) \cdot t$ and hence TB empties at time $b/(\lambda_p - \lambda_t)$. The maximum burst size b' then becomes $b/(1 - \lambda_t/\lambda_p)$.

2. **Long-term output smoothness**: Over a large time duration T, the number of packets sent out by the Leaky Bucket, $n(T)$, is $\leq \lambda_t \cdot T = n_t$. This relationship is also true for any time duration T' *starting from zero or any epoch when token buffer becomes empty*. It is assumed here that the token buffer is empty at $t = 0$.

3. **Short-term burstiness**: Over durations smaller than T mentioned in the previous item and exceeding the maximum burst size, Leaky Bucket output can be modeled as a Linear Bounded Arrival Process (LBAP) with parameters (σ, ρ)[13]. Here, σ represents the maximum burst size b' and ρ represents the token rate λ_t.

In terms of the smoothness definition given earlier, we can state that for any T starting from 0 (or from any epoch when token buffer is empty), LBP output is (n_t, T) smooth.

9.3.2 Jumping Window Shapers

A jumping window regulator divides the time line into fixed-size windows of length w and limits the number of cells accepted from a source within any window to a maximum number m. The traffic generated of a jumping window can have a worst-case burst length of $2m$. This happens when two bursts of size m are released next to each other, the first one at the end of its window and the second one at the beginning of the next window. Like a Leaky Bucket, a jumping window regulator can also be implemented with two counters.

9.3.3 Moving Window Shapers

Similar to a jumping window, in a moving window the number of arrivals in a time window w is limited to a maximum number m. The difference is that each cell is remembered for exactly one window width. That is, if we slide a window of size w on the time axis, the number of cells admitted within a window period can never exceed m irrespective of the position of the window. Hence, the worst-case burst size in a moving window regulator never exceeds m. Compared to a jumping window shaper, traffic generated of a moving window shaper is smoother. This smoothness, however, comes at the cost of added complexity in implementation. Since the departure time of each cell is remembered for a duration of one window period, the implementation complexity depends on m, the maximum number of cells released within a window period.

9.3.4 Exponentially Weighted Moving Average Scheme

Exponentially Weighted Moving Average Scheme (EWMA) is a window-based scheme where the maximum number of cells permitted within a fixed time window is limited. If we consider the connection time to consist of consecutive windows of the same size, the maximum number of cells accepted in the ith window N_i is a function of the mean number of cells per window N, and an exponentially weighted sum of the cells accepted in the preceding windows is as given below:

$$N_i = \frac{(N-(1-\gamma)(\gamma X_{i-1}+....+\gamma^{i-1}X_1))-\gamma^i S_0}{(1-\gamma)},$$

where S_0 is the initial value for the EWMA. The weight factor γ decides the number of relevant preceding windows which influence the number of packets permitted in the current window. A nonzero value of γ permits more burstiness. For a value of $\gamma = 0.8$, up to $5N$ packets can occur in the first window. Thus, a large value of γ increases the reaction time and it is shown in [2] that the dynamic behavior of EWMA is the worst. Moreover, the implementation complexity of this scheme is higher than LB and other window-based schemes.

9.4   Desirable Properties of a Traffic Shaper

A good shaping mechanism should exhibit the following properties:

- The traffic envelope it enforces on a source should be easy to describe.

- It should be simple to implement and easy to police.

- It should be able to capture a wide range of traffic characteristics.

Although the shaping mechanisms described above satisfy the first and second requirements, they do not quite meet the third one. Traffic envelopes defined by a single Leaky Bucket, jumping window, or moving window is often not adequate for precise characterization of the bursty and variable rate traffic generated by multimedia applications. This mismatch between the original traffic form and that enforced by the shaper can have serious implications on system performance. Let us consider an example to better understand the problem.

Example: Consider an MPEG-coded video stream. From uncompressed video data, an MPEG encoder produces a coded bit stream representing a sequence of encoded frames. There are three types of encoded frames: I (intracoded), P (predicted), and B (bidirectional). The sequence of encoded frames is specified by two parameters: M, the distance between I and P frames, and N, the distance between I frames. For example, when M is 2 and N is 5, the sequence of encoded frames is IBPBIBPB ... (see Fig. 9.2). The pattern IBPB repeats indefinitely. The interarrival time τ between two successive frames is fixed, and depends on the frame rate.

In general, an I frame is much larger than a P frame (in size), and a P frame is much larger than a B frame. Typically, the size of an I frame is larger than the size of a B frame by an order of magnitude. Let us assume that $|I|$, $|P|$, and $|B|$ be the sizes of I, P, and B frames, respectively [3]

Let us consider the problem of choosing a moving window shaper for this source. One good set of parameters is $w = \tau$ and $m = |I|$. Clearly, with this choice of parameters, there will be no delay in the shaper. However, this traffic envelope grossly overestimates the

---

[3] For simplicity, we assume that the sizes of all I frames are the same and so are the sizes of all P and B frames. In general, $|I|$, $|P|$, and $|B|$ are random variables. However, it is not unreasonable to assume that $|I|$ is larger than $|P|$ and $|P|$ is larger than $|B|$.

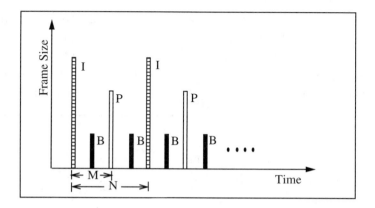

Fig. 9.2. An Example of an MPEG Coded Stream

traffic generated by the source. In fact, this is a peak rate approximation of the original source. An alternative set of parameters is $w = \tau$ and $m = (|I| + |P| + 2|B|)/4$. With this shaping envelope, the average rate of traffic generated by the original source and that estimated from the traffic envelope are the same. In other words, it is an average rate approximation of the source. It smoothes the traffic generated by the original source to an equivalent source with the same average rate by holding the frames in the shaper buffer. Here, an I frame may be delayed by $\tau \lfloor 4|I|/(|I| + |P| + 2|B|) \rfloor$ time units in the shaper buffer.

Clearly, none of the choices is satisfactory. With the peak rate approximation of the source, there is no delay in shaper. However, this traffic envelope grossly overestimates the resource requirement of the source, leading to network underutilization. With the average-rate approximation of the source, network resource utilization is high, but only at the expense of a higher shaper delay. Hence, it is important that the traffic envelope captures the characteristics of the original source as closely as possible. The traffic envelopes enforced by a single Leaky Bucket, moving window, and jumping window are too simple for an accurate characterization of bursty sources. We can do better if we use multiple shapers to shape a traffic source.

9.5 Composite Shapers

All the shapers described in the previous section enforce a specific rate constraint on a source, typically a declared peak or average rate. However, most applications generate inherently bursty traffic. That is, the difference between the peak rate and the mean rate of traffic generation is quite high. Hence, enforcing an average rate results in a higher delay in the shaper buffer and a peak rate enforcement leads to overallocation of system resources (and consequently lower utilization of the system). To alleviate this problem, or in other words to enforce a traffic envelope that is close to the original shape of the traffic and yet simple to specify and monitor, we can use multiple shapers to enforce multiple rate constraints. That is, we can choose multiple

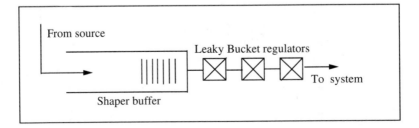

Fig. 9.3. Composite Leaky Bucket

Leaky Buckets, moving windows, and jumping windows enforcing different rate constraints over different time intervals. For example, two Leaky Buckets arranged in series can be used to enforce a short-term peak rate and a long-term average rate on a source. Composite shapers provide us with a much richer and larger set of traffic envelopes, with a marginal increase in complexity.

Example: To appreciate the effectiveness of a composite shaper in better characterizing a bursty source, let us consider the same example as above. A dual-moving-window shaper with parameters $(w_1 = 4 \times \tau, m_1 = |I| + |P| + 2|B|)$ and $(w_2 = \tau, m_2 = |I|)$ can capture the original characteristics of the source much more accurately than either one of the moving windows alone. The first shaper enforces the longer-term average rate, while the second one controls the short-term peak rate of the source. Now, the cells generated from the I frame would not be held up in the shaper buffer for $\tau \lfloor 4|I|/(|I|+|P|+2|B|) \rfloor$ time units, as is the case when we use a single moving window with $w = \tau$ and $m = (|I|+|P|+2|B|)/4$. Also, unlike the traffic envelope of the moving window with $w_2 = \tau$ and $m_2 = |I|$, the composite traffic envelope does not overestimate the traffic generated by the source. An even more precise characterization can be done with three moving window regulators with parameters $(w_1 = 4 \times \tau, m_1 = |I| + |P| + 2|B|)$, $(w_2 = 2 \times \tau, m_2 = |I| + |B|)$, and $(w_3 = \tau, m_3 = |I|)$. With a better characterization of a traffic source, a more efficient utilization of the shared resources is possible.

Although developing techniques for choosing the right shaping mechanism and shaper parameters for a traffic source is an interesting and important subject of research, it is not the focus of this book. Our objective is to study the performance of the network subsystem, and for our purposes shapers are the traffic sources that feed the network. Hence, our interest is in characterizing the traffic generated by the shapers so that they can be used to model the traffic arrivals in the network. Also, since we are interested in the worst-case behavior, we concentrate on the worst-case bursty traffic generated by the shapers. In the following, we derive the exact forms of the worst-case traffic envelopes enforced by composite Leaky Bucket, moving window, and jumping window shapers.

9.5.1 Composite Leaky Bucket

In a composite Leaky Bucket shaper, multiple simple Leaky Buckets are arranged in cascade (see Fig. 9.3). The data generated by the source is first buffered in the shaper buffer. Fixed-length cells are dispatched into the system if and only if there is at least one token in each of the Leaky Buckets. A single Leaky Bucket generates the worst-case bursty traffic when the system starts with a full bucket of tokens, and dispatches a cell whenever there is a token.

This worst-case behavior of a Leaky Bucket is characterized by a traffic envelope that starts with a burst that is equal to the bucket size, followed by a straight line [4] of slope equal to the rate of token generation. The traffic envelope enforced by a composite Leaky Bucket is the intersection of the traffic envelopes of the constituent Leaky Buckets.

Example: In Fig. 9.4, a composite Leaky Bucket consisting of Leaky Buckets LB_1, LB_2, LB_3, and LB_4 is shown. The composite traffic envelope is marked by the dark line.

---

[4]Strictly speaking, the traffic envelope due to each Leaky Bucket is a burst followed by a staircase function. For ease of exposition, we have approximated the staircase function by a straight line with the same slope. This simplification is only for the purpose of explanation. The results derived later takes into consideration the staircase function.

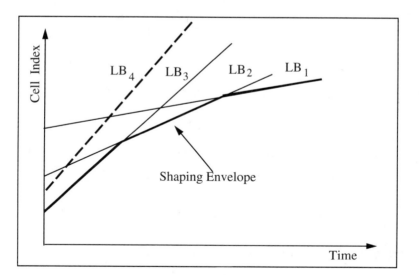

Fig. 9.4. **Shaping with Multiple Leaky Buckets**

The exact shape of the envelope depends on the number of components and the associated parameters. Inappropriate choices of shaper parameters may give rise to redundant components which may not have any role in defining the traffic envelope. For example, LB_4 is a redundant component in the composite shaper shown in Fig. 9.4. We call a set of Leaky Buckets an *essential set* if none of the buckets is redundant.

Let us consider n Leaky Buckets (b_i, t_i), $i = 1, 2, \ldots, n$. Without loss of generality, we number the buckets in such a fashion so that $t_i \geq t_j$, for $i < j$. We will show that if these Leaky Buckets form an *essential set*, then $b_i > b_j$ and $t_i > t_j$ for $i < j$. It can be shown that if two Leaky Buckets (b_1, t_1) and (b_2, t_2) form an essential set, then $b_1 > b_2$ and $t_1 > t_2$[14].

By using this result repeatedly, we can show that a set of Leaky Buckets (b_i, t_i), where $i = 1, 2, \ldots n$, form an essential set; then, $b_1 > b_2 > \cdots > b_n$ and $t_1 > t_2 > \cdots > t_n$.

To capture the worst-case bursty behavior, we assume that all the buckets are full and cells are released to the network as long as there is at least one token in each of the buckets. The traffic envelope of a composite shaper consisting of an essential set of Leaky Buckets can be formally stated, using the definition of a composite Leaky Bucket as given in the sequel.

An n-component composite Leaky Bucket is an essential set of n Leaky Buckets $(b_1, t_1), (b_2, t_2), \ldots, (b_n, t_n)$, where $b_i > b_j$ and $t_i > t_j$ for $i < j$. For the purpose of mathematical convenience, we assume that the n-component shaper includes another pseudo Leaky Bucket (b_{n+1}, t_{n+1}), where $b_{n+1} = 0$ and $t_{n+1} = 0$.

Let us consider an n-component composite Leaky Bucket. Let us define

$$
B_k = \begin{cases}
\infty & k = 0, \\[2mm]
\left\lfloor \dfrac{b_k t_k - b_{k+1} t_{k+1}}{t_k - t_{k+1}} \right\rfloor & k = 1, 2, \ldots, n, \\[2mm]
0 & k = n + 1.
\end{cases}
$$

Then the departure time of the ith cell from the composite shaper, denoted by $a(i)$, can be expressed as

$$
a(i) = \sum_{k=1}^{n+1} (i - b_k + 1)\, t_k\, [U(i - B_k) - U(i - B_{k-1})], \quad i = 0, 1, \ldots, \infty
$$

where $U(x)$ is the unit step function defined as

$$
U(x) = \begin{cases}
0 & x < 0, \\
1 & x \geq 0.
\end{cases}
$$

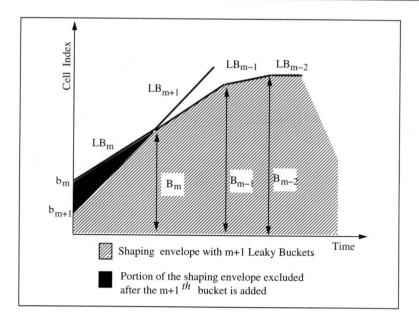

Fig. 9.5. Traffic Envelope after Adding a $(m+1)^{th}$ Bucket.

This result can be proved by induction [14].

If we consider the base case, for $n = 1$, we have $B_0 = \infty$, $B_1 = b_1$, and $B_2 = 0$. Therefore,

$$a(i) = (i - b_1 + 1)\, t_1\, U(i - b_1).$$

This allows a burst of size b_1 to depart at time 0 and a cell after every t_1 henceforth. Clearly, the traffic envelope captures the characteristics of the traffic generated by a Leaky Bucket with parameters b_1 and t_1. Hence, the hypothesis holds in the base case.

To proceed with the hypothesis inductively, assume that the theorem holds for all $n \leq m$. To prove that it holds for all n, we need to show that it holds for $n = m + 1$.

Fig. 9.5 shows the traffic envelope before and after the addition of the $(m+1)^{th}$ bucket. Since the set of buckets constitute an essential set, $b_{i+1} < b_i$ for $i = 1, 2, \ldots m$. Therefore, the effect of the $(m + 1)^{th}$ bucket is observed from time 0 to the time when the traffic envelope due to bucket $m + 1$ intersects the composite traffic envelope due to Leaky Buckets 1 through m (see Fig. 9.5). We observe that this crossover point is really the point of intersection between the traffic envelopes of the mth and the $(m+1)^{th}$ Leaky Buckets. Using simple geometry, we can find that they intersect at the departure instant of the $\lfloor(b_m t_m - b_{m+1} t_{m+1})/(t_m - t_{m+1})\rfloor$th cell, which, by definition, is B_m.

In other words, the bucket $m+1$ excludes the segment marked by the solid shadow from the shaping envelope as shown in Fig. 9.5. The new segment can be expressed as

$$(i - b_{m+1} + 1)\ t_{m+1}\ [U(i - B_{m+1}) - U(i - B_m)]$$

The composite traffic envelope of buckets 1 through m is a piecewise linear function joining the points of intersections of the traffic envelopes of ith and $(i+1)^{th}$ buckets, for $i = 1, 2, \ldots m - 1$. By adding the new segment to that, we get the composite traffic envelope due to $m + 1$ buckets.

$$
\begin{aligned}
a(i) &= \sum_{k=1}^{m+1} (i - b_k + 1)\ t_k\ [U(i - B_k) - U(i - B_{k-1})] \\
&\quad + (i - b_{m+1} + 1)\ t_{m+1}\ [U(i - B_{m+1}) - U(i - B_m)] \\
&= \sum_{k=1}^{m+2} (i - b_k + 1)\ t_k\ [U(i - B_k) - U(i - B_{k-1})] \quad (since\ b_{m+2} = 0)
\end{aligned}
$$

This essentially completes the proof.

9.5.2 Composite Moving Window

A single moving window (w, m) generates the worst-case bursty traffic when a burst of m cells is released at the beginning of each window. Hence, the worst-case traffic envelope of a single moving window is characterized by a staircase function with step height m and step width w. In a composite moving window shaper, multiple moving window regulators are arranged in cascade. The traffic envelope defined by a composite moving window is the intersection of the traffic envelopes of the constituent shapers. The following example explains it in more detail.

Example: Fig. 9.6 shows the worst-case traffic envelope of a composite shaper consisting of moving windows $MW_1 = (w_1, m_1)$, $MW_2 = (w_2, m_2)$, $MW_3 = (w_3, m_3)$, where $w_1 = 3 \times w_2$, $w_2 = 4 \times w_3$ and $m_1 = 2 \times m_2$, $m_2 = 2 \times m_3$. In this particular example, traffic is shaped over three different time windows. The first moving window limits the number of cells dispatched in any time window of size w_1 to m_1. However, MW_1 does not impose any restriction on how these m_1 cells are dispatched. In the worstcase, they

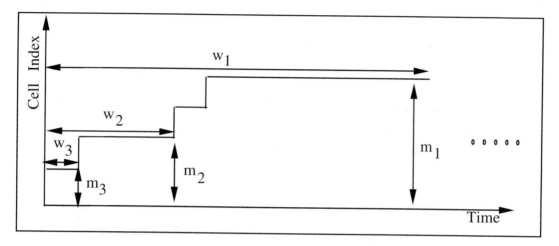

Fig. 9.6. Traffic Envelope of a Composite Moving Window

may be dispatched as a single burst of size m_1. Moving window MW_2 determines the burst size distribution within w_1. Window w_1 can be broken down into three windows of duration w_2 each. The maximum amount of traffic that can be dispatched during any time interval w_2 is limited to m_2 by MW_2. Hence, m_2 cells are dispatched in each of the first two w_2 intervals. Since $m_1 = 2 \times m_2$, no cell is dispatched in the third w_2 window to satisfy the constraint imposed by the first moving window. Similarly, the second moving window limits the maximum number of cells released in a window of length $w_2 = 4 \times w_3$ to $m_2 = 2 \times m_3$. Hence, m_3 cells are dispatched in each of the first two w_3 windows within a w_2 window. In the remaining two w_3 windows, no cells are dispatched to satisfy the constraint imposed by MW_2.

The shape of the worst-case traffic envelope of a composite moving window shaper can be stated succinctly. In order to do so, let us define a composite moving window shaper.

An n-component composite moving window shaper consists of n simple moving windows (w_k, m_k), $k = 1, \ldots, n$, where $w_i \geq w_j$, $m_i \geq m_j$, and $m_i/w_i \leq m_j/w_j$, for $1 \leq i < j \leq n$. For the sake of mathematical convenience we assume that an n-component composite shaper also includes another pseudo moving window (m_0, w_0) such that $m_0/m_1 = 0$. We also assume, for simplicity of exposition, that m_{i+1} divides m_i and w_{i+1} divides w_i, for $i = 1, 2, \ldots, n - 1$.

Consider an n-component moving window shaper. If $a(i)$ is the departure time of the ith cell from the shaper, then

$$a(i) = \sum_{k=1}^{n} \left(\left\lfloor \frac{i}{m_k} \right\rfloor - \left\lfloor \frac{i}{m_{k-1}} \right\rfloor \frac{m_{k-1}}{m_k} \right) w_k, \qquad i = 0, 1, \ldots, \infty$$

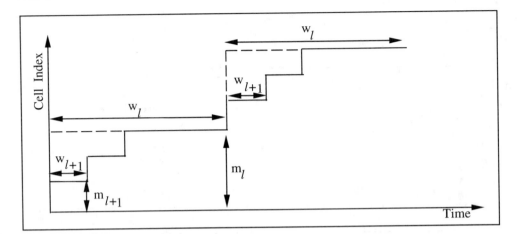

Fig. 9.7. Traffic Envelope after Adding the $(l+1)^{th}$ **Moving Window**

This can also be proved by induction [14].

If we look at the base case for $n = 1$, we have $a(i) = \left\lfloor \frac{i}{m_1} \right\rfloor w_1$. This means that a burst of size m_1 appear at times kw_1, $k = 0, 1, \ldots, \infty$. Clearly, this represents the traffic envelope due to a single moving window with parameters (w_1, m_1). Hence, the premise holds in the base case.

In order to prove this by induction, assume that the premise holds for all $n \leq l$. To prove that it holds for all n, we need to show that it holds for $n = l + 1$.

Consider the effect of adding the $(l + 1)^{th}$ moving window. In the worstcase, the burst always comes at the beginning of a window. Therefore, as shown in Fig. 9.7, bursts of size m_l cells appear at the beginning of each window of length w_l, for m_{l-1}/m_l windows. Now, from the hypothesis, the arrival time of the ith cell is given by

$$a(i) = \sum_{k=1}^{l} \left(\left\lfloor \frac{i}{m_k} \right\rfloor - \left\lfloor \frac{i}{m_{k-1}} \right\rfloor \frac{m_{k-1}}{m_k} \right) w_k.$$

If a new shaper (w_{l+1}, m_{l+1}) is added, the burst appearing at the beginning of each w_l window will spread out into m_l/m_{l+1} bursts of size m_{l+1} each and separated by w_{l+1}, as shown in Fig. 9.7. Due to this spreading out of the bursts, the arrival time of the ith cell will be postponed by

$$\left(\left\lfloor \frac{i}{m_{l+1}} \right\rfloor - \left\lfloor \frac{i}{m_l} \right\rfloor \frac{m_l}{m_{l+1}} \right) w_{l+1}$$

Hence the arrival time of the ith cell after the addition of the $(l+1)^{th}$ moving window is

$$
\begin{aligned}
a(i) \; = \; & \sum_{k=1}^{l} \left(\left\lfloor \frac{i}{m_k} \right\rfloor - \left\lfloor \frac{i}{m_{k-1}} \right\rfloor \frac{m_{k-1}}{m_k} \right) w_k \\
& + \left(\left\lfloor \frac{i}{m_{l+1}} \right\rfloor - \left\lfloor \frac{i}{m_l} \right\rfloor \frac{m_l}{m_{l+1}} \right) w_{l+1} \\
= \; & \sum_{k=1}^{l+1} \left(\left\lfloor \frac{i}{m_k} \right\rfloor - \left\lfloor \frac{i}{m_{k-1}} \right\rfloor \frac{m_{k-1}}{m_k} \right) w_k
\end{aligned}
$$

This essentially completes the proof.

9.5.3 Composite Jumping Window

Although moving and jumping window shapers appear to be quite similar, their worst-case traffic envelopes can be quite different. In a single moving window shaper, two full-size bursts are always separated by at least one window length. However, in a jumping window shaper, two bursts can appear next to each other: one at the end of a window and the other at the beginning of the next window. Similar cases are possible in composite jumping window shapers. Hence, unlike in moving window shapers, where the worst-case bursty behavior occurs when bursts appear at the earliest possible instants, in jumping windows the worst-case occurs when the first of the two consecutive bursts arrives at the end of its window, and the next arrives at the beginning of the next window.

Example: Fig. 9.8 shows the traffic envelope of a composite shaper consisting of jumping windows $JW_1 = (w_1, m_1)$, $JW_2 = (w_2, m_2)$, $JW_3 = (w_3, m_3)$, where $w_1 = 3 \times w_2$, $w_2 = 4 \times w_3$ and $m_1 = 2 \times m_2$, $m_2 = 2 \times m_3$ in the interval $[0, 2w_1]$. If we had only one shaper (w_1, m_1), two bursts of size m_1 cells each could have appeared next to each other at w_1^- and and w_1. However, jumping window JW_2 mandates that the maximum size of the bursts can only be $m_2 = m_1/2$. Hence, each of the bursts of size m_1 has to be broken down into two bursts of size m_2 each. In the worst-case, they can appear at times $w_1 - w_2$, w_1^-, w_1, and $w_1 + w_2$. However, jumping window JW_3 restricts the size of each burst to $m_3 = m_2/2$ cells only. Hence, each of the bursts of size m_2 has to be further broken down into bursts of size m_3. Consequently, in the worst-case, the first m_1 cells are released as four separate bursts of size m_3 cells each at times $w_1 - w_2 - w_3$, $w_1 - w_2$, $w_1 - w_3$, and w_1^-. The second batch of m_1 cells are released as four separate bursts of size m_3 each at times w_1, $w_1 + w_3$, $w_1 + w_2$, and $w_1 + w_2 + w_3$ (see Fig. 9.8). The subsequent batches of m_1 cells can be released starting at time $2w_1$ and following the constraints imposed by JW_is, for $i = 1, 2, 3$.

The exact form of the worst-case traffic envelope as defined by a composite jumping window can be stated using the following definition of a

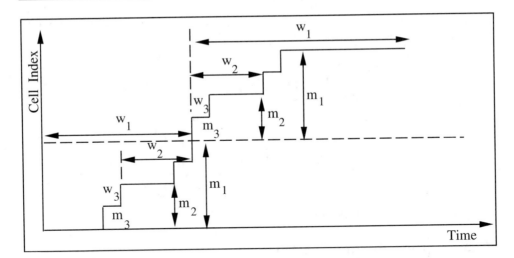

Fig. 9.8. Traffic Envelope of a Composite Jumping Window Shaper

composite jumping window shaper.

An n-component composite jumping window shaper consists of n simple jumping windows (w_k, m_k), $k = 1, \ldots, n$, where $w_i \geq w_j$, $m_i \geq m_j$, and $m_i/w_i \leq m_j/w_j$, for $1 \leq i < j \leq n$. For the sake of mathematical convenience we assume that an n-component composite shaper also includes another pseudo jumping window (m_0, w_0) such that $m_0/m_1 = 0$. We also assume for simplicity of exposition that m_{i+1} divides m_i, and w_{i+1} divides w_i, for $i = 1, 2, \ldots, n - 1$.

The worst-case departure time $a(i)$ of the ith cell, $i = 0, 1, \ldots, \infty$, from an n-component composite jumping window shaper is given by

$$
a(i) = \begin{cases}
\displaystyle\sum_{k=1}^{n} \left\{ \left(\left\lfloor \frac{i}{m_k} \right\rfloor + 1 \right) - \left(\left\lfloor \frac{i}{m_{k-1}} \right\rfloor + 1 \right) \frac{m_{k-1}}{m_k} \right\} w_k, & 0 \leq i < m_1 \\[4ex]
\displaystyle\sum_{k=1}^{n} \left(\left\lfloor \frac{i}{m_k} \right\rfloor - \left\lfloor \frac{i}{m_{k-1}} \right\rfloor \frac{m_{k-1}}{m_k} \right) w_k, & m_1 \leq i < \infty.
\end{cases}
$$

While proving this formally, the reader should remember that the main difference is that in the case of the jumping window, the first batch of bursts is released at the end of the first outer window. The rest of the batches are dispatched starting at the beginning of the subsequent outer windows.

9.6 Shaping and BW Allocation

The bandwidth that needs to be allocated to the shaped stream depends on the shaper parameters. For instance, a LB produces a stream which requires, at minimum, bandwidth equal to the token arrival rate to be allocated at the access multiplexer. A larger token arrival rate reduces the access delay at the policer but needs a larger bandwidth allocation. For a source characterized by a peak rate λ_p and burstiness $\hat{r}$, bandwidth allocation λ_{bw} is such that $\lambda_p/\hat{r} \leq \lambda_t \leq \lambda_{bw} \leq \lambda_p$. At the access multiplexer, the capacity of the output link $\lambda_o = \sum_{i=1}^{m} \lambda_{bw}(i)$ for m streams multiplexed to the same output. Since most multimedia traffic sources are bursty in nature, a large statistical multiplexing gain is possible only if λ_t is near the average arrival rate $\lambda_a = \lambda_p/\hat{r}$. On the other hand, smaller λ_t means larger access delay and/or violation probability incurred by the source. A lenient enforcement policy can increase the delay at the multiplexing/switching nodes due to buffer overflows. Thus, there is a trade-off between the access delay introduced by the policer and the network delay at the switches. From the end user's point of view, the delay incurred by the application includes the access delay and the network delay. For a constant bandwidth allocation, the effect of input rate control can be summarized by the following observations [6,7].

1. The total delay experienced by a cell is the sum of the access delay due to queuing at the shaper and the network delay at the switch. The policer simply transfers the network delay on to the input side, thereby avoiding overflow losses/delays within the network. Thus, unless the source has a large buffer and can tolerate excess delay, the input rate control as performed by the LB can hardly improve the network performance [7]. For many real-time applications, this access delay could be prohibitive.

2. A stringent input rate control may unnecessarily increase the user end-to-end delay by a significant amount [7].

3. The minimum total average delay is achieved when no traffic enforcement is invoked [6,7]. This observation is applicable when the network bandwidth is considerably greater than the source transmission rate, in which case the effect of individual streams is smoothed by statistical multiplexing. Nevertheless, to check excessive burstiness and prolonged rate violations, an input policer is practically needed.

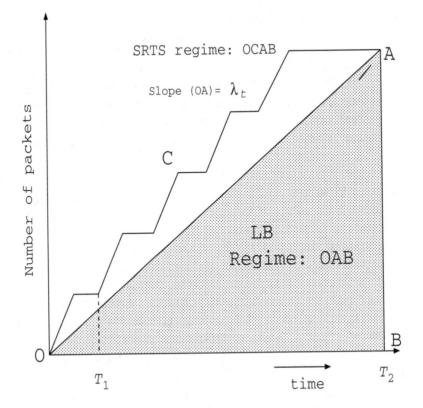

Fig. 9.9. Permitted Number of Packets versus Time

It is evident from the aforementioned points that the access delay introduced by the traffic policer can be significant. One way of reducing the access delay would be to permit more short-term burstiness subject to:

- Maximum burst size should be bounded and burst arrivals must be peak rate enforced.

- Number of arrivals over a larger time duration to be bounded at the average policing rate.

LB and the EWMA mechanisms perform these in different ways. The short-term burstiness permitted by the LB is decided by the size of the token buffer b. As explained earlier, over any time duration T starting from 0 (or any epoch when the token buffer becomes empty), the number of packets admitted into the network is bounded by $\lambda_t * T$. With reference to Fig. 9.9

which shows the number of admitted packets versus time, the operating region for LB operation is below the line OA corresponding to the average policing rate. A source is permitted to send a burst only if it remains inactive for a sufficient amount of time to gather enough tokens in the token buffer. Thus, the operating point is always below the line OA. A well-behaved source transmitting uniformly at the token arrival rate will operate along OA.

The short-term burstiness in the EWMA mechanism is influenced by the factor γ as described earlier in Section 9.3.4. The dynamic response for the EWMA is however poor for reasonable values of γ. EWMA output is not peak rate enforced, and the implementation complexity is also considerable compared to the other schemes.

9.7 Shift Register Traffic Shaper (SRTS)

The guiding principles in the design of Shift Register Traffic Shaper (SRTS) are:

1. Permit short-term burstiness but bound long-term behavior so that the number of packets admitted over a long time is the same as that admitted by an equivalent Leaky Bucket.

2. Accommodate variable burstiness easily.

3. Enforce peak rate policing.

4. Have two or more windows so that the shaper behavior can be more flexibly set, unlike the EWMA which has only one control parameter γ.

5. Use shift register and counters for easy implementation.

6. Adopt a less stringent attitude towards short-term burstiness to reduce access delays.

The advantage that is foreseen in *permitting controlled burstiness* is improvement of the statistical multiplexing gain at the switches. *This is of utmost relevance in the current scenario since most of the multimedia traffic sources are bursty in nature.* These include naturally stream-based sources, which are also rendered bursty by the efficient compression and coding mechanisms employed.

In Fig. 9.9, the operating region of the LB is depicted. The previous section described how LB introduces access delays which can become prohibitive for real-time applications. With an aim to *reduce the access delays*, what we need is a traffic shaper which performs like the LB over longer durations, but allows short-term burstiness in a more liberal sense than is permitted by the LB. With reference to Fig. 9.9, we attempt to operate above line OA over short durations while being confined to the LB bound over a large interval (say OB). As mentioned in the previous section, OA is the upper boundary for LB operation. A typical upper boundary for the proposed shaper can be the piecewise linear line OCA. Thus, by virtue of its short-term operation above line OA, short-term burstiness is more flexibly permitted by the proposed shaper. In the case of LB, a stream has to gather enough tokens by remaining inactive before it can afford to drive in a burst of data. On the contrary, a larger operating region of SRTS permits the source to have short-term overdrafts as long as it confines within the operating region. A simple implementation of the scheme using two windows is outlined in the following section.

9.7.1   SRTS Shaper

The Shift Register Traffic Shaper (SRTS) makes use of the temporal profile of the packet stream admitted by the shaper over the immediate past N time slots, where a time slot τ refers to the reciprocal of the peak rate. This temporal history can be maintained by a shift register, with 1 bit corresponding to every packet sent. The shift register is shifted right every time slot τ. The entry of the bits into the shift register is as per the following:

Let $f_d = 1$ if the data buffer is not empty, and 0 otherwise. Similarly, let f_a denote the admit control function defined as $f_a = (n(T_1) < n_1)$ and $(n(T_2) < n_2)$ and $(n(T_3) < n_3) \cdots$, depending on the number of windows. Here T_i refers to a time window. The size of the corresponding window is denoted by W_i and the maximum number of packets permitted in W_i by N_{Wi} (note that $N_{Wi} = n_i$). The data bit shifted in is *1* if $f_d = 1$ and $f_a = 1$. It is 0 otherwise.

Thus, the bit contents of the shift register at any instant provide an image of the history of the packets sent. All the time durations mentioned with reference to the shift register start from the time point corresponding to the entry point of the shift register. To determine the number of packets in any time duration, a counter is used which is incremented whenever a '1' enters the shift register and decremented when a '1' shifts out of the right

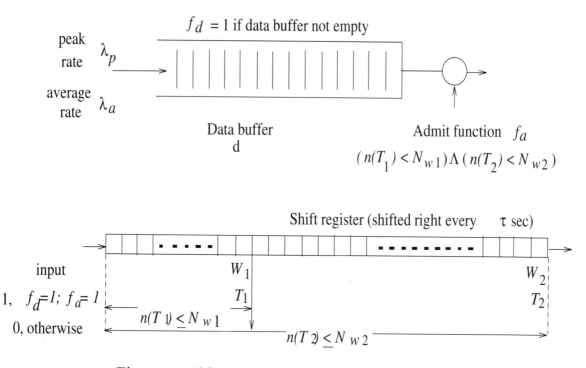

Fig. 9.10. Shift Register Traffic Shaper (SRTS)

edge of the corresponding window monitored by the counter.

Fig. 9.10 describes an enforcement scheme using two windows. This scheme generates an $(n_1, T_1; n_2, T_2)$ smooth traffic, which means that over any period of duration T_1, the number of packets $n(T_1) \leq n_1$, and over any period of duration T_2, the number of packets $n(T_2) \leq n_2$. Even though we have described the scheme with two windows, further flexibility in handling the burstiness is possible using an appropriate number of windows. Since the restriction on the number of packets permitted in a time window is enforced at the entry point of the shift register and the window shifts to the right every τ seconds, the smoothness is guaranteed over *any time window over the entire duration of the connection*.

One limitation that arises in the above arrangement is due to the discretization of time into slots of τ. A slot is termed active if a cell is transmitted during that slot and is idle otherwise. Since the cell arrival instant need not synchronize with the output slots, a cell arriving during an idle slot will have to wait until the end of that slot for transmission. This limitation is removed in the current scheme by using "soft" discretization. If a cell arrives

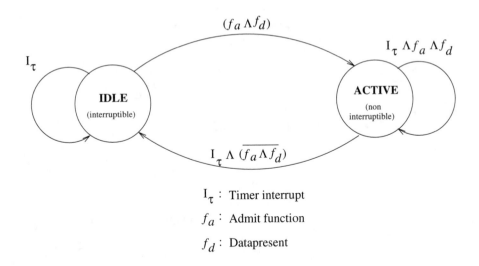

I_τ : Timer interrupt

f_a : Admit function

f_d : Datapresent

Fig. 9.11. FSM Describing the Transitions between Idle and Active States

during an idle slot, say after τ' elapses (out of τ), the idle slot is frozen and an active slot is initiated immediately. At the termination of this active slot, if either data is absent or the admit function is false, the residual idle slot of duration $(\tau - \tau')$ commences. The end of a slot is indicated by the timer interrupt shown in Fig. 9.11. The shift register is shifted right at the end of every slot, active or passive. The essence of the above arrangement is that an idle slot is interruptible whereas an active slot is not. Every time an idle slot is interrupted, the residual idle time is saved for future use up.

The modification described above is illustrated as an FSM in Fig. 9.11. The key features are:

- Idle to Active state transition is fired by the event $(f_a \wedge f_d)$ where f_a: admit function and f_d : data present flag.
  The following actions ensue:

  1. Save residual time by freezing the counter.

  2. Initiate transmission and go to the active state.

  3. Every slot timer interrupt in the idle state will cause transition to itself after resetting the counter.

- Active to Idle state transition is fired by the timer interrupt.

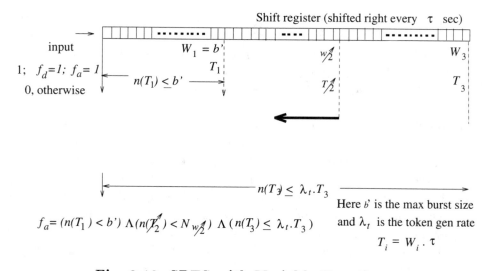

$$f_a = (n(T_1) < b') \wedge (n(T_2) < N_{w/2}) \wedge (n(T_3) \le \lambda_t . T_3)$$

Here b' is the max burst size and λ_t is the token gen rate

$$T_i = W_i . \tau$$

Fig. 9.12. SRTS with Variable Burstiness

1. **if** $((f_a \wedge f_d) = 1$, initiate another active slot.

2. **else** initiate an idle slot and go to idle state.

9.7.2 Providing Adjustable Burstiness

Using three counters and the associated SRTS parameters N_{W1}, W_1, N_{W2}, W_2 and N_{W3}, W_3, it is possible to tune the burstiness at the output of the SRTS while complying with the LB bounds over a predecided time duration. Window parameters can be derived from the key observations about the characteristics of the LBP output.

LBP has essentially two parameters: the bucket size b which decides the maximum burst size and the token arrival rate λ_t which provides a measure of the effective bandwidth allotted to the source. The model used here has three parameters: one window, W_1, which limits the maximum burst size, and a second window (W_3) for long-term average policing that corresponds conceptually to the two LBP parameters. The third window, namely W_2, is the one for providing the variable burstiness feature. An adjustable burstiness feature can be provided in SRTS by the following choice of parameters.

1. The parameters of the smallest window T_1 are chosen as $W_1 = b'$ and $N_{W1} = b'$. This bounds the maximum burst size.

2. Window-3 parameters can enforce the average policing characteristics

exhibited by the LBP over large time durations. If λ_{eff} is the effective bandwidth allotted for the bursty source(λ_p, λ_a), then the token arrival rate λ_t of the equivalent Leaky Bucket should be equal to the effective bandwidth. Thus, the window parameters are chosen as follows: for W_3 = large value T, $N_{W3} = \lambda_{eff} \cdot \tau \cdot W_3$.

3. Window-2, the main control parameter of the shaper, can be suitably tuned to incorporate the burstiness control feature. If we assume a LBAP(σ, ρ) for the output of the LBP over durations larger than and of the order of the maximum burst size, σ will be b' and ρ equals λ_t. Then for a chosen value of W_2, $N_{W2} = b' + \lambda_t \cdot (W_2 - W_1) \cdot \tau$. The region of operation to permit higher burstiness is shown by the shaded arrow in Fig. 9.12. The burstiness can be varied by adjusting N_{W2} or W_2. For instance, increasing N_{W2} or reducing W_2 increases the output burstiness.

Example For a bursty model with a mean ON period of 200 msec, a minimum intercell time τ of 10 msec, and burstiness 5, $\lambda_p = 100$ and $\lambda_a = 20$. If we choose λ_{eff} to be 40, for a bucket size (of an equivalent LBP) of 18, max burst size $b' = b/(1 - \lambda_t/\lambda_p) = 30$. Thus $W_1 = N_{W1} = 30$. For $W_2 = 75$, $N_{W2} = 30 + 45 \cdot 40/100 = 48$. W_3 corresponds to the large duration over which the average policing is enforced.

For a choice of $W_3 = 450$, $N_{W3} = \lambda_{eff} \cdot \tau \cdot W_3 = 450*40/100 = 180$.

The exact choice of W_2 and W_3 is currently arbitrary and can be tailored to suit the specific application stream. The only criteria is that over W_2, we assume the equivalent LBP to generate a LBAP stream whereas over the larger window W_3, an averaging property is expected. The influence of the source leading to a judicious choice of W_2 and W_3 is yet to be investigated.

9.7.3 Performance Study and Results

The performance characteristics of SRTS have been studied via simulation in [9]. We discuss the controlling effect of shaper parameters on the input traffic characteristics. SRTS shaper and a LB shaper are compared with respect to the mean and peak rate policing behavior to understand the respective delay and loss as the performance parameters.

The source is assumed to be of ON-OFF bursty type. Three simulation experiments are performed as detailed below. In all the cases, $W_1 = N_{W1} = 30$; $W_3 = 450, N_{W3} = 180$; $N_{W2} = 48$; Size of control window W_2 is a variable parameter. Each simulation run is performed with 10^7 packets. These values are chosen based on the discussion in the previous section.

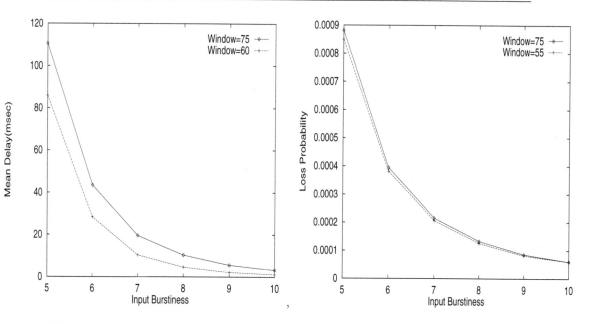

Fig. 9.13. (a)Mean Delay and (b)Loss Characteristics versus Input Burstiness

Experiment 1   In this experiment, we study the delay characteristics of the traffic shaper as a function of the input burstiness for different window parameters. The size of the data buffer is very large to keep losses close to zero. The input burstiness is varied by adjusting the ON period, keeping the OFF period constant. Intercell time is 10 msec and hence $\lambda_p = 100$. Since the long-term average policed rate is λ_t, the range of ON period variation is such that λ_a remains $\leq \lambda_t$ for stability. Thus $(T_{ON}/(T_{ON} + T_{OFF}) \cdot 100) < \lambda_t$, which is fixed at 40. Input burstiness is varied from 5 to 10 by keeping the OFF period constant at 800 msec and adjusting the ON period. Fig. 9.13(a) gives the delay distribution for window sizes of 75 and 60. The number of simulation runs are such that the results are accurate to within 5% with 95% confidence level.

Experiment 2   In this experiment, we study the loss characteristics incurred by SRTS shaping as a function of the input burstiness for different window parameters. Data buffer size is finite. In this case, the input burstiness is varied by keeping the ON period constant at 200 msec and varying the OFF period.

Simulation is conducted for a sufficient number of packets to yield loss probability values of up to 10^{-6} [see Fig. 9.13(b)].

Experiment 3   In this experiment, we study the output burstiness as a function of window parameters, for the same source burstiness. Since the output stream is of an arbitrary nature, unlike the input stream which is described by a bursty ON-OFF model parameter, we use a ratio of Variance to Mean of cell interarrival times [15,16] for characterizing the burstiness. We will use the term "burst factor" for this ratio to differentiate this definition of burstiness. Fig. 9.14(a) presents the result for two source ON-OFF characteristics.

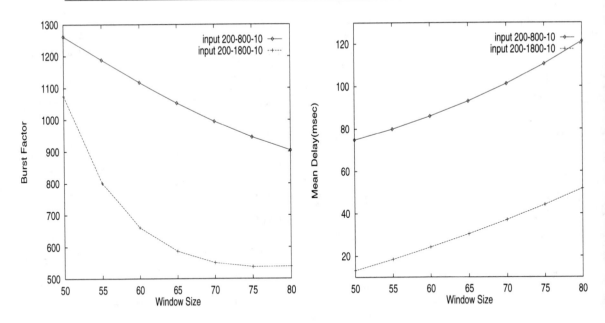

Fig. 9.14. (a) Output Burst Factor and (b) Mean Delay versus Window Size

Keeping the ON time at 200 msec, measurements are taken for two OFF period values, namely 800 msec and 1800 msec, respectively.

Fig. 9.14(b) illustrates the effect of window size on mean delay. The number of simulation runs are such that the results are accurate to within 5% with 95% confidence level.

An increase in input burstiness causes a reduction in the mean delay. This is expected since a larger burstiness implies a shorter source active period for a constant OFF period. As can be seen in Fig. 9.13(a), a smaller window size W_2 for the same N_{W2} admits more bursty streams than would be admitted by a correspondingly larger window size for the same N_{W2}. For the finite buffer case, the loss characteristics are presented in Fig. 9.13(b). For reasons similar to the results in the previous experiment, a smaller window reduces the losses. The difference is, however, not as pronounced as in the previous case.

The output burst factor variation demonstrated in Fig. 9.14(a) is a significant result in concurrence with our concept of a "controllable" burstiness. A shaper with a larger control window size generates a smoother output stream. The burstiness of the output can be tuned to provide higher bandwidth utilization at the switches. The results of Fig. 9.14(b) provide a means of selecting the window parameters suitable for the delay requirements of the application. By judiciously selecting the window-2 parameters, namely W_2 and N_{W2}, it is possible to tune the shaper behavior based on the application characteristics and the performance requirements. Although the general influence of the parameters is apparent, the precise correspondence between the source behavior and the window parameters needs to be established for different practical sources.

9.7.4   Comparison of SRTS and LB Policing

For comparing the performance of SRTS with the LBP scheme, the parameters of the two schemes have to be chosen to establish a functional equivalence. We use SRTS with two windows to obtain the transfer characteristics OCA depicted in Fig. 9.9. The shaping parameters are the window sizes W_1, W_2 and the maximum number of packets permitted in each window N_{W1}, N_{W2}. The window parameters can be derived from the key observations made earlier regarding the LBP scheme.

The maximum burst size b' for the LBP is $b' = b/(1 - \lambda_t/\lambda_p)$. If we observe the number of packets within a window of size, say W, the maximum number of packets allowed N_W within W is:

$$\begin{aligned}
&\text{for } W \leq b', \quad N_W = W; &(a)\\
&\text{for } W > b', \quad N_W = b' + \lambda_t \cdot (W - b') \cdot \tau; &(b)\\
&\text{for } W \gg b', \quad N_W \cong W \cdot \tau \cdot \lambda_t; &(c)
\end{aligned}$$

The values assumed for the LBP in the current simulation are $b = 18$, $\lambda_p = 100$, and $\lambda_t = 40$. Then max burst size $b' = b/(1 - \lambda_t/\lambda_p) = 30$. The first window W_1 is chosen as 50 to satisfy (b). Thus, to admit more short-term burstiness than what is permitted by the LBP, N_{W1} should be $\geq 30 + 20 \cdot 40/100 = 38$. For the current simulation, we have chosen this value of 38 for N_{W1}. For the LBP, the distribution of these packets within W_1 should be subject to operation within the shaded region in Fig. 9.9 whereas for the SRTS, they can be more flexibly distributed since the SRTS operating regime is bigger than that of LBP. Window-2 parameters can enforce the average policing characteristics exhibited by the LBP over large time durations. Hence the window size, in this case, follows (c). Consequently, the number of packets policed over a time duration $T_2 (= W_2 \cdot \tau)$ for the LBP and the SRTS are identical. For the current study, we have chosen $W_2 = 10 \cdot W_1 = 500$ and $N_{W2} = 500 \cdot \tau \cdot \lambda_t = 200$.

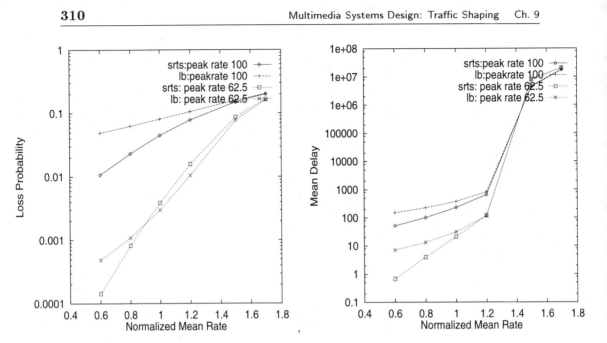

Fig. 9.15. (a)Loss and (b)Delay Characteristics versus Normalized Mean Rate

The exact choice of W_1 and W_2 is currently arbitrary and can be tailored to suit the application stream. The only criteria is that over W_1, we assume the "equivalent" LBP to generate a LBAP stream whereas over the larger window W_2, an averaging property is expected.

To understand the effectiveness of SRTS and LBP as mean and peak rate policers, two simulation experiments are performed. The source model is the bursty ON-OFF model explained earlier. Since we intend to vary the burstiness of the source, the mean ON time is kept at 200 msec. The OFF times and τ_p are appropriately adjusted to obtain the required mean rate. SRTS is a mean as well as peak rate policer. In the two experiments, we assume an overdimensioning factor $C = 1.5$ relating the policed rate and the mean rate of the source (as in [2]). The peak enforced rate is 100, and hence the minimum delay between consecutive packets at the output of the shaper τ is 10 ms. Each simulation run is performed with 10^7 packets.

Experiment 1 In this experiment, we study the loss and delay characteristics for different source mean rates. The mean rate variation is achieved by varying the OFF time, keeping mean ON time = 200 and mean policed rate $\lambda_t = 40$. With the overdimensioning factor of 1.5, the negotiated mean rate = 26.67. The OFF time is varied such that $\lambda_p/(1 + \frac{(T_{OFF})}{(200)}) \leq 26.67$. Thus, $T_{OFF} > 550$ for a well-behaved source. The X-axis shows

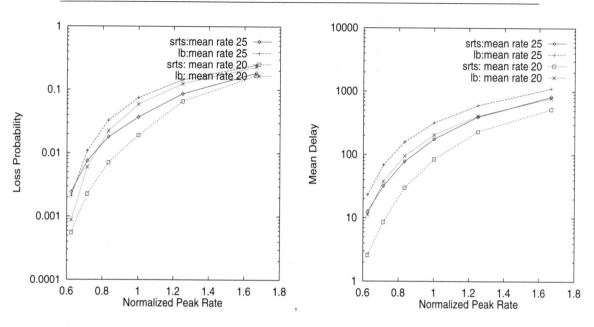

Fig. 9.16. (a)Loss and (b)Delay Characteristics versus Normalized Peak Rate

the normalized mean rate. For the first part which estimates the violation probability, a finite data buffer of size 20 is assumed. In a practical case, the size can be based on the maximum access delay that can be tolerated by a particular application. For the second part of the experiment which studies the access delay, the size of the data buffer is kept very large so as to keep losses close to zero. The experiment is performed for two values of the peak rate: $100(\tau_p = 10)$ and $62.5(\tau_p = 16)$. The results are shown in Fig. 9.15.

Experiment 2 In this experiment, we study the loss and delay characteristics for different source peak rates. Thus, we compare the peak rate enforcement provided by the SRTS and the LBP. For each run, the peak rate and the OFF duration are adjusted to keep the mean rate constant. The X-axis plots the normalized peak rates. The experiment is repeated for two values of the mean rate 25 and 20. Both of these values are within the negotiated rate of 26.67. Other parameters are as in the previous experiment. The results are shown in Fig. 9.16.

With reference to Fig. 9.15(a), for an input stream with peak rate 100 (corresponding to the peak rate limit built in the shaper), SRTS has a much smaller loss probability for mean rates up to the policed rate (1.5 * source mean). Beyond this, both curves converge quickly. At the lower peak rate of 62.5, however, there is a crossover between the SRTS and LBP loss curves. We attribute this to the fact that the source traffic is smooth in this region, and the advantage of SRTS in favoring short-term burstiness is not being used. In both cases, the steeper gradient of the SRTS curve is an indicator of its effectiveness as a mean rate policer. The flexible admission of short-term burstiness results in a lower access delay for the SRTS. This fact is evident from Fig. 9.15(b). For well-behaved sources with mean rates below the negotiated value, the lower the mean rate, the better the performance of the SRTS. This is true from the point of view of loss probability as well as access delay. At 0.6 times the mean rate, the access delay introduced by the SRTS is an order of magnitude less than that introduced by the equivalent LBP.

Fig. 9.16 depicts the response of the shapers to peak rate violation. For the loss curves, violation is more gradual than in the mean rate case. For our simulation which assumed a data buffer of size 20, SRTS yields lower values of violation probability than the LBP for traffic conforming to the negotiated rate. This is due to the more liberal admission policy for burstiness existing over short durations. The access delay curves for the two shapers are almost parallel to each other. As in the previous case, SRTS shaped streams have a consistently smaller access delay compared to the LBP case. However, compared to the delay characteristics for mean rate violation behavior, peak rate violation curves for SRTS as well as LBP do not exhibit steep gradients.

The advantages of the SRTS policy in terms of lower violation probability and access delay for traffic *within the negotiated rates* are due to the larger operating regime shown in Fig. 9.9. The above advantage of the SRTS, however, comes at a cost. The SRTS output is burstier than its LB counterpart. This would necessitate a more careful buffering and scheduling design at the switches to prevent congestion at the intermediate nodes. Since the network link transmission rate is generally much higher than the maximum source transmission rate, we expect that the fluctuations at the SRTS output will be effectively smoothed out by the statistical multiplexing effect at the switches. Also, since the maximum burst size is limited and the long-term behavior is bounded, the buffers and the schedulers can be dimensioned appropriately at the switches to provide the required loss and delay guarantees.

From the point of view of minimizing congestion within the network, the policy adopted by the LB is quite effective. LB reduces the delays within the network by transferring them on to the input side. However, its stringent enforcement increases the access delay and hence raises questions regarding the suitability of LB for real-time traffic. We showed through this study that the access delays can be reduced by adopting a more liberal attitude over shorter durations while maintaining the LB bounds over larger durations. For the same bandwidth allocation at the switches, such a policy is shown to perform better for real-time source traffic.

9.8 Summary

In this chapter, we discussed shaping traffic for the purpose of policing and characterization. We discussed simple shaping mechanisms such as Leaky Buckets, moving and jumping windows, and characterized the traffic envelopes defined by composition of multiple shapers. We will use these traffic envelopes to model input traffic to the network in the following chapters.

Shaping mechanisms have been proposed and analyzed by several authors [2,17]. However, most of these studies investigate different aspects of simple shapers such as a single Leaky Bucket or single jumping and moving window. The contribution of this chapter is in the characterization of the traffic envelopes defined by composite shapers. We believe that the characterization of traffic generated by composite shapers will be extremely useful in developing an end-to-end quality of service architecture.

We then discussed a flexible traffic shaper and compared its performance with a LBP. The motivation for the new scheme is derived from the output characteristics exhibited by the LBP. Two main goals were set. One is to provide an adjustable burstiness feature so that higher bandwidth utilization, along with reasonable guarantees, can be obtained. The second goal was to reduce the access delays for real-time traffic by being more liberal in permitting short-term burstiness. The window-based shaping policy adopted in the SRTS scheme can be used to achieve both goals.

The performance of the proposed shaper was studied in two parts. In the first we studied the effect of window parameters on input characteristics and demonstrated the adjustable burstiness feature. In the second part, we compared the loss and delay performance of a 2-window SRTS and a LBP. By adopting a more liberal, yet bounded, attitude over short durations, SRTS reduces the access delays for time-critical traffic.

For providing the desired utilization and guarantees, a traffic shaper must work in unison with the buffer management and scheduling schemes at the switches. A composite study involving the shaper and the scheduler is necessary to see the effect of SRTS shaping on end-to-end performance.

REFERENCES

1. S. Radhakrishnan and S. V. Raghavan. Network Support for Distributed Multimedia - Issues and Trends, Proceedings of SEACOMM'94, International Conference on Communications and Computer Networks, Kuala Lumpur, Malaysia, October, 1994.

2. Erwin P.Rathgeb. Modeling and Performance Comparison Of Policing Mechanisms for ATM Networks, IEEE Journal on Selected Areas in Communications, Vol. 9, No. 3, pp. 325-334, April 1991.

3. Krishna Bala, Israel Cidon, and K.Sohraby. Congestion Control for High-Speed Packet Switched Networks, IEEE INFOCOM, pp. 520-526, 1990.

4. A.E. Eckberg, D.T. Luan, and D.M. Lucantoni. Bandwidth Management: A Congestion Control Strategy for Broadband Packet Networks-Characterizing the Throughput-burstiness Filter, Computer Networks and ISDN Systems, Vol. 20, pp. 415-423, 1990.

5. M. Sidi, W. Liu, and I. Cidon and I. Gopal. Congestion Control through Input Rate Regulation, Proceedings of GLOBECOM'89, Dallas, Texas, pp. 1764-1768, November 1989.

6. Masayuki Murata, Yoshihiro Ohba, and Hideo Miyahara. Analysis of Flow Enforcement Algorithm for Bursty Traffic in ATM Networks, Proceedings of IEEE INFOCOM'92, Firenze, Italy, pp. 2453-2462, May 1992.

7. San-qi Li and Song Chong. Fundamental Limits of Input Rate Control in High-Speed Network, Proceedings of IEEE INFOCOM'93, San Francisco, California, pp. 662-671, March 1993.

8. S. Radhakrishnan, S. V. Raghavan, and Ashok K. Agrawala. A Flexible Traffic Shaper with Variable Burstiness for High-Speed Networks, Proceedings of the JENC6 International Conference to be held in Tel Aviv, Israel, May 1995.

9. S. Radhakrishnan, S. V. Raghavan, Ashok K. Agrawala. A Flexible Traffic Shaper for High-Speed Networks: Design and Comparative Study with Leaky Bucket, Computer Networks and ISDN Systems, Vol. 28, pp. 453-469, 1996.

10. D. Saha, S. Mukherjee, and S. K. Tripathi. Multi-rate Traffic Shaping and End-to-end Performance Guarantees in ATM Networks, Proceedings of International Conference on Network Protocols, 1994.

11. A. L. Elwalid and D. Mitra. Effective Bandwidth of General Markovian Traffic Sources and Admission Control of High-Speed Networks, Proceedings of IEEE INFOCOM'93, San Francisco, California, pp. 256-265, March 1993.

12. R. Guerin, H. Ahmadi, and M. Naghshineh. Equivalent Capacity and its Application to Bandwidth Allocation in High-Speed Networks, IEEE Journal on Selected Areas in Communications, Vol. 9, No. 7, pp. 968-981, September 1991.

13. R. L. Cruz. A Calculus for Network Delay, Part I: Network Elements in Isolation, IEEE Transactions on Information Theory, Vol. 37, No. 1, pp. 114-131, January 1991.

14. Debanjan Saha. Supporting Distributed Multimedia Applications on ATM Networks, Ph.D. Thesis, University of Maryland, College Park, Maryland, 1995.

15. J. Y. Hui and E. Arthurs. A Broadband Packet Switch for Integrated Transport, IEEE Journal on Selected Areas in Communications, Vol. 5, pp. 1264-1273, October 1987.

16. K. Sriram and W. Whitt. Characterizing Superposition Arrival Processes in Packet Multiplexers for Voice and Data, IEEE Journal on Selected Areas in Communications, Vol. 4, pp. 833-846, September 1986.

17. H. J. Chao. Architecture Design for Regulating and Scheduling User's Traffic in ATM Networks, Proceedings of SIGCOMM, 1992.

Exercises

1. Write a simulator to graphically describe the departure process from a Leaky Bucket. Use the ON-OFF traffic models discussed in Chapter 7.

2. Try to relate Jackson's theorem in queuing networks to the phenomenon occurring in traffic shapers. If we focus our attention only on the simple Poisson behavior of the input process, what can you say about the departure process?

3. For an MPEG trace (Star Wars for example), compare the output from all the traffic shapers discussed in this chapter.

Chapter 10

Multimedia Systems Design: Scheduling

10.1 Multiplexing and Scheduling

The heart of a quality of service architecture providing deterministic guarantees on performance is the multiplexing policy used at the switching nodes. Multiplexing is the allocation of link capacity to competing connections. The manner in which multiplexing is performed has a profound effect on the end-to-end performance of the system. Since each connection might have different traffic characteristics and service requirements, it is important that the multiplexing discipline treats them differently, in accordance with their negotiated quality of service. However, this flexibility should not compromise the integrity of the scheme; that is, a few connections should not be able to degrade service to other connections to the extent that the performance guarantees are violated. Also, the scheme should be analyzable since performance guarantees are to be given. Finally, it should be simple enough for implementation in high-speed switches.

10.2 Current State of Art

In the last several years, a number of multiplexing disciplines have been proposed [1]. Based on the performance guarantees they provide, these schemes can be broadly categorized into two classes: ones that provide guarantees on maximum delay at the switching nodes and ones that guarantee a minimum throughput. In the following, we briefly explain working principles of the representative schemes from each class and examine their merits and shortcomings.

10.2.1 Delay Guarantee

The multiplexing disciplines providing delay guarantees typically use priority-based scheduling to bound the worst-case delay encountered by a cell belonging to a connection at a particular switch. Depending on the nature of priority assignment, they can be further subdivided into static priority schemes and dynamic priority schemes. In a static priority scheme [2], each connection is statically assigned a priority at the time of connection setup. When a cell from a certain connection arrives at the multiplexing node, it is stamped with the priority label associated with its connection, and is added to a common queue. The cells are served according to their priority order. There are other alternative approaches to implement a static priority scheduler. In a dynamic priority scheduler, the priority assigned to cells belonging to a particular connection can be potentially different, depending on the state of the server and that of the connections. For example, an Earliest Deadline First scheduler [3] uses a real or a virtual deadline as the priority label for a cell. Here again, cells are put in a common queue and served in the priority order. Knowing the exact arrival patterns of cells from different connections, it is possible to bound the worst-case delay suffered by cells from a particular connection in both static and dynamic priority scheduling. The end-to-end queuing delay suffered by a cell passing through multiple multiplexing nodes, each employing deadline or priority scheduling, is the sum of the worst-case delays encountered at each node. One of the serious problems with the schemes described above is that they require traffic reshaping at each node. Priority scheduling completely destroys the original shape of the traffic envelope. Since these schemes require that the exact form of the traffic envelope be known at each node in order to guarantee worst-case delay bounds, traffic has to be reshaped into its original form as it exits at a multiplexing node.

10.2.2 Throughput Guarantee

The multiplexing disciplines providing throughput guarantees [4,5,6,7,8] use weighted fair queuing and frame-based scheduling to guarantee a minimum rate of service at each node. Knowing the traffic envelope, this rate guarantee can be translated into guarantees on other performance metrics, such as delay, delay jitter, worst-case backlog, etc. Unlike the disciplines providing delay guarantees, in rate-based schemes, worst-case end-to-end queuing delay is equal to the delay suffered at the bottleneck node only, not the sum of the worst-case delays at each intermediate node. Rate-based schemes are also more fair in terms of distributing excess bandwidth. In a delay-based scheme employing priority scheduling, excess bandwidth is consumed by the connections with the highest priorities, whereas in rate-based schemes it can be distributed more evenly and predictably.

Based on implementation strategies, rate-based schemes can be further classified into two categories: 1) priority queue implementation, and 2) frame-based implementation.

The most popular examples of priority queue implementations are virtual clock [7], packet-by-packet generalized processor sharing (PGPS) [6,9], self-clocked fair queuing (SFQ) [10], etc. In virtual clock, every connection has a clock associated with it that ticks at a potentially different rate. When a cell from a certain connection arrives at the system, it is stamped according to an algorithm that is independent of the arrivals from other connections and dependent only on the history of arrivals in the connection concerned, and the rate of service allocated to the connection. The stamped cells enter a queue common to all connections, and are served in the order of stamped value. Both PGPS and SFQ are similar to virtual clock in the sense that they all stamp the cells at their arrival, put all cells in a common queue, and serve them in the order of stamped value. However, they differ in the stamping algorithms they use. While these schemes are extremely flexible in terms of allocating bandwidth in very fine granularity and fair distribution of bandwidth among active connections, they are costly in terms of implementation. Maintaining a priority queue in the switches is expensive. In some cases, the overhead of the stamping algorithm also can be quite high.

Frame-based mechanisms are much simpler to implement. The most popular frame-based schemes are Stop-and-Go (SG) [5,11] and Hierarchical-Round-Robin (HRR) [4]. Both SG and HRR use a multilevel framing strategy. For simplicity, we just describe one-level framing. In a framing strategy, the time axis is divided into a period of some constant length, called a frame. Bandwidth is allocated to each connection as a certain fraction of frame time. In SG, at each multiplexing node, the arriving frames of each incoming link are mapped onto the departing frames on the outgoing links. All the cells from one arriving frame of an incoming link and going to a certain outgoing link are put into the corresponding departing frame on the outgoing link. In some sense, SG emulates circuit switching on a packet-switched network. One-level HRR is equivalent to a non-work-conserving Round Robin service discipline. Each connection is assigned a fraction of the total available bandwidth and receives that bandwidth in each frame, if it has sufficient cells available for service. The server ensures that no connection gets more

bandwidth than what is allocated to it, even if it has spare capacity and
the connection is backlogged. Both SG and HRR are non-work-conserving
service disciplines and, hence, fail to exploit the multiplexing gains of ATM.
Another important drawback of SG and HRR, and all framing strategies for
that matter, is that they couple the service delay with bandwidth allocation
granularity. The delay encountered by a cell in a SG and HRR is bounded
by frame size multiplied by a constant factor (in SG, the constant is in between 2 and 3; in HRR, it is 2). Hence, the smaller the frame size is, the
lower is the delay. However, granularity of bandwidth allocation is inversely
proportional to the frame size, resulting in an undesirable coupling between
delay and bandwidth allocation granularity.

10.3 Scheduling Policies: Two Approaches

We will discuss two approaches to scheduling in high-speed environments.
One approach is a compromise solution between the traditional First Come/First
Served (FCFS) and Round Robin (RR), called Generalized Round Robin
(GRR) [12]; the other is based on a time-line divide-and-allocate policy in-
spired by the traditional Round Robin, but moderated by fair queuing, called
Carry-Over Round Robin (CORR) [8,13].

10.4 Generalized Round Robin (GRR)

Assume a source is characterized by $(\lambda_p, \lambda_a, I, b)$ where λ_p is the peak rate
($\tau_p = 1/\lambda_p$ is the minimum interarrival time between two consecutive packets), λ_a is the average rate, I is the time interval over which the average rate
is specified, and b is the maximum burst size. For exploiting the burstiness
of the shaped traffic effectively, some amount of statistical sharing capability is desirable at the switch/multiplexer. From the point of view of offering
performance guarantees, some degree of isolation is desirable.

The work-conserving schedulers for homogeneous traffic are fundamentally based on two policies: FCFS (First Come/First Served) and RR (Round
Robin). Whereas FCFS provides statistical sharing and minimum average
delay, RR offers isolation and fairness. While no guarantees can be provided
using FCFS, RR can provide throughput and delay guarantees. We discuss
a scheme called Generalized Round Robin(GRR) for efficient scheduling of
bursty traffic generated by a traffic shaper. GRR schemes can operate between the FCFS and RR extremities, providing a performance that is tunable for an optimum balance between sharing (FCFS characteristics) and

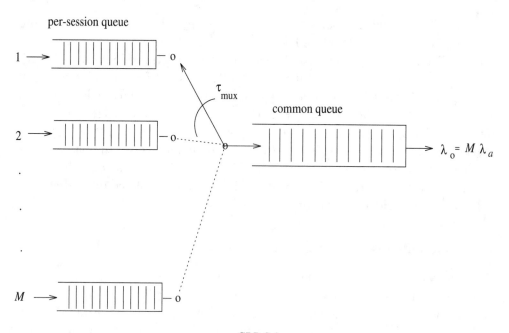

GRR Scheme

Proposal I :   multiplexing rate $\tau_p < \tau_{mux} < \tau_a$

Proposal II : multiplexing rate = τ_a; quantum size $1 < q < \tau_a/\tau_p$

Fig. 10.1. Generalized Round Robin (GRR) Scheme

isolation (RR characteristics).

Consider the general scheduling setup shown in Fig. 10.1, consisting of M per-session queues, a sampler, and a common queue. The inputs are characterized by $(\lambda_p, \lambda_a, I, b)$ bound. The time is slotted and input arrival instants occur at the end of the respective slots. Per-session queues correspond to the RR queues and the common queue is similar to the FCFS queue. The behavior for different multiplexing rates is as follows:

1. If each per-session queue is sampled every τ_a/M, where τ_a/M is also the time taken to transmit a packet on the output link of bandwidth $\lambda_a.M$, then the common queue is not required and the setup reduces to the plain RR.

2. If we assume that the input stream arrivals are synchronous, then sampling the per-session queues at τ_p/M gives plain FCFS operation. For

Fig. 10.2. Regime of the Generalized Round Robin

arrivals occurring at one instant, the service order is however prioritized as per the sampling order. If the input streams are not synchronous, then for the above sampling rate, service is FCFS with a resolution of τ_p. As $\lambda_{mux} \to \infty$, service $\to$ FCFS, and since each input queue is guaranteed to be serviced within a time $\leq \tau_p$, per-session queues are practically not needed and are similar (if not identical) to the FCFS arrangement.

Approach 1: In order to operate in the shaded region shown in Fig. 10.2 so that the statistical sharing of the FCFS and the isolation property of the RR can be optimally combined, one samples each per-session queue at a rate of λ_{mux} (or adjacent queues served every τ_{mux}/M) with $\tau_p \leq \tau_{mux} \leq \tau_a$. In this case, both per-session queue and the common queue are required. Statistical sharing in the common queue emulates the FCFS behavior and sampling the per-session queue emulates the RR behavior. A behavior intermediate to pure FCFS and pure RR is predicted. The relation between the tuning parameter τ_{mux} and the average delay is discussed later.

Approach 2: Every τ_a sec, the maximum number of packets in the bursty arrival case is τ_a/τ_p. In plain RR, in every sampling, we remove one packet, transmit it, and then sample the next per-session queue. With reference to the setup shown in Fig. 10.1, one removes up to "q" packets, if available at the sampling instant, from the per-session queue and copies into the common queue. Here, $1 \leq q \leq \tau_a/\tau_p$. With $q = 1$, we have RR operation and $q = \tau_a/\tau_p$, an operation similar to FCFS (though not identical). Thus, "q" is a tuning parameter for operating in the shaded region of Fig. 10.2.

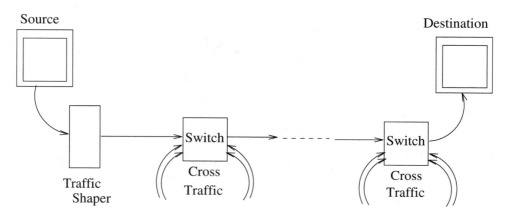

Fig. 10.3. Application of GRR in Multimedia Communication

In both of the above cases, by appropriately tuning the sampling parameter (λ_{mux} or "q"), we can operate anywhere in the regime for the statistical guarantees depicted in Fig. 10.2.

Applications of GRR: Consider the end-to-end view of a multimedia application supported over a network (see Fig. 10.3). The overall delay, as perceived by the application end user, comprises the access delay in the traffic shaper and switching delays in the intermediate nodes. Most multimedia sources exhibit bursty behavior. They are either naturally bursty or rendered so by the coding and compression mechanisms employed. A large class of these applications come under the paradigm of playback applications defined in [14]. Playback applications can be thought of as consisting of many application units, each of which are packetized and transmitted over the network, and are required to be reconstructed and played within a delay bound. For this reason, it is necessary to provide deterministic or statistical delay guarantees for these application units. The possibility of "statistical" guarantees is due to two facts. One is that the end user in multimedia applications is more often a human being and can tolerate some amount of distortion. The second reason is that the similarity between application units permits approximate reconstruction of occasionally lost packets.

From the application viewpoint, it is desirable to transport the bursts across the network with as little dispersion as possible. The practical difficulty in doing so is the possible congestion and consequent losses at the switches, where many streams contend for the link bandwidth. For loss-free switching, a RR policy in conjunction with non-bursty streams is ideal. But

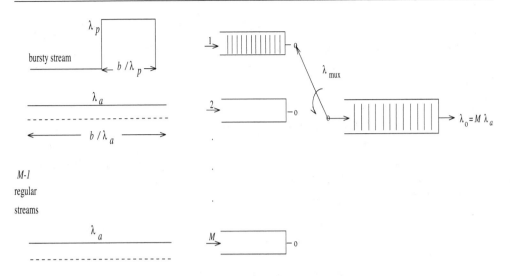

Fig. 10.4. Analysis of GRR Scheduling

this would necessitate strict average rate enforcement by the traffic shaper, resulting in increased access delay. Such a scheme is also inefficient due to the absence of statistical sharing of the link bandwidth. On the other extreme, a bursty source and FCFS scheduling at the switches can derive the benefit of complete sharing and minimum delay, but at the possibility of congestion. A traffic shaper which permits some amount of burstiness (LB or SRTS) at the network access and GRR at the switches provides a good compromise between these two extremes. We believe this tunability is of potential application in multimedia networking, where a wide range of applications with different QoS requirements must be supported.

10.5 Analysis of GRR

We assume an M-input multiplexer which is fed by a bursty stream. Following the $(\lambda_p, \lambda_a, I, b)$ characterization defined earlier, a worst-case burst stream will generate a burst of size b at rate λ_p followed by a quiescent period of $b(\frac{1}{\lambda_a} - \frac{1}{\lambda_p})$ as shown in Fig. 10.4. In this case, the length of the averaging interval I is $\frac{b}{\lambda_a}$. The burst is modeled as a continuous fluid flowing at rate λ_p for a duration b/λ_p. We assume that the other $(M-1)$ streams are well-behaved, each generating fluid at rate λ_a. For stability, the total capacity of the output link λ_o should be greater than $(M.\lambda_a)$. The sampling rate λ_{mux} should be greater than λ_a for stability. Due to this, the per-session queues of the well-behaved streams will be empty. Let $\lambda_m = min(\lambda_{mux}, \lambda_p)$. The maximum delay experienced by the burst in per-session queue (psQ):

$$D_{burst}^{psQ} = b.(\frac{1}{\lambda_m} - \frac{1}{\lambda_p}) \tag{10.1}$$

Since input rate for the $M - 1$ regular streams is $\lambda_a < \lambda_{mux}$, flow rate for these streams from per-session queue to common queue is λ_a. The last unit of the burst sees a backlog of $[\lambda_{mux} + (M-1).\lambda_a - \lambda_o].(b/\lambda_m)$ in the common queue. Thus, the maximum delay suffered by the burst in the common queue (cQ) is:

$$D_{burst}^{cQ} = b.(\frac{1}{\lambda_o} + \frac{(M-1)\lambda_a}{\lambda_o\lambda_m} - \frac{1}{\lambda_m}) \tag{10.2}$$

The total delay for the burst is obtained as:

$$D_{burst}^{tot} = D_{burst}^{psQ} + D_{burst}^{cQ} = b.(\frac{1}{\lambda_o} + \frac{(M-1)/M}{\lambda_m} - \frac{1}{\lambda_p}) \tag{10.3}$$

The above expression illustrates the effect of $(M-1)$ cross traffic streams on the delay caused to a bursty stream.

For the well-behaved (wb) stream, the only delay is that in the common queue and is given by

$$D_{wb}^{tot} = b.(\frac{1}{\lambda_o} + \frac{(M-1)\lambda_a}{\lambda_o\lambda_m} - \frac{1}{\lambda_m}) \tag{10.4}$$

If we assume λ_o to be $M.\lambda_a$, then the expressions for delays reduce to

$$D_{burst}^{tot} = (\frac{1}{M\lambda_a} + \frac{(M-1)/M}{\lambda_m} - \frac{1}{\lambda_p}) \tag{10.5}$$

$$D_{wb}^{tot} = \frac{b}{M}(\frac{1}{\lambda_a} - \frac{1}{\lambda_m}) \tag{10.6}$$

These delays are plotted as a function of λ_m in Fig. 10.5 for different M and as a function of input burstiness for different λ_{mux} in Fig. 10.6.

From the discussions, it is clear that:

1. For $\lambda_{mux} = \lambda_a$, GRR $\Rightarrow$ RR.

2. For $\lambda_{mux} = \lambda_p$, GRR $\Rightarrow$ FCFS.

Scheme	D_{burst}^{tot}	D_{wb}^{tot}
RR	$b.[\frac{1}{\lambda_a} - \frac{1}{\lambda_p}]$	0
GRR	$b.[\frac{1}{M\lambda_a} + \frac{(M-1)/M}{\lambda_m} - \frac{1}{\lambda_p}]$	$\frac{b}{M}[\frac{1}{\lambda_a} - \frac{1}{\lambda_m}]$
FCFS	$\frac{b}{M}[\frac{1}{\lambda_a} - \frac{1}{\lambda_p}]$	$\frac{b}{M}[\frac{1}{\lambda_a} - \frac{1}{\lambda_p}]$

Table 10.1. Expressions for Delay in RR, GRR, and FCFS

3. For $\lambda_a < \lambda_{mux} < \lambda_p$, an operation intermediate between FCFS and RR is obtained. The corresponding expressions for delay are given in Table 10.1. Fig. 10.5 depicts the delays suffered by the bursty and well-behaved streams as the multiplexing rate λ_{mux} varies from λ_a (RR operation) to λ_p (FCFS operation). The burstiness λ_p/λ_a is kept as 10 for Fig. 10.5. Thus, *the left edge of the graph corresponds to RR and the right edge to FCFS operation.* For the case of $M = 5$, the normalized delay for the bursty stream is 0.9 for RR operation ($\lambda_{mux} = \lambda_a$), 0.14 for FCFS operation ($\lambda_{mux} = \lambda_p = 10.\lambda_a$), and 0.3 for GRR with $\lambda_{mux} = 4.\lambda_a$. Since the reduction in delay for GRR and FCFS is equally shared by the well-behaved streams, their delays increase slightly. It is seen that as the number of streams M increases, delays reduce for both the bursty as well as well-behaved streams.

4. Fig. 10.6 illustrates the variation of delay suffered by the bursty stream with its burstiness (ratio of peak to average rates). For the RR case, the delay increase is maximum, whereas for FCFS (which promotes burstiness), the delay increase is minimum. The region of operation of GRR is bounded by the RR and FCFS curves. The graphs for GRR clearly demonstrate that the delay can be precisely tuned to confine anywhere in the region bounded by RR and FCFS.

5. Since input characteristics are bounded by traffic shaping, the queues, (both per-session queues and the common queue) can be properly di-

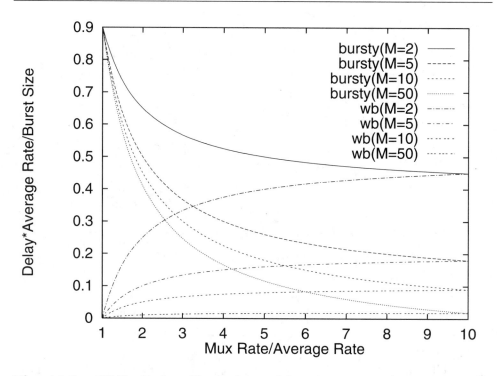

Fig. 10.5. GRR: Delay Variation with Mux Rate (Peak Rate = 10.aver rate)

mensioned for loss-free operation. Using appropriately sized queues, individual streams can be provided statistical loss guarantees of the type $Prob[loss < \epsilon] > .95$.

6. The cost for flexibility is the higher buffer requirement for loss-free operation of GRR. It can be seen easily that the total buffer requirement maximizes for $\lambda_{mux} = \sqrt{\lambda_a . \lambda_p}$ and maximum size $= 2Mb(1 - \sqrt{\frac{\lambda_a}{\lambda_p}})$. For FCFS and RR, total buffer size $= Mb(1 - \frac{\lambda_a}{\lambda_p})$.

7. The operation with $\lambda_{mux} = \lambda_p$ yields pure FCFS behavior only for the continuous model. For discrete streams, maximum error is limited to the minimum interpacket time τ_p. For $\lambda_{mux} \to \infty$, the discretized version also tends to FCFS.

8. In general, if there are k streams generating bursty output with the bursts occurring simultaneously, and $M - k$ regular streams, then during the burst processing period, each bursty stream dynamically gets

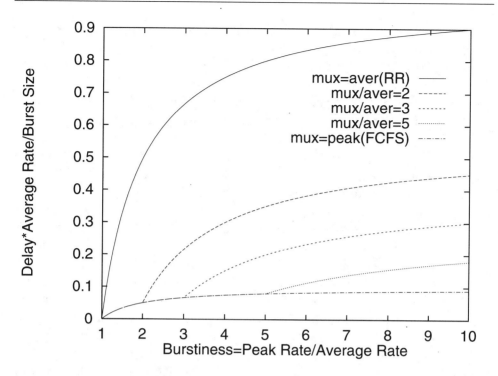

Fig. 10.6. GRR: Delay Variation with Burstiness (M=10)

◦ bandwidth share of $\lambda_m/(k.\lambda_m + (M-k).\lambda_a)$. Thus, this scheme has a dynamic burst priority feature. In the limit, when all streams are bursty and all bursts occur simultaneously, GRR behaves like a RR.

10.6 CORR Scheduling Algorithm

Like simple Round Robin scheduling, CORR (Carry Over Round Robin) divides the time line into allocation cycles. The maximum length of an allocation cycle is T. Let us assume that the cell transmission time is the basic unit of time. Hence, the maximum number of cells (or slots) transmitted during one cycle is T. At the time of admission, each connection C_i is allocated a rate R_i expressed in cells per cycle. Unlike simple Round Robin schemes, where R_is have to be integers, CORR allows R_is to be real. Since R_is can take real values, the granularity of bandwidth allocation can be arbitrarily small, irrespective of the length of the allocation cycle. The goal of the scheduling algorithm is to allocate each connection C_i close to R_i slots in each cycle and exactly R_i slots per cycle over a longer time frame.

It also distributes the excess bandwidth among the active connections C_is in the proportion of their respective R_is.

The CORR scheduler consists of three asynchronous events — *Initialize*, *Enqueue*, and *Dispatch*. The event *Initialize* is invoked when a new connection is admitted. If a connection is admissible[1], it is simply added to the connection list $\{C\}$. The connection list is ordered in the decreasing order of $R_i - \lfloor R_i \rfloor$, that is, the fractional part of R_i. The event *Enqueue* is activated at the arrival of a packet. It puts the packet in the appropriate connection queue and updates the cell count of the connection. The most important event in the scheduler is *Dispatch*. The event *Dispatch* is invoked at the beginning of a busy period. Before explaining the task performed by *Dispatch*, let us introduce the variables and constants used in the algorithm and the basic intuition behind it.

For each connection C_i, the scheduler maintains a separate queue, n_i keeps the count of the waiting cells, and r_i holds the number of slots currently credited to it. Note that r_i's can be real as well as negative fractions. A negative value of r_i signifies that the connection has been allocated more slots than it deserves. A positive value of r_i reflects the current legitimate requirements of the connection. In order to allocate slots to meet the requirements of the connection as closely as possible, CORR divides each allocation cycle into two subcycles — a *major cycle* and a *minor cycle*. In the major cycle, the integral requirement of each connection is satisfied first. Slots left over from the major cycle are allocated in the minor cycle to connections with still-unfulfilled fractional requirements. Obviously, a fraction of a slot cannot be allocated. Hence, eligible connections are allocated a full slot each in the minor cycle whenever slots are available. However, all the connections with fractional requirements may not be allocated a slot in the minor cycle. The connections that get a slot in the minor cycle oversatisfy their requirements and carry a debit to the next cycle. The eligible connections that do not get a slot in the minor cycle carry a credit to the next cycle. The allocations for the next cycle are adjusted to reflect the debit and credit carried over from the last cycle. Following is a detailed description of the steps taken in the *Dispatch* event.

At the beginning of a busy period, all r_i's are set to 0 and a new cycle is initiated. The cycles continue until the end of the busy period. At the beginning of each cycle, the current number of unallocated slots t is initialized to T, and the major cycle is initiated. In the major cycle, the *dispatcher*

---

[1] We discuss admission control later.

cycles through the connection list and, for each connection C_i, updates r_i to $r_i + R_i$. If the number of cells queued in the connection queue, n_i, is less than the updated value of r_i, r_i is set to n_i. This is to make sure that a connection cannot accumulate credits. The minimum of t and $\lfloor r_i \rfloor$ cells are dispatched from the connection queue of C_i. The variables are appropriately adjusted after dispatching the cells. A minor cycle starts with the slots left over from the preceding major cycle. Again, the *dispatcher* walks through the connection list. As long as there are slots left, a connection is deemed eligible for dispatching if and only if 1) it has queued packets, and 2) its r_i is greater than zero. If there is no eligible connection, or if t reaches zero, the cycle ends. Note that the length of the major and minor cycles may be different in different allocation cycles.

Example: Let us consider a CORR scheduler with cycle length $T = 4$ and serving three connections C_1, C_2, and C_3 with $R_1 = 2$, $R_2 = 1.5$, and $R_3 = 0.5$, respectively. In an ideal system where fractional slots can be allocated, slots can be allocated to the connections in a fashion shown in Fig. 10.7, resulting in full utilization of the system. CORR also achieves full utilization, but with a different allocation of slots.

For ease of exposition, let us assume that all three connections are backlogged starting from the beginning of the busy period. In the major cycle of the first cycle, CORR allocates C_1, C_2, and C_3, $\lfloor R_1 \rfloor = 2$, $\lfloor R_2 \rfloor = 1$, and $\lfloor R_3 \rfloor = 0$ slots, respectively. Hence, at the beginning of the first minor cycle, $t = 1$, $r_1 = 0.0$, $r_2 = 0.5$, and $r_3 = 0.5$. The only slot left over for the minor cycle goes to C_2. Consequently, at the end of the first cycle, $r_1 = 0.0$, $r_2 = -0.5$, and $r_3 = 0.5$, and the adjusted requirements for the second cycle are

$$r_1 = r_1 + R_1 = 0.0 + 2.0 = 2.0$$
$$r_2 = r_2 + R_2 = -0.5 + 1.5 = 1.0$$
$$r_3 = r_3 + R_3 = 0.5 + 0.5 = 1.0$$

Since all the r_is are integral, they are all satisfied in the major cycle.

10.6.1 Discussion

The main attraction of CORR is its simplicity. In terms of complexity, CORR is comparable to Round Robin and frame-based mechanisms. However, CORR does not suffer from the shortcomings of Round Robin and frame-based schedulers. By allowing the number of slots allocated to a connection in an allocation cycle to be a real number instead of an integer, we break the coupling between the service delay and bandwidth allocation granularity. Also, unlike frame-based mechanisms such as SG and HRR, CORR is work conserving as it is capable of exploiting the multiplexing gains of packet switching. In the following, we briefly outline a hardware implementation of CORR scheduling. Later in the chapter we discuss some of its basic properties.

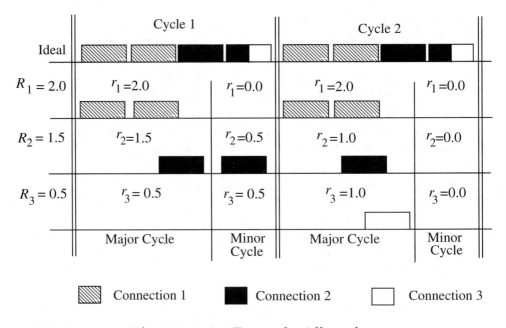

Fig. 10.7. An Example Allocation

10.6.2   Implementation in a Switch

A design for implementation of CORR scheduling in an output buffered switch is outlined in Fig. 10.8. The buffer manager consists of a cell pool, a table lookup memory, an idle-address-FIFO, and a processor. The cells are stored in the cell pool. The table lookup memory, referred to as *connection table*, stores necessary control information. The idle-address-FIFO contains addresses of the current empty cell locations in the cell pool.

The buffer manager maintains a virtual queue for each connection by linking the cells through pointers. The cells stored in the cell buffer are tagged with the pointer to the next cell from the same connection, if any. When a cell arrives, it is stored in the cell pool at the address given by the idle-address-FIFO. While the cell is being written into the cell pool, its connection identifier is extracted by the processor and the corresponding entry in the connection table is accessed to retrieve connection-specific state information. The connection state is updated to reflect the new arrival, and the pointers are suitably adjusted to add the arriving cell at the end of the connection queue.

The connection table stores the state information of all connections. The state of a connection consists of Head and Tail pointers to the corresponding

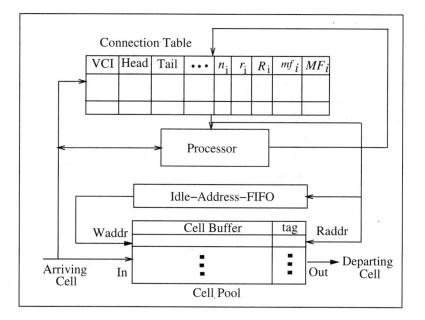

Fig. 10.8. Architecture of the Buffer Manager

connection queue and a few connection-specific constants and variables. The constants and variables important to the scheduling algorithm are R_i, r_i, and n_i. A cell from a connection is considered eligible for dispatching in a major cycle if n_i is greater than zero and r_i is greater than one. Similarly, a connection is considered eligible for dispatching in a minor cycle if n_i is greater than zero and r_i is greater than zero. We keep two one-bit flags, MF and mf, to indicate whether a connection is eligible for dispatching in the major and minor cycles, respectively. These flags are set/reset by local logic to save processor cycles, and are used for fast indexing to the connection states of the eligible connections during the major and minor cycles.

Once an eligible connection is selected, the processor extracts the buffer address of the cell at the head of the connection queue from the connection and dispatch it on the output link. The buffer address of the next cell in the queue, if any, is written into the Head field of the corresponding entry in the connection table. The processor also makes necessary changes to the state information stored in the connection table.

10.6.3 Basic Properties

In this section, we discuss some of the basic properties of the scheduling algorithm. A connection is said to be in the busy period if the connection queue is nonempty. The system is said to be in the busy period if at least one of the connections is in its busy period. Note that a particular connection can switch between busy and idle periods even when the system is in the same busy period. We can state the departure time of a specific cell belonging to a particular connection as follows:

Assume that a connection enters a busy period at time 0. Let $d(i)$ be the latest time by which the ith cell, starting from the beginning of the current busy period, departs the system. Then $d(i)$ can be expressed as

$$d(i) = \left\lceil \frac{i + 1 + \delta}{R} \right\rceil T, \quad i = 0, 1, \ldots, \infty,$$

where R is the rate allocated to the connection, T is the maximum length of the allocation cycle, and $\delta = max_k\{kR - \lfloor kR \rfloor\}$, $k = 1, 2, \ldots$.

Since a cell may leave the system at any time during an allocation cycle, we capture the worst-case situation by assuming that all the cells served during an allocation cycle leave the system at the end of the cycle. Now, when a connection enters a busy period, the lowest value of r is $-\delta$. If cell i departs at the end of the Lth cycle from the beginning of the connection busy period, the number of slots allocated by the scheduler is $L \times R - \delta$, and the number of slots consumed is $i + 1$ (assuming packet numbers start from 0). In the worst-case,

$$1 > L \times R - \delta - (i + 1) \geq 0.$$

This implies that
$$\frac{i + 1 + \delta + 1}{R} > L \geq \frac{i + 1 + \delta}{R}.$$

From the above inequality and noting that L is an integer and $d(i) = L \times T$, we get

$$d(i) = \left\lceil \frac{i + 1 + \delta}{R} \right\rceil T.$$

10.7 Summary

In this chapter, we presented a generalized scheduling methodology named GRR for homogeneous multiplexing of bursty streams. The motivation for the scheme came from the performance extremities offered by the FCFS and RR schemes and the need for tuning the performance between sharing and isolation. Multimedia traffic is generally bursty in nature. Bursts could be packets belonging to a single frame in the case of video traffic. Since the burst sizes and rates are policed and bounded by the traffic shaper, it will be desirable to dynamically assign a higher priority for bursts. GRR achieves precisely this. In spite of the simplicity of the model, we see that GRR operates in the regime bounded by FCFS and RR and the operation is tunable. Using a deterministic flow model, we have obtained worst-case delay bounds for bursty and well-behaved streams.

We also presented a cell scheduling discipline designed to provide deterministic performance guarantees on a per-connection basis. We gave a detailed description of the algorithm and discussed some of its basic properties. These results are used in the next chapter to derive delay bounds and to analyze fairness properties of the algorithm.

It is clear from the discussion above that CORR is a simple extension of the Round Robin discipline. It can be implemented using a two-phase Round Robin scheduler and is much simpler compared to the priority queuing mechanisms. In terms of complexity, CORR is comparable to frame-based mechanisms such as SG and HRR. However, CORR does not suffer from the typical shortcomings of frame-based scheduling. It is work conserving, and hence can exploit the multiplexing gains of ATM. Also, unlike most frame-based schemes, CORR does not suffer from the undesirable coupling between delay and bandwidth allocation granularity.

REFERENCES

1. C. M. Aras, J. F. Kurose, D. S. Reeves, and H. Schulzrinne. Real-Time Communication in Packet-Switched Networks, IEEE Transactions on Information Theory, Vol. 82, No. 1, 1994.

2. H. Zhang and D. Ferrari. Rate Controlled Static Priority Queuing, Proceedings of INFOCOM, 1993.

3. L. Georgiadis, R. Guerin, and A. Parekh. Optimal Multiplexing on Single Link: Delay and Buffer Requirements, Proceedings of INFOCOM, 1994.

4. C. R. Kalmanek, H. Kanakia, and S. Keshav, Rate Controlled Servers for Very High-Speed Networks, Proceedings of GLOBECOM, 1990.

5. S. J. Golestani. A Framing Strategy for Congestion Management, IEEE Journal on Selected Areas of Communication, Vol. 9, No. 7, 1991.

6. A. K. Parekh and R. G. Gallager. A Generalized Processor Sharing Approach to Flow Control in Integrated Services Network: The Single Node Case, IEEE/ACM Transactions on Networking, Vol. 1, No. 1, 1993.

7. L. Zhang. Virtual Clock: A New Traffic Control Algorithm for Packet Switching Networks, Proceedings of SIGCOMM, 1990.

8. D. Saha, S. Mukherjee, and S. K. Tripathi. Multi-rate Traffic Shaping and End-to-end Performance Guarantees in ATM Networks, Proceedings of the International Conference on Network Protocols, 1994.

9. A. Demers, S. Keshav, and S. Shenkar. Analysis and Simulation of Fair Queuing Algorithm, Proceedings of SIGCOMM, 1989.

10. S.J. Golestani. A Self-Clocked Fair Queuing Scheme for Broadband Applications, Proceedings of INFOCOM, 1993.

11. S. J. Golestani. Congestion Free Communication in High-Speed Packet Networks, IEEE Transactions on Communications, Vol. 32, No. 12, 1991.

12. S. Radhakrishnan, S. V. Raghavan, and Ashok K. Agrawala. A Flexible Traffic Shaper for High-Speed Networks: Design and Comparative Study with Leaky Bucket, Computer Networks and ISDN Systems, Vol. 28, pp. 453-469, 1996.

13. Debanjan Saha. Supporting Distributed Multimedia Applications on ATM Networks, Ph. D. Thesis, University of Maryland, College Park, Maryland, 1995.

14. David Clark, Scott Shenker, and Lixia Zhang. Supporting Real-Time Applications in an Integrated Services Packet Network: Architecture and Mechanism, Proceedings of ACM SIGCOMM'92, Baltimore, Maryland, pp.14-26, August 1992.

Exercises

1. For deterministic traffic, derive an expression for a departure time of the ith cell, given that the scheduler operates as GRR.

Chapter 11

Multimedia Systems Design: Congestion Control

11.1 Congestion Control in Multimedia Communications

So far, we have studied the traffic behavior, buffer allocations to suit such traffic, methods of shaping traffic, and techniques to ensure that resources are allocated for a given media and its flow. In a typical multimedia scenario, a heterogeneous mix of video, voice, and data traffic with Quality of Service (QoS) demands assigns new responsibilities on the network. This chapter deals with one of the key issues involved in the development of network support for multimedia communications, viz., Congestion Control.

The Congestion Control problem is one of the challenging problems facing the designers of multimedia networks. Proper control of congestion is *sine qua non* for providing performance guarantees for all the services supported by the network. In this chapter, we present a general framework for controlling congestion, in light of what we discussed in the previous chapters on traffic analysis, buffer design, traffic shaping, and scheduling.

11.2 Congestion: What and Why?

We discuss the potential reasons for congestion, classification of congestion, and why congestion control is fundamentally much harder at high-speeds. Multimedia sources such as voice and video are bursty in nature. There may be many bursts during a call and the bursts themselves may have a variable number of cells. The call duration, burst duration, and cell duration form a hierarchy. For the duration of a call, the burst-level and cell-level behavior are illustrated in Fig. 11.1. Since the idea of high-speed networks, such as ATM, is to provide bandwidth on demand, the effective bandwidth provided

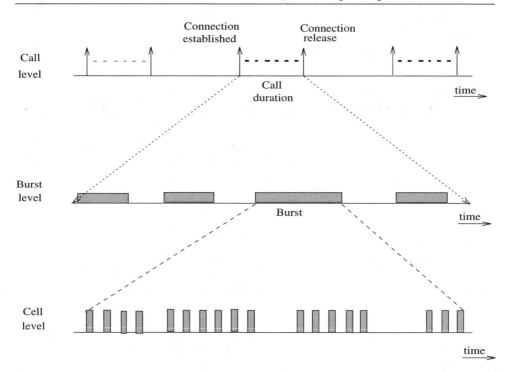

Fig. 11.1. Illustration of Traffic Generated by a Typical Multimedia Source

to a source could be much less than its peak rate. Statistical multiplexing, used in the switching nodes, provides higher bandwidth utilization at the cost of possible degradation in performance due to congestion. The consequence of congestion is delay/loss of cells, leading to a deterioration in the perceived quality of presentation.

Congestion can be roughly classified, based on its duration, as short-term, medium-term, and long-term congestion. Short-term congestion persists, by its nature, for durations of the order of cell transmission times. However, if not immediately controlled, it can lead to congestion sustaining over larger durations-resulting in objectionable levels of losses and delays. Medium-term congestion persists over durations of the order of propagation delays. Congestion lasting for durations of the order of call time and beyond can be classified as long-term congestion. Each of these congestions needs a different control mechanism, as we shall see in Section 11.3.

Congestion control is hard at high-speeds for the following reasons:

1. The switching technology should cope with transmission speeds. As a result, processing at the switches should be simple and fast. When many bursty sources are multiplexed, losses due to overflows is possible.

2. The increase in the ratio between the propagation time and the transmission time is another factor which makes congestion control at high-speeds extremely difficult.

Example: Let two adjacent switching nodes be separated by a 100 km cable; packet size is 53 bytes (the value agreed upon for ATM) and propagation delay is 5 μsec/km. For a 1 Mb/sec channel, cell transmission time is 0.484 msec, whereas at 1 Gb/sec, cell transmission time becomes 0.484 μsec. Since propagation delay remains the same at 0.5 msec, the propagation time to transmission time ratio has now increased thousandfold. This means that before any congestion information can travel back to the source, more than a thousand cells have already been put into the pipeline. Thus, any of the techniques successfully employed at Mbit speeds and below become totally ineffective at Gbit speeds, since the congestion information could become late or obsolete by the time it reaches the source!

Reactive versus Preventive Congestion Control: *Reactive control* is based on the use of feedback information from the congested node to the source nodes for throttling their traffic flows. Due to reasons stated in the previous section, such a scheme is ineffective at high-speeds. The alternative strategy is *preventive control*. By employing effective schemes at the network entry points, preventive control prevents the network from reaching disagreeable levels of congestion. As we are looking at the design of high-speed networks for multimedia, we discuss only preventive control schemes.

11.3 A General Framework for Congestion Control

A general framework for control congestion at all time scales is presented in Fig. 11.2 [1]. The y-axis gives the duration of congestion and the corresponding rectangular boxes contain the schemes to be employed for controlling congestion at that level. For guaranteeing a congestion-free environment, we need to tackle the problem at multiple levels. In the following, we will discuss only the schemes which have been proposed over the past few years in the context of real-time communication with performance guarantees. As shown in Fig. 11.2, admission control works at the call level whereas policing, priority control, and cell discarding operate at the cell level.

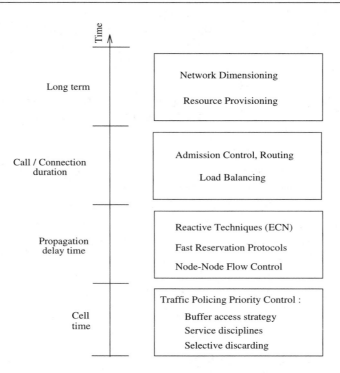

Fig. 11.2. A General Framework for Congestion Control

Congestion control at the cell-level is the most challenging issue at high-speeds. This is due to the latency effects explained earlier. Since reaction times are much larger than the transmission times, only preventive techniques are effective for cell-level congestion. The main preventive congestion control schemes are *admission control, traffic policing, priority scheduling,* and *adaptive routing.*

Admission Control: This can prevent congestion by limiting the number of connections in the network so that performance requirements of all the admitted connections can be satisfied. The user, while requesting for a connection, specifies the characteristics of the source and the expected QoS parameters. Admission Control is the decision-making process whether to admit the user or not. Conditions to be satisfied during admission control are:

- Network should be able to provide the requested QoS requirements, at least within the tolerance range specified.

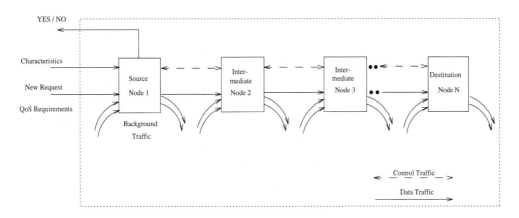

Fig. 11.3. Call setup over a typical source-destination path

- QoS guarantees provided to existing users should not be violated.

Admission Control is performed based on the currently existing traffic in the network and user-specified traffic and QoS parameters, subject to the above two conditions. This decision has to be made at the sending node and every node along the route to the requested destination. If at least one node in the route between the sender and receiver is unable to honor the request, admission is denied.

The process of deciding whether a call can be admitted into the network is designated as the Call Admission Control problem (CAC). CAC requires the concurrence of all the nodes situated along the path from source to destination before admitting the new connection. On the other hand, Node Admission Control (NAC) refers to the process of deciding whether a node can admit a new connection with a QoS requirement while continuing to provide guarantees to existing connections.

Let the new connection request be associated with input source characteristics vector $\vec{S}$ and QoS requirement vector $\vec{Q}$. The source characteristics may consist of peak transmission rate p, average rate m, averaging interval τ, and the maximum packet size k. Thus, the source characteristics vector may be specified as $\vec{S} = <p, m, \tau, k>$. The elements of $\vec{Q}$ are throughput bound t, delay bound d, and jitter bound j. A typical source-destination path over which a call has to be setup is shown in Fig. 11.3. The node where the call originates is called the source node. The QoS associated with the new call has to be agreed upon by all the intermediate nodes before the call can be admitted. Moreover, there may be *existing traffic*. Background

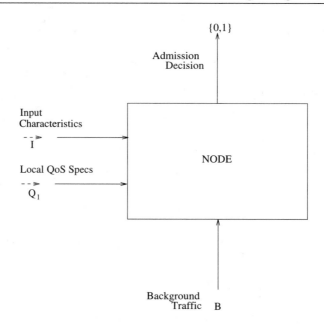

Fig. 11.4. Node Admission Control Problem

traffic shown refers to the *existing traffic* at any node and is denoted by B. For the QoS specified, viz., $\vec{Q} =< t, d, j >$, the CAC function can be stated as follows:

$$\mathcal{F}_{CAC} \longrightarrow \text{YES, if}$$
$$minimum\{t_i\} \geq t, \sum_{i=1}^{N} d_i \leq d \text{ and } \sum_{i=1}^{N} j_i \leq j;$$

where t_i, d_i, j_i are the throughput, delay and jitter to be provided by node i.

If the global information regarding the nature and number of connections at all the nodes are available at the source, then deriving the CAC function becomes a local computation problem at the source. This is however not practicable because:

1. There could be a wide variety of multimedia applications with diverse requirements traversing each node at any instant. Also, classifying as well as broadcasting the information in real-time is nontrivial.

2. Large latency at gigabit speeds causes the information received at other nodes to be obsolete and inconsistent.

Thus, the CAC problem has to be decomposed into individual Node Admission Control (NAC) problems. NAC resolves the local admission control problem at each node. In this case, the local QoS bounds to be satisfied by each node have to be derived from the user-specified bounds. In practice, a resource reservation protocol performs this task in one round-trip propagation through the nodes in the source-destination path. The NAC problem can be stated as:

$$\mathcal{F}_{NAC} : \{\vec{I}, \mathrm{B}, \vec{Q}_l\} \longrightarrow \{0, 1\}$$

where $\vec{I}$ is the input characteristics at that node, B denotes the background traffic, and $\vec{Q}_l$ represents the local QoS bounds to be met at that node. At the source node where the call originates, $\vec{I}$ is synonymous to $\vec{S}$ described earlier. The NAC problem is depicted in Fig. 11.4.

A conceptual model of the ideal NAC is as shown in Fig. 11.5. q_0, $q_1,....,q_M$ denote the QoS requirements of the requesting connection as well as the M existing connections. A scheduling function $\mathcal{S}$ schedules the traffic from these connections. The loss and delay characteristics of each is derived by the QoS analyzer. The connection request is honored if and only if the QoS guarantees are satisfied for all $M + 1$ connections.

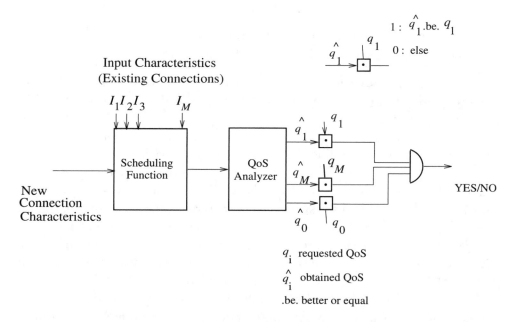

Fig. 11.5. **Model of an Ideal Node Admission Controller**

The admission control in the TENET scheme [2] clearly maps on to the model shown above. Various tests ensure the QoS guarantees of each individual connection. The technique for satisfying QoS guarantees for a connections may be *deterministic*, *statistical*, or *best effort*.

Admission Control in the TENET schemes   In the TENET approach, services are classified into three categories; hard guaranteed or deterministic service, service with statistical guarantees, and best effort service with no guarantees. A Multiclass Earliest Due Date (EDD) discipline is assumed at the switches. Admission Control performed at each switch during the channel establishment phase consists of three tests.

- *deterministic test* checks whether accepting a new request with deterministic delay bound would still keep the worst-case utilization by the deterministic channels below 1.

- *statistical test* checks whether accepting a new channel would still keep the probability of violating the delay bounds below the specified value.

- *buffer space test* checks for sufficient buffer space to retain the packets of the new channel so that scheduler saturation as defined in [2] can be avoided.

These three tests to be performed in the switching nodes are fairly simple and hence can be easily computed in real-time.

Issues in Admission Control   One issue in admission control is that the parameters specified by the user may not be correct. If they are conservative, network utilization will be low. Should we admit new traffic, taking into consideration the statistical smoothing effects, when the number of connections are large? Providing performance guarantees and maximizing link utilization, at the same time, is still an open problem. Yet another issue in admission control is whether the traffic existing in the network can be calculated from the user-specified characteristics or be based on actual measurements. Admission Control based on actual measurement has been suggested in [3,4,5]. An approach based on measurement would achieve a higher utilization. The traffic can be monitored over an observation interval (window), and a decision can be made based on the past behavior. The optimum size of the window for credible results remains to be investigated. Whether the measured approach can be adopted in a system providing hard guarantees is yet to be ascertained.

Traffic Enforcement Traffic enforcement and shaping schemes have been extensively studied from the point of view of their effectiveness in smoothing the burstiness of the input stream. The enforcement schemes police the source streams to check for their compliance with the pre-declared values throughout the life of the connection. Policing schemes come under two categories: one, the Leaky Bucket and its variants, and the other, window-based schemes.

Priority Scheduling In a multimedia network, different streams may have widely different characteristics and diverse QoS requirements. Some applications are delay sensitive whereas some are loss sensitive. The sensitivity value of each will also depend on the QoS requirements set by the application. In practice, different grades of services will be offered at appropriately rated tariff for the user to choose. Thus, a prioritized scheduler in place of normal FCFS can give preferential treatment for cells belonging to higher priority applications. Priority scheduling is implemented using a queuing strategy consisting of a service discipline (time or delay priority) and a buffer allocation policy (space priority) [6]. The service discipline is concerned with the decision of selecting the next packet for service, whereas the buffer management decides which incoming packet to accept. In a high-speed environment supporting multimedia, the diverse QoS requirements of different applications can be efficiently achieved through the use of priority buffer access control along with adequate traffic policing at the ingress of the network. Different buffer allocation strategies and their performance comparison for FCFS service are studied in [6]. In case of buffer overflow, cells to be discarded can be selectively discarded based on their priority [7,8]. Selective discarding based on priority can improve the quality of transmission of voice and video-based applications.

ATM provides only one bit for priority information. Simplicity of the priority scheme in ATM is in accordance with the spirit of ATM; that the protocol at the switches should be simple and fast. In a multimedia environment priority policies, apart from throughput guarantees, should also provide delay and jitter guarantees. Many scheduling schemes have been proposed to meet the delay and jitter guarantees of multimedia applications [2,3,9]. Based on the relationship between the status of the input queues and the scheduling operation, there are two categories of scheduling disciplines:

- Work conserving, in which the scheduler is never idle as long as there is at least one packet in the queue.

- Non-work conserving, on the other hand, may have idle periods even when there are packets in the queue. Non-work conserving schedulers have been shown to be quite effective in providing tight delay and jitter bounds. However, they are difficult to implement.

A comparative study of some of the scheduling disciplines for performance guarantees can be found in [10].

Adaptive Routing   Adaptive routing aims at relieving congestion by providing alternate routes for the congesting sources. By quickly withdrawing the cells from the congested node, proliferation of congestion is effectively checked. However, this approach is difficult at high-speeds. Since performance guarantees need resource provisioning, real-time services use a connection-oriented approach. Adaptive routing in networks such as ATM is still an open research issue.

11.4   Summary

This chapter presented the congestion problem in high-speed networks for multimedia communications and some of the solutions. Congestion continues to be one of the key issues to be addressed in future networks. The transition to high-speeds has made congestion control increasingly difficult due to latency effects. Older and proven reactive control schemes have been shown to be ineffective at high-speeds. Preventive control needs a multi-pronged approach to check congestion. Admission Control at the time of connection request, traffic policing at the edges of the network, and priority scheduling strategies at the switches are some of the open loop solutions. The area of congestion control is fertile, with a lot of potential for research.

REFERENCES

1. Henry Gilbert, Osama Aboul-Magd, and Van Phung. Developing a Cohesive Traffic Management Strategy for ATM Networks, IEEE Communications, Vol. 30, N. 10, pp. 36-45, October 1991.

2. Domenico Ferrari and Dinesh C. Verma. A Scheme for Real-Time Channel Establishment in Wide-Area Networks, IEEE Journal of Selected Areas in Communications, Vol. 8, No. 3, pp. 368-379, April 1990.

3. David Clark, Scott Shenker, and Lixia Zhang. Supporting Real-Time Applications in an Integrated Services Packet Network: Architecture and Mechanism, Proceedings of ACM SIGCOMM'92, Baltimore, Maryland, pp. 14-26, August 1992.

4. Jay Hyman, Aurel A. Lazar, and Giovanni Pacifici. Joint Scheduling and Admission Control for ATS-based Switching Nodes, Proceedings of ACM SIGCOMM'92, Baltimore, Maryland, August 1992.

5. H. Saito and K. Shiomoto, Dynamic Call Admission Control in ATM Networks, IEEE Journal of Selected Areas in Communications, Vol. 9, No. 7, pp. 982-989, September 1991.

6. Y.M. Lin and John A.Silvester. Priority Queuing Strategies and Buffer Allocation Protocols for Traffic Control at an ATM Integrated Broadband Switching Systems, IEEE Journal of Selected Areas in Communications, Vol. 9, No. 9, pp. 1524-1536, December 1991.

7. David W. Petr and Victor S. Frost. Optimal Packet Discarding:An ATM-Oriented Analysis Model and Initial Results, IEEE INFOCOM, pp. 537-542, 1990.

8. N. Yin, S. Q. Li, and T. E. Stern. Congestion Control for Packet Voice by Selective Packet Discarding, IEEE Transaction on Communications, Vol. 38, No. 5, pp. 674-683, May 1990.

9. J. M. Hyman, A. A. Lazar, and G. Pacifici. Real-Time Scheduling with Quality of Service Constraints, IEEE Journal of Selected Areas in Communications, Vol. 9, No. 7, pp. 1052-1063, September 1991.

10. Hui Zhang and Srinivasan Keshav. Comparison of Rate-based Service Disciplines, Proceedings of ACM SIGCOMM'91, Zurich, Switzerland, pp. 113-122, September 1991.

Chapter 12

Multimedia Systems Design: System Software Trends

12.1 Introduction

Multimedia applications typically involve moving large volumes of time-sensitive data between devices and peripherals attached to the same host or to different hosts. For example, in a video recording application, data captured from a camera is compressed and coded by a CODEC and stored on a disk, all of which can be done on the same host. Alternatively, images can be captured by a camera attached to one host, compressed by a CODEC in another, and stored on a disk in yet another host, all connected via a network. In either case, providing adequate system support requires an infrastructure that is capable of moving hundreds and thousands of megabytes of data from one end to the other in a timely and orderly manner. Although we have witnessed great gains in hardware performance in recent years, software performance has not improved commensurately. The inadequacy of the current generation of operating systems (OSs) in supporting I/O-intensive applications is a major deterrent in the widespread deployment of multimedia applications.

The current generation of operating systems fails to provide the sheer performance required or the predictability of performance desired by multimedia applications. Although it is not immediately obvious, both these limitations arise due to the processor-centric viewpoint adapted by current OSs. The processor-centric viewpoint is embodied in the notion of a process. A process, by definition, is an instantiation of the current state of a computation and a place to keep a record of resources reserved for the computation. The most important omission from this notion, we believe, is that a process says very little about communications and I/O operations that take place.

346

Nothing is indicated about what resources are to be used for communications and I/O and their expected usage pattern. Implicit resource demands of communications and I/O make it hard to design OSs which would provide predictable performance. Another aspect of the processor-centric viewpoint of current operating systems is shown by how I/O operations occur. In current systems, the main processors and memory subsystems are involved in initiating I/O operations and moving data even when applications do little or no data manipulation. A canonical example would be the I/O operations observed for an application that is recording scenes captured by a camera and in a file saved on a disk. In this application, every data byte would pass over the processor memory and would be delivered to an application that runs at a main processor. This path, as one would expect, remains the principle bottleneck for high-performance desired for multimedia servers.

12.2 Kernel Support for QoS

In traditional operating systems, input/output (I/O) subsystems implement a *push-pull* environment that provides system calls to allow user applications to *pull* data from or *push* data to a device. These services are implemented as code-to-code control transfers and as memory-to-memory buffer copies. In computing environments that supports streams, such as Unix, these are combined. The major advantage in such cases is the ability of the applications to do transformations on data on the fly. Applications such as *FTP, Web Server (thru HTML), On-Demand Video, etc.* use the traditional *push-pull* technique. Obviously, performance of these become limited, and can be improved, if *streamed*. Kernel support for *streams* with on-the-fly transformations are the key elements to the performance of multimedia systems.

12.3 Current State of Art

Operating systems have become faster over the years but the gap between the raw hardwares capabilities and what is made available to the users has grown over the years [1]. For instance, microprocessors have improved their MIPS rating every year roughly by 55% or more. As a result of this improvement in the computing power, computationally intensive applications have shown impressive gains. However, the improvement in performance is rather meager for I/O-intensive applications, where the performance of OS remains the bottleneck. This fact is most evident when we examine the performance of applications moving large volumes of data, e.g., World-

Wide-Web browser application. As we move to multimedia applications that generate and consume a large amount of time-critical data, the performance gap is expected to widen even further. For example, Video-On-Demand servers serving a metropolitan area or a large campus have to be capable of serving upwards of 1000 video/audio streams. The total demand on the I/O subsystem it would place would exceed a few gigabits/sec[1]. With compressed video traffic, total throughput desired at a client is not a challenge, but the requirements of the client's operating system are no less stringent because of the real-time nature of the data being displayed.

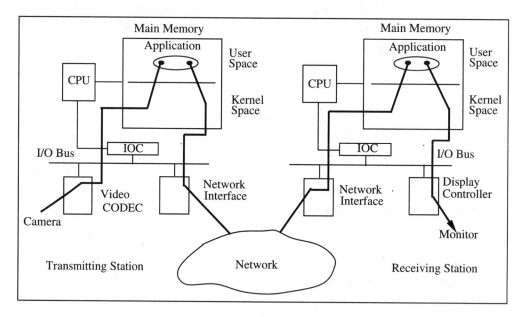

Fig. 12.1. A Video Playback Environment

In the past decade of OS research, OS performance has improved only marginally with the innovations that have happened. Over the past decade we have gone from having a monolithic OS such as Unix to micro-kernels implementing many traditional OS services in user space [2]. In the past few years there has been a significant growth in the number of micro-kernels [3,4]. The current practice to structure a micro-kernel-based operating sys-

---

[1]In arriving at this estimate, we have assumed that each stream is encoding an image sequences with full TV-size images and 30 frames/sec rate. If the stream is compressed with MPEG-2 at 3 Mbps rate, which gives an NTSC-type quality, the total data rate required for the server would be 3 Gbps I/O rate.

tem as one or more server address spaces solves some of the flexibility and
extensibility problems of the monolithic OS. However, the communication
overhead incurred in contacting servers can lead to poor performance. To
alleviate this problem, in some of the recent architectures OS services have
been added back into the kernel [5,6,7,8,9,10,11]. To tailor OS services to specific application needs, some of these kernels allow user processes to extend
kernel services by dynamically loading user code into the kernel. It is unclear
at this point if these extensible kernels will be successful in achieving their
goal in combining the flexibility of the micro-kernels with the performance of
monolithic OSs without compromising safety. We have learned much from
these efforts about how to design lean kernels that are easy to build and
maintain. In that process, the performance has surely improved, but the
improvement lags behind the one observed for the hardware. RoadRunner
proposes a new set of abstractions that have the potential of achieving some
of the performance-related goals that have eluded us so far [12].

In order to understand why OS performance lags, let us consider in detail
typical activities that takes place in OS while supporting a basic multimedia
application. Shown in Fig. 12.1 is the application that captures a sequence
of images at one of the network nodes and displays in real-time these images
at another node. As shown in the figure, typical of current system architectures, the data captured are first copied from the adapters buffers to the
kernel's communication buffers in main memory. From there the data are
copied again into the buffer in user's address space. To move data across
the network, one would then have to make a system call and transfer data
once again through the kernel space. The data buffer is copied from the
user space back into kernel space (as a chain of *mbufs*), and from there onto
the buffer on the network adapter. Thus, the same data were copied four
times before being sent out on the network. This is wasteful of host bus,
processor, and memory bandwidth. Moreover, data movement also harms
the cache performance. The processor's primary and secondary caches are
filled with data that is used only once, leading to flushing of caches of other
data, which would generate more processor stalls later for other programs.
On the other hand, if the data transferred is allowed to bypass the cache, the
networked application will experience increased latency due to cache misses
when processing message headers and control messages.

Frequent context switches is another leading cause of the poor performance [13,14,15] with large I/O data transfers. Measurements have shown
that only about 15% of the total time is spent in protocol-specific processing.
The rest is spent equally divided between data copying, checksum operations,

and the overhead of context switching. In the above example, every copy of data buffer also requires a context switch between user and kernel processes. These context switches cannot be avoided because protection boundaries are being crossed in copying data from user to kernel and kernel to user space. The trend in microprocessor technology towards a larger set of registers, deeper pipelines, and multiple instruction issues is going to further increase the cost of a context switch.

Several recent works [15, 16, 17, 18, 19] address the problem of data copying across domain boundaries. Although their solutions improve performance in some isolated case studies, it is not clear at this time if theses approaches will be successful as general-purpose mechanisms. The increasing gap between processor speeds and memory bandwidth also means the cost of delivering data to a wrong place in the memory hierarchy would also rise proportionately. Carter et. al. [20] proposes to address this problem by integrating memory controller with the network interface. In order to reduce the frequency of context switches required, Bershad et. al. [6] proposes building extensible kernels that would include some part of an application to run in the kernel. Fall and Pasquale [15] propose a Peer-to-Peer I/O model where most of the data flow occurs through the kernel and does not require extra copies or context switch between users/kernel. Although the approach would lead to higher performance for I/O-intensive applications, it also increases the complexity of the kernel and thus may adversely affect the performance of the kernel and other applications.

The trend in microprocessor technology is always towards cheaper and faster microprocessors, and most devices nowadays are equipped with on-board processors powerful enough to do some extra processing tasks. Taking advantage of this trend, one could make devices that generate and consume data independently instead of application-driven push-pull control. Data could be transferred from one device to another without processor or main memory getting in the way. Such devices would not only move data but also do rate matching and recover from occasional data losses. Once the connection is established by an application program running at the processor between two devices, there would be no further need to involve the main processor in the data transfer. In the context of the example shown above, a connection would be established between the camera controller and the network controller and then each frame would be captured at a rate at which the network agrees to push it out. Once the context is established, the controllers would never need to interrupt the kernel until one desires to terminate the capture mode or wishes to exchange control information such as controls for camera positioning.

Smart devices capable of direct data transfer address the problem only partially. A disk controller that stores a file would also require someone to manage disk space (allocate disk sectors, link them in a file system, etc.) If this is provided by an OS service, each data transfer would still require some action from a processor. We define a new term, autonomous devices, for a device that can be a source or a sink of data without repeated interactions with the main processor, i.e., OS services. Several recent works on redesigning workstations to be Desk Area Networks [21,22,23,24] have explored the notion of using direct transfers between certain types of devices, such as a camera and a display.

12.4 Integrated I/O for Multimedia Operating System

Input/Output processing should integrate the notion of direct transfer more deeply in the OS system. For example, one such implementation called Road-Runner [12] unifies I/O and communication under the same abstraction and treats them as schedulable events. It uses a new abstraction, called a *MAP*, that replaces the abstraction of a process. A MAP, by definition, is a record of computation where the computation is viewed as being performed by a collection of autonomous, communicating entities. A MAP explicitly keeps states of communication channels between connected entities and resources reserved for the purpose. The entities connected are generically some type of data manipulation procedures that could either be run at one of the main processors or at microprocessors normally used as device controllers. In the later case, a MAP records information needed to facilitate communications between autonomous devices. The notion of MAP and its implications on performance of multimedia applications are explored later in the proposal.

Allowing autonomy in I/O operations and taking a communications-oriented viewpoint in building an OS are possibly the main directions of current research efforts. In the case of multimedia, additional research goals are:

> **Scalability:** A scalable system is one that is capable of running on hardware platforms designed for many different functionalities. For instance, we would like to use the same OS to control a networked camera, a set-top box controlling TV and other home devices, a workstation, and a multiprocessor server machine. Another requirement for scalability is the ability to run on target systems that are modu-

lar and allow future additions of new types of processors and devices. The scalability is important because it leads to the preservation of our investment in software and eases the task of building a new generation of target systems.

Performance: Since many multimedia applications involve movement of large amounts of data, high performance of the I/O subsystem is going to be a key to building an operating system for multimedia applications. The current generation of operating systems perform rather badly in this respect, and this was one of the two main motivating factors for suggesting a new OS. The I/O performance needs to improve at least by an order of magnitude before cost-effective multimedia servers are used on a wide scale for video-on-demand service and distance-learning applications.

Predictability: Multimedia applications require predictable quality of service and not just "high" average throughput or "low" latency. Video images to be displayed in real-time would suffer not only if the data coming in from a network or a disk is lost, but also if the data arrives too late. Although many types of quality of service guarantees desired (such as peak or average rate, or acceptable cell loss rates) have been discussed in the literature, so far no one to our knowledge has incorporated a need to provide predictability as a fundamental OS design principle. It is a worthwhile goal to design an operating system where it is natural to provide such performance guarantees to all applications.

12.5   Design Principles

Three central tenets guiding our design effort are: giving a central role to communications, allowing autonomous device operations, and providing direct control of I/O to applications. These design principles are discussed below.

- **Central Role of Communications:** *Operating systems should be more concerned with communications than computations.*

- **Autonomy of Devices:** *Operating systems are NOT an I/O director but a facilitator.*

- **Translucent OS:** *The best OS is the one that is hardly ever there.*

Central Role of Communications: Recent operating systems research has been focused on interprocess communications and network communications. The effort has led to lower latencies and higher throughput over a single connection. We believe that it is now the right time to take a more global view of the communications involved in carrying out a computation.In doing so, one of the biases that needs to be removed is the process-centered view of communications. So far the resources required for communications are identified only implicitly. An OS scheduler does not know what effect the running of a particular process would have on the communications among various processes. An OS scheduler may be able to use information about communications, if available, in many different ways. The scheduler may schedule tasks intelligently by knowing producer/consumer relationships, list of recipients for any communication, the frequency and the desired quality of service, and resources required for successful communications. Because a process only keeps a record of one endpoint of a communication channel, currently a global picture can only emerge by examining all processes, and that is something that a scheduler does not have enough time for.

An abstraction can address this by keeping a record of global communications required by an application [25]. The abstraction records the topology of interconnections between processing modules, resource demands, and the quality of service required for these communication paths. It differs from the concept of a process group in that it makes communications among processes a first-class object. Explicit and centralized information regarding communications required makes it easier to ensure that communications occur in time and resources used are globally optimized. With this change in the framework of providing OS services, it is expected that the user-level performance would be less chaotic and the OS would be able to provide quality of service guarantees to real-time multimedia applications.

Autonomy of Devices: Currently, I/O performance limited by many factors such as MIPS required for data movement, operating system kernel overhead, the limited bandwidth of I/O buses, or the limited bandwidth of the host memory. The autonomy principle outlined here enhances performance by avoiding going through these subsystems as fast as possible. The architecture, which is sometimes referred to as a Desk-Area Network (DAN) system, replaces a shared I/O and/or memory-processor bus with a switching hub that allows multiple simultaneous communication paths between modules. We believe that this is the future trend for workstation architectures. Although the DAN architecture leads one to the notion of autonomy, the autonomy principle is also useful with the traditional bus-based architecture. Conversely, some DAN systems have been built where main processor is still the central bottleneck [22].

A device is a source or a sink of data. A monitor, keyboard, mouse, disk, tape drives, and network adapters are all devices.[2] In the standard model of a computation, application proceeds by directing a device to do something. The operation that is requested is at a high level of abstraction (e.g., read line from the named file, open file for reading). This request would be translated into a system call. The OS kernel would handle the system call by breaking down the operation in a sequence of low-level commands to a device. Transferring large amounts of data, such as listing a file, thus involves repeatedly transferring control to kernel as well as passing a data through the processor. Matching a rate of flow between devices is done by buffering data in the kernel and sometimes in the application space as well. This type of device is referred to as a passive device.

The notion of autonomous devices is defined as follows. An active device is defined as one that is capable of handling data transfers, of buffering data, and matching rates with flow control mechanisms. An autonomous device is defined as a type of active device that is capable of de-multiplexing traffic according to application-specific contexts provided to it by a processor when a connection is initialized. Autonomous devices may also include simple data manipulation capabilities such as byte swapping, checksum operation, and more complex actions such as BITBLT operations used in bit-mapped display devices. In this model, the OS is viewed as the one that established connections and necessary contexts at devices. The control may be transferred to an OS only in emergencies and not during the data flow.

Translucent OS: In the traditional model, an application currently executing is given unfettered accesses only to CPU and its register set, except for some special registers and some privileged instructions. Any access to I/O devices has to go through the kernel and hence requires a context switch. What would be desirable is a direct access to devices. As in the case of conventional DMA, application should have DDA (Direct Device Access). The term, application channel in [7], refers to the concept and the mechanism that would allow applications direct access to network devices in a controlled fashion. We propose to expand the concept to include other I/O devices, in particular autonomous devices. Giving unfettered access to all I/O devices

---

[2]Main memory could also be treated as an autonomous device. A discussion of how this could be done and its implications on system performance are discussed in [25].

could be risky and may cause a complex run-time system to be included with every application. Yet, the advantages are large enough to justify a cautious exploration in a direction when some applications are granted direct I/O access to devices such as networks, disk storage, keyboards, mouse, and monitor.

12.6   Summary

An ideal multimedia system is yet to come, but the current research directions seem to indicate the possibility of a flexible computing environment (with emphasis on efficient input/output) being "just around the corner". Initial attempts such as RoadRunner are a modest step in this direction. Also, the fact that OSs have not caught up with the processor speed upgrades over the years indicates that there is a lot of room for the future designer. We hope that the material presented in this book will help the reader come out with innovative ways and means of contributing to the creation of a versatile multimedia system.

REFERENCES

1. John Ousterhout. Why Aren't Operating Systems Getting Faster As Fast As Hardware?, Proceedings of the USENIX Summer Conference, 1990.

2. M. Accetta, R. Baron, W. Bolosky, D. Golub, R. Rashid, A. Tevanin, and M. Young. Mach: A New Kernel Foundation for UNIX Development, Proceedings of the USENIX, 1986.

3. J.M. Phelan, J. Arendt, and G.R. Ormsby. An OS/2 Personality on Mach, Proceedings of the USENIX Mach Symposium, 1993.

4. M. Rozier, V. Abrossimov, F. Armand, I. Boule, M. Giend, M. Guillemont, F. Herrmann, P. Leonard, S. Langois, and W. Neuhauser. The Chorus Distributed Operating System, Computing Systems, Vol. 1, No. 4, 1988.

5. J. Carter, B. Ford, M. Hiber, R. Kuramkote, J. Law, J. Lepreau, D. Orr, L. Stoller, and M. Swanson. Flex:A tool for building efficient and flexible systems, In Proceedings of IEEE Workshop on Workstation Operating Systems, 1993.

6. B. Bershad, C. Chanmers, S. Eggers, C. Maeda, D. McNamee, P. Pyzemyslaw , S. Savage, and S. Emin Gon. SPIN - An Extensible Microkernel for Application-Specific Operating System Services, Department of Computer Science and Engineering FR-35, TR-94-03-03, University of Washington, 1994.

7. A.B. Montz, D. Mosberger, S.W. O'Malley, L.L. Peterson, T.A. Proebsting, and J.H. Hartman. SPIN: A Communications-Oriented Operating System, Department of Computer Science, TR-94-20, University of Arizona, 1994.

8. R. Pike, D. Presotto, K. Thompson, and H. Trickey. Plan 9 from Bell Labs, Proceedings of the Summer UK UNIX User's Group, 1990.

9. David Presotto. Multiprocessor Streams for Plan-9, Proceedings of the Summer UK UNIX User's Group, 1990.

10. P. Druschel, L. Peterson, and N.C. Hutchinson. Beyond micro-kernel design: Decoupling modularity and protection in Lipto, In Proceedings of ICDCS, 1992.

11. H. Massalin. Synthesis: An Efficient Implementation of Fundamental Operating System Services, PhD thesis, Columbia University, 1992.

12. Debanjan Saha, Hemant Kanakia, and Satish K. Tripathi. RoadRunner: An OS for Multimedia, Unpublished Report of University of Maryland, 1996.

13. J. Mogul and A. Borg. The Effect of Context Switches on Cache Performance, Proceedings of the ASPLOS-IV, 1991.

14. P. Druschel and L. Peterson. Fbufs: A High-Bandwidth Cross-Domain Transfer Facility, Proceedings of the SOSP, 1993

15. K. Fall and J. Pasquale. Exploiting In-Kernel Data Paths to Improve I/O Throughput and CPU Availability, Proceedings of the USENIX Winter Conference, 1993.

16. David Clark. The Structuring of Systems Using Upcalls, Proceedings of the SOSP, 1985.

17. J.B. Chen and B.N. Bershad. The Impact of Operating System Structure on Memory System Performance, In Proceedings of SOSP, 1993.

18. P. Druschel, M. Abbott, M. Pagels, and L. Peterson. Analysis of I/O Subsystem Design for Multimedia Workstations, Proceedings of the Workshop on Network and Operating System Support for Digital Audio and Video, 1992.

19. P. Druschel and L. Peterson. Fbufs: A High-Bandwidth Cross-Domain Transfer Facility, Proceedings of the SOSP, 1993.

20. J.B. Carter, A. Davis, R. Kuramkote, C.-C. Kuo, L.B. Stoller, and M. Swanson. Avalanche: A Communication and Memory Architecture for Scalable Parallel Computing, Draft Report, Computer Systems Laboratory, University of Utah, 1995.

21. G. Finn. An Integration of Network Communication with Workstation Architecture, Computer Communication Review, Vol. 21, No. 5, October 1991.

22. J. Adam, H. Houh, M. Ismert, and D. Tennenhuse. A Network Architecture for Distributed Multimedia Systems, Proceedings of the Multimedia Computing and Systems, 1994.

23. S. Wray, T. Glauert, and A. Hopper. Networked Multimedia: The Medusa Environment, IEEE Multimedia, Vol. 1, No. 4, 1994.

24. M. Hayter and M. Derek. The Desk Area Network, Operating Systems Review, Vol. 25, No. 4, 1991.

25. Debanjan Saha. Supporting Distributed Multimedia Applications on ATM Networks, Ph. D. Thesis, University of Maryland, College Park, Maryland, 1995.

Appendix A

Multimedia Systems Technology: Standards

A.1 Introduction

Apart from the networking standards, the field of multimedia is inspired by several standards that span voice, image, graphics, video, and interchange formats. Moreover, there are at least four different types of standards bodies whose standards impact the growth of multimedia. They are International Standards bodies such as CCITT or ISO, Cooperative Standards bodies such as ATM Forum and IMA Forum, the ubiquitous Internet RFCs, and the proprietary standards of manufacturers. In this chapter, we discuss the standards from these organizations that are relevant to multimedia systems.

A.2 Standards and Standard Makers

Standards are agreements to produce or design things in a particular way for some purpose. For example, the main electric supply in India is supplied at a standard voltage, and through plugs and sockets of a standardized design. Thus, when we normally move from one house to another, a table fan that we take from the old house to the new house should plug into a socket provided in the new house, and work when we switch it on. But when we move to a different country, say Europe, the same standard may not apply. This is because the voltages, socket type, shape, and size are all different. If we imagine the same standard all over the world, things could be easy for a common user. When we talk about standards in computer networks, we expect to see that the procedures followed for the applications (transferring files for example) remain the same.

It is important that a terminal produced by one manufacturer interfaces to the computer system produced by a different manufacturer. For this, we need standards. Perhaps the situation is even worse if a person wants to buy a system from manufacturer X, a database package from manufacturer Y, and a graphics package from yet another manufacturer Z. Unless there is an open standard to which each one of the manufacturers X, Y, and Z make their respective products, interworking will be hard. There could be a certain amount of cooperation between the manufacturers for a specific application or a set of applications, but to make it global there should be internationally accepted standards.

There are several standards makers and their operations range from hardware-level interconnection to cooperation at the level of application.

1. *International Telecommunications Union* or *ITU* is an intergovernmental organization founded in 1865 to harmonize the activities of European telegraph systems. In 1947 it became an agency of the United Nations, specializing in telecommunications. Its two standards committees are CCITT (now ITU-T) and CCIR (International Radio Consultative Committee). The meeting of these committees are normally attended by national telecommunications administrations amongst others. From its European origin, it has become a worldwide organization dealing with technical, political, and financial issues in communications.

2. *International Standards Organization* or *ISO* is an independent international agency with the aim of developing and promoting standards throughout the world. It was founded in 1947. There are some 90 national standards bodies which constitute its membership. It covers standards in all fields except electrical and electronic engineering, where the International Electrotechnical Commission has the responsibility. There are some 165 technical committees (TCs) operating through a hierarchy of structures to draft and finalize proposals.

3. *International Telegraph and Telephone Consultative Committee* or *also known as CCITT* is a part of the ITU. It was formed in 1956 to ensure cooperation among the previously separate committees dealing with telegraph, data, and telephone issues respectively. Its members include national telecommunications, administrations, major telecommunications carriers, and a number of other organizations, including user groups. It is organized into a number of study groups (SGs) which

keep existing recommendations up-to-date and produce new recommendations when required. Every four years, there is a planery session of the CCITT to approve the work carried out in the foregoing period and to specify its work program for the next period. The recommendations themselves are issued in the form of "Colored Books". The contents of the books serve an important purpose in guiding European telecommunications service providers and suppliers. Increasingly, CCITT cooperates with the ISO. The Study Group XVIII on Digital Networks concentrates on ISDN.

4. *British Standards Institution (BSI)* is the recognized U.K. organization for the formation of national standards. It participates in ISO, through BSI committees that are restricted to professional bodies or trade associations. The BSI operates through a hierarchy of committees and working groups. Committees of interest to the information technology area are: IST - Information Systems Technology and AMT - Advanced Manufacturing Technology. Work on LAN and related standards are carried out by IST.

5. *The European Computer Manufacturers Association (ECMA)* is a group setup and managed by a number of companies developing and marketing computer systems in Europe. Its purpose when it was setup in 1961 was to develop data processing standards, and was instrumental in assisting ISO in this field. As with other organizations, its work is carried out by technical committees which themselves setup working groups for particular tasks. Its committees, however, meet more frequently than those of the other organizations.

6. *Institute of Electrical and Electronics Engineers* or *IEEE* is a U.S.-based professional body. It gained a wider scope in 1965 with its responsibilities to provide data processing guidance to the Government. It has produced standards known as FIPS (Federal Information Processing Standards), which are observed by all government agencies in their data processing work. Many of these standards contract to industry to produce standards as required.

7. *American National Standards Institute (ANSI)* is the U.S. counterpart of BSI. It also has a committee/subcommittee structure where standardization for the data transmission industry is governed by the X3 committee. Its subcommittees are very active, and many of its ex-

perts take part in ISO work. In fact, ANSI has the secretariat of the ISO TC97 committee. There is also an American National Bureau of Standards (NBS), which is active in standardization in the information technology area. Standards developed by both ANSI and NBS are often adopted by industry.

8. *The International Federation for Information Processing* (IFIP) is an international federation of professionals and technical groups with interests in promoting information science and technology and assisting in research, development, and education. Each country is represented by one full member. For example, the Computer Society of India is the Indian member. The IFIP has several Technical Committees (TCs) which promote special areas. The TC6 is on data communication.

A.3   CCITT Standards

CCITT standards appear in series identified by an alphabet. Each series deals with standards relating to a service, technology, or interface. In every series, the related standards will be referred to by their identification numbers. For example, CCITT standard F.711 refers to the F-series recommendations and a particular standard with number 711.

F700 Series: This series deals with audio-, video-, and graphics-based services. For each service, there are individual standards. F.711 deals with Audiographic Conference Teleservice for ISDN, F.720 deals with Videotelephony Services General, F.721 deals with Videotelephony Teleservices for ISDN, F.722 deals with Videotelephony Services General, F.730 deals with Videoconference Service General, and F.732 deals with Broadband Videoconference Services, and F.740 deals with Audiovisual Interactive Services (AVIS).

G700 Series: This series deals with voice coding standards. G711 deals with 64 kbit/s Pulse Code Modulation (PCM) audio encoding, G721 deals with 32 kbit/s adaptive differential pulse code modulation (ADPCM) for audio encoding, G722 deals with 7 KHz audio encoding within 64 kbit/s, and G725 deals with system aspects of the use of 7 kHz audio codec within 64 kbit/s.

H - Series: This series deals with procedures and formats for providing audio and video services using ISDN channels. We will discuss H221, H242, H261, H263, and H320.

H.221   This deals with frame structure for a 64 to 1920 kbit/s channel in audiovisual teleservices. It defines a frame structure for audiovisual teleservices in single or multiple B[1] or H0[2] channels, or a single H11 or H12 channel, which make the best use of the characteristics and properties of the audio and video encoding algorithms. It offers several advantages: it takes into account Recommendations G.704, X.301/I.461, etc.; it may allow the use of existing hardware and software; it may be implemented on a single microprocessor using well-known hardware principles. H221 is a synchronous procedure. The exact time of a configuration change is the same in the transmitter and the receiver. It needs no return link for audiovisual signal transmission, since a configuration is signaled by repeatedly transmitted codewords. It is very secure in case of transmission errors, since the code controlling the multiplex is protected by double-error correcting code. It allows synchronization of multiple 64 kbit/s or 384 kbit/s connections and the control of the multiplexing of audio, video, data, and other signals within the synchronized multiconnection structure in the case of multimedia services such as videoconferencing. It can be used in multipoint configurations, where no dialogue is needed to negotiate the use of a data channel. It provides a variety of data bit rates (from 300 b/s up to almost 2 Mb/s) to the user.

H.242:   This deals with audiovisual communication using digital channels up to 2 Mbit/s. Recommendation H.242 should be associated with Recommendations G.725, H.221, and H.230. A number of applications utilizing narrow (3 kHz) and wideband (7 kHz) speech together with video and/or data have been identified, including high-quality telephony, audio, and videoconferencing (with or without various kinds of telematic aids), audiographic conferencing, and so on. More applications will undoubtedly emerge in the future. To provide these services, a scheme is recommended in which a channel accommodates speech, and optionally video and/or data at several rates, in a number of different modes. Signaling procedures are required to establish a compatible mode upon call setup, to switch between modes during a call and to allow for call transfer. Some services will require only a single channel which, according to the procedures in Recommendation H.242, could be a B (64 kbit/s), a H0 (384 kbit/s), a H11 (1536 kbit/s), or a H12 (1920 kbit/s). Other services will require the establishment of two or more connections with B or H0 channels. In such cases, the first established connection

---

[1]B channel is a user channel that can be used to carry digital data.

[2]H channels are provided for user information at higher bit-rates.

is hereafter called the initial channel while the others are called additional channels. All audio and audiovisual terminals using G.722 audio coding, G.711 speech coding, or other standardized audio codings at lower bit-rates should be compatible to permit connection between any two terminals. This implied that a common mode of operation has to be established for the call. The initial mode might be the only one used during a call or, alternatively, switching to another mode can occur as needed depending on the capabilities of the terminals. Thus, for these terminals an in-channel procedure for dynamic mode switching is required. Recommendation H.242 develops these considerations and describes recommended in-channel procedures.

H.261: Recommendation H.261 describes the video coding and decoding methods for the moving picture component of audiovisual services at the rate of $p \times 64$ kbit/s, where p is in the range 1 to 30. It describes the video source coder, the video multiplex coder, and the transmission coder. This standard is intended for carrying video over ISDN - in particular for videophone and for videoconferencing applications. Videophone is less demanding of image quality, and can be achieved for $p = 1$ or 2. For videoconferencing applications (where there is more than one person in the field of view), higher picture quality is required and p must be at least 6. H.261 defines two picture formats: CIF (Common Intermediate Format) has 288 lines by 360 pixels/line of luminance information and 144×180 of chrominance information; and QCIF (Quarter Common Intermediate Format) which is 144 lines by 180 pixels/line of luminance and 72×90 of chrominance. The choice of CIF or QCIF depends on available channel capacity. The algorithm includes a mechanism which optimizes bandwidth usage by trading picture quality against motion, so that a quickly changing picture will have a lower quality than a relatively static picture. H.261 used in this way is thus a constant-bit-rate encoding rather than a constant-quality, variable-bit-rate encoding. H.261 codecs have been implemented in VLSI and are now used in commercial products.

H.263: Recommendation H.263 is a low bit-rate video standard for teleconferencing applications that has both MPEG-1 and MPEG-2 features [6,7]. It operates at 64 Kbps. The video coding of H.263 is based on that of H.261. In fact, H.263 is an extension of H.261 and describes a hybrid DPCM/DCT video coding method. Both H.261 and H.263 use techniques such as DCT, motion compensation, variable-length coding, and scalar quantization. Both use the concept of macroblock structure.

The idea of a PB frame in H.263 is interesting. The PB frame consists of two pictures being coded as one unit. The name PB is derived from the MPEG terminology of P-pictures and B-pictures. Thus, a PB frame consists of one P-picture that is predicted from the last decoded P-picture and one B-picture that is predicted from both the last decoded P-picture and the P-picture currently being decoded. This last picture is called a B-picture because parts of it may be bidirectionally predicted from the past and future P-picture.

It has been shown that the H.263 system typically outperforms H.261 by 2.5 to 1. That means, for a given picture quality, the H.261 bit-rate is approximately 2.5 times that of H.263 codec.

H.320: Recommendation H.320 covers the technical requirements for narrow-band visual telephone services defined in H.200/AV.120 Series Recommendations, where channel rates do not exceed 1920 kbits per second. Note - It is anticipated that Recommendation H.320 will be extended to a number of recommendations, each of which would cover a single videoconferencing or videophone service (narrowband, broadband, etc.). However, large parts of these recommendations would have identical wording, while in the points of divergence the actual choices between alternatives have not yet been made; for the time being, therefore, it is convenient to treat all the text in a single recommendation. The service requirements for visual telephone services are presented in Recommendation H.200/AV.120-Series; video and audio coding systems and other technical set aspects common to audiovisual services are covered in other recommendations in the H.200/AV.200-Series

T - Series: This deal with compression and coding of images. In particular, Recommendation T.80 deals with the basic principles and common components for image compression and communication; Recommendation T.81 deals with digital compression and encoding of continuous tone still images; Recommendation T.82 deals with progressive compression techniques for bi-level images, and Recommendation T.83 deals with compliance testing. Recommendations T121 to T124 deal with network-independent audio conferencing protocols.

X.400 - Message Handling System: This is the standard for the exchange of multimedia messages by store-and-forward transfer. The aim of the X.400 standards is to provide an international service for the exchange of electronic messages without restriction on the types of encoded information conveyed.

X.400 makes a clear distinction between message envelope, which controls the message transfer process, and message content, which is passed transparently from originator to recipient. The most common content type in use is the interpersonal-messaging content type - this format divides content into two parts: heading and body. Heading fields (with labels such as 'from', 'to', and 'subject') convey standard items of information. The message body consists of one or more body parts, each of which may contain a different type of encoded information. A number of body part types are defined as 'basic' in X.400: IA5Text, Teletex, Voice, G3Facsimile, G4Class1, Videotex, Message, and File Transfer. In addition to these, the Externally Defined body part type allows any identified data format to be conveyed, such as word processing and spreadsheet formats. A format is identified by the assignment of a globally unique Object Identifier. Commercial organizations can acquire Object Identifiers at nominal cost from their national standards organizations. Alternatively, the File Transfer body part type may be used for the transfer of structured and unstructured data.

X.400 has two further features that make it especially suitable for the conveyance of multimedia information. First, it uses ASN.1 [3], which guarantees data transparency and offers a choice of encodings, including a space-optimized "packed encoding". Second, it uses the Reliable Transfer Application Service Element to provide a very tolerant data transfer mechanism with recovery from connection failure. This is especially important for large multimedia messages.

A.4   ISO Standards

ISO standards include ISO 10744, and ISO 12087-3. These standards deal with hypermedia documents and image interchange facility.

ISO 10744:   This describes the SGML-based standard for hypermedia documents. HyTime (Hypermedia/Time-Based Structuring Language) is a standardized infrastructure for the representation of integrated, open hypermedia documents. It was developed principally by ANSI Committee X3V1.8M, and was subsequently adopted by ISO. The HyTime standard specifies how certain concepts common to all hypermedia documents can be represented using SGML. These concepts include: association of objects within documents with hyperlinks, placement, and interrelation of objects in space, and time logical structure of the document to include of nontextual data in the document. An "object" in HyTime is part of a document, and is unrestricted in form - it may be video, audio, text, a program, graphics, etc. SGML (Stan-

---

[3]Abstract Syntax Notation.

dard Generalized Markup Language: ISO 8879) is used to specify document markup schemes called Document Type Definitions (DTDs). HyTime is not itself a DTD, but provides constructs and guidelines for making DTDs for describing Hypermedia documents. For instance, the Standard Music Description Language (SMDL: ISO/IEC Committee Draft 10743) defines a DTD which is an application of HyTime. HyTime consists of six modules:

- **Base module:** This provides facilities required by other modules, including "xenoforms" for specifying application-defined expressions, and identification of policies for coping with changes to a document; (activity tracking).

- **Finite Coordinate Space module:** This allows for an object to be scheduled in time and/or space (which HyTime treats equivalently) within a bounding box called an "event".

- **Location Address module:** The standard specifies how to identify locations of document objects by name, by coordinate location, or by semantic construct. Five different types of hyperlink are provided for.

- **Event Projection:** module. This specifies how events in a source Finite Coordinate Space (FCS) are to be mapped onto a target FCS.

- **Object Modification module:** This allows for individual objects to be modified before rendition, in an object-specific way.

ISO 12087-3: This describes Image Interchange Facility. The Image Interchange Facility (IIF) is part of the first International Image Processing and Interchange Standard (IPI), and comprises both a data format definition and a gateway functional specification. The main component of the IIF is the definition of a data format for exchanging arbitrarily structured image data. The IIF defines a format that can be used across application boundaries and that can easily be integrated into international communication services. Besides the definition of a file format, there are definitions of parsers, generators, and format converters to enhance open image communication. The IIF approach clearly distinguishes between the image structure (a data-type-oriented description of the image), image attributes (expressing colorimetric and geometric semantics), the sequential data organization (managing data partitioning and periodicity organization), and the data encoding/compression. The syntax specification and the data encoding of syntax entities use ASN.1 and the Basic Encoding Rules, respectively. For the compressed representation, the following standards are referenced: JBIG, Facsimile Group 3 and 4, JPEG, and MPEG. Besides the data format specification, the IIF also encompasses functionality for generating and parsing image data, and for compressing and decompressing. It is also useful in the exchange of image data between the application program and the Programmer's Imaging Kernel System (PIKS), which is Part 2 of the IPI standard, and storage/communication devices. This functionality is located in the so-called IIF Gateway. The IIF gateway controls the import and export of image data to and from applications, as well as to and from the PIKS. The IIF may serve as a future image content architecture of the Open Document Architecture (ODA). Work is ongoing to develop a (multimedia) electronic mail application on top of X.400, using IIF.

A.5   Joint CCITT and ISO Standards

CCITT and ISO have a joint study group that recommends multimedia standards that are endorsed by both the bodies. The popular JPEG, MHEG, and ODA standards are of this category.

JPEG (CCITT and ISO)   (see also Chapter 3): JPEG is a standardized image compression mechanism. JPEG stands for Joint Photographic Experts Group, the original name of the committee that wrote the standard. JPEG is designed for compressing either full-color (24 bit) or grey-scale digital images of "natural" (real-world) scenes. JPEG does not handle black-and-white (one bit/pixel) images, nor does it handle motion picture compression. JPEG is "lossy", meaning that the image you get out of decompression is not quite identical to what you originally put in. The algorithm achieves much of its compression by exploiting known limitations of the human eye, notably the fact that small color details are not perceived as well as small details of light and dark. Thus, JPEG is intended for compressing images that will be looked at by humans. A useful property of JPEG is that the degree of lossiness can be varied by adjusting compression parameters. This means that the image compression can trade-off file size against output image quality. One can make extremely small files if one does not mind poor quality; this is useful for indexing image archives, making thumbnail views or icons, etc. Conversely, if one is not happy with the output quality at the default compression setting, one can jack up the quality until one is satisfied, and accept lesser compression. Although it handles color files well, it is limited in handling black-and-white and files with sharp edges (files come out very large). The processing costs, even on up-to-date computers, is also high.

MHEG - (CCITT T.170 and ISO (JTC1/SC2/WG12)): MHEG stands for the Multimedia and Hypermedia Information Coding Experts Group. This group is developing a standard "Coded Representation of Multimedia and Hypermedia Information", commonly called MHEG. The standard is in two parts - part one being object representations and part two being hyperlinking. MHEG is suited to interactive hypermedia applications such as on-line textbooks and encyclopedia. It is also suited for many of the interactive multimedia applications currently available (in platform-specific form) on CD-ROM. MHEG could, for instance, be used as the data structuring standard for a future home entertainment interactive multimedia appliance. To address such markets, MHEG represents objects in a non-revisable form, and is therefore unsuitable as an input format for hypermedia authoring applications: its place is perhaps more as an output format for such tools. MHEG is thus not a multimedia document processing format - instead it provides rules for the structure of multimedia objects, which permits the objects to be represented in a convenient form (e.g., video objects could be MPEG encoded). It uses ASN.1 as a base syntax to represent object structure, but allows for the use of other syntax notations - an SGML syntax is also specified. MHEG objects (which may be textual information, graphics, video, audio, etc.) may be of four types: input object (i.e., a user control such as a button or menu), output object (e.g., graphics, audio visual display, text), interactive object (a "composite" object containing both input and output objects), and hyperobject (a "composite" object containing both input and output objects, with links between them). MHEG supports various synchronization modes for presenting output objects in these relationships.

ODA (Office [Open] Document Architecture and Interchange Format): The ODA standard is concerned with the open interchange of documents. The ODA standards are part of a group of related standards concerned with documents, their content, and how they may be conveyed between systems. SGML (Standard Generalized Markup Language) and various related standards are other members of this group. Through the standards, a wide range of documents from simple text-only documents (such as office memoranda and letters), to complex documents (such as technical reports) may be encoded. These complex documents may contain text, raster graphics, and computer graphics and may well require complex layout specifications. The ODA standards support a very wide range of features and tend to be abstract in nature, hence industry experts have clarified the concept by defining Document Application Profiles (DAPs). These subsets provide support for document interchange between similar systems, which have a more restricted range of features. These DAPs will be published as ISO standards known as International Standardized Profiles (ISPs). The current target for ODA implementors is seen as the open interchange of mixed-content 'word processor' documents. The future for ODA is not as limited as this might suggest, as a number of major suppliers are known to have products under development. However, strong support for SGML and SDIF (SGML Data Interchange Format) is lacking, reflecting the fact that few SGML suppliers are associated with OSI.

A.6   Internet Standards

IP Multicast - RFC 1112:   IP multicasting is the transmission of an IP datagram to a host group, which is a set of hosts identified by a single IP destination address. A multicast datagram is delivered to all members of a destination host group. The membership of the host group is dynamic. A host group may be transient or permanent. Multicasting of this nature is essential to optimize bandwidth usage for multiparty conferencing applications.

Internet forwarding of IP multicast datagrams is handled by multicast routers. The special routing requirements of multicast IP can be met in several different ways. There are extensions to the Open Shortest Path First (OSPF) and Border Gateway Protocol (BGP) routing methods, and a relatively new routing method (CBT - Core Based Trees). CBT is likely to be adopted as the appropriate method of routing multicast IP.

MIME - RFC 1341:   Multipurpose Internet Mail Extensions (MIME) supports not only several predefined types of nontextual message contents, such as 8-bit 8000Hz-sampled μ-LAW audio, GIF image files, and PostScript programs, but also permits you to define your own types of message parts. A typical MIME mail reader can:

- Display GIF, JPEG, and PBM encoded images using, for example, 'xv' in X windows.

- Display PostScript parts (e.g., something that prints to a PostScript printer, that invokes GhostScript on an X windows display, or that uses Display PostScript.)

- Obtain external parts via Internet FTP or via mail server.

- Play audio parts on workstations that support digital audio.

MIME is designed to provide facilities to include multiple objects in a single message, to represent body text in character sets other than US-ASCII, to represent formatted multifont text messages, to represent nontextual material such as images and audio fragments, and generally to facilitate later extensions defining new types of Internet mail for use by cooperating mail agents.

RFC 822 defines a message representation protocol which specifies considerable detail about message headers, but which leaves the message content, or message body, as flat ASCII text. RFC1341 redefines the format of message bodies to allow multipart textual and nontextual message bodies to be represented and exchanged without loss of information. This is based on earlier work documented in RFC 934 and RFC 1049, but extends and revises that work. Because RFC 822 said so little about message bodies, RFC 1341 is largely orthogonal to (rather than a revision of) RFC 822. An associated document, RFC1342, extends Internet mail header fields to permit other than US-ASCII text data.

RTP: Real-Time Transport Protocol is a transport protocol for audio and videoconferences and other multiparticipant real-time applications. Services typically required by multimedia conferences are playout synchronization, demultiplexing, media identification, and active-party identification. RTP is not restricted to multimedia conferences, however, and other real-time services such as data acquisition and control may use its services. RTP uses the services of an end-to-end transport protocol such as UDP, TCP, OSI TPx, ST-2, or the like. The services used are: end-to-end delivery, framing, demutliplexing, and multicast. The network is not assumed to be reliable and is expected to lose, corrupt, delay, and reorder packets. RTP is supported by a real-time control protocol (RTCP). Conferences encompassing several media are managed by a reliable conference protocol not discussed in the RTP draft.

The design goals of RTP are:

- media flexibility

- extensible

- independent of lower-layer protocols

- gateway compatible

- bandwidth efficient

- international

- processing efficient

- implementable

Services provided are:

- framing

- demultiplexing by conference/association

- demultiplexing by media source

- demultiplexing by media encoding

- synchronization between source(s) and destination(s)

- error detection

- encryption

- quality-of-service monitoring

RTP consists primarily of protocol header for real-time data packets. In the typical case, the RTP header is just 8 octets long and composed of the following fields:

- protocol version (2 bits, value 1)

- flow identifier (6 bits)

- option present bit

- synchronization bit (marks end of synchronization unit)

- content type index (6 bits)

- packet sequence number (16 bits)

- timestamp, middle 32 bits of NTP-format timestamp

ST-2 RFC 1190:   This is Internet Stream Protocol, Version 2 (ST-2), an IP-layer protocol that provides end-to-end guaranteed service across an internet. ST-2 is an internet protocol at the same layer as IP. It differs from IP in that it requires routers to maintain state information describing the streams of packets flowing through them. ST-2 incorporates the concept of streams across an internet. Every intervening ST entity maintains state information for each stream that passes through it. The stream state includes forwarding information, including multicast support for efficiency (required for multi-participant conferencing) and resource information which allows network or link bandwidth and queues to be assigned to a specific stream. Pre-allocation allows data packets to be forwarded with low delay, low overhead, and low probability of loss due to congestion. It also allows ST-2 to give a real-time application to the guaranteed and predictable communication characteristics it requires. The data stream in an ST-2 connection is essentially one-way, except that there is a reverse-direction channel for control messages.

Transport protocols above ST-2 of interest to multimedia applications include Packet Video Protocol (PVP) and the Network Voice Protocol (NVP), which are end-to-end protocols used directly by applications.

A.7   Proprietary Standards

Bento - Apple Computer: Bento is a specification for the format of "object containers" and an associated API. In this context, an "object" such as a word-processor document or a movie clip that typically comprises some metadata (data about the object's format) and a value (the content of the object). A "container" is some form of data storage or transmission (e.g., a file or part of a mail message). Bento containers are defined by a set of rules for storing multiple objects in such a container. Bento does not require individual objects to be "Bento-aware".

Bento can store objects in compressed or encrypted form, where compression/encryption algorithms may be specified externally. It can store external references to data - for instance, to a large movie file (perhaps itself part of a Bento container) stored on a fileserver - and can also store a limited-resolution version for use when the fileserver version is unavailable.

Unlike other similar standards such as ASN.1 and ODA, Bento allows for the storage of multimedia objects in a medium-specific interleaved layout (say, on a CD-ROM) suitable for "just-in-time" real-time display.

The Bento specification contains an API and is platform independent. It is suitable for random-access reading (when a container is in RAM or on disk). It has an "update-in-place" mechanism supported in the API, but not yet in format specification or implementation. It has a globally unique naming system for objects and their properties. Names can be allocated locally for casual use or registered for common use. Objects are extensible - new information may be added to an object without disrupting applications which do not understand the new information. It supports links between objects. provides recursive access to embedded Bento containers, and can store a single object in several different formats (e.g., with different byte ordering). It is not a general-purpose object database mechanism.

GIF (Graphic Interchange Format):   The Graphics Interchange Format defines a protocol intended for on-line transmission and interchange of raster graphic data in a way that is independent of the hardware used in their creation or display. The Graphics Interchange Format is defined in terms of blocks and subblocks which contain relevant parameters and data used in the reproduction of a graphic. A GIF Data Stream is a sequence of protocol blocks and subblocks representing a collection of graphics. In general, the graphics in a data stream are assumed to be related to some degree, and to share some control information. A data stream may originate locally, as when read from a file, or it may originate remotely, as when transmitted over a data communications line. The format is defined with the assumption that an error-free Transport Level Protocol is used for communications; the Format makes no provisions for error detection and error correction.

The GIF format utilizes color tables to render raster-based graphics. The concept of both global and local color tables are supported to enable the optimization of data streams. The decoder of an image may use a color table with as many colors as its hardware is able to support; if an image contains more colors than the hardware can support, algorithms not defined in the 'standard' must be employed to render the image. The maximum number of colors supported by the 'standard' is 256.

QuickTime - Apple Computer: This is a file format for the storage and interchange of sequenced data, with cross-platform support. A QuickTime movie contains time-based data which may represent sound, video, or other time-sequenced information such as financial data or lab results. A movie consists of one or more tracks, each track being a single data stream.

A QuickTime movie file on an Apple Macintosh consists of a "resource fork" containing the movie resources and a "data fork" containing the actual movie data or references to external data sources such as a video tape. To facilitate the exchange of data with systems which use single fork files, it is possible to combine these into a file which uses only the data fork . Movie resources are built up from basic units called atoms, which describe the format, size, and content of the movie storage element. It is possible to nest atoms within "container" atoms, which may themselves contain other container atoms.

One type of container atom is the "movie" atom which defines the time-scale, duration and display characteristics for the entire movie file. It also contains one or more track atoms for the movie. A track atom defines a single track of a movie, and is independent of any other tracks in the movie carrying its own temporal and spatial information. Track atoms contain status information relating to the creation or editing of the track, priority in relation to other tracks, and display and masking characteristics. They also contain media atoms which define the data for a track. Media atoms contain information relating to the type of data (sound, animation, text, etc.) and information relating to the QuickTime system component (i.e., driver) that is to handle the data. Component-specific information is contained in a media information atom which is used to map media time and media data.

The above is a very simplistic view of a QuickTime movie resource. In fact there are many more atom types which define a wide variety of features and functions, including a TEXT media atom which allows displayed text to change with time, and user-defined data atoms called "derived media types". These allow for the custom handling of data by overriding the media handler with a user-supplied driver.

The actual movie data referred to by the movie resources may reside in the same file as the movie resource (a "self contained" movie), or more commonly it may reside in another file or on an external device.

RIFF - Microsoft and IBM: This is a file structure for multimedia resources. RIFF (Resource Interchange File Format) is a family of file structures rather than a single format. RIFF file architecture is suitable for the following multimedia tasks:

- Playing back multimedia data

- Recording multimedia data

- Exchanging multimedia data between applications and across platforms

A RIFF file consists of a number of "chunks" which identify, delimit, and contain each resource stored in the file. Each chunk is defined as four characters (the chunk type) identifying how the data stored in the chunk is represented; a 32 bit unsigned number representing the size of the data stored in the chunk; the binary data contained in the store. There are two special chunks which allow nesting of multiple chunks. These are the "RIFF" chunk, which combines multiple chunks into a "form", and "LIST" which is a list or sequence of chunks. Certain chunk types (including all form and list types) should be globally unique. To guarantee this uniqueness there is a registration scheme run by Microsoft, where new chunk types may be registered and a list of current registrations may be obtained. The definition of a particular RIFF form typically includes a unique four character code identifying the form type, a list of mandatory chunks, a list of optional chunks, and a required order for the chunks. Currently registered "forms" are PAL Palette File Format (.PAL files), RDIB RIFF Device Independent Bitmap Format (.DIB files), RMID RIFF MIDI Format (.MID files), RMMP RIFF Multimedia Movie File Format, and WAVE Waveform Audio Format (.WAV files).

The RIFF "LIST" chunk is identified by a four character "list type" code. If an application recognizes the list type, it should know how to interpret the sequence of chunks although any application may read through the nested chunks and identify them individually. RIFX is a counterpart to RIFF that uses the Motorola integer byte ordering format rather than the Intel format. There are no currently defined RIFX forms or lists. RIFF files are supported in Windows 3.1 under MS DOS, and by MMPM/2 under OS/2. There is no sign yet of RIFF being adopted on hardware platforms other than the PC.

A.8   Summary

In this chapter, we discussed the role of standardization bodies and looked at some specific standards that are directly relevant to multimedia systems.

Acronyms

AAL	ATM Adaptation Layer
ACK	Acknowledgement
ADC	Analog to Digital Converter
AM	Amplitude Modulation
ANSI	American National Standards Institute
API	Application Program Interface
ARP	Address Resolution Protocol
ARQ	Automatic Repeat Request
ASCII	American Standards Committee for Information Interchange
ATDM	Asynchronous Time Division Multiplexing
ATM	Asynchronous Transfer Mode
UNI	User Network Interface
AU	Administrative Unit
B-ISDN	Broadband ISDN
BER	Bit Error Rate
BGP	Border Gateway Protocol
BSC	Binary Synchronous Communication
CAC	Connection Admission Control
CBR	Constant Bit Rate
CCITT	International Telegraph and Telephone Consultative Committee
CD	Carrier Detect/Collision Detection

CD-ROM	Compact Disc-Read Only Memory
CDMA	Code Division Multiple Access
CGA	Color Graphics Adaptor
CLNP	ConnectionLess Network Protocol
CLNS	ConnectionLess Network Service
CMIP	Common Management Information Protocol
CMIS	Common Management Information System
CPU	Central Processing Unit
CRC	Cyclic Redundancy Check
CSCW	Computer-Supported Cooperative Working
CSMA-CD	Carrier Sense Multiple Access with Collision Detection
DARPA	Defence Advanced Research Projects Agency
DAT	Digital Audio Tape
DBMS	Data Base Management System
DCE	Data Circuit Terminating Equipment
DCT	Discrete Cosine Transformation
DFT	Discrete Fourier Transform
DIS	Draft International Standard
DM	Distributed Memory
DNS	Domain Name Service
DQDB	Distributed Queue Dual Bus
DSP	Digital Signal Processing
DTE	Data Terminal Equipment
DUI	Data Unit Identifier
DVMRP	Distance Vector Multicast Routing Protocol
EGA	Enhanced Graphics Adapter
EGP	Exterior Gateway Protocol

ETSI	European Telecommunications Standards Institute
FAT	File Allocation Table
FCFS	First Come First Served
FCS	Frame Check Sequence
FDDI	Fiber Distributed Data Interface
FDM	Frequency Division Multiplexing
FDMA	Frequency Division Multiple Access
FEC	Forward Error Correction
FFT	Fast Fourier Transform
FTP	File Transfer Protocol
GBps	GigaBytes per second
GHZ	Gigahertz
GIF	Graphics Interchange Format
GKS	Graphical Kernal System
GUI	Graphical User Interface
Gbps	Gigabits per second
HDLC	High-level Data Link Control
HDTV	High Definition Television
HEC	Header Error Checksum
HTML	HyperText Markup Language
HTTP	HyperText Transfer Protocol
Hz	Hertz
IDI	Initial Domain Identifier
IDP	Initial Domain Part
IDRP	Inter Domain Routing Protocol
IEEE	Institute of Electrical and Electronics Engineers
IETF	Internet Engineering Task Force
IP	Internet Protocol
IPC	Interprocess Communication
IPX	Internetwork Packet Exchange [Novell]

IS	Information System
IS	International Standard
ISDN	Integrated Services Digital Network
ISO	International Standards Organization
ITU	International Telecommunications Union
IWU	Interworking Unit
JPEG	Joint Photographic Experts Group
KBps	KiloBytes per second
KHz	KiloHertz
Kbps	Kilobits per second
LAN	Local Area Network
LAP	Link Access Procedure
LCN	Logical Channel Number
LLC	Logical Link Control
LPC	Local Procedure Call
MAC	Medium Access Control
MAN	Metropolitan Area Network
MBps	MegaBytes per second
MIB	Management Information Base
MPEG	Moving Picture Experts Group
MS	Message Store
MTA	Message Transfer Agent
Mbps	Megabits per second
Modem	Modulator/demodulator
N-ISDN	Narrowband ISDN
NAK	Negative AcKnowledgement
NETBLT	Network Block Transfer
NFS	Network File System
NSAP	Network Service Access Point
NTP	Network Time Protocol
OSPF	Open Shortest Path First

PABX	Private Automatic Branch Exchange
PAL	Programming Array Logic
PCI	Protocol Connection Identifier
PCM	Pulse Code Modulation
PDU	Protocol Data Unit
PER	Packet Error Rate
PLP	Packet Level Protocol
PMD	Physical Medium Dependent
PVC	Permanent Virtual Connection (Circuit)
QoS	Quality of Service
RAID	Redundant Array of Inexpensive Disks
RFC	Request For Comment
RIP	Routing Information Protocol
RPC	Remote Procedure Call
RSVP	ReSource ReserVation Protocol
SAP	Service Access Point
SAR	Segmentation And Reassembly
SDH	Synchronous Digital Heirarchy
SDLC	Synchronous Data Link Control
SDU	Service Data Unit
SMDS	Switched Multimegabit Data Service
SMT	Station Management
SMTP	Simple Mail Transfer Protocol
SNA	Systems Network Architecture [IBM]
SNMP	Simple Network Management Protocol
SONET	Synchronous Optical NETwork
SPX	Sequenced Packet Exchange [Novell]
SQL	Structured Query Language
STDM	Synchronous Time Division Multiplexing
STP	Shielded Twisted Pair
THz	Tera Hertz

SVC	Switched Virtual Connection
SVGA	Super VGA
TCP	Transmission Control Protocol
TDM	Time-Division Multiplexing
TFTP	Trivial File Transfer Protocol
TP	Twisted Pair
TP 4	Transport Protocol class 4
TPDU	Transport Protocol Data Unit
TRT	Token Rotation Time
TTRT	Target TRT
TV	TeleVision
UA	User Agent
UDP	User Datagram Protocol
UTP	UnTwisted Shielded Pair
VBR	Variable Bit Rate
VC	Virtual Connection
VCC	Virtual Channel Connection
VCI	Virtual Channel Identifier
VGA	Video Graphics Adaptor
VLSI	Very Large Scale Integration
VPI	Virtual Path Identifier
WAIS	Wide Area Information Service
WAN	Wide Area Network
WORM	Write Once Read Many
WWW	World Wide Web
WYSIWYG	What You See Is What You Get

Glossary

10Base2: A type of Ethernet that operates at 10 Mbps, with a maximum length of 200 m.

10Base5: A type of Ethernet that operates at 10 Mbps, with a maximum length of 500 m.

10BaseT: A type of Ethernet that is similar to unshielded twisted pair(UTP) that operates at 10 Mbps, with a maximum length of 100 m from a node to the hub.

Asynchronous Transmission: Transmission of individual bytes without time-dependency between the bytes.

A-to-D: Conversion from an analog signal to a digital signal.

B-frame: A kind of frame in MPEG coded stream. B-pictures achieve the highest amount of compression and require both a past and a future reference frame. Bi-directional pictures (B-Pictures) are never used as a reference.

Bit-Rate: The number of bits transmitted per second.

Bridge: A device that connects two or more local area networks and forwards packets among them. Bridges operate at the media access control level.

Broadcasting: It is the delivery of a copy of a given packet to all hosts attached to a given network.

Burstiness: It is the ratio of the peak bit-rate to the mean bit-rate of a traffic source.

Bus: A shared communication path interconnecting one or more devices.

Cable TV: A system of broadcasting television programs by cable to subscribers.

Cache: A memory that is smaller and faster than main memory and that is interposed between the CPU and the main memory. The cache acts as a buffer for recently used memory locations.

Cell: A cell is a fixed size unit of data.

Circuit Switching: A circuit switched network is one in which each connection results in a physical communication channel being setup through the network from the calling to the called subscriber equipment.

Client-Server: The model of interaction in a distributed system in which a program at one site sends a request to a program at another site and awaits a response. The requesting program is called a Client. The program satisfying the request is called a Server.

Compression: A *transformation of number of bits* that represent the information produced by a source, for compaction and hence efficient transmission.

Data: Basic unit of multimedia information that has the physical form of a file.

Defacto Standard: A standard that exists in practice; may not be a formal international standards document.

Digital Signal: A signal which is represented as a series of bits.

Digitization: Conversion of an analog signal to all-digital form by quantizing the magnitude of the signal at regular intervals into its equivalent binary form.

E-mail: A system in which messages, usually stored as files of text, are sent and received.

Ethernet: A local area network, developed by Xerox, DEC, and Intel. Later it became IEEE Standard 802.3.

Frame Relay: Frame Relay is a simple connection-oriented, virtual circuit packet service. Frame Relay provides both switched virtual connections (SVCs) and permanent virtual circuits (PVCs), and keeps the data and the signaling information separate.

Graphics: Basic unit of multimedia information that has the physical form of the output as displayed on a monitor.

H.261: A standard developed by CCITT Study Group XV and known popularly as Video Coded for Audiovisual Services at $p \times 64$ kbps.

Huffman Coding: An entropy coding method specified in the JPEG standard. Huffman coding requires that one or more sets of Huffman code tables be specified by the application. The same tables are used for compression and decompression of the image. Huffman tables may be predefined and used within an application as defaults, or computed specifically for a given image in an initial statistics-gathering pass prior to compression. Such choices are the responsibility of JPEG applications.

IEEE 802.2: The Standard produced by the IEEE, to describe the upper part of the data link layer, which uses the LLC (Logical Link Control) protocol.

IEEE 802.3: The IEEE Standard for 1-persistent CSMA/CD local area network. This Standard is adopted by the Ethernet LANs.

IEEE 802.4: The Standard produced by the IEEE for Token Bus LANs.

IEEE 802.5: The IEEE standard for Token Ring local area networks.

I-frame: The I-Frame is the first frame of each *GOP* in MPEG-coded streams. The Intra-pictures (I-Frames) provide reference points for random access and are subjected to moderate compression. From compression point of view, I-pictures are equivalent to *images* and can be DCT encoded using a JPEG-like algorithm.

Image: Basic unit of multimedia information that has the physical form of a photograph.

Macroblock: In the case of motion video compression based on MPEG, motion-compensation units, called Macroblocks of size 16 × 16 are used. This size is arrived at based on a trade-off between coding gain provided by motion information and the cost associated with coding the motion information.

MBONE: A Multicast Back**bone** is a cooperative agreement among sites to forward multicast datagrams across the Internet by the use of IP tunneling.

Modem: Modem stands for **Modulator-Dem**odulator. A device that enables a machine or terminal to establish a connection and transfer data through telephone lines or leased lines.

Motion Compensation: The technique used to compress video efficiently when a picture is coded with respect to a reference.

Motion Vector: The motion vector extracts motion information from a video sequence. If we use the block matching technique, the motion vector is obtained by minimizing a cost function measuring the mismatch between a block and each predictor candidate.

Multicasting: Multicasting is a technique that allows copies of a single packet to be passed to a selected subset of all possible destinations.

Multimedia: Literally multimedia means many media or multiple media. A medium as used here refers to data, digitized voice, digitized images, full-motion video, and graphics.

Netscape: A browser for the World Wide Web from Netscape Communications Inc.

Octet: Another (networking) term for a byte.

P-frame: A kind of frame in an MPEG coded stream. Prediction pictures are coded with reference to a past picture (intra(I) or predicted(P)) and can in general be used as a reference for future predicted pictures.

Pixel: Picture element that constitutes the basic unit of display on a CRT screen.

Protocol: Formal description of message formats and the rules to be followed by two or more machines in order to exchange messages.

Quantization: The phase in which the output of the picture processing phase of the compression process, which are coefficients expressed as real numbers, are mapped onto integers; quantization may result in a reduction of precision.

Resolution: The resolution of a display is the number of dots per inch (or pixels per inch) supported by the display.

Sampling: Conversion of uncompressed analog signals into the digital counterpart.

Synchronous Transmission: Data communications in which transmissions are sent at a fixed rate, with the sending and receiving devices synchronized.

Token Ring: A medium access control technique for ring topology. A token circulates around the ring. A station may transmit by seizing the token, inserting a packet onto the ring, and then retransmitting the token.

Token Bus: A medium access control technique for bus topology. Stations form a logical ring around which a token is passed. A station receiving the token may transmit data, and then pass the token on to the next station in the ring.

Video: Basic unit of multimedia information that has a physical form of a movie that we can see.

Voice: Basic unit of multimedia information that has a physical form of speech that we can hear.

World Wide Web(WWW): A networked hypertext protocol and user interface.

X.21: The CCITT standard defining the interface between DTE and a Digital Interface Unit (DIU).

X.25: The CCITT standard defining the interface between a packet-type DTE and a public data network.

Index